*Abortion:*
*The Clash of*
*Absolutes*

# ABORTION
## The Clash of Absolutes

LAURENCE H. TRIBE

*W. W. NORTON & COMPANY*

*New York   London*

Printed in the United States of America.

First published as a Norton paperback 1991.

The text of this book is composed in Century Old Style,
with the display set in Radiant Bold Condensed.
Composition and manufacturing by the Haddon Craftsmen, Inc.
Book design by Margaret Wagner.


Library of Congress Cataloging-in-Publication Data
Tribe, Laurence H.
Abortion: the clash of absolutes/Laurence H. Tribe.
p.  cm.
1. Abortion—Political aspects—United States     2. Abortion—
Government policy—United States.     3. Abortion—Moral and ethical
aspects.     4. Abortion—Law and legislation—United States.
I. Title.
HQ767.5.U5T73      1990
363.4'6—dc20           90–32205

ISBN 0-393-30699-2

W. W. Norton & Company, Inc., 500 Fifth Avenue, New York, N.Y. 10110
W. W. Norton & Company Ltd, 10 Coptic Street, London WC1A 1PU

4 5 6 7 8 9 0

*For Carolyn*

*Also by Laurence H. Tribe*

*AMERICAN CONSTITUTIONAL LAW*

*GOD SAVE THIS HONORABLE COURT:*
*How the Choice of Supreme Court Justices*
*Shapes Our History*

*CONSTITUTIONAL CHOICES*

*WHEN VALUES CONFLICT:*
*Essays on Environmental Analysis,*
*Discourse, and Decision (coeditor)*

*CHANNELING TECHNOLOGY THROUGH LAW*

# Contents

# Acknowledgments

This book could not have been written without the tireless and meticulous collaboration and assistance of Peter Rubin in every phase of the project, from the initial research to the preparation of successive drafts. Peter's penetrating mind, his lucid style, and his exacting standards made an enormous difference in shaping my effort to explore and synthesize the many subtle strands of the abortion debate and in carrying that effort to conclusion.

Very special gratitude also goes to my wife, Carolyn, whose deep insight and analytic clarity, in conversations with me over the past twenty-five years and especially over the past twenty-five weeks, have been vital to whatever understanding I have achieved in this perplexing area.

Gene Sperling should also be singled out for particular thanks. His always impressive command of the politics and rhetoric of this complex subject and his acute sense of symbolism and psychology proved enormously helpful.

For especially significant editing help, I thank Don Chesebro, Ken Chesebro, and Thomas Aylesworth, all of whom read through the manuscript with a skeptical eye and an active pen; Hilary Hinzmann, my editor at Norton, whose eye was every bit as acute and who made many perceptive suggestions; and the president of Norton, Donald Lamm, whose insight and oversight were crucial in helping this book take shape.

Several of my current students at Harvard Law School should also be singled out for thanks; their energetic and thorough research, their intelligent editing suggestions, and their careful proofreading all made a great difference. Those students are Michael A. Albert, Frank Cooper, Kevin M. Downey, David C. Finn, David T. Goldberg, David Jones, Robert Malley, Shaun P. Martin, and Radhika Rao—and especially Ellen

M. Bublick, Michael C. Dorf, Barack H. Obama, Ashar Qureshi, Jerri-Lynn Scofield, and Lisa B. Shelkrot.

Nearly all the students in my fall 1989 constitutional law course at Harvard Law School were also helpful as I sought to explore with them the complexities of this intractable topic. And three of my colleagues (Kathleen Sullivan, Susan Estrich, and Frank Michelman) helped greatly through the writings they have been good enough to share with me from time to time.

Finally, I thank Leslie Sterling and Mark Weltner, whose free-lance typing was accompanied by the critical sense that only unusually intelligent nonlawyers could bring to this effort. I greatly appreciate the very able assistance of Lynne Sikorski, without whom much of my other work would have ground to a halt while I wrote this book. And I am especially grateful for the extraordinary help and perceptiveness of my secretary and assistant, Jamie Silverstein, several of whose turns of phrase irresistibly worked their way into the manuscript, and whose photographic memory and unparalleled tact and cheer made pleasurable what might otherwise have been a painful project.

Laurence H. Tribe
*Cambridge, Massachusetts*
*February 1990*

*Abortion:*
*The Clash of*
*Absolutes*

# 1

# Approaching Abortion Anew

This book is about a clash of absolutes, of life against liberty.

No right is more basic than the right to live. And the untimely death of a young child is among life's most awful tragedies. To cause such a death is a great wrong. And if infanticide is wrong, is the destruction of a fetus at eight months of gestation, or at five, any different?

Nothing is more devastating than a life without liberty. A life in which one can be forced into parenthood is just such a life. Rape is among the most profound denials of liberty, and compelling a woman to bear a rapist's child is an assault on her humanity. How different is it to force her to remain pregnant and become a mother just because efforts at birth control accidentally failed? From her point of view, the pregnancy is also unsought. From the perspective of the fetus, how the pregnancy began surely makes no difference.

If forcing a woman to continue a pregnancy that will almost certainly kill her is impermissible, how different is it to compel her to continue a pregnancy that will probably shorten her life? Or a pregnancy that will leave her life a shambles?

Are there ways of approaching issues like abortion that avoid pitting these absolutes against one another? Ways of choosing that maintain respect for the deepest values on both sides of the equation? Ways that face the realities of sex and power that underlie the struggle?

Famous legal cases in our nation's history, cases like *United States of America v. Richard M. Nixon,*[1] in which the Supreme Court compelled President Nixon to turn over the Watergate tapes, often have titles in which the names of the parties who are identified on either side of the "versus" tell us about real people or institutions and the real interests they represent.

The principal case that lies behind this book is named *Jane Roe v. Henry Wade,*[2] a case in which the Supreme Court said that except in narrow circumstances, the Constitution of the United States does not permit the government to interfere with a woman's right to choose abortion.

*Roe v. Wade* is many things. It is a legal decision by the Supreme Court; a rallying cry for both sides in the abortion debate. But it is also, and was at first, an entirely human story, one that has become by now familiar to many, a story similar to other stories repeated all over the United States every day.

"Jane Roe" is not a real person's name at all, but a pseudonym. The woman who sought an abortion in that case wanted for a time to remain anonymous. "Henry Wade" is the real name of a Texas official, a Dallas county prosecutor who is sued almost every week. His name appears on one side of the "versus" in scores of cases, defending the laws of Texas that it is his duty to enforce. But although Henry Wade is real, Wade's executive powers (unlike those of Richard Nixon in *United States v. Nixon*) were not at issue in the case of *Roe v. Wade.* Rather, the interests opposed to those of the anonymous Ms. Roe were those of the unborn, for the people of Texas had decided, through their state legislature, to protect unborn lives.

Why did the woman in *Roe v. Wade* want to conceal her real name? Presumably she did not wish to broadcast either the fact of her pregnancy or her decision to end it. Not long after the Supreme Court's decision in *Roe v. Wade,* "Jane Roe" revealed who she really was. Her real name was Norma McCorvey. She explained that as she walked home from work late one summer evening in 1969, twenty-five years old and unmarried, she became the victim of a gang rape. Her anguish grew several weeks later, she said, when she learned to her dismay that she was pregnant.

Abortion was illegal (except to save the woman's life) in Texas where she lived, and she lacked the resources to travel to a place where a legal abortion might be obtained. Although McCorvey was unable under Texas law to terminate her own unwanted pregnancy, she was willing to challenge the Texas abortion ban for the sake of other women. Norma McCorvey's only condition for going ahead with the legal challenge was that she remain anonymous. Thus she was named "Jane Roe" in the lawsuit.

McCorvey had little education, and did not realize the attention that her case might receive. When her lawyer informed her that the case would be presented to the Supreme Court of the United States, McCorvey was dismayed. "My God," she said, "all those people are so important. They don't have time to listen to some little old Texas girl who got in trouble."

In a different sort of society, a woman who had in fact been raped might not feel ashamed, as if the rape were somehow her fault. She might not be driven to hide her "shameful" secret behind the anonymity of a fictitious name.

A decade and a half after the Court handed down its decision in *Roe v. Wade* McCorvey explained, with embarrassment, that she had not been raped after all; she had made up the story to hide the fact that she had gotten "in trouble" in the more usual way. Many reacted with dismay. How could the heroine of the most important abortion rights case have deceived the advocates of such rights? Few asked why she had felt a *need* to deceive them. In a different sort of society the life she would have faced as an unwed mother might not have been nearly so lonely. In such a society she might not have made up a story about how she became pregnant. In such a society she might not even have chosen an abortion.

It seems telling that in *Roe v. Wade* both the woman on one side of the "versus" ("Roe") and the fetus on the other (represented by Wade) are nameless. In much of the debate over abortion in our society, one side or the other is reduced to ghostly anonymity. Many who can readily envision the concrete humanity of a fetus, who hold its picture high and weep, barely see the woman who carries it and her human plight. To them she becomes an all but invisible abstraction. Many others, who can readily envision the woman and her body, who cry out for her right to control her destiny, barely envision the fetus within that woman and do not imagine as real the life it might have been allowed to lead. For them, the life of the fetus becomes an equally invisible abstraction.

Who knows the names of the countless women who have died from painful and illegal abortions? What of the names of the countless babies who would have been born but for all the abortions, legal as well as illegal, that have been performed in recent decades? Melissa Able would have been aborted if Sandra Race Cano, the "Mary Doe" in the case of *Doe v. Bolton,*[3] another abortion case decided by the Supreme Court on the same day as *Roe v. Wade,* had been able to obtain in Georgia the abortion she sought there. Because abortion was so heavily restricted, Cano (already a mother of three children) ended up giving birth to a daughter—Able—whom she put up for adoption. Biological mother and daughter have since met; indeed, for several months they even lived in the same house. Remarkably Cano and Able are now playing out on a personal level the clash of absolutes with which so many of us are familiar.

Although she was once a key pro-choice litigant, Cano believes today that abortion should be illegal. She is now active in the pro-life movement. Her daughter Able (herself now a mother) disagrees. Able knows she would never have been born if abortion rights had been established sooner, but she told a newspaper interviewer in November 1989 that she believes women have the right to choose. Indeed, of her own mother she says, "If she'd had an abortion she would have had her right."[4] Cano, Able and McCorvey are three real individuals. That the names of millions of others—the women, the fetuses who were not born, and the many who were born but unwanted—are not known to us should not make them any the less real.

We must see the reality that "Roe" and "Wade" stand for if we are to move beyond the clash of absolutes. Giving voice to the human reality on each side of the "versus," keeping both the woman and the fetus in focus at the same time, may be the only way to avoid the no-win battle that mercilessly pits women against their unborn children and leaves us all impoverished losers.

America is at a crossroads. In 1989 the sixteen-year era of judicial protection of legal abortion rights that began with the Supreme Court's 1973 decision in *Roe v. Wade* ended with that Court's five to four decision upholding certain state regulations of abortion in the case of *Webster v. Reproductive Health Services.* A right that, since the time of Watergate and Vietnam, had been kept by judges from the rough-and-tumble of local politics—the woman's right to decide for herself whether to terminate a pregnancy—is now subject to regulation, and possibly even prohibition, by our elected representatives. A right that many Americans took for granted is now in a real sense up for grabs. Anyone who doubts that this is the meaning of *Webster* need look no further than the morning newspaper. As the 1990s dawn, the complexion of politics in America is changing daily, and the shadow of the question of abortion rights grows, with widespread significance for our society. Even as the public agenda is stretched to address such new questions as the right to die, no issue threatens to divide us politically in quite as powerful a way as the abortion issue does.

Our national institutions are braced for a seemingly endless clash of absolutes. The political stage is already dominated by the well-rehearsed and deeply felt arguments, on either side of the abortion issue, that we have come to know so well. The debate is unending. None of its participants ever seems even mildly persuaded by the arguments of the other side. As the apparently irresistible force of the pro-life movement bears down on the seemingly immovable object of abortion rights, local politics may at times be overwhelmed by the kind of single-issue campaigning that has already distorted the face of national elections. If this happens, the losers will be the democratic process and the American people.

For most Americans the years after *Roe* and the legalization of abortion in the United States were not a time to face carefully or to discuss dispassionately the many subtle and complex legal and moral questions that abortion as a public issue presents. For those who were convinced that abortion should never have been proclaimed a "right" at all, those years were a time for quiet lament or vigorous protest. For those who assumed that abortion would indefinitely remain a judicially declared legal right, and to whom this was unobjectionable, there was no need to consider the question of the proper government treatment of abortion.

With the legal status of abortion snatched from the political dueling ground by the Court's 1973 *Roe* decision, the public stage was left largely to those who believed most strongly that abortion was wrong absolutely, that it was immoral to let each woman choose for herself, and that therefore the law should be changed to make it possible for abortion to be criminalized once again.

The debate was thus controlled by those willing to wage the only political campaign that our constitutional structure made available—a political campaign to transform the federal judiciary—and by those who opposed them. Since it was judges who had read abortion rights *into* the Constitution, abortion opponents believed, we needed judges who would read abortion back *out* of it. For a time some urged a constitutional amendment that would effectively have prohibited abortion or would at least have returned the question to each state's legislature, but the considerable political consensus and effort required for enactment of any such amendment proved elusive. The argument was polarized; its terms became static. For all its other significance, the *Webster* decision presents an opportunity for all of us to examine the bitter and divisive public question of abortion "policy."

This book challenges the inevitability of permanent conflict on that question and tries to lay the groundwork for moving on. The face of the abortion argument need not remain frozen. The thinking on all sides of the issue is likely to be recast by social and technological change. If we examine critically both the pro-choice and the pro-life arguments, we may discover areas in which the two sides can find common ground and, of course, some areas in which they cannot. We will also explore approaches to the abortion issue that, while recognizing the necessary conflict between the position for life and the case for choice, might serve as a means for getting beyond that conflict.

Inevitably then, this is a book about constitutional law. Since it first came before the Supreme Court, the question of abortion in our country has been about the Constitution. Whom does it protect? How do we decide whom it protects, and how much protection it provides? Among the most pressing questions to arise in the wake of the abortion debate are the extent to which our Constitution limits the competing rights and interests of women and unborn children and the role judges should play in umpiring the political struggles over such issues or even removing them from the fray of politics.

This book will explore the legal framework in which the constitutional question of abortion rights must be decided. It will trace the development of the constitutional law of privacy from the Supreme Court's decisions of the 1920s about child rearing through its abortion jurisprudence of the 1970s and 1980s. It will also look at the implications of various competing constitutional theories for the abortion question and how judicial responses to abortion affect the fabric of other key constitutional rights: the right to raise our children as we see fit; the freedom of speech; the right to choose those with whom we will share our lives.

This is also intended as a book about morality. By offering several perspectives from which to view the question of abortion, some rooted in philosophy, some springing from recent developments in science and technology, we may come to see new ways to understand the issue. This book must also touch, as any genuine look at abortion must, deep and difficult questions about birth and death, about life and its inception, about sexuality and gender, about the distribution of power.

Ultimately some may be persuaded that we need not cling so fiercely to one or the other extreme, that there is room for movement toward healing our divisions over the abortion question, based on shared values and goals. If each of us reexamines the complex issues that make up the question of abortion, we may yet find more common ground than we currently imagine. And perhaps we may resist the cruel compromises that offer only an illusion of reasonable accommodation.

It is not this book's goal to "prove" to anyone the correctness of any particular position in the abortion debate. It seems doubtful that anything like "proof" is attainable on this subject. Each side can benefit, though, from recognizing the strengths of the other's arguments and the weaknesses of its own. We may then be able to loosen the logjam that the abortion debate has become. And then, perhaps, we will be able, if not to resolve, at least to make our way through the question of abortion.

For those who have not really made up their minds about abortion or who once thought they had but are no longer so sure, this book is an invitation to grapple with a problem that will not go away and that is transforming our politics.

For those whose minds are made up, this book offers a window into the way the "other side" sees things, an understanding of why you have not been able to persuade opponents, and some insights into what they believe and, perhaps, why.

And for those who have no thought of taking sides, this book tells a story fascinating in itself, a story of how law, politics, sex, medicine, and moral fervor have become woven into a rich and multihued tapestry of our times.

# 2

# From <u>Roe</u> to <u>Webster</u>

On January 22, 1973, the Supreme Court handed down its decision in the case of *Roe v. Wade*,[1] announcing that the United States Constitution protects a woman's right to decide whether to end a pregnancy. The constitutional question the Court answered in *Roe* is at the center of one of the most intense legal and political debates in American history, and as the 1990s begin, a changing Supreme Court is again being asked to reconsider the issue.

The *Roe* case presented a challenge to a Texas statute, substantially unchanged since 1857, that made it a crime to "procure an abortion" except where it was "procured or attempted by medical advice for the purpose of saving the life of the mother."[2] The Court's decision about this law had been long awaited. *Roe v. Wade* had been argued in 1971, and then, under a procedure used in only a few of the roughly 150 cases the Supreme Court hears every year, it was held over by the justices and argued a second time in 1972. *Roe*'s significance was certainly not lost on the Court or on the journalists who filled the press section in the Supreme Court chamber.

To understand the analysis on the basis of which the Court that day protected the right to choose abortion, we must first understand a basic point of constitutional law.

The Supreme Court has distinguished certain rights or liberties as "fundamental." Other rights—the "right" to drive a car, say—may be abridged by government as part of a rational scheme to achieve some collective good. For example, some people (like children, or people with poor eyesight, or people who exceed their quota of traffic violations) may be denied the liberty to drive simply because the state has a rational reason, such as the promotion of highway safety.

Fundamental rights or liberties, however—for example, the right to free speech—can be abridged by government only when demonstrably necessary to achieve a "compelling" objective. The Supreme Court rarely finds such compelling necessity, so the choice of which test to apply usually resolves the case. If the Court decides to treat a right as "fundamental," that right becomes very difficult to abridge. An abridgment of a fundamental right is almost never upheld. On the other hand, if a right is not deemed fundamental, virtually any government action that abridges that right is upheld. Government is free to abridge a nonfundamental right for almost any reason.

## *The* Roe *Opinion*

The Court's decision in *Roe v. Wade* was notable in the first instance for the lopsided vote in favor of the right to choose (seven to two) and the fact that members of the Court regarded as conservative backed that right. Justice Harry Blackmun, a Republican appointed to the Supreme Court by President Richard M. Nixon, delivered the opinion he had written for himself and six other members of the Court, including the conservative chief justice, Warren Burger. Justice Blackmun had been a judge on the United States Court of Appeals, the second-highest court in the United States, before his appointment in 1970 to the Supreme Court. Before becoming a judge, he had served for nine years as general counsel for the Mayo Clinic and the Mayo Foundation in Rochester, Minnesota. Justice Blackmun has always been regarded as an extraordinarily kind man. He is more judicious than political. While at the time of his appointment he was described as a "conservative," he has undergone something of a transformation in philosophy on the bench—in part, perhaps, as a result of the reaction to his decision in *Roe.* Eighty-two as this book goes to press, Justice Blackmun has become a fairly solid member of the Court's "liberal" wing.

In *Roe* Justice Blackmun wrote that a woman's right to decide whether or not to terminate her pregnancy is a fundamental right, part of a "right of privacy" the Court had recognized in earlier cases. Therefore, under *Roe,* only a compelling reason will allow government to interfere with the exercise of that right.

The Court's opinion spells this out. During the first third, or trimester, of pregnancy, government may not interfere with a woman's decision to terminate a pregnancy in any way except to insist that it be performed by a licensed physician.

In the second trimester government has the power to regulate abortion only in ways designed to preserve and protect the *woman's* health. The Court wrote that this goal becomes compelling at the end of the first trimester because before that time abortion is less hazardous for the woman than childbirth. *Roe* says that during the second trimester the only permissible abortion regulations are those designed to ensure that the procedure is performed safely, because the only compelling reason the government has for involvement in the pregnant woman's decision during this period is the protection of her health.

After fetal viability, the point at which the fetus is capable of surviving outside the womb, at approximately the beginning of the final third of a fetus's gestation, protection of fetal life also becomes a compelling reason sufficient under *Roe* to justify interference with the exercise of the right to choose abortion. At that point the government can also regulate, or even prohibit, abortion in order to protect fetal life unless the abortion is necessary to preserve the life or health of the woman.

Just as the Court held that the right to abortion was not absolute— that protection of the fetus need not necessarily await live birth—it also held that a state or local government could not overcome the woman's right "by adopting one theory of life,"[3] the theory that life begins at conception.

Justice William Rehnquist filed a dissenting opinion. Another Nixon appointee, Justice Rehnquist is a remarkably talented jurist who was at the time of *Roe v. Wade* regarded as clearly the most conservative member of the Supreme Court. During the two terms of the Reagan presidency, Justice Rehnquist (once presented by his law clerks with a Lone Ranger doll because of his frequent role as the "lone dissenter") was joined by other justices who shared his philosophy. In 1986 President Reagan elevated him to chief justice at age sixty-one, making him, in essence, "the first among equals." The chief justice wields the considerable power, when he is in the majority, to assign the opinion in a case to a particular justice. As the Court enters the 1990s, Chief Justice Rehnquist frequently exercises this prerogative as the head of a fairly reliable five-member conservative majority. Chief Justice Rehnquist is known for his good personal relations with colleagues despite ideological differences. Indeed, the justice with whom he is reported to have been most friendly during his tenure on the bench is the Court's most noted liberal member, William J. Brennan, Jr.

In *Roe v. Wade* Justice Rehnquist protested the Court's requirement of a compelling reason to justify regulation of abortion and argued that the right to choose whether to end a pregnancy is not "fundamental." Although he conceded it was "a form of 'liberty,' "[4] he argued that it should receive no greater protection than any other liberty abridged by routine social and economic legislation. Justice Byron White filed a very similar dissenting opinion.[5] A Rhodes scholar and former professional football player (indeed, a member of the Pro Football Hall of Fame) Justice White served before his appointment to the Court as deputy attorney general under Robert Kennedy in the Department of Justice. Although he was appointed by President John F. Kennedy to the Supreme Court at the age of forty-three in 1962, and was initially regarded as quite liberal except in criminal law matters, Justice White is now a reliable conservative vote. He is, however, no radical, adhering to some well-settled doctrines with which his more activist conservative colleagues would do away.

Parts of the *Roe* decision almost seemed to suggest that the right to decide about abortion belonged to the doctor, perhaps reflecting Justice Blackmun's background as lawyer for the Mayo Clinic. At one point Justice Blackmun wrote that "[t]he decision vindicates the right of the physician to administer medical treatment according to his professional judgment."[6] However, other parts of the opinion, and subsequent decisions of the Court, made clear that the right in question was that of the pregnant woman. As Justice Lewis Powell later wrote for the Court,[7] "we held in *Roe v. Wade* that the right of privacy, grounded in the concept of personal liberty guaranteed by the Constitution, encompasses a woman's right to decide whether to terminate her pregnancy."

Justice Powell, a gracious southerner appointed by President Nixon and sworn in on the same day as his more conservative colleague William Rehnquist, was already sixty-five years old when he ascended the bench in 1972. Justice Powell's time on the Supreme Court capped a distinguished career in the law that included a term as president of the American Bar Association. Despite four years of service in the U.S. Army Air Forces, Justice Powell has led something of a sheltered life. He once asked one of his law clerks, working in informal attire on a Saturday, "Are those what they call 'blue jeans?' "[8] Justice Powell retired from the Court in 1987.

*Roe*'s immediate effect was to enunciate a principle under which the existing abortion legislation in at least forty-nine states and the District of Columbia was invalid. Apparently only the law of New York state would survive. In the months and years that followed, many pre-*Roe* abortion statutes were struck down on the strength of *Roe v. Wade*. Some were judicially invalidated; others were repealed outright or replaced with new laws; still others were left on the books but were no longer enforced.

## Supreme Court Decisions in the Years Following Roe

In subsequent cases—*Roe*'s "progeny"—the Supreme Court issued a series of opinions both reaffirming the rules of *Roe* and, over a gradually growing number of dissents, applying them to specific cases.

In its first post-*Roe* abortion ruling, the 1976 case of *Planned Parenthood v. Danforth,*[9] the Court explained that government may not interfere with a woman's abortion decision by giving a veto over the abortion to the man who shares responsibility for the woman's pregnancy or even, in the case of a woman below the age of majority, by conferring an absolute veto on the young woman's parents.

The Court has held, though, that the government's interest in protecting immature minors is sufficient to uphold certain requirements of parental involvement in minors' decision making. But as the Court held in the 1983 case of *City of Akron v. Akron Center for Reproductive Health, Inc.,* [10] requirements of parental consent must provide for an alternative form of approval—by a judge—for a minor who is sufficiently mature to make the decision herself or who has a good reason for not seeking parental consent and can demonstrate that an abortion would be in her best interests. In addition, a parental consent rule must be accompanied by procedures ensuring that the judicial bypass will be accomplished quickly and confidentially.[11]

In terms of a woman's own decision to end a pregnancy, government may insist that she certify in writing prior to an abortion "that her consent is informed and freely given and is not the result of coercion."[12] Legislative attempts to specify the information to be provided to a pregnant woman (details about fetal development, for instance) have nonetheless been struck down because they were designed "to influence the woman's informed choice between abortion or childbirth."[13] In a series of cases culminating in *Thornburgh v. American College of Obstetricians and Gynecologists* in 1986, the Court struck down state laws requiring that a woman seeking an abortion be given detailed descriptions of fetal development, informed of particular physical and psychological risks associated with abortion, and reminded of the availability of assistance from the father or from social service agencies should she decide to give birth. The Court has also held that government cannot impose a fixed waiting period on a consenting woman who seeks an abortion.[14]

In the second trimester the government is permitted to adopt reasonable regulations specifically calculated to promote safe abortions. But requiring that abortions be performed in hospitals, or only with the approval of another doctor or committee in addition to the woman's physician, has been ruled impermissible, as has any requirement that the abortion procedure employ a technique that is not widely available.[15]

Government may impose record-keeping requirements that are designed to preserve maternal health and ensure the confidentiality of information about the patient. However, the Supreme Court has shown no tolerance for "extreme" reporting requirements that would make available to the public detailed information about the woman, the physician, and the circumstances of the abortion. The Court in the *Thornburgh* case perceived in such requirements a design to facilitate public exposure and harassment of women seeking to exercise their constitutional right to control their reproductive destiny.[16]

Although a physician may be required to exercise due care to preserve the life of a "viable" fetus—that is, a fetus that can survive outside the womb—the Court has held that requiring such care is unconstitutional if it poses any additional risk to the pregnant woman's health. Thus, the Court said in *Thornburgh,* a statute that requires a doctor to take greater care whenever the fetus *"may be* viable" impermissibly suggests that the physician may be forced to make a "'trade-off' between the woman's health and additional percentage points of fetal survival."[17] When the fetus *is* viable, however, government may require that a second doctor be present to provide additional protection for the life of the fetus, so long as the requirement contains a "medical emergency" exception to ensure that attention to the fetus is not achieved at the expense of increased risk to the woman's health.[18]

Interestingly, one of the parties for whom a leading abortion case is named is Richard Thornburgh, who was in the lawsuit because at the time it began he was governor of Pennsylvania, the state whose legislation was at issue in the case. He was subsequently appointed attorney general of the United States by President Reagan, a position which he retained in the Bush Administration. Thornburgh has himself been mentioned as a possible nominee for any Supreme Court vacancy that might occur during President Bush's term of office.

In general, the pattern of litigation before the Court in the years following *Roe* was quite predictable. Antiabortion legislatures would enact restrictions, ones less stringent than those previously invalidated, that would themselves ultimately be challenged and, in most cases, invalidated.

The only real exceptions to this rule were decisions in which a majority of the Supreme Court upheld government decisions to provide needy women with money or public services to cover the expense of childbirth but not to fund the less expensive choice of abortion. In 1977, in *Maher v. Roe,* [19] the Supreme Court upheld a Connecticut regulation that denied state Medicaid funding (money provided under the joint state-federal program to reimburse medical expenses of the needy) from being used for "non-therapeutic" abortions—that is, abortions not necessary to protect the life or health of the woman. At the same time the Court held in the companion case of *Poelker v. Doe* [20] that a city-owned public hospital that provided childbirth services was not constitutionally compelled to provide nontherapeutic abortions. The Court extended the reasoning of these cases in 1980 to the denial of federal Medicaid funds even for some medically necessary abortions in the case of *Harris v. McRae.* [21]

The Court in these cases distinguished between *direct* interference with a woman's right to choose abortion and the *indirect* deterrence of the abortion choice resulting from government's decision to pay for health care that is related to childbirth by a poor woman but to provide no parallel support for the same woman if she chooses to have an abortion. The question of public funding for abortion has been a primary battleground in the abortion dispute ever since 1976. Still, in the years following *Roe* one could safely predict that *direct* restrictions on abortion would be overturned.

## Political Responses to the Court's Decision

The main consequence of the decision in *Roe,* aside from the statement of a principle under which almost no existing government regulation of abortion could be upheld, was to galvanize a right-to-life movement that had, of course, predated *Roe* in nascent form but that gained cohesion largely by virtue of the Supreme Court's ruling. This group harnessed the power of single-issue politics to elect public officials who believed, as they did, that abortion was murder and that it should be outlawed. Ironically, *Roe* contributed to the success of this movement because it prevented government from legislatively restricting access to abortion. Those who did not agree with the right-to-life position thus could vote for pro-life candidates with whom they otherwise agreed without concern that antiabortion views would actually be enacted into enforceable laws.

Because *Roe*'s recognition of a constitutionally protected right to decide whether or not to terminate a pregnancy shut the door to direct political action to restrict abortion, the right-to-life forces had open to them only two avenues for a change in the law. The first and perhaps most obvious recourse was to try to amend the Constitution. This is, purposely, a burdensome process. Under Article V of the Constitution, unless the legislatures of two-thirds of the states demand a constitutional convention—something that has never happened—a proposed amendment requires passage by two-thirds of both the House of Representatives and the Senate and ratification by the legislatures of, or by special conventions in, three-fourths of the states. To convey some idea of the degree of difficulty this entails, in the two hundred years since the Bill of Rights was ratified, the Constitution has been amended only sixteen times. Several attempts at constitutional amendment were put forward by antiabortion groups, but it became evident quite quickly that the considerable political consensus necessary to enact such an amendment simply did not exist.

The second avenue open to the right-to-life forces was to try to remake the federal judiciary by seating new judges who would interpret the Constitution as *not* protecting abortion rights. Supporters of the right-to-life position took this road as well. A valuable interim goal was the appointment of antiabortion lower court judges (they are charged with interpreting the Supreme Court's decisions and applying their reasoning to new situations) who would restrict in application the scope of the Supreme Court's abortion rulings. The ultimate goal was to capture a majority on the Supreme Court to overrule *Roe v. Wade*—an entirely legitimate objective, many believe, under our form of government.

Under the Constitution federal judges are nominated by the President and are subject to confirmation by the Senate. The members of the federal judiciary serve for life. Since the resignation, retirement, or death of the members of the Supreme Court and other federal courts cannot be predicted, the war to transform the judiciary has necessarily been one of attrition. And the only way to fight the war was to elect a President.

That is precisely what the antiabortion forces did. In 1980 they helped elect Ronald Reagan to the presidency. President Reagan, who believed as they did, carried out the right-to-life plan to alter the face of the federal judiciary. The most significant litmus test for would-be judges on the federal Court of Appeals or the Supreme Court under Reagan was opposition to *Roe v. Wade*. [22] During his eight years in office President Reagan appointed more than half the members of the federal bench. More important, he appointed three new Supreme Court justices, replacing three of the members of *Roe*'s seven to two majority.

The declining size of the Supreme Court majority for vindicating abortion rights in cases decided during the 1980s spoke volumes about the effectiveness of Reagan's appointments. In 1981, when Justice Potter Stewart retired, President Reagan appointed Sandra Day O'Connor, the first woman ever to serve on the Supreme Court, to fill Stewart's seat. By coincidence, Justice O'Connor was a Stanford Law School classmate of Justice Rehnquist's. Active in Republican politics in Arizona, she had served, prior to her appointment to the Supreme Court, in the state senate and as a state judge there. Justice O'Connor is seen as a generally conservative jurist, but not predictably so where women's rights are involved.

Justice O'Connor, who was fifty-one years old at the time of her appointment, joined Justices Rehnquist and White in dissent in the first abortion case on which she sat, *City of Akron v. Akron Center for Reproductive Health, Inc.,* in 1983. In that case the Supreme Court, over Justice O'Connor's dissent, struck down a number of provisions in a city ordinance, including a parental consent requirement and a requirement that a physician make specified statements to the pregnant woman describing the fetus before performing an abortion. The law struck down in *Akron* also mandated a twenty-four-hour waiting period and required that all second-trimester abortions be performed in hospitals.

When Chief Justice Burger retired in 1986, President Reagan elevated the most staunchly conservative justice, William Rehnquist, to fill his seat and appointed Judge Antonin Scalia, then fifty, to fill Rehnquist's chair. Justice Scalia, who has brought vitality and candor to the Court, has a brilliant and incisive conservative mind. From his short time on the Court it is apparent that he will make a powerful and influential contribution to its jurisprudence. A former editor of the *Harvard Law Review,* Justice Scalia was serving on the United States Court of Appeals at the time of his appointment to the Supreme Court. Before becoming a judge, Justice Scalia was a law professor at the University of Chicago and at the University of Virginia.

After the retirement of Justice Lewis Powell in 1987, President Reagan nominated Judge Robert Bork, then sixty, for the Court. Bork, who failed to be confirmed by the Senate after a massive nationwide campaign by his opponents, is a strong conservative who at the time was a sitting judge on the United States Court of Appeals. He had been a law professor at Yale, where he specialized in antitrust law, and had served under President Nixon as the solicitor general of the United States, the third-ranking person in the Justice Department and the person responsible for arguing the position of the United States government in cases before the Supreme Court. Judge Bork was regarded by many as the leading conservative constitutional scholar and had published on a variety of key issues. He was perhaps best known for his vigorous arguments that individual rights should be limited by the "original intent" of the Constitution's framers and that federal courts should exercise "judicial restraint" by interfering less frequently with the activities of elected officials.

The question of whether the Senate acted wisely in rejecting Bork for a lifetime seat on the Court will probably be debated for decades. In his own attack on the Senate's action, published in the 1989 book *The Tempting of America,* Judge Bork argues in considerable detail that his rejection was symptomatic of a still-dominant "liberal" ethos about the proper role of judge-made law in our political life.

That characterization was disputed in a 1989 book by a bright young journalist named Ethan Bronner. That book, *The Battle for Justice,* does criticize the personal attacks on Judge Bork's character used by groups opposing Bork's appointment, primarily some of those in the civil rights community. But Bronner makes a powerful case that Bork's own long campaign to cut back on constitutional protections that most Americans had long come to accept as basic was the primary reason for the Senate's ultimate rejection of his nomination.

When the Senate finally rejected Judge Bork, Reagan announced that his second nominee would be Judge Douglas Ginsburg. A colleague of Judge Bork on the Court of Appeals, the then forty-one-year-old Judge Ginsburg was a former head of the Justice Department's Antitrust Division and a former professor at Harvard Law School. His name was withdrawn when ideological conservative support evaporated after revelations that he had smoked marijuana while a law professor.

President Reagan then nominated, and the Senate confirmed, his final appointment, Anthony Kennedy, then fifty-one. At the time of his nomination Justice Kennedy sat on the United States Court of Appeals in California, a position to which he had been appointed in 1975 by President Gerald Ford. His opinions on the appeals court suggested a more flexible conservatism than that of Judge Bork, but in his first three terms on the Supreme Court he voted fairly consistently with the most doctrinaire conservatives, Justice Scalia and Chief Justice Rehnquist. Justice Kennedy's tenure on the Court is likely to be a long one, however, and it is probably too early to make any definitive statement about his jurisprudence.

After Justice Kennedy was sworn in, there remained on the Court, therefore, only four justices who had previously expressed their commitment to the constitutional protection of abortion rights. Three were members of the *Roe* majority: *Roe*'s author, Justice Harry Blackmun, whose age as this book goes to press is eighty-two; Justice William J. Brennan, Jr., eighty-four, who served on the Court from 1956 to 1990; and Justice Thurgood Marshall, eighty-two. They were joined by Justice John Paul Stevens, who was appointed by President Ford at the age of fifty-five in 1975, a moderate Republican who has voted consistently since taking his place on the Court in favor of recognizing the right to choose abortion.

After Justice O'Connor's appointment the seven-justice majority for reaffirming *Roe* had shrunk, in the *Akron* case, to six to three. When *Thornburgh v. American College of Obstetricians and Gynecologists* was decided in 1986, that majority had narrowed, through an apparent change of sentiment by Chief Justice Burger, to five to four. When Rehnquist was elevated to chief justice and Justice Scalia took his place on the Court, most observers concluded that Chief Justice Burger had been replaced by another solid vote to overturn *Roe,* with the margin left five to four in favor of *Roe.*

The antiabortion campaign to alter the complexion of the American judiciary truly bore fruit in 1989, in the landmark decision of *William*

*Webster v. Reproductive Health Services.*[23] The *Webster* case presented an abortion clinic's challenge to a Missouri abortion law. The government of Missouri (William Webster is the state's attorney general) and the Bush administration both urged the Court to take the *Webster* case as an occasion to reconsider its decision in *Roe v. Wade.*

In a different setting, the *Webster* case might have been routine, presenting another in a series of post-*Roe* challenges to a variety of abortion restrictions. The Missouri law includes a restriction on the performance of abortions in public institutions, even when the woman would be paying her own bill; a preamble in the statute that declares that "the life of each human being begins at conception"; and a regulatory requirement that a number of tests of fetal viability be performed when a woman seeking an abortion is believed to be twenty weeks pregnant.

What made the *Webster* case so critical was the change in the composition of the Supreme Court. This was to be the first public test of the positions of Justice Scalia and Justice Kennedy on the question of abortion since they had become members of the Court. While Justice Scalia had expressed scholarly opposition to *Roe* before his appointment to the Supreme Court, Justice Kennedy, though conservative, seemed more of a question mark. And, notwithstanding her dissents in previous abortion cases, Justice O'Connor had scrupulously avoided joining any opinion expressly calling for *Roe*'s reversal. The depth of her opposition to *Roe* was thus unknown.

With only four solid votes to reaffirm *Roe,* the tenuous nature of the constitutional right to choose to terminate a pregnancy was evident to anyone who could count. The interest in the case was reflected in the number of friend of the court ("amicus") briefs submitted on behalf of individuals or organizations not parties to the case but with an interest in its outcome. *Webster* produced a record number: Seventy-eight amicus briefs were filed, surpassing by twenty the previous record of fifty-eight, which had been held for the thirteen preceding years by the landmark affirmative-action case, *Regents of the University of California v. Bakke.*[24]

## The Webster Case

While the Missouri law in *Webster* contains a number of provisions, most of the shouting was about a portion of the statute that requires testing for fetal viability—to determine if a fetus which a woman wants to abort is able to survive outside the womb.

The viability testing provision is not a model of clarity. It provides that a physician may not perform an abortion on a woman whom he or she believes to be twenty weeks or more pregnant unless the doctor

first undertakes certain tests "to determine if the unborn child is viable."
The statute then appears to contradict itself. On one hand, it states that
the physician must "us[e] and exercis[e] that degree of care, skill, and
proficiency commonly exercised by the ordinary skillful, careful and prudent physician engaged in similar practice under the same or similar
conditions." On the other hand, it mandates that "[i]n making this determination of viability, the physician *shall perform* . . . such medical examinations and tests as are necessary to make a finding of the gestational
age, height, and lung maturity of the unborn child."[25]

The contradiction is that the tests required by the latter provision
would *never* be used by a prudent physician on a fetus that seemed about
twenty weeks old. This is because tests of fetal weight are not accurate
in that age range, and amniocentesis, the only currently available procedure for testing fetal lung capacity, "is contrary to accepted medical
practice until 28–30 weeks of gestation, and imposes significant health
risks for both the pregnant woman and the fetus."[26]

Although the law is not perfectly clear, two things are certain. First, if
the statute were read to require that these *specific* tests be performed at
around twenty weeks of pregnancy, a time at which some of them pose
significant health risks to the pregnant woman without even being useful
in determining whether a fetus is viable, it would be struck down, not
just under *Roe,* but under the most lenient standard of review ever used
by the Court inasmuch as the requirement would then serve no rational
purpose at all. If the statute really mandated these specific tests, it
would serve only to harm pregnant women without advancing the government's interest in preserving fetal life. It would therefore be deemed
unconstitutional quite apart from *Roe.*

Second, if the Missouri statute were construed to require only those
tests that would *actually* be helpful in determining fetal viability, prior to
*Webster* it would have been upheld even under *Roe.* For although the
tests are required when the physician believes the woman is twenty
weeks pregnant—not the twenty-four weeks that, according to nearly all
physicians at the beginning of the 1990s, mark the earliest point at which
a fetus may be "viable"—there is a roughly four-week margin of error in
determining a fetus's actual gestational age. Because government is recognized by *Roe* to have a compelling interest in ensuring that no abortions occur after viability (except to preserve the woman's life or
health), the regulation, read in this way, does not conflict with *Roe.*

A badly splintered Court upheld Missouri's regulation. However, no
single opinion, no single piece of reasoning, was endorsed by a majority
of the justices. Chief Justice Rehnquist, in an opinion joined by Justice
White, the other *Roe* dissenter, and by Justice Kennedy, strained in
interpreting the regulation in order to make a bold statement. With some

difficulty, the chief justice first construed the statute to require only those tests to determine fetal viability warranted by a doctor's "reasonable and professional skill and judgment" in the circumstances.[27] Thus, he concluded that the statute need not automatically be struck down. He next pointed out that the tests—designed to protect fetal life, *not* the life or health of the pregnant woman—add to the cost of abortion. This added cost, according to the chief justice, would be forbidden by *Roe* if it were deliberately imposed on a *second*-trimester abortion. Because some of the viability tests required by Missouri will turn out to have been conducted in cases where the fetus's *actual* gestational age was less than initially estimated by the doctor, so that the pregnancy was really in its second trimester, the chief justice concluded that the Missouri regulation conflicts with the framework set out in *Roe v. Wade.*

This was an extremely tenuous, if not altogether circular, form of argument. It went out of its way to read *Roe* far more sweepingly than necessary. But it did permit these three justices to make their point. Chief Justice Rehnquist explained that in view of the conflict with *Roe* (the conflict he had stretched both the Missouri statute and the *Roe* decision to create) either the viability testing provision or the trimester framework set out in *Roe* had to be abandoned. The three justices thus had their opportunity to attack *Roe.*[28]

Chief Justice Rehnquist's opinion concluded that government has an interest in protecting potential human life not just after viability but *throughout pregnancy* and that that interest is sufficient to permit Missouri's regulatory interference with the exercise of the abortion right. Although it did not expressly say so, his plurality opinion (the opinion representing the views of the largest number of justices voting with the majority, three in this instance) suggested that the Court need not examine closely the strength of the government's reasons for limiting access to abortion. It described a woman's right to decide whether to terminate a pregnancy as a mere "liberty interest,"[29] harking back to Justice Rehnquist's *Roe* dissent, a right apparently no different from her "right" to drive a car, say, or open a store, or work as a dentist.

One member of the Court, Justice Scalia, went further. In a blistering opinion he wrote that instead of merely gutting the central point of *Roe*'s protection of a special liberty interest, as he understood the plurality to be doing, he would expressly overrule *Roe v. Wade.* Thus, four justices voted to uphold the regulation essentially on the ground that the right to decide whether or not to terminate a pregnancy, unlike the right to assemble, speak freely, or be secure in one's home, merits no special protection from government.

Four other justices left no doubt they would strive to protect, as special, the right to choose abortion recognized in *Roe.* In *Webster* Justices Brennan and Marshall joined an opinion written by Justice Blackmun voting to strike down much of the regulation because of its interference with that right. Justice Stevens wrote separately to argue that the viability testing provisions are unconstitutionally burdensome and would be indefensible even if there were no special protection for the abortion right and that the plurality had construed *Roe* in a strained way just to reach the question whether *Roe* should be overruled. These four Justices continued to insist that the right to decide whether to end a pregnancy *is* fundamental.

This left the fate of *Roe v. Wade* and of the constitutional protection of abortion rights as of late 1989 in the hands of Justice O'Connor, who has displayed a distinctive view of the meaning of *Roe* and its progeny. For her, those cases mean only that a regulation imposed on an otherwise lawful abortion is unconstitutional if it imposes what she describes as an "undue burden" on a woman's abortion decision. By deciding that the viability testing provisions of the Missouri law did not "unduly" burden that decision and, thus, that the law did not come into conflict with the Court's previous rulings on the question of abortion, Justice O'Connor was able to vote to uphold the regulation without concluding that *Roe* should be expressly overruled.

With four apparent votes to overturn *Roe* and four to uphold it, Justice O'Connor in 1989 became the swing vote on the permissibility of state abortion legislation. As long as she would continue to find in abortion regulations no "undue burden", they would be upheld. And although *Roe v. Wade* will never be blotted from the history books and indeed may perhaps never be expressly overruled, there is likely nonetheless to be substantial practical infringement on the right for which *Roe* once stood. Beyond this Justice O'Connor has retained the option of reconsidering the very existence of the right to abortion recognized in *Roe* and its progeny.

Some commentators immediately after *Webster* tried to downplay the decision's significance. Some suggested that because the framework of *Roe* remained technically undisturbed, the *Webster* decision represented no change in the law. The distinguished legal philosopher Ronald Dworkin, for example, wrote that because the main opinion was joined by only three justices, "it is wrong to assert, as many commentators have, that its remarks about *Roe v. Wade* have already changed constitutional law."[30] But if constitutional law is as constitutional law does, then after *Webster, Roe* is not what it once was.

*Webster* was and remains an open invitation to state legislators to see just how strictly they can regulate abortion without Justice O'Connor's finding the burden on the abortion right "undue." Indeed, the four members of the Court who expressly reject *Roe,* whether in whole or in part, could not have made their invitation much clearer.

Justice Scalia bluntly denounced the Court's failure to resolve *Roe*'s status decisively in *Webster*. He predicted—wrongly, it turns out—that the decision's ambiguous outcome would "doubtless be heralded as a triumph of judicial statesmanship."[31] He made it plain that he saw the Court's action as more cowardly than statesmanlike,[32] and he went so far as to dismiss Justice O'Connor's contrary assertion as one that "cannot be taken seriously."[33] After launching several further (and equally pointed) attacks upon Justice O'Connor in particular[34] and after slamming her views as "irrational,"[35] Justice Scalia left no doubt where *he* thought the Court was heading with respect to abortion: "It . . . appears that the mansion of constitutionalized abortion-law, constructed overnight in *Roe v. Wade,* must be disassembled door-jamb by door-jamb, and never entirely brought down, no matter how wrong it may be."[36]

*Webster* suggests that the constitutional tide turned in 1989 for state regulation of abortion. After years of striking down state restrictions on abortion, the Court finally upheld one. The change has been confirmed by the Court's post-*Webster* decisions dealing with abortion. In the 1990 case of *Hodgson v. Minnesota,* [37] the Court by a five-to-four vote upheld a Minnesota law requiring a minor seeking an abortion to do one of two things: either agree to have *both* her parents notified forty-eight hours before undergoing the procedure, or obtain a court order sanctioning the abortion. On the same day, in *Ohio v. Akron Center for Reproductive Health,* [38] the court voted, six to three, to uphold a requirement that a physician inform at least one parent of a pregnant minor before performing an abortion on her.

The Minnesota law at issue in *Hodgson* actually contained two provisions for parental notification. The first required that both parents of a pregnant minor be notified before an abortion could be performed, with no exceptions. Justice O'Connor, the only swing vote in *Hodgson*, found this requirement invalid, and the Court's four more liberal members joined her in striking it down. But the second provision in *Hodgson* said that if the first, very strict two-parent notification rule was declared invalid by any court, then a pregnant minor seeking an abortion would have the choice of informing both parents or seeking a court order authorizing the abortion. Justice O'Connor joined her four most conservative colleagues in ruling that this requirement was constitutional. Remarkably, her decision to invalidate the strict two-parent Minnesota notice requirement was not based squarely on a conclusion that the statute "unduly burdened" the abortion right. Rather Justice O'Connor seemed to imply that, especially since the law made no exception to its notification requirement even for the case of abusive parents, the provision failed adequately to serve the purposes put forward by the state to justify it.[39] Indeed, the only right with which Justice O'Connor explicitly found the Minnesota law to interfere was the right of the *family* to decide as it best saw fit—by which she presumably meant one parent's right not to be forced to consult an absent or perhaps abusive other parent.[40] While Justice O'Connor in *Hodgson* thus did vote to strike down an abortion restriction for the first time, her opinion in that case suggests no firm line beyond which she will not tolerate the regulation of abortion.

After *Webster* the race is on to see how great the sea change has been. It is a race whose intensity has not been diminished by the Court's subsequent pronouncements on abortion. State legislatures, full of pro-life candidates elected when their antiabortion views could affect nothing, have set out to test the new Court's limits. The political battle for reproductive autonomy has been taken to the streets, in demonstrations and counterdemonstrations.

Even more frightening to pro-choice advocates, some state law enforcement officials, in Louisiana, for example, with less publicity (and less political risk) have sought permission to enforce old abortion statutes—some enacted in the mid-nineteenth century—that had been judicially nullified based on the Supreme Court's decision in *Roe.* These law enforcement officials argue that *Webster* overruled *Roe* without saying so and that consequently there is no longer any basis for continuing the injunctions against old abortion laws.

*Webster* did not overrule *Roe*—indeed all the justices went out of their way to make that clear—so these challenges defy the Constitution as the Supreme Court interpreted it as of the date *Webster* was decided. Still, it is chilling to think of such antiquated, disused criminal laws being enforced against women who seek abortions today without even a current legislative enactment declaring abortion a crime.

Most of the attempts to resuscitate these laws seem doomed to fail. Old abortion statutes have often been superseded by specific enactments—for example, certain types of parental or judicial consent provisions—that implicitly repealed the earlier prohibitions on abortion. In addition, without contemporary reenactment, statutes enacted at a time when abortion meant something radically different, both in terms of women's health and safety and in terms of what we now understand about the process of fetal development—especially statutes originally enacted simply to protect pregnant women's health—might not give potential defendants as much notice as the Constitution requires of exactly *what* conduct is criminal.

The fact that some of these laws were never enacted by a legislature that even took into account the constitutional significance of an abortion right also might lead a court to conclude that their enactment did not satisfy the requirements of due process of law mandated by the Fourteenth Amendment to the Constitution. For these reasons, an attempt to enforce laws such as these that impose a crushing burden on a person's autonomy and that were enacted as long ago as the 1850s, would have serious constitutional difficulty. But this is by no means a settled question.

In early 1990, a federal court in Louisiana ruled that that state's pre-Civil War antiabortion law had been impliedly repealed by later, inconsistent enactments and thus could not be enforced.[41] But if *Roe* is overruled, there are likely to be many more enforcement efforts of this sort, and some may succeed. Pre-*Roe* laws and subsequently enacted abortion statutes that are unconstitutional under *Roe* remain at least arguably on the books in thirty-three states.

The future of *Roe* became even cloudier in 1990 with the surprise retirement of Justice William Brennan and his replacement on the bench by President Bush's appointee, fifty-one-year-old United States Court of Appeals Judge David H. Souter. Justice Brennan—one of the giants in the public life of this century, who sat on the High Court for thirty-four years—was a staunch defender of reproductive rights, and one of the four justices who at the time of his retirement adhered to the view first put forward in *Roe.* While his confirmation hearings suggest that Justice Souter may well be a brilliant jurist, and is likely to be a moderate conservative, his views on abortion rights—the focus of much of those hearings—remained unknown when he took his seat on the Court. No case likely to be decided in Justice Souter's first year on the Court presents him with a good opportunity to express his views on the merits of *Roe,* but if he joins his conservative brethren (Chief Justice Rehnquist and Justices White, Scalia, and Kennedy) when the abortion right next reaches the Court, then *Roe* would effectively be overruled whatever Justice O'Connor's equivocations might lead her to do—at least in the absence of a switch by one of the four justices who have appeared to indicate that they would vote to overturn *Roe*.

To consider whether *Roe* was rightly decided in the first place, we must examine competing views about what the Constitution does or doesn't say about abortion. Before considering that question, however, we should look at the history of the legal treatment of abortion in the United States and at the responses of other nations and cultures to the abortion question.

# 3

# Two Centuries of Abortion in America

If all law tells a story, the story of abortion in America is not a simple one. Retelling it may help set the contemporary clash over abortion rights in a broader framework by revealing how it has been shaped and where it originated. That story may also help us see that while the clash over abortion is one of absolutes, absolutes themselves may be contingent; they arise out of particular social contexts, problems, and concerns that change as society changes.

Current debate in America concerning abortion appears to pose an insoluble conflict between two fundamental values: the right of a fetus to live and the right of a woman to determine her own fate. The contemporary citizen seeking an ethical solution to the abortion dilemma must, it seems, navigate like Ulysses between the Scylla of infanticide and the Charybdis of women's bondage.

This vision of abortion almost totally obscures the fact that these competing values are in significant part peculiar to late-twentieth-century America. Far from being inevitable outgrowths of the natural order of things, these competing values are socially constructed.

To assert that the forms of our thinking on abortion may be new and that the values underlying the abortion debate are social constructs is not to deny, of course, that they express fundamental beliefs about the way people should live. It does not denigrate such beliefs to acknowledge that they are historically created and dependent upon particular experiences and modes of understanding. Yet if we recognize the nature of our beliefs, we may ultimately be better able to discern the social agendas implicit in the positions taken on each side of the abortion question.

## *From the Revolution Onward*

In early post-Revolution America, abortion, at least early in pregnancy, was neither prohibited nor uncommon. Each American jurisdiction— that is, each of the states—was governed by the common law, the cor- pus of English judge-made law that had evolved over the centuries preceding the Revolution, as supplemented by legislated laws. At the time of the Revolution and of the adoption of the United States Constitu- tion—indeed, until 1821—no state had enacted a statute outlawing abor- tion.

Under common law, abortion was permitted until "quickening," the time when the first movement of the fetus was perceived by the woman. In practice this meant that abortion was unrestricted until the fourth or fifth month of pregnancy. This rule was supported by a number of ra- tionales. For some, fetal movement signified that the fetus had a soul. For others, especially those in the medical profession, performance of an abortion before quickening was deemed to present little danger to the woman's health. At the most pragmatic level, the distinction was rooted in the scientific limitations of the time: Before quickening, no one could know for sure if a woman was pregnant. If it could not be known that a woman was pregnant, it could not be proved that an abortion had been performed and certainly not that one had been intentionally performed.[1] The common law also provided that even when an illegal abortion was performed, the woman involved was immune from prosecution.[2]

Because postquickening abortion was considered a crime, we know that the first American lawmakers valued fetal life. But we cannot know with certainty how high a value they put on it. During the early history of the United States abortion was at worst considered a misdemeanor of- fense. This may mean that society attached little moral significance or legal importance to the fetus. But it could also reflect judicial and legisla- tive restraint in the face of great uncertainty about the existence and development of the unborn. The laws that society makes must be about actions that human beings can control. No rational society makes laws it cannot hope to enforce.

Abortion of unwanted pregnancies apparently was not unusual in the United States during the late eighteenth and early nineteenth centuries. At the beginning of this period American attitudes toward sexuality be- came more liberal. Indeed, one historian, Michael Gordon, has calculated that three of ten women in late-eighteenth-century New England were pregnant at the time they married. This was more than three times the rate of pregnancy among brides a hundred years before.[3] That there was a decline in the overall birthrate during this same period suggests an increase in the use of both birth control and abortion.

Eighteenth- and nineteenth-century American society was predominantly rural. Such societies typically value children as a source of economic strength, and the United States was no exception. For this reason abortions were sought primarily by single women.[4] A woman generally resorted to abortion to conceal the sexual behavior that resulted in her pregnancy. Abortion as such was not perceived as a great moral issue. Abortion was the subject of debate only in terms of the illicit sexual behavior that occasioned it, behavior so harshly condemned at times that society's rebuke must have been a terrible thing for women to endure.[5]

The regulation of abortion by statute began in America in the nineteenth century. The earliest laws were primarily about women's health.[6] Nineteenth-century abortion methods were as dangerous as one might imagine. When one considers that it was popular to administer poisons to pregnant women to induce abortion (on the dubious theory that a dosage sufficient to kill the fetus might spare the woman), it is understandable that America's first statutory abortion regulation, enacted by the state of Connecticut in 1821, prohibited only the inducement of abortion through the use of dangerous poisons.

The Connecticut statute applied, even then, only to postquickening abortions, testimony to the strength of the view that a woman should be able to end an unwanted, unconfirmed early pregnancy.[7] Indeed, America's first abortion statutes dealt primarily with postquickening abortion.

Mortality from surgical abortion was also extremely high. Statistics from New York in the early nineteenth century demonstrate a *30 percent death rate* from infections after abortional surgery, even when performed in hospitals. In contrast, the mortality rate in cases of childbirth was *under 3 percent.* Even so, by 1840 only eight states had enacted any kind of statutory restriction on abortion.

Between 1800 and 1900 the rate of fertility—the average number of children born to each woman—for white American women (the only group for which statistics are readily available) dropped almost 50 percent, from 7.04 to 3.56 children.[8] This drop coincided with an increase in the visibility of abortion. The popular press carried advertisements for home abortifacients and remedies to relieve "menstrual blockage."[9] These home remedies were often unsafe and ineffective and ranged from strenuous exercise to soap solutions and mild poisons to physical intrusions into the uterus. The rate of abortion increased, and by the middle of the nineteenth century there was, by some estimates, one induced abortion for every four live births.[10]

## The Role of the Medical Profession

When restrictive abortion laws were finally enacted in the United States in the mid-nineteenth century, the force behind them was neither religious belief nor a popular moral crusade. Rather, our strict abortion laws were the product of lobbying by the organized medical profession and reflected increased professionalization of the practice of medicine.

The motivations that lay behind the physicians' movement to outlaw abortion seem quite complex. "Regular" physicians—generally those who were trained in the more rigorous medical schools and who subscribed to the scientific method[11]—were certainly concerned about the safety of abortions to the women who underwent them. In the face of a rapidly swelling number of irregular physicians and apothecaries promising miraculous abortional procedures, the profession also felt the need to police its boundaries. In part to legitimize and consolidate the medical profession,[12] physicians were eager to halt the competition in abortion services from medical irregulars.[13]

In the mid-nineteenth century regular physicians were the members of society most vocally committed to defending the value of human life.[14] In 1857 Dr. Horatio Storer, a specialist in obstetrics and gynecology who was then the leading American advocate for the criminalization of abortion, launched a national drive by the ten-year-old American Medical Association (AMA) to end legal abortion.[15] At its annual convention in 1859 the AMA called for the "general suppression" of abortions, including those performed before quickening.[16] The physicians organized an effective media and lobbying campaign that focused on the fetus's right to life. Over time their efforts altered the prevailing attitudes about the practice in the United States.

A moral component to the doctors' campaign cannot be denied. The movement to end competition for abortion services by having abortion declared criminal was motivated by a reluctance to perform abortions. On a professional level, adherence to the Hippocratic oath and to the ethical vision it implies underlay an important part of the movement to distinguish the regulars from other providers of medical services during this period. The oath expressly forbids giving a woman "an instrument to produce abortion," and it has been interpreted to forbid inducing abortion by any method.

In personal terms, advances in science had given many doctors moral misgivings about abortion. Specifically their more science-based view of human development as a continuous process rather than as a sudden event led them to question the relevance of the distinction between quick and nonquick fetuses.[17]

## The Position of the Roman Catholic Church

The Roman Catholic Church, currently the best-known organized opponent of abortion, was notably absent from the nineteenth-century debate on the subject. The belief that abortion is murder was not yet a part of church dogma.

To be sure, there was debate within the church on the issue, and some Catholic clergy vehemently opposed abortion. But the traditional Catholic position on abortion—similar to that taken by Aristotle and by some rabbinic scholars in the Jewish tradition—was that a fetus was not a human being until the time of "animation." Under Catholic doctrine, a male fetus became animated—that is, infused with a soul—at forty days after conception. A female fetus was believed to become animated at a gestational age of eighty days.

Although Catholicism traditionally forbade even early abortion, such abortion was condemned in essentially the same way that the church condemned, and continues to condemn, masturbation and contraception. It held that these acts interfered with the procreative purpose of sexual activity; but a fetus was not considered a person early in pregnancy, and early abortion was not deemed homicide.

Only in the late nineteenth century, following the discovery of fertilization, did the debate about abortion within the church tip in favor of its now familiar position that human life begins at conception. This shift was given a strong push by the theological acceptance of the Immaculate Conception of Mary, not to be confused with the doctrine of the Miraculous Conception, Mary's pregnancy with Jesus. In 1701 Pope Clement XI declared the Immaculate Conception a feast of universal obligation. In 1854 Pius IX incorporated into Catholic dogma the teaching that Mary was without sin from the moment of her conception.[18] These beliefs were not easily squared with the view that the fetus did not acquire a soul until later in pregnancy.

It was only in 1869 that Pius IX promulgated the papal enactment *Apostolicace sedis,* which abandoned the limitation under which excommunication was to be imposed only for those abortions of "ensouled" fetuses.[19] (This strict rule had first been in effect for two years in the late sixteenth century. The papal bull that contained the original declaration, *Effraenatam,* was issued by Pope Sixtus V in 1588. But it did not gain acceptance with contemporary theologians and it was repealed two years later by the new pope, Gregory XIV.[20]) Only at this point, well after the movement to criminalize abortion was under way in America, and only by implication, was the groundwork laid within the church for the theological position that all abortion is homicide.

Nor were the other organized religions at the forefront of the movement to outlaw most abortion in the United States. Historian James Mohr tells us that the religious press did not address abortion until after the Civil War. While religious opposition to abortion grew more vocal toward the end of the century, the clergy were influenced by the medical profession, not the other way around.

## Social and Demographic Forces

In any event, the doctors' campaign was by no means a pure question of abstract morality—for any segment of society. The movement also reflected (and appealed to) concerns spurred by a metamorphosis in the social meaning of abortion.[21] As increasing numbers of married white middle-class Protestant women chose to interrupt pregnancies, abortion took on for powerful groups new and threatening significance.[22]

By 1860 the birthrate among white Americans of British and northern European descent had declined significantly by comparison with that of the newly arrived, predominantly Catholic groups, in part as a result of an increased rate of abortion among the more established Americans. In 1855, for example, the birthrate among thirty- to thirty-four-year-old Irish immigrant women in Buffalo was more than twice that for native-born white Protestant women.[23]

Doctors used the transformation in the demographics of abortion to awaken among the Protestant middle and upper classes racist fears regarding the ethnic makeup of the United States. Eugenic concerns, expressed as a fear of race suicide through the failure to have enough children, motivated and were relied upon by physicians advocating abortion restrictions. An 1865 tract by antiabortion physician Horatio Storer, for example, asserts that abortion is "infinitely more frequent among Protestant women than among Catholic."[24] Another physician voiced concern about the threat to what he called "our most intelligent communities."[25] Physicians at the time also expressed particular concern about abortion among women of "high repute."[26]

Protestant fears of race suicide were far more prominent in the mid-nineteenth-century movement against abortion than was religious antiabortion sentiment of any kind. Indeed, historian Mohr concludes that such opposition to abortion as *was* expressed by Protestant clergy was motivated more by the declining birthrates of adherents than by moral opposition to the practice.

## The Early Role of Women's Concerns

Declining birthrates also threatened a different kind of revolution in the social order. A central theme throughout the history of abortion in America is that women who are able to control their reproductive destinies gain freedom to pursue personal missions other than the traditional one in the home. The physicians' campaign for abortion regulation urged that abortion posed a threat to traditional sex roles.

An 1871 report of the American Medical Association Committee on Criminal Abortion is a disturbing example of this appeal. This report describes the woman seeking an abortion as "unmindful of the course marked out for her by Providence" and characterizes her as selfish and immoral. The report reflects a vision in which female sexuality cannot honorably be divorced from the traditional role of wife and mother: "She yields to the pleasures—but shrinks from the pains and responsibilities of maternity. . . . Let not the husband of such a wife flatter himself that he possesses her affection. Nor can she in turn ever merit even the respect of a virtuous husband. She sinks into old age like a withered tree, stripped of its foliage; with the stain of blood upon her soul, she dies without the hand of affection to smooth her pillow."[27] What is most striking about this vision is the attempt to pit husbands, who must often have participated in decisions to terminate pregnancy, against their wives.

The fears of dislocation in traditional family structures were no doubt reinforced by an increase in the percentage of women who worked. The urbanization of America during this period increased the number of working-class women forced to supplement their husbands' wages with incomes of their own. The dramatically transformed terms in which abortion was depicted and the altered terms through which the woman who would choose an abortion was described reflect a graphic, sometimes desperate effort to reassert traditional social control and male dominance.

Intriguingly, abortion rights, despite this link to the control of women by men, were not really on the agenda of the early feminists. For them questions of reproduction were primarily about avoiding death in childbirth. To this end they advocated "voluntary motherhood," primarily through sexual abstinence. Within the context of nineteenth-century morality, the feminists attempted to seize a high ground of sorts by arguing that women were by nature morally superior; women could oppose abortion because unlike men, women were thought willing to abstain from sex and were viewed to be by nature nurturing.

## The Nineteenth-Century Laws

The nineteenth-century physicians' campaign mobilized public opinion. Within less than two decades, more than forty antiabortion statutes had been passed in the United States. The structure of these laws tells the story of their purpose. In general, mid-to-late-nineteenth-century abortion legislation abandoned the distinction between quick and nonquick fetuses. Like some earlier laws that had been supported by regular physicians, these statutes tended to have exceptions for "therapeutic" abortion. Typically abortion would be permitted when necessary *in the opinion of a physician* to preserve the life of the woman. (Ten states required the concurrence of a second physician.)[28]

The regular physicians succeeded in their movement to obtain control of the practice of abortion; the social metamorphosis of the abortion question into a matter of "medical judgment" had taken hold. The laws reflecting and reinforcing this metamorphosis sent out a powerful signal about the role of the medical profession.

Laws dating from this period may appear familiar. Although the issue is clouded by subsequent enactments that worked to repeal inconsistent earlier laws, versions of these laws arguably remain on the books in more than thirty states today. As the preceding chapter noted, if *Roe v. Wade* were overruled, it will be urged that some of these laws—designed more to protect the medical profession than to safeguard *either* women *or* the unborn—will be enforceable even without reenactment by any twentieth-century legislature.

## The Early Twentieth Century to 1950

With antiabortion laws firmly in place in the United States, the early twentieth century was remarkably free from debate about abortion, remarkably so because it appears that women continued to have abortions in roughly the same proportions as they had before criminalization. Although the data on this subject are not completely reliable, it seems that as many as one in three pregnancies was terminated by induced abortion during this era.[29]

A large number of abortions, primarily those involving privileged women, were performed by sympathetic physicians who found that they could interpret the exception for therapeutic abortions as broadly or narrowly as conscience demanded.[30] Some physicians vigorously resisted legislative efforts to specify what circumstances would justify abortion.[31] Many adopted a loose personal definition of which conditions threatened a woman's life.

Indeed, throughout the period of criminalized abortion in America the scope of the therapeutic abortion evolved, reflecting broader issues in society. In the 1930s poverty became a widely accepted basis for providing a therapeutic abortion. In the 1940s and 1950s some doctors performed abortions for psychiatric reasons.

Most abortions, and a particularly high percentage of those performed on poor women and women in rural areas, were performed illegally. The tale of death that illegal abortions caused is well known; the personal tragedies that tale recounts were widespread, and evident in every social stratum. Paradoxically the tale has been so often told that many listeners have become anesthetized to the human pain it reflects.

Notwithstanding the criminalization of abortion and the wide-scale practice of illegal abortion, there were few indictments and disproportionately fewer convictions for abortion during this period. For example, in Minnesota between 1911 and 1930 there were only 100 indictments for abortion, and only 31 of these led to convictions. In Michigan between 1893 and 1932, 156 indictments for unlawful abortion were handed down, with only 40 resulting in conviction.[32]

Most Americans were apparently content to live with this hypocrisy. The major "punishments" for abortion, punishments disproportionately borne by underprivileged women, remained the mutilations or deaths that often attended the illegal terminations of unwanted pregnancies.

## The Modern Era: From the 1950s to the 1970s

The modern era of debate on the abortion question began in the 1950s. As advances in medical care increased the safety of those pregnancies in which women experienced life-threatening complications, doctors found it less easy to justify abortions for these women, or for the vast majority of others, on the theory that pregnancy put their lives in danger. The legitimate availability of "legal" abortions therefore shrank. Scrutiny of medical abortion decisions, on the other hand, grew dramatically.

As medicine itself grew ever more bureaucratic, hospitals established review boards to decide in each case whether an abortion was "necessary."[33] Whatever the intent behind the development of these boards, individual doctors who had previously made abortion decisions privately were now subject to the approval of a public review board. As the number of therapeutic abortions being performed plummeted, doctors insisted that the laws on abortion be clarified both in order to prevent lawsuits based on differing interpretations of the "preservation of the woman's life" language in state abortion statutes and because of a perception that hospital review boards were arbitrarily limiting—for non-health-related reasons—the number of therapeutic abortions that could be performed.[34]

The American Law Institute (ALI), an influential body of legal academics and practicing lawyers mostly from major urban centers, responded in 1959 by suggesting a revision in its widely copied Model Penal Code. The proposed revision, which later grew in legislative influence, included three now familiar defenses to a charge of criminal abortion: first, that continuation of the pregnancy "would gravely impair the physical or mental health of the mother"; second, that the child was likely to be born with "grave physical or mental defects"; and third, that the pregnancy resulted from rape or incest. This Model Code required a certification by two doctors stating the circumstances justifying the abortion. Even this quite conservative and cautious proposal for reform, put forward by a professional elite of doctors and lawyers, was slightly ahead of its time.

The climate that permitted a broad reexamination of America's abortion laws in the 1960s was not born of any single event, nor did it grow from any single vision. Doctors, who had been at the forefront of the battle to criminalize abortion, began to focus on closer comparisons of the relative health-related dangers of aborting a pregnancy, versus carrying it to term.[35] With rapid medical progress, abortion had become a comparatively safe procedure, especially during the early months of pregnancy. Whereas in 1955 roughly a hundred out of every hundred thousand legal abortions resulted in the woman's death along with that of the fetus, by 1972 that grim number had fallen to three out of a hundred thousand.[36]

At the same time the physicians' concept of "health" was expanding to include the pregnant woman's overall mental state. Thus, in cases of rape and incest doctors began to include psychological harm in their calculations of the costs associated with childbirth. Perhaps most important in altering the views of the medical community, however, was a focus on the child's "quality of life."

## Two Tragic Episodes

Two widely reported tragic episodes at this time helped transform medical opinion about abortion. The first involved the tranquilizer thalidomide. Banned in the United States but marketed in Europe, thalidomide caused horrendous birth defects when taken by pregnant women. In the late 1950s and early 1960s ingestion of thalidomide by pregnant women in Europe resulted in the births of many badly deformed children. Infants were born with seallike flippers instead of arms or with shortened thighs and twisted legs. Others were missing ears or had paralyzed faces.[37]

In 1962 an American woman, Sherri Finkbine, a mother of four from Arizona, discovered early in her fifth pregnancy that a tranquilizer she had taken was thalidomide that her husband had brought back from overseas. Upon the advice of her physician, Finkbine scheduled a legal abortion, to be performed at a local hospital.

Hoping to warn other pregnant women of the dangers of the drug she had taken, she informed a friend at a newspaper. The resulting front-page news story created enough controversy to dissuade the hospital from performing the abortion that had been scheduled. No physician had argued that Finkbine's own health was at risk. Yet she had received permission for a "legal" abortion with little difficulty, from a doctor who had seen her only a few times previously. Finkbine found herself unable, even after bringing a court challenge, to have an abortion legally. She was ultimately forced to go to Sweden to obtain a legal abortion. The embryo, the doctor told her later, had been horribly deformed.[38] The Finkbine case left in its wake a controversy in the medical community over the proper reach of the exceptions physicians were morally and legally allowed to make under the criminal abortion laws.

The rubella, or German measles, outbreak of 1962–65 provided the second major impetus in the American medical community for abortion reform. The occurrence of rubella during pregnancy also causes severe birth defects; when contracted by a woman in early pregnancy, rubella can cause blindness, deafness, and severe mental retardation in her child. As a result of the 1962–65 epidemic, some fifteen thousand babies were born with birth defects. Physicians, already moved by changing scientific realities, reacted to the restrictive abortion laws that permitted this tragedy.[39] The medical profession, to which we owe most of America's laws against abortion, now mobilized in favor of easing the restrictions, on the basis of the belief of doctors that on many levels abortion might be less tragic than childbirth.

During the rubella episode some doctors and hospitals performed abortions even in cases not strictly permitted by statute. After pressure was brought by Dr. James McNulty, a Catholic physician on the California State Medical Board, an investigation led to charges against nine physicians, who became known as the San Francisco Nine. Their experience deterred other doctors in California from performing such abortions. This strengthened the pioneering efforts to pass a reform measure, the Therapeutic Abortion Act, in the California legislature.[40]

Indeed, in 1970 a Minnesota physician, Dr. Jane Hodgson, now an abortion rights advocate whose name appears on the first abortion case presented to the Supreme Court after *Webster,* was convicted for performing an abortion on a twenty-three-year-old mother who had contracted German measles, a conviction reversed after the Supreme Court's *Roe* decision. Hers was the first conviction of a doctor for performing an abortion in a hospital in United States history.[41]

The events of the early and mid-1960s exposed the fact that legal abortion remained available for a variety of conditions that were not explicitly included in the statute books. Similarly, physicians who took a broad view of what counted as an abortion to " save the life" of a woman were amazed and distressed by the outcry surrounding the abortions in the Finkbine case and the rubella epidemic.

Faced with the possibility of legal liability in an area that they had always considered the domain of professional judgment, physicians now pressed legislatures to codify the practices the profession had engaged in for the preceding decades.[42] In 1967 the AMA issued a statement favoring liberalization of the abortion laws, and in 1970 it recognized the legitimacy of abortion, limited only by the "sound clinical judgment" of a physician.[43] Indeed, a majority of doctors around that time appear to have favored the right to abortion on request.[44]

Unlike the nineteenth-century physicians' campaign on abortion, the climate in the late-1960s for reconsideration of abortion laws was less a creation of physicians than a response to popular interest in the question. The Finkbine case had attracted the attention of the general population and had angered many people who believed that, in this of all cases, legal abortion should have been available. A Gallup poll taken shortly after the incident revealed that 52 percent of Americans supported Sherri Finkbine's abortion, while only 32 percent opposed it.[45]

## Women in the Modern Period

A crucial social development was the change in the kinds of lives that many women chose to lead or often were economically forced to lead during this period. Increasing numbers of women entered the work force or undertook higher education. From 1950 to 1970 the percentage of white married women working outside the home nearly doubled, and in the 1970s college enrollment among white women increased 57 percent. Among black women it increased 112 percent.[46] By 1970, 43.3 percent of working-age women were in the work force.[47] Large numbers of women sought jobs outside those areas traditionally reserved for women, jobs in which continuity was important either for obtaining seniority rights or for achieving advancement and promotion. As it had during the nineteenth century, the fertility rate among American women dropped precipitously during the 1960s and 1970s: from an average of 3.7 children in the mid-1950s to 2.4 in 1970, to about 1.8 in 1975.[48] This change corresponded with an increase in the number of young women choosing to delay marriage and childbearing.

As this increasing number of women entered the work force, they confronted the glaring disparity between men's and women's treatment and compensation in the workplace. Because women increasingly defined themselves by their careers, groups of economically powerful and politically active women came to feel more strongly that control of reproduction was critical to the achievement of parity in the labor market.[49] The development of new contraceptive techniques like the birth control pill and the intrauterine device (IUD) helped make possible the dramatic changes in the life style of women in America. But the freedom of women to work as equals with men outside the home led to an increase in women's reliance on *all* types of fertility control, including abortion.

The beliefs of many of those who first supported and led the reexamination of abortion law were shaped less by ideology—feminism or libertarianism, for example—than by a simple awareness, often firsthand, of the real pain that was being inflicted by the regime of criminal abortion laws. Pat Maginnis, for example, the founder of the Society for Humane Abortion in California, had had to go to Mexico in 1957 to obtain an abortion. Even more influential was her experience as a medical technician stationed in the Panama Canal Zone for the Women's Army Corps. Interviewed by Lawrence Lader for his 1973 book *Abortion II,* Maginnis recalled: "I saw the brutality of the system—a soldier's wife who had attempted suicide after being refused abortion, held captive like an animal in the hospital ward, literally forced by the staff to continue a pregnancy she hated."[50]

Journalist Susan Brownmiller had a horrid experience traveling to Puerto Rico, where she had to plead with doctors for an illegal abortion.[51] Gloria Steinem, the widely known feminist and cofounder of *Ms.* magazine, had an abortion overseas in the 1950s after considering suicide and the inducement of a miscarriage through reckless horseback riding.[52] Steinem has written about a transformative experience she had many years later at an early feminist meeting she covered for *New York* magazine at which women spoke openly about their frightening and humiliating experiences with abortion: "Suddenly, I was no longer learning intellectually what was wrong. I knew. I had had an abortion when I was newly out of college, and had told no one. If one in three or four adult women shares this experience, why should each of us be made to feel criminal and alone? How much power would we ever have if we had no power over the fate of our own bodies?"[53]

Some doctors, nurses, and hospital emergency workers who had seen the brutality imposed by illegal abortions sought now to liberalize abortion laws. Another profession often witness to the humiliation, pain, and death caused by criminal abortion laws was the clergy. In a world where women were afraid to admit not only to having had an abortion but, indeed, to having engaged in any sexual activity not intended to lead to pregnancy, it was often members of the clergy who saw and heard firsthand the stories of brutal back-alley abortions that many women kept secret even from their friends and families.

In May 1967 twenty-one members of the clergy made a stunning announcement, reported on page one of the *New York Times,* offering to refer women to doctors they knew to be performing safe and legitimate abortions.[54] Their organization, the Clergy Consultation Service on Abortion, soon spread across the country with thousands of clergy participating as "gentle lawbreakers," referring women to doctors in Puerto Rico, in Great Britain, and even within the United States.[55] In Michigan alone, a hundred members of the clergy, including a few Catholic priests, gave such referrals.[56]

These clergy served as a form of *Consumers Report* for abortion. A pregnant woman, scared for her life and virtually penniless from the trip to Mexico or Puerto Rico, could at least have assurance that the doctor she was going to see was legitimate, that the facilities were safe and clean. This movement among the clergy also lent moral legitimacy to those who would reform the law of abortion.

The climate for change was thus set by those who had directly seen the reality of the pain of illegal abortion in the lives of real women. In a time when the market on visual reality has been effectively cornered by those who oppose abortion—with grim photographs of aborted fetuses, or with films that show fetuses writhing in what appears to be pain during abortion procedures—we would do well to remember and to try to envision the disfigurement, destruction, and death wrought by the butchery of the black-market back-alley abortion. Photographs of the corpses of women killed in this way, some of them crouching in contorted poses, others ironically curled into fetal positions themselves, are at least as shocking as any picture of a dead fetus. That such photographs are seen more rarely must not be permitted to obscure the genuine tragedies they reflect. Many of the women who suffered were not anesthetized; we should not be either.

## The Role of Poverty, Race, and Population Concerns

There were many other forces underlying popular support of abortion reform in general during the 1960s. Greater sensitivity to issues of poverty and race heightened awareness of the unequal quality and availability of abortion services to women according to social class and skin color. By the late 1960s as many as 1,200,000 women were undergoing illegal abortions each year: more than one criminal abortion a minute.[57] The operation, of course, was not free, nor was its quality unrelated to the money one could afford to spend on it. The price for an abortion varied tremendously: from a thousand dollars for an operation using advanced medical technology to less than a hundred dollars in poorer areas of the United States.[58]

The movement toward relaxation of restrictions on abortion also took place in a context of growing concern in America about worldwide overpopulation. Between the two World Wars the focus of population theory underwent radical change. Economists now argued that the key to economic prosperity and equality was a low birthrate.[59]

After 1950, increased U.S. contact with the developing nations reinforced this impression. In 1954 biologist Paul Ehrlich published a widely noted pamphlet, *The Population Bomb,* in which he asserts that population "threatens to create an explosion as disruptive and dangerous as the explosion of the atom." Indeed, in what must be regarded as a measure of the consensus on this issue and of its importance, former Presidents Harry Truman and Dwight Eisenhower became cochairmen of Planned Parenthood/World Population in 1965.

## The Legislative Crescendo: 1967–1973

The movement to reform strict abortion laws that began in the 1950s came to a head in the years between 1967 and 1973. From 1967 onward a rapidly increasing number of state legislatures passed cautious reforms of their harsh antiabortion statutes, primarily along the lines suggested in the ALI revision to the Model Penal Code. In the aftermath of the German measles epidemic, Colorado and California both passed reform bills, with then Governor Ronald Reagan unenthusiastically signing the California bill. In North Carolina, one of the first three states to pass a reform bill similar to that proposed by the ALI, many of the legislators were influenced by visits to institutions where abandoned children in near-vegetative states were kept.[60] In the 1967 session alone twenty-eight state legislatures considered liberalization bills; by 1970 twelve had passed them.[61]

These reform laws, actively supported by medical, women's, and religious groups, were generally based on the ALI model statute. Their thrust was to create exceptions to the strict prohibitions on abortion so as to make it legal when the fetus had a serious physical or mental defect, when a physician thought that an abortion was necessary to protect the mental or physical health of the pregnant woman from grave impairment, and in cases of rape or incest.[62] The results were not always benign.

The Georgia reform law, for example, based on the ALI statute (and ultimately struck down in *Doe v. Bolton,* the less famous companion case to *Roe v. Wade* ), was enacted primarily to protect doctors from prosecution while preventing nonresidents from flocking to Georgia to receive abortions.[63] The statute required the pregnant woman to swear under oath that she was a resident of Georgia and the doctor to certify that he believed her. It imposed extremely intrusive and burdensome regulations, requiring the woman to obtain the approval of three doctors and a hospital review board.[64]

The law also required that in cases of rape, the solicitor general of the local judicial circuit in which the rape was alleged give a statement that there was probable cause to believe that a rape had, in fact, occurred. The statute expressly permitted anyone who was a close relative to sue to vindicate any right the fetus might have to prevent the abortion. It also allowed—in a sense, invited—hospitals to refuse to admit abortion patients, and doctors to refuse to perform abortions, on moral or religious grounds. And of course, it continued to prohibit almost all abortion.[65]

While many of the supporters of these new laws hoped that the statutes would give doctors latitude to make humane exceptions on the
ground of health—especially the flexible ground of mental health—the
result may have been just the opposite. Two years after the enactment
of Colorado's reform provision, one of the statute's sponsors observed
of its poor performance that its effect was that "19 of every 20 women
seeking legal abortions are being turned away."[66] Some thought that the
new laws, by putting a spotlight on abortion, actually resulted in a *decrease* in the number of legal abortions.

The *New York Times* reported that only forty-five legal abortions had
been performed in Denver in the first five months after the passage of
Colorado's reform legislation.[67] "We tried to change a cruel, outmoded,
inhuman law," lamented Representative Richard Lamm, the future governor of Colorado; "what we got was a cruel, outmoded, inhuman law."[68]

While a hundred thousand illegal abortions took place annually in
California, just over two thousand took place legally in the first half of
1968 under the new reform law.[69] The law didn't even make exceptions
for those whom it might have seemed intended to protect. A seventeen-
year-old girl who was impregnated by an older man driving her home
from a baby-sitting job was denied an abortion. In an effort to induce an
abortion herself, she jumped off her garage and died from the resulting
injuries.[70]

The laws were particularly unhelpful to poorer women. A legal abortion under the reform laws tended to cost between six and seven hundred dollars (the equivalent of between twenty-one and twenty-five hundred dollars in 1989 dollars[71]) with a hundred dollars just for a required
letter from a psychiatrist.[72] Most poor women could not even consider
legal abortion in reform states. A back-alley abortion could be had for
one-third the cost of an average legal abortion. So it seems the reform
laws didn't work. This gave steam to a movement for the repeal of
criminal prohibitions on abortion, at least in the early months of pregnancy.

## Reform Versus Repeal

Women's groups, which had not played a very active role in the movement for reform, by now almost universally supported complete repeal.[73] To abortion rights activist Lawrence Lader, "[t]he most puzzling
issue in the revolt against abortion laws [was] why women suffered
quietly for so long."[74] The societal taboo on women's sexuality appears
to have been the blanket that for many years smothered the open ex-

pression by women of their deep concern about criminalized abortion—notwithstanding the staggering number of women who had personally endured the frightening, humiliating, and dangerous experience of obtaining the procedure illegally and the many men who knew, or suspected, the pain their lovers or wives had undergone. As University of California sociologist Kristin Luker has written, the prohibition on abortion seems to have been more strongly linked to questions of sexuality than to ultimate issues of human life.[75]

One woman who had an illegal abortion explained, "Nobody talked about it. Each one of us thought that we were a separate little person who was the only one who had ever done such a thing."[76] Women had yet to overcome the shame associated with the illicit sexuality that led to abortion.[77] As Marcia Cohen has described, television reports on abortion, then as now, routinely showed women who had had abortions in silhouette, like drug addicts or paid informants.[78]

A radical group of feminists called the Redstockings tried to fight this tendency by holding "speak-outs" across the country where women would describe in public their experiences with illegal abortions.[79] Other feminist groups also recognized the importance of this approach. But society's disapproval of nonprocreative sexual activity by women had an effect even on feminists who were politically active.

With the exception of Margaret Sanger's fight for access to contraception during the first half of the twentieth century,[80] the women's movement had acted on the premise that avoiding sexual issues would enhance its credibility and keep political debate about issues concerning women focused on economic and political freedom. Even in the early and mid-1960s this belief had a strong silencing effect. Prominent feminist Jean Faust described the situation: "We were all blocked at first by traditional labels. We were afraid of being called 'loose women' if we included abortion in our platform."[81]

In Betty Friedan's classic work *The Feminine Mystique,* published in 1963, there was little direct mention of abortion or birth control. In a chapter devoted to sexuality, Friedan's tone seems almost puritanical. Observing the apparent paradox of the increase in women's sexual frustration in a society that was becoming more and more sexually open, Friedan remarks only "that several generations of able American women have been successfully reduced to sex creatures, sex-seekers. But . . . [i]nstead of fulfilling the promise of infinite orgiastic bliss, sex in the America of the feminine mystique is becoming a strangely joyless national compulsion, if not a contemptuous mockery."[82] Whether she avoided the issues of birth control or abortion consciously, for strategic reasons, or unreflectively, out of a social taboo so strong it defied open recognition, the result was that even women as conscious of the predicament of womankind as Friedan said little or nothing, at least publicly, on the topic that today virtually *defines* the women's movement.

Despite this silence, Friedan's book, which sold nearly two million copies, was a powerful force in the movement toward the political empowerment of women in support of abortion rights. The book caused many women to rethink the meaning of their assigned sexual roles. And it made Friedan the symbol of the feminist movement. When she later threw her weight behind abortion rights, her influence was great.

Perhaps the turning point for reproductive choice as a women's issue took place at the 1967 national conference of the year-old National Organization for Women (NOW). After an intense debate many of the younger women, led by the forty-five-year-old Friedan, succeeded in having the "Right of Women to Control their Reproductive Lives" included in NOW's Women's Bill of Rights.[83]

This development greatly concerned the mainstream professional women in NOW. They worried that the focus on abortion could jeopardize the dignity of the movement and distract from their economic goals. Indeed, many delegates resigned.[84] Still, more and more women added their energies to the movement for abortion rights. Many women who believed in reproductive freedom would be silent on the issue no longer.

The movement for repeal of abortion laws benefited not only from the participation of women's groups but also from the incorporation of feminist theory. The idea of repealing abortion laws was consistent with the view that women had a *right* to a legal and safe abortion. For many women, more reform of abortion laws was not enough, for it would simply mean that (primarily male) physicians would have wider latitude to make a decision that these women believed was the business only of the pregnant woman. The necessity of a doctor's approval, even under reformed abortion laws, reinforced the traditional role of the woman as dependent, without control over her future.[85]

## Growth of the Repeal Movement

Ironically, the physicians' reform movement itself lent credibility to the cause of outright repeal; the question of the proper scope of medical discretion in providing abortions really only begged the further question of why it should be a matter of *medical* discretion at all. While the belief that elective abortion was every woman's right originated with radical feminists, by the late 1960s it had become dominant within the movement against restrictive abortion laws.[86]

Activists, dissatisfied with reform laws, sought repeal. Ruth Smith, former executive director of the Association for the Study of Abortion, Dr. Lonny Myers, founder of the Illinois Committee for Medical Control of Abortion, and abortion rights advocate Lawrence Lader called a national conference on abortion law in Chicago in 1969. They used this conference to create the National Association for the Repeal of Abortion Laws (NARAL—after 1973 the National Abortion Rights Action League), which was to become the principal national lobbying group for grass-roots pro-choice organizations around the country.[87]

Support for total repeal of abortion laws also came from some unexpected sources. Lyndon Johnson had appointed a Presidential Advisory Council on the Status of Women, with former Senator Maurine Neuberger of Oregon as its chairwoman. Its report, released in 1968, called for the repeal of all abortion laws.[88] This was the first time a major figure in the federal government had taken this position.

One influential voice was that of the Jesuit law professor and future congressman Robert F. Drinan. Drinan, an early opponent of the Clergy Consultation Service,[89] condemned governmental imposition of norms and judgments describing who was fit to be born and who was not. Consequently, he objected to abortion law reform.

Yet in September 1967 Drinan surprisingly stated that he had come to believe that even though *reform* laws were immoral, the *repeal* of the government prohibition of abortion in the first twenty-six weeks of pregnancy was acceptable because "[u]nder this arrangement the law would not be required to approve or disapprove the choices of parents and physicians as to who may be born or not born."[90]

As advocates of legalized abortion gathered strength, they attracted the early support of feminists, lawyers, and health and welfare workers. The repeal movement also achieved credibility through public endorsement by liberal clergy, including the Episcopalians, the United Church of Christ, the United Methodist Church, and the United Presbyterian Church, and by such respected groups as Church Women United and the YWCA.[91]

After having kept its distance for several decades, the population control movement also openly acknowledged abortion as a significant factor in controlling fertility. In 1969 Planned Parenthood publicly supported the repeal of criminal abortion statutes, and in 1972 the Commission on Population Growth issued a favorable report on abortion reform.[92]

In 1970 Hawaii became the first state in the nation to repeal its criminal abortion law, legalizing abortions performed before the twentieth week of pregnancy.[93] While Hawaii had seemed to be headed for a reform law similar to that enacted in other states, Father Drinan's view convinced both the superintendent of the Catholic school system and State Senator Vincent Yano (a Catholic with 10 children who had been awarded the honor of Knight of the Pope) that repeal was the least evil of the various unsatisfactory solutions to the abortion problem.[94]

Yano, along with an experienced lobbyist named Joan Hayes, promoted the repeal law.[95] The bill was signed into law by a governor who, despite being Catholic, stated that it was best for laws to be silent on abortion both to prevent the maimings and deaths caused by dangerous illegal abortions and to respect the separation of church and state.[96] Hawaii's repeal measure did contain a residency requirement. The fact that even a state so distant from the others as Hawaii was concerned about being an "abortion mill" for the rest of the country was testimony to how far women would go to obtain safe abortions.

In New York, which also repealed its abortion law in 1970, the view that repeal was less objectionable than reform also proved influential. The most dramatic example of the power of this position in New York was provided by Assemblyman Martin Ginsberg.

The previous year the New York legislature had considered and almost passed a reform law, supported by then Governor Nelson Rockefeller, that permitted abortion in cases of serious fetal deformity. Ginsberg, who had been crippled as an infant by polio, played an important role in defeating the bill by helping to convince 14 erstwhile supporters to change their votes. He asked what such a law would say to those "already in this world . . . malformed or abnormal" about their right to live. "God saw fit to let me live in this form and condition . . . so I could be here on April 17 to speak on this specific bill."[97]

By 1970, however, Ginsberg, like Drinan, had come to the conclusion that repeal, though not reform, was acceptable because repeal did not represent a government policy that singled out those who might be disabled as less worthy of life.[98]

The contest over the repeal of New York's criminal abortion law was particularly fierce. The battle lines were drawn for the first time in the way that has become so familiar to all of us in the years since *Roe.* For the first time a strong feminist bloc made its political presence felt. On the other side, the Roman Catholic Church took a strong public position against legalization.

The forces opposing repeal included among their targets those Catholic legislators, like Mary Anne Krupsak, subsequently New York's lieutenant governor, who took a position in favor of abortion rights. As a result of her stance, Krupsak's father's neighborhood business was picketed, even by her in-laws, and she was singled out by the bishop of

Albany in a day of mourning for legislators who supported the legalization of "murder."[99]

In an interesting shift on the race suicide theme that had animated debate in the nineteenth century, some black legislators felt pressure to oppose the repeal because of "black genocide" concerns expressed by black militants. The *New York Times,* however, reported that minority group coalitions supported reform of abortion laws. They were no doubt aware that it was nonwhites who "most often became statistics in the grim catalogue of women killed by illegal abortions." In fact, a NOW survey in Buffalo showing that 75 percent of blacks favored repeal helped convince black assemblymen to vote for repeal.[100]

After the repeal measure passed the New York Senate (by a vote of 31 to 26), it needed 76 of 150 votes to pass in the Assembly. As the final votes were being counted on April 9, 1970, it became apparent that the repeal bill would fail by a single vote. Yet unknown to anyone, one assemblyman who had opposed repeal was privately feeling tortured by his opposition to legalized abortion.

Because Assemblyman George Michaels represented a conservative district with a constituency that was about 65 percent Catholic, his opposition to repeal seemed almost automatic.[101] However, Michaels's son, who was working as an intern in a Cincinnati ghetto, had made his parents aware of the human suffering he had seen as a result of criminal abortion laws. When Assemblyman Michaels tried to explain to his family that his vote was not so important because repeal would pass anyway in a few years, his wife had replied, "In the meantime, thousands of women will be butchered in underworld abortion."[102]

Having cast his vote against repeal, Michaels thought of this as he watched the final votes being counted. Just as the speaker was to proclaim defeat of the bill, Michaels approached the microphone. As The *New York Times* described the moment:

> Assemblyman George M. Michaels of Auburn, his hands trembling and tears welling in his eyes, stopped the roll-call only seconds before the clerk was to announce that the reform bill had been defeated for lack of a single vote. . . . "I realize, Mr. Speaker," Mr. Michaels said, "that I am terminating my political career, but I cannot in good conscience sit here and allow my vote to be the one that defeats this bill—I ask that my vote be changed from 'no' to 'yes.' "[103]

The floor of the legislature erupted with pro-repeal legislators, aides and lobbyists bursting into tears at the last-minute victory.

Michaels paid a political price for his vote. His own party refused to endorse him,[104] and he was defeated for reelection in the primary.[105] But he has never expressed regrets. Michaels said later to Lawrence Lader: "I had spent 37 months in the Marines in World War II, much of it in combat in the Pacific under mortar fire. This [feeling before I switched my vote] was worse than anything. It was the summit of my life."[106]

Another assemblyman from a heavily Catholic district told papers anonymously: "My wife (a Catholic and a school teacher) prayed for me and said vote for the bill. . . . She had a 12 year old girl in a class who was pregnant. What can you do?"[107]

In the same year Alaska joined New York and Hawaii in repealing its abortion law. As a result of a popular referendum, the state of Washington soon followed.

## *The Road Not Taken: What If the Court Had Not Stepped In?*

How might the story of abortion have unfolded if it had been left to the legislatures to decide? What of this road not taken? It is worth asking whether continued legislative action might have spared us, as Professor Mary Ann Glendon of Harvard Law School contends, what Dean Guido Calabresi of Yale Law School has called the "sense of desperate embattlement" that has marked the abortion debate since the Supreme Court's 1973 decision in *Roe.*

Professor Glendon has argued that the *Roe* decision interrupted an evolutionary process within state legislatures. She observes that between 1967 and 1973, nineteen states had reformed their abortion laws. She posits that this represented a trend and observes that such laws were also enacted in Western Europe in the subsequent period.[108]

During the 1970s and 1980s this argument gained currency. It has frequently been invoked to persuade even those who favor the right to choose abortion that *Roe* should be overruled and abortion regulation returned to the states. Indeed, Professor Glendon has argued that in such a circumstance, abortion would continue to be freely available— through legislation—during the first trimester of pregnancy.[109] But the history of abortion law reform in the United States seriously undermines this claim.

As we have seen, the types of reforms passed by most states hardly increased access to abortion, even in cases where there might have been widespread support for use of the procedure. Further, the movement for the repeal of criminal abortion laws, although it had some successes, was by no means overwhelmingly victorious. If the razor-thin margin of victory in liberal New York were not enough to demonstrate the point, it emerges with clarity as soon as one recalls that measures to repeal abortion restrictions were defeated in several other states during this same period. Indeed, two years after the legalization of early-term abortion in New York, the legislature voted to repeal in part the *new,* more permissive abortion law. The right to choose abortion was preserved only when Republican Governor Rockefeller—over the protest of President Nixon, who was then seeking Catholic support—vetoed this measure.[110]

In the early 1970s a movement in opposition to laws providing greater access to abortion was also in its nascent stages. In 1971 John C. Willke, a Cincinnati physician and the father of the National Right to Life Committee, published with his wife a *Handbook on Abortion,* with arguments against abortion as well as pictures of aborted fetuses. While this movement did not gain its real intensity before *Roe v. Wade* was decided, it, too, was not without its victories.

In Michigan Willke helped defeat a 1972 referendum that would have legalized abortion in the first twenty weeks of pregnancy. While a *Detroit News* poll during the month preceding the vote showed 59 percent support for the measure, the referendum lost by a vote of 62 percent to 38 percent.[111] The pro-life activists in Michigan were funded in part by solicitations in all Catholic parishes.[112] Willke and his wife distributed a glossy color "fetus brochure" entitled *Life and Death* with which Michigan was blitzed in the final weeks of the election. The brochure, the cover of which contrasted a color photograph of a child born at twenty-one weeks of pregnancy with a grisly one of a fetus aborted by saline injection, was distributed to a large majority of the two million households in the state. The Willkes' brochure helped achieve similar success in North Dakota, where it was even more widely distributed and where a referendum on abortion was defeated by an even wider margin.[113]

In addition, the availability of safe, legal abortion in some states might well have drained vitality from the movement for further reform elsewhere. Well-to-do women who sought access to abortion services but who could afford to travel out of state to obtain them might no longer have felt a need to press for abortion law reform at home. Indeed, even in states with laws based upon the ALI provision, many of the obstacles to abortion that remained (such as the requirement that women obtain signed statements from doctors, and the need to employ effective advocates before hospital review boards) were most easily met by members of this group. The continued local restrictions on abortion were far more devastating to the poor, precisely those who lacked the political power to effect change. It is obviously easier for a suburban woman of means to find a psychiatrist who will say that she would be emotionally crippled by continued pregnancy than it is for a woman struggling to make ends meet in the inner city to do so.

So it seems a serious mistake to assume that the partial success of legislative reform movements in a few key states would have been replicated elsewhere if *Roe v. Wade* had not intervened. Instead, there might well have been a dislocation in the democratic process, as economically and politically powerful groups not gravely burdened by local abortion regulations chose to spend their energies on what, to them, were more pressing concerns. In this perhaps limited sense, leaving the question of abortion in the legislative arena might actually have disserved many of the values of democracy.[114] Indeed, it is instructive in this regard that between 1971 and 1973 not one additional state moved to repeal its criminal prohibition on abortion early in pregnancy.

Thus, when one hears that a consensus for increased access to abortion early in pregnancy was building in America in the early 1970s, and this is cited as evidence that *Roe* could be overruled in a supposed victory for democracy over judicial imperialism without a meaningful decline in the availability of abortion services, one should look to the story that was being told by the law when the *Roe* decision was handed down. In 1973 only four states, two of them (Alaska and Hawaii) geographically remote from the rest of the nation, guaranteed a woman by law the right to choose for herself whether to terminate her pregnancy. There is little evidence that the United States was on the verge of emerging, in the early 1970s, from the long shadow of shame that had branded women as blameworthy for extramarital sex and nonprocreative sex and that condemned them for choosing abortion even when the choice was a painful and profoundly reluctant one.

# 4

# Locating Abortion on the World Map

Abortion is an option to which people of all times and places have resorted, with or without religious consent, legal approval, or medical supervision. Anthropologist George Devereux has concluded that "abortion is an absolutely universal phenomenon."[1]

Abortion is a practice meaning different things for different people, an act whose significance has shifted as it has become the concern of successive sets of social actors. Although our society now grounds its discussion of abortion in terms of individual rights and is polarized around seemingly irreconcilable claims—a woman's right to privacy and autonomy versus a fetus's right to life—and although the people who have appropriated either side of the debate are mainly lawmakers, women's organizations, physicians, and religious groups, in numerous other societies this is not the case.

Like our examination of the American history of abortion in the preceding chapter, this look at the treatment of abortion by various groups and countries may serve a dual purpose. First, the concrete realization that other groups view abortion in ways very different from ours may help us to approach anew our own understanding of some of the implications of various possible solutions to the abortion question.

Second, we shall see in some cases that moral tales societies tell themselves about abortion, the stories they incorporate in ethical or legal norms, are designed to serve apparently unrelated needs that those societies feel. Indeed, as was the case in the United States in the nineteenth century, even the identity of the participants in the abortion debate may reveal a great deal about unspoken concerns that underlie one or another abortion policy. While the views most of us hold about abortion, whether pro-life or pro-choice or a mix of both, are not *obvious* rationalizations for policies that serve nonabortion-related interests, our views about what is the right way for American society to treat abortion may well reflect deeply held, sometimes hidden, views about the needs of society.

## *A Glimpse at Preliterate Societies*

Some early attitudes about abortion may survive in the various approaches taken to it by the relatively few preliterate societies that exist today in isolated areas of the world. In many cases, anthropological research tells us not so much about law as about custom, custom often inferred from the observation of individual instances of abortion. Still, the work of anthropologists reveals that members of preliterate cultures take a variety of approaches to abortion, and a variety of considerations may justify terminating a pregnancy. Ultimately the treatment of abortion in these societies appears to reflect pragmatic societal needs at least as much as it reflects moral or metaphysical concerns.

In some cultures the decision to end a pregnancy is strictly the choice of the woman. For example, among the Kafir tribe in Central Asia there is no taboo or restriction at all with regard to abortion.[2] This attitude seems to be the exception, however. Whether or not abortion is justified in some situations, it appears generally in most cultures to be considered a "wrong." It is sometimes difficult, however, to separate a society's view of its own practices from the value judgments placed on them by those Western researchers who report them.[3]

The high rates of maternal mortality during childbirth in preliterate societies may play a role in justifying abortion. In some societies women choose abortion, or are made to abort, because they are too young, too old, too small, or too sick to bear children.[4] On the other hand, primitive methods of abortion can also present a significant risk to the pregnant woman's health. This appears to explain some cultural restrictions on the availability of abortion. Some societies in which this may be a concern have created elaborate superstitions surrounding the effects of abortion on the health of women.[5]

Economic strain is a theme that informs the abortion debate in the most traditional as well as the most developed societies. Child-spacing concerns are particularly acute in migratory societies that hunt and gather since an individual mother is greatly limited in the number of children she can both nurse and transport.[6]

Some preliterate cultures enforce child spacing through a taboo on sexual activity by women during the pregnancy and breast-feeding periods.[7] Women in these societies may choose, or may be pressured, to abort to avoid the long period of abstinence from sexual relations, or they may be required to abort if they have violated the taboo.[8]

In other preliterate societies the concern about economic strain justifies eugenic abortion policies. For example, among the Masai of East Africa, abortion is mandated when a fetus is fathered by an old, weak, or infirm man. (In a number of societies infanticide likewise is permitted for eugenic reasons.[9]) In some preliterate societies in which natural resources are severely limited, the choice between abortion and childbirth has stark implications for the entire society. Abortion is often viewed as an acceptable means of limiting the number of individuals demanding a slice of a constantly shrinking pie.[10] On the Pacific island of Nukuoro, for example, the tribal chief decides whether or not a woman should have an abortion on the basis of the community's ability to support an additional member.[11]

The practice of abortion to conserve resources is not limited to those groups whose circumstances are marginal or destitute. The Tikopian people, on the Pacific island of Tikopia, intent on preserving a consistently high quality of life, use abortion, along with contraception and infanticide, as a means of keeping population down.[12] These examples reflect a pattern that is the mirror image of that found in agricultural economies where children are valued because they represent additional labor, an economic asset.

Another concern that animates the practice of abortion in some preliterate societies is that of lineage and honor. As with economic necessity, depending on the situation this concern can militate in favor of or against abortion. In societies in which there is a male-dominated, gender-based hierarchy, a woman's decision to abort may be considered an insult to her husband and his family. In the Xhosa tribe of South Africa the chief is reported to collect a fine as compensation for the loss of a follower from any woman who terminates a pregnancy.[13] By contrast, in order to protect dynastic lines, some societies may permit men to force women to have abortions in certain situations.[14] Some groups consider it wrong *not* to abort an illegitimate fetus, and the husband of a pregnant woman will in some circumstances force an abortion in a case of adultery.[15] Within societies that place special emphasis on lineage and honor, women may induce abortion to express hostility toward their husbands or to guard against discovery of sexual activities disapproved of by the existing social order.[16] Indeed, "improper" paternity may be the most common rationale for abortion in traditional societies.

Some preliterate societies believe that abortion can cause various supernatural evils to be visited upon individuals or the entire community. The penalties for abortion in these societies may be imposed upon the woman, her family, and anyone helping in the abortion. They can range from social ostracism to beatings to death.[17] Among the Mojo of South America a woman who aborts is drowned in the belief that this is necessary to prevent an outbreak of dysentery in the village.[18]

## Classical Cultures

Preliterate societies are often denigrated as "primitive," but on the subject of abortion their practices seem no more arbitrary than those of the ancient Greeks and Romans, which have informed the modern abortion debate. Advocates for choice have observed (and Supreme Court Justice Harry Blackmun wrote in *Roe v. Wade*) that the ancient Greeks and Romans had a permissive attitude toward abortion. In classical societies it appears to have been the father who had the right to determine whether there was to be an abortion.[19]

In his *Republic* Plato writes that abortion should be compelled in any woman who becomes pregnant after the age of forty.[20] Aristotle believed that the state should fix the number of children a married couple could have. If a woman became pregnant after having her allotted number of children, Aristotle thought that she should be compelled to abort her pregnancy "before she felt the life."[21] While Hippocrates disapproved of abortion, his was a minority position in ancient Greece.

This permissive attitude toward abortion seems the product of a view that the fetus was simply a part of the pregnant woman's body.[22] It may be that the practice of abortion was considered wrong in ancient Rome, but it was certainly not considered seriously so. Indeed, Seneca tells us (though with disapproval) that it was common practice for a woman to induce abortion in order to maintain the beauty of her figure.[23]

## Abortion in the Soviet Union and Eastern Europe

In the twentieth century abortion regulation has often been an instrument of government control of society. That reality is perhaps best illustrated by abortion policy in the Soviet Union and the Eastern bloc, at least prior to the radical transformation under Mikhail Gorbachev in 1989. Events in this area of the world are unfolding so rapidly as this book goes to press that it is hard to imagine the Soviet and Eastern

European treatment of abortion, or of almost anything else, for that matter, remaining static. Yet it remains informative to consider recent abortion policies in these countries.

Perhaps the most striking and remarked-upon aspect of abortion in the Soviet Union has been its sheer prevalence.[24] Even by notoriously understated official reports, the Soviet Union over a substantial period of time averaged between one and two abortions for every live birth; by contrast, in 1985 the United States averaged one abortion for each 2.3 live births.[25] More candid assessments estimate that two in three, or even four in five, pregnancies of Soviet women (or at least of ethnic Russian women) end in induced abortion, producing an average of up to nine abortions over the course of a Soviet woman's lifetime.[26]

The enormous scale of abortion in the Soviet Union is more a result of the unavailability of adequate contraceptive techniques than of any respect for the right of women to control their bodies. The first Soviet abortion decree, issued in 1920, was cast solely in terms of public health. Calling abortion a necessary "evil," the proclamation alluded to the pervasiveness of illegal abortion in a country torn by famine and civil war and suggested that abortion was a symptom of the social illnesses that lingered from the czarist regime and for which socialism would soon find the cure.[27]

Even Soviet women's organizations, which along with physicians' groups had pressed for the 1920 decree,[28] reflected this tone and did not argue for legal abortion in terms of equality or liberty.[29] Rather, they argued that legalization was necessary to prevent the carnage of illegal abortions and to help keep women in the labor force. Some women (including Lenin's wife, Krupskaya, a champion of birth control and a supporter of legal abortion) actually derided as "bourgeois selfishness" the notion that women should control their own bodies.[30]

Those opposing legalized abortion argued not in terms of the right to life of the unborn child but in terms of the duty of the mother to perform her "natural" role in society, that of bearing children. The socialist state, they believed, had a right to the "natural" increase of the labor force occasioned by this role.[31]

In 1936 Joseph Stalin outlawed abortion. He proclaimed that socialism had solved the underlying problems that had caused abortion and he exhorted Soviet women to fulfill their natural role and "give the nation a new group of heroes."[32] In Stalin's words, woman "is mother . . . she gives life, and this is certainly *not* a private matter but one of great social importance."[33]

Even Stalin, however, could not prevent illegal abortion in a country where contraceptive devices were virtually nonexistent, where the practice of abortion as birth control was deeply rooted, and where the necessities of life, urban housing in particular, were so hard to come by. Two decades later, after Stalin's death, abortion was relegalized, again for "public health reasons."[34]

Perhaps reflecting the lack of emphasis on abortion as an exercise of a woman's rights, the actual practice of legal abortion in the Soviet Union has shown little concern for the well-being of women. The medical establishment seems tied to the traditional view of maternity as the proper vocation for women[35] and does not go out of its way to make the procedure as tolerable as possible. First-person accounts of abortion clinics in the Soviet Union report that the medical personnel are unfriendly, even abusive, and that privacy is nonexistent. It has also been reported that the procedure is performed with ineffective anesthesia, or with no anesthesia at all, unless the woman reaches a private agreement with—in other words, bribes—a doctor.[36]

Where such a private agreement is reached, the pregnant woman enters the Soviet hospital feigning some other kind of condition. In exchange for payment, she is then afforded better accommodations, more courteous treatment, and more privacy. The abortion is typically performed at night. It is estimated that in the Soviet Union illegal abortions are about three or four times more common than legal procedures.[37]

Most of the Eastern bloc countries followed the Soviet Union's lead in the post-Stalin era in decriminalizing abortion, while requiring that it be performed in state hospitals by state-licensed doctors. The Czechoslovakian law permitting abortion for "social reasons" was imported from the USSR in 1957. Hungary's abortion laws were radically liberalized in 1956; more permissive laws were enacted in Poland and Bulgaria.[38]

By acknowledging abortion as an inevitability rather than a right, Eastern European countries retained for themselves the power to regulate abortion in the interests of state population policy. In many Eastern bloc countries, including Poland, Hungary, and Czechoslovakia, women have been required to obtain official permission from local committees in order to receive legal abortions, and even where approval is relatively pro forma and a right to appeal an unfavorable decision to a regional committee is preserved, the process has given the government a framework through which radical changes in abortion law can be effected with a minimum of ceremony.

Perhaps the best example of autocracy in abortion legislation has been Romania, which in 1966, in an attempt to increase population, banned all abortions for "social reasons," as well as all contraception. This meant that a pregnant woman could not get an abortion unless she already had four children; later the quota was raised to five children. According to one source, women who were age twenty-five and childless were forced to pay special tax penalties of between 10 and 15 percent of their salaries.[39]

Abortion was actively prosecuted under this regime in Romania. But as might be expected, falsified medical reports, general physician corruption, and widespread illegal abortions undermined the effectiveness of this policy. Because illegal private abortions performed by doctors or nurses were extremely expensive, costing more than three times the monthly salary of an average worker, thousands of women resorted to amateur abortionists.[40]

The government fought hard against attempts to get around the law. Women were watched at work for signs of pregnancy; those who tested positive were closely monitored. Miscarriages were investigated.[41] Measures became so extreme, according to a number of reports, that apparently many women were forced to submit to medical examinations every three months for any sign that they had had abortions.[42]

Despite the severity of its law, Romania was still said to have had one of the highest rates of abortion in Europe.[43] One commentator has also suggested that there was a high rate of infanticide or at least of infant death from delay in seeking treatment of common infant illnesses.[44] Moreover, by 1988 Romanian orphanages were filled beyond capacity with children who had been abandoned.[45] Perhaps this experience reflects women's reluctance to bear or to raise children in a society in which life is so completely controlled by the state. It is not surprising that one of the first acts of Romania's new government following the bloody Romanian revolution of late 1989 was the legalization of abortion.[46]

It should not be assumed from this example that the democratization of Eastern Europe, and perhaps of the Soviet Union, will predictably lead to fewer restrictions on, and better conditions for, abortion. The discussion of abortion may take on the character of free debate found in Western nations, with all the difficult questions it involves. But although women may feel freer to come forward and urge that society recognize abortion as a matter of right, openness also means a resurgence of those who long for more traditional ways and who have strong opinions about the traditional or natural role of women.

For example, in ardently Roman Catholic Poland the rise of Solidarity, which is closely associated with the church, has led to efforts to restrict abortion. Solidarity itself appears to be sharply divided, with a number of its partisans having presented a bill in Parliament that would revoke the permissive abortion laws currently in effect.[47] Eduard Shevardnadze, the Soviet foreign minister, added to the emerging dialogue in a 1987 speech in which he criticized abortion as stemming from "thoughtlessness and egoism." Shevardnadze called abortion an "important right to be used, not abused," and clearly suggested that, when practiced on a mass scale, abortion becomes an "antistate" evil.[48]

## Lessons from Nazi Germany

If the Soviet and Eastern European history of treating abortion as a matter of state population policy raises serious moral problems, the abortion policies of Nazi Germany best exemplify the potential evil of entrusting government with the power to say which pregnancies are to be terminated and which are not. Nazi social policy, like that of Romania, vigorously asserted the state's right to ensure population growth. But Nazi policy went even further. Following the maxim that "Your body does not belong to you," it proclaimed the utter absence of any individual right in the matter and made clear that abortion constituted a governmental tool for furthering Nazi theories of "Aryan" supremacy and genetic purity.[49]

Nazi propaganda constantly emphasized the duty of "Aryans" to have large families.[50] Family planning clinics were shut down, often on the ground of alleged ties with communism. The Third Reich made every effort to control contraception, ultimately banning the production and distribution of contraceptives in 1941.[51] The state, largely at the behest of SS leader Heinrich Himmler, abandoned its commitment to "bourgeois" marriage and undertook to promote the "voluntary" impregnation of "suitable women."[52] Allowances were paid to women, married or not, for having children.

Abortion and even its facilitation were, in general, serious criminal offenses in Nazi Germany; a network of spies and secret police sought out abortionists, and prosecutions were frequent.[53] By 1943 the penalty for performing an abortion on a ":genetically fit" woman was death; those on whose premises abortions were performed risked prison sentences.[54]

As early as 1933 the Nazis embarked on a policy of mandatory sterilization for "genetically defective" women. Hitler wrote that "there is only one infamy, namely for parents who are ill or show genetic defects to bring children into the world."[55] The sterilization laws were applied by a network of 205 "Hereditary Health Courts," with appeal as a matter of right to one of 26 "Higher Eugenics Courts."[56]

By 1938 Jews had been clearly defined as within the "genetically defective" group, and the state readily acquiesced in abortions by this group, for an abortion by such a woman was regarded as an incremental improvement in the "hereditary health" of the nation.[57] This complemented the policy of enforced sterilizations.

Although the birthrate clearly increased in the years before the Second World War, there is no evidence that Nazi policy had an appreciable effect on the number of illegal abortions, which hovered between an estimated five hundred thousand and one million annually.[58]

## Modern Asia: Japan

Supporters of free access to abortion have often pointed to Japan as an example of a modern state's successful implementation of a liberal abortion policy. While abortions are readily available in Japan, and in fact have at times been a mainstay of Japanese birth control, the history of and responses to Japan's abortion policy are not quite as consistent as many commentators would have one believe.[59]

Abortion has been known in Japan since at least the medieval period, and it has been documented that in the late Tokugawa era (1603–1867) abortion—and infanticide, particularly female infanticide—were extensively practiced.[60] Prohibitions against abortion coincided with the Meiji restoration of the nineteenth century. On the eve of the twentieth century Japan adopted a penal code heavily influenced by that of France. Like that Catholic nation, Japan criminalized abortion.[61]

After the Second World War Japan liberalized its abortion policy, but in a rather roundabout manner. In 1948 the government passed the Eugenic Protection Laws, which permitted abortions to "prevent the increase of the inferior descendants from the standpoint of eugenic protection and to protect the life and health of the mother."[62] The next year the act was amended to include economic hardship among the "health" considerations that would justify a legal abortion, effectively making abortions available upon request for Japanese women.[63]

Because there is an unusual level of fear in Japan about the safety of the pill, abortion has emerged as a—if not the—primary means of birth control.[64] Apparently, and remarkably, the medical profession has worked to prevent the introduction of other means of birth control in order to prevent competition with its extremely profitable abortion business.[65] However, the ready availability and employment of abortion do not mean that there is no societal disapproval of abortion in Japan. Attitude surveys among the Japanese generally show a mixed response to the practice.[66] And although religion apparently is not a significant factor in reducing the number of abortions in Japan,[67] there is opposition to abortion from some religious groups.[68]

Buddhism claims a multiplicity of adherents in Japan. While the Buddhist religion is opposed in spirit to the practice of abortion, its position does not have the kind of impact upon policy decisions that religious teaching does in the West. Buddhist clergy are not given to declarations of dogma or to taking direct stands on political issues. Still, compassion is a central virtue in Buddhist belief, implying an obligation to overcome egoism and to care for the fetus. Abortion, in other words, violates the Buddhist ideal of self-sacrifice. Its price is the woman's entrapment in the perpetual cycle of birth and rebirth.[69]

The Japanese Buddhists have a number of devotional practices that demonstrate their opposition to abortion, while possibly mitigating the sense that it can do permanent harm. As early as the Tokugawa period an aborted fetus came to be known as *mizuko* (water child or unseeing child). It was believed that the soul of the aborted child is sent back to a children's limbo, whence it might later be reborn into the family that earlier rejected it. The practice of erecting both statues of Jizō, the guardian of children, to honor fetus souls and tumuli containing the bones of aborted fetuses also dates from this era. This practice continues today, and monuments to *mizuko* have been built as recently as 1974 at the Hase Temple in Kamakura. Memorial services for the souls of aborted fetuses are fairly common in contemporary Japan.[70]

Shinto beliefs also have antiabortion implications. According to Shinto doctrine, both objects and the spirits of the dead can act upon the mundane world. A fetus that has been the victim of an abortion can, in this way, avenge itself on the woman who committed the abortion. An offering, *kuyō,* made to the fetus may help mollify it.[71]

While both Buddhist and Shinto beliefs tend to align in opposition to abortion, the only Japanese religious group with a highly articulate and vocal antiabortion position is the Seichō no Ie, the "Home of Infinite Life, Wisdom and Abundance." Holding a combination of Christian, Buddhist, and Shinto beliefs, Seichō is a relatively small but politically active group. *What's Important,* the group's central pronouncement on abortion, unequivocally states that abortion is infanticide. Moreover, this book argues that because the fetus's soul is immortal, the fetus is capable of wreaking revenge on the mother who aborts it.[72]

Most Japanese approve of abortion but only if there are medical or economic reasons justifying it. Arguments in favor of legalized abortion as a function of a woman's right to bodily autonomy are almost completely absent in Japan.[73]

## Abortion in China

Abortion has an equally ancient history in China, where in premodern times it was seen as a self-inflicted punishment meted out to the fetus's parents rather than as a crime against God or society. As in Japan, the criminalization of abortion came about as a consequence of Western influence at the turn of the twentieth century. The impetus in China's case, however, was external pressure to modernize, one of the prerequisites for the withdrawal of the Western powers.[74]

Abortion in postrevolutionary China has had a checkered history. In 1953 the People's Republic of China somewhat loosened its restrictions on abortion, apparently out of a desire to ameliorate the effects of illegal abortions.[75] Governmental policies on abortion since that time, much like those in Eastern Europe, have been dependent upon the economic and population goals of the Communist party.

For instance, after the Great Leap Forward (1958–1962), when population was regarded as growing too rapidly, restrictions on abortion were further relaxed.[76] High population growth continued and in recent years, in the face of growing alarm, China has adopted a one child per family policy. A multiplicity of measures, including financial incentives and compulsory abortions, are being used to "encourage" each family to have only one child.[77]

China's compulsory scheme has been met with widespread domestic resistance, particularly in rural areas; international opprobrium has also been harsh.[78] Domestic Chinese resistance to abortion in general, and to compulsory abortion in particular, grows from traditional Chinese values.[79] The Confucian ideal has always been that a large, complex, and extended joint family (a *jia*) is the basic unit of society and that each male should have as many sons as possible.

China's one family, one child and compulsory abortion policies greatly undermine the well-being of the couples who bear a female child. Under the traditional view, the failure to bear a son is a tragic failure, leaving no one to carry on the family name, to perpetuate "the incense smoke at the ancestral shrine" or to care for the couple during old age or in times of distress.[80] Prevented by the state from having additional children, couples to whom daughters are born have increasingly resorted to the drowning or abandonment of their infant girls, thus entitling them to another attempt at a son, greatly adding to the age-old practice of female infanticide. In addition to the obvious brutality of this result, many demographers are concerned that the practice will lead to significant male-female imbalances in the not too distant future.[81]

As in Stalin's Russia and Nazi Germany, in the Chinese context neither those advocating abortion nor those opposing it use the language of "rights" that characterizes the abortion debate in the United States. Scant attention is paid either to the right of the woman to have her child or to her right to terminate her pregnancy—or to any right of the fetus to be born. Rather, the conflict is structured almost wholly in terms of corporate groups, like the state and the family, and centers on the needs of and the duties owed to such groups.

## The Indian Subcontinent

India, like China and Japan, makes no real effort to curb abortion. In 1971 India passed the Medical Termination of Pregnancy Act, which permits abortions when it is likely that the child will be born with significant physical or mental abnormalities or when the birth poses a threat to the physical or mental health of the woman. This latter category was intended to be extremely broad and has in practice been interpreted so liberally as to provide fairly unfettered access to abortions in India.[82]

An examination of the legislative history of the act suggests that the legalization of abortion was viewed by the Indian Parliament largely as a solution to India's mounting health, population, and illegal abortion problems.[83] Abortion is not regarded as a corollary to a woman's natural right to bodily autonomy except by a very small group of Westernized middle-class urban feminists.

Despite legalization and a high incidence of abortion, opposition to the practice is fairly widespread. Throughout the Vedas, the classical Hindu religious texts, pejorative references to abortion abound. It has been called embryo murder and an act inimical to the very principle of creation. Most traditional Hindu lawgivers treated abortion as a crime and ranked it among such other crimes as murder, incest, and adultery.[84]

This traditional opposition to abortion does not fully explain the Hindu stance on the subject. Even among traditional Hindu lawgivers, some, like Manu (c. 200 B.C.), considered abortion little more than a misdemeanor.[85] Moreover, within the Hindu belief system there is a fundamental difference between the ideal and the permissible, that is, between the behavior required of a saint and that required from an ordinary person. Ordinary Hindus are not expected to live up to Vedic strictures on abortion. For most contemporary Hindus, abortion appears a necessary evil.

Fervent opposition to abortion in India comes from its Muslim and tribal minorities. Tribal groups see the government's authorization of abortion as an attempt to undermine their growing demographic strength. The basis for Muslim opposition to abortion is somewhat more complex.

In recent years hadith (traditions derived from the Prophet Muhammad's life) have become the basis for the widespread approval of birth control in Islamic nations.[86] Certain forms of contraception, particularly withdrawal, were practiced by Arabs during the early Islamic era. These were apparently condoned by Muhammad.[87] In 1937 the grand mufti of Egypt issued a *fatwa* (opinion) that declared birth control permissible. Expanding upon the subject of abortion, he pointed out that the majority of Islamic jurists were opposed to abortion except when it was necessitated by concerns for the baby or the pregnant woman's life.[88] In 1964, however, the grand mufti of Jordan declared that it is permissible to seek an abortion as long as the embryo is "unformed," that is, within 120 days of conception. To justify his position, the grand mufti pointed to the social utility of abortion.[89] On the whole, Islam appears to espouse a view, reminiscent of some others we have seen, that strictly forbids abortion after the embryo has acquired a soul, something said to take place any time between 40 and 120 days after conception.[90]

While the general body of current Islamic jurists is not actively opposed to abortion, there exists an extremely vocal minority that is unalterably opposed to all forms of birth control, including abortion. Taking their cue from the Qur'anic injunction "Kill not your children for fear of poverty. We provide for them and for you,"[91] such Muslim scholars have argued that all forms of birth control, including abortion, are types of infanticide.

This has been the view espoused by the Deobandi school, which is extremely influential in India. Such fervent opposition to abortion has been particularly marked in the writings of Maulana Syed Abul'Ala Maudoodi, a leading Pakistani Deobandi scholar held in high esteem in both India and Pakistan. Under the influence of the Deobandi school, Muslim leaders and Muslim groups in India have been vociferously opposed to abortion as a form of murder.[92] And in almost wholly Muslim Pakistan the triumph of the conservative Muslim jurists has been virtually total.

This religiously motivated opposition to abortion is compounded by the relatively low status of women in Muslim India and Pakistan. Women are deemed to be appendages to men, and their main function is considered childbearing. Moreover, women are viewed as essentially sexual beings whose impulses may easily lead them astray and bring dishonor, *be-izzati*, to their kinsmen.[93] As such, abortion and the image of female sexual autonomy that it conjures up are anathema to the traditional Indian or Pakistani Muslim male.

## The Fate of Female Fetuses in Asia

In recent years the abortion debate in India and, indeed, in much of Asia has been redirected by the injection of a new and disturbing element. In most Asian societies there is a marked preference for sons. For Indian parents, for example, not only does a son present an economic asset (he will support them in their old age) but for the Hindu majority, a son is also necessary for certain religious rites, including the lighting of his parents' funeral pyres.[94] Conversely, a daughter is not only a drain on familial resources (a dowry must be provided for her) but also, in terms of popular superstition, a *punishment* for her parents' sins.[95]

With the development of amniocentesis and other techniques, it is now relatively easy to determine the sex of a fetus, and it is becoming easier to do so at ever-earlier stages of pregnancy. In a number of Asian countries the use of amniocentesis to determine the gender of an embryo and the consequent abortion of female fetuses have become, in a modern variation on the traditional evil of female infanticide, increasingly common.[96]

The problem of female feticide has been most markedly manifested in India, where there exists both a particularly strong preference for sons *and* fairly free access both to amniocentesis and to abortions. Amniocentesis and abortion clinics offering to guarantee the birth of much desired sons have mushroomed all over the Indian landscape, both urban and rural. It is not surprising that with such ready availability of amniocentesis the number of female fetuses aborted has risen dramatically. A significant proportion of abortions in India are undertaken for sex-discriminatory reasons.[97]

This trend toward sex-specific abortion is causing great concern. Not only is the male to female ratio in the Indian population shifting (the 1981 census showed the ratio to be 1,000 males to 935 females, and preliminary statistics show that it has been shifting rapidly since then), but the discriminatory use of abortion also raises significant moral and ethical concerns about abortion upon request.[98] The rise in sex-discriminatory abortions has forced almost all engaged in the abortion debate in India to reconsider their positions.

The dilemma is particularly acute for Asian feminists and others who see abortion in terms of a woman's right to bodily autonomy. Such

groups' support for abortion seems to put them in the highly problematic position of defending a woman's right to discriminate against
female fetuses and, by implication, against baby girls and adult women.
Some feminists have responded to this seeming paradox by demanding
that the government prohibit sex-discriminatory abortions, while others
urge that the issue is not *why* abortion choices are made but *who* is to
make them and insist that the regime of readily available abortions must
continue.[99]

Among the solutions put forward to curb sex-selective abortion, the
most prominent involves restrictions on the availability of amniocentesis
and other sex determination tests. The medical community has been
opposed to a total ban on such tests since they are also useful for detect-
ing certain genetic disorders. Restricted access to sex-determination
tests has emerged as the most viable answer. As early as 1975 government hospitals discontinued such tests for sex-selection purposes.[100]

In 1988 the Government of the Indian state of Maharashtra passed a
law permitting amniocentesis only if the woman is at least thirty-five
years old or has a medical or family history suggesting the likelihood of
genetic disorders.

Response to this new Maharashtra law has been less than enthusiastic. Those concerned with the demographic implications of sex-discriminatory abortions and feminist groups that believe that this practice
oppresses women point out that women can easily go to other states to
have such tests performed, a concern reminiscent of our own federal
system. Moreover, since the object of the legislation is an essentially
"private" procedure between doctor and patient, enforcement presents
a significant problem. Opponents of sex-discriminatory abortions have
gone on to demand more stringent nationwide legislation.

Groups that continue to support abortion upon request argue that the
Maharashtra legislation impinges upon the intimate relationship between doctor and patient and unduly restricts the right of a woman to
have an abortion for her own reasons. Some have gone so far as to avow
that since women are so oppressed in Indian society, sex-discriminatory
abortions may very well be a benefit to the female fetus.[101]

## Great Britain

Although India's history has defied Britain's proud boast that the sun
never sets upon the British Empire, not even a cursory review of foreign
abortion policy would be complete without several stops in the Commonwealth. In light of our shared common law tradition, it is not surpris-

ing that the history of abortion legislation in Great Britain, Australia, and Canada should present many parallels to our own. Not only is the evolution of law somewhat similar, but current attitudes and debate, particularly the division between liberal pro-choice and conservative pro-life factions, also bear a significant resemblance to the American situation.

Britain departed from its common law tradition earlier than did the United States. Abortion law became more stringent in 1803, when abortion was criminalized. Punishment for abortion before quickening was set at exile, whipping, or imprisonment.[102] Postquickening abortion was sanctionable with death.[103] It was not until 1838 that the concept of quickening was subtracted from British legal calculations on abortion. At the same time, punishment by death was also eliminated.[104] It is not entirely clear what the basis for these early British laws was. At least one authority suggests that passage of the act prohibiting abortion was primarily motivated by the deaths of pregnant women caused by the poisonous abortifacient herbs and pills available in the nineteenth century.[105]

Under the Offenses Against the Person Act of 1861 anyone procuring an "unlawful" abortion, *including the woman herself,* could be sentenced to life imprisonment, while an aider or abettor could be punished with three years' in prison.[106] The broadly worded act did not specify which abortions were "unlawful," or, indeed, whether an abortion could possibly *be* lawful.

With the advance of medical science, it became clear that there were situations in which an abortion might save a pregnant woman's life. In response to such developments, Parliament passed the 1929 Infant Life (Preservation) Act, which states that a termination of pregnancy, particularly with a viable fetus, is unlawful except when proved to have been done in good faith to preserve the life of the woman. This law raised more questions than it answered, requiring women and doctors to negotiate the murky waters of good faith, viability, and necessity.[107]

It was not until 1938 in a case against Aleck Bourne, a consultant obstetrician, that anything like an authoritative interpretation of the 1861 statute became available. Dr. Bourne performed an abortion on a fourteen-year-old victim of a rape committed by two soldiers. The attorney general decided to prosecute. In acquitting Dr. Bourne, Britain's Justice MacNaughton said that in certain situations doctors may act to safeguard a woman's health, both physical and mental, as well as to save her life. In fact in certain circumstances, he averred, a doctor may have an affirmative duty to terminate a woman's pregnancy.[108]

The *Bourne* case put a judicial gloss on the literal terms of the 1861 act. MacNaughton's liberal opinion, however, did little to clarify the precise scope of British law on abortion, and for the next few decades the availability of abortions was to vary greatly with the circumstances of individual women.[109]

In the generally liberal mood of the 1960s Parliament passed the British Abortion Act of 1967.[110] This act, still in force as of 1990, was a remarkably liberal document for its time, permitting abortion until viability as long as two doctors certify that the risk to the life or mental or physical health of the woman, or to her existing children, would be greater if the pregnancy were to continue than if it were to be terminated.[111] Given the relative safety of early abortion compared with carrying a child to term, this statute provides in practice for early abortion upon request. The line of viability is provided by the still-valid Infant Life (Preservation) Act, which has been interpreted to restrict abortion after twenty-eight weeks of gestational age. While the Abortion Act, which was sponsored in Parliament by David Steel, did not vest decision making in the hands of women, it was nevertheless seen as a victory for female bodily autonomy. The act applies only in Great Britain—that is, in England, Scotland, and Wales. In Northern Ireland, the 1861 act, as construed in the *Bourne* case, is still in force.

The British act has been extremely influential and has served as a model for legislation in a number of countries. Since passage of the bill Britain has had a fairly high rate of legal abortion. In 1987 alone 174,276 abortions were performed in Britain.[112] A significant proportion of Great Britain's legal abortions have been performed upon foreign women, primarily from neighboring Ireland, where abortion is illegal, and from Spain, where abortion was prohibited until 1985.[113] As of 1988, 15,500 of the abortions performed in Britain were performed upon non-British Europeans.[114]

Since its passage in 1967 the act has met with significant opposition from antiabortion groups. The Society for the Protection of Unborn Children, the most significant of these groups, has been the source of a number of attempts to pass laws to restrict access to abortions.[115] The society's latest move has been the introduction of a bill in Parliament that seeks to restrict the availability of abortions to the first eighteen weeks. The bill has recently passed its first vote required for enactment in the House of Commons, by a margin of 251 to 196. Whether it will become law is, at this writing, still open to question.

## Australia

Australia owes its abortion laws largely to Britain. The situation in Australia, however, is a particularly confusing one. Australia, like the United

States, has a federal structure. The absence of a supreme court to announce national legal standards and rights, and the national legislature's
failure to come up with national abortion legislation, have left each of the
states free to implement its own abortion regime.[116] All six states and
the Northern Territory more or less inherited Britain's 1861 Offenses
Against the Person Act. The only state that still maintains that act with
anything like its original vigor is Queensland. South Australia and the
Northern Territory have both passed more liberal legislation based on
the 1967 British Abortion Act, in 1969 and 1973 respectively. Victoria
and the other states have circumvented the problem by construing the
1861 statute liberally.[117]

There is significant pressure for national legislation and standards in
Australia. The issue is a particularly pressing one considering that federal funding for abortion is widely available in Australia. In a recent
decision a judge in Victoria determined, in the context of deciding if a
husband could prevent his wife from having an abortion, that the fetus
had no right to be born.[118] Public reaction to this case may precipitate a
national legislative solution.

## *Revisiting North America: Canada*

Canada, like Australia, inherited the 1861 Offenses Against the Person
Act. In 1892 the Canadian legislature criminalized the possession of all
"obscene" materials, including in this ban all contraceptives and abortifacients. In this regard Canadian law at the turn of the century had less in
common with the laws of Britain than it did with the notorious Comstock
antiobscenity laws of the United States.

In 1969, following a gradual liberalization of Canadian abortion law,
Canada adopted a fairly permissive statute that allowed abortions in
hospitals that had appointed committees of no fewer than three physicians when such committees determined that continuation of a pregnancy would be likely to endanger the life or health of the pregnant
woman. In the aftermath of the act the number of legal abortions in
Canada increased (from eleven thousand in 1970 to forty-three thousand
in 1973).

Canada's laws might have continued to evolve legislatively had it not
been for Dr. Henry Morgentaler. A pro-choice Quebec physician who
had consistently provided easy access to abortions, he was charged
repeatedly for violations of the 1969 statute. In 1988, in an appeal from
one of Morgentaler's convictions, the Supreme Court of Canada invoked
the U.S. Supreme Court's *Roe* decision and held the 1969 statute to be
an impermissible restriction on a woman's right to have an abortion, an

aspect of the "right to security of the person," which is guaranteed by the 1982 Canadian Charter of Rights and Freedoms. In her concurring opinion in *Morgentaler v. Regina,* Justice Bertha Wilson, now one of three women on Canada's Supreme Court, wrote:

> The history of the struggle for human rights . . . has been the history of men struggling to assert their dignity and common humanity against an overbearing state apparatus. The more recent struggle for women's rights has been a struggle . . . to achieve a place for women in a man's world, to . . . place women in the same position as men. It has *not* been a struggle to define the rights of women in relation to their special place in the societal structure and in relation to the biological distinction between the two sexes. . . . The right to reproduce or not reproduce which is in issue in this case is one such right and is properly perceived as an integral part of modern woman's struggle to assert *her* dignity and worth as a human being.[119]

The decision of the Supreme Court of Canada in the *Morgentaler* case left that nation without any abortion law, effectively making abortion available on request in Canada.[120] But the ruling was deferential to the legislature, and it did not obviate the possibility of future legislation regulating women's rights to an abortion; it discarded only the particular balance struck by the 1969 statute. Thus, there was immense pressure on the Parliament of Canada to fill the legal vacuum with a solution that would satisfy both the court and antiabortion groups. Throughout 1988 and 1989, however, the Canadian Parliament was unable to reach any agreement on the issue.[121]

The pressure to find some agreement became even more acute when the Canadian Supreme Court delivered its opinion in the *Chantal Daigle* case in November 1989.[122] Daigle was being sued by her estranged lover, Jean-Guy Tremblay, who demanded that she carry his child to full term. In denying him the injunction he sought, the Supreme Court of Canada averred that the *Quebec* Charter of Rights guarantees the right to life of persons but that a fetus is not a person for purposes of the charter. The court, however, refused to rule on whether the fetus was a person for the purposes of the *Canadian* Charter of Rights.[123]

This decision was another spur to antiabortion groups, and as this book goes to press in early 1990, the already politicized issue of abortion occupies political center stage in Canada. On November 28, 1989, Prime Minister Brian Mulroney won approval in principle in the Canadian House of Commons for a bill that would make abortion legal only upon recommendation of a doctor.

## Western Europe

The nations of Western Europe also share with a great many Americans a common heritage. The most detailed examination of abortion law in Western Europe is that undertaken by Harvard Law Professor Mary Ann Glendon in her influential 1987 book *Abortion and Divorce in Western Law.* Professor Glendon describes how the Western European nations, with which we share fundamental values and democratic traditions, have charted a course quite different from our own.

As in the United States, most Western European countries adopted restrictive abortion policies in the nineteenth century only to liberalize them in the twentieth. Within the 20 years from 1967 to 1987 a vast majority of the countries of Western Europe abandoned strict antiabortion laws through legislative reform.[124]

These laws are not uniform. Of the eighteen European countries surveyed by Professor Glendon, only two, Belgium and Ireland, virtually outlaw abortion. Even in these countries there is apparently an affirmative defense of necessity, that the abortion was performed in order to prevent the death or serious injury of the pregnant woman. In Ireland, by a two-thirds vote in a popular referendum in 1983, the ban on abortion has been incorporated in the constitution.[125]

Most Western European countries have adopted a system in which abortion is available for a limited number of reasons enumerated by law. In a few countries—Portugal, Spain, and Switzerland—the allowable reasons resemble those included in America's ALI-inspired reform provisions of the late 1960s. These limit legal abortion to cases of rape or incest, situations in which the health of the woman is endangered, and cases in which the fetus is likely to have a serious disease or defect.[126] Interestingly, the Swiss law dates from 1942, twenty-five years before any other Western European jurisdiction liberalized its abortion law. In the years of strict abortion restriction in the United States wealthy women seeking abortions sometimes traveled to Switzerland to obtain them in cantons where the "health" of the pregnant woman is interpreted broadly.

In other countries the list of grounds justifying abortion is more expansive and includes serious economic and social hardship for the pregnant woman and her family. In some countries the applicable statute mandates that this factor, including the effect on the woman's life of having a child, be considered in evaluating the woman's mental health. In others it constitutes a separate ground justifying abortion. In some countries—Italy, France, and the Netherlands—the ground ("distress" or "emergency") is so broad as to offer no meaningful standard.[127]

Typically, abortion on economic or social grounds in these nations will require certification by two physicians or by a physician other than the one who performs the procedure. However, in France and Italy the pregnant woman is permitted to determine for herself whether her situation falls within the statutory exception. In the Netherlands the woman is supposed to make the determination in consultation with her doctor. In many of these countries a pregnant woman must undergo mandatory counseling or a waiting period or receive certain prescribed information before she is allowed to have an abortion.[128]

Another group of five European countries—Austria, Denmark, Greece, Norway, and Sweden—permit early abortion for any reason. Some of these countries require that the woman be given information or "guidance" prior to the procedure. All these countries limit free access to abortion to the early weeks of pregnancy, usually the first twelve weeks, but as late as the eighteenth week in the case of Sweden.[129]

Whatever the regime, most Western European countries impose additional restrictions on abortion, for example approval by a committee, later in pregnancy. The list of reasons that will justify an abortion also tends to narrow as the pregnancy progresses. Abortion is, however, still generally available, on at least some grounds, through the end of the second trimester.

For Professor Glendon, the European laws represent a compromise that has spared those countries the upheaval and turmoil that have accompanied debate over the abortion question in the United States since the decision in *Roe.* [130] She argues that these statutes send an important constitutive message that "combine[s] compassion with affirmation of life"[131] and that they demonstrate the "commitment of society as a whole to help minimize occasions for tragic choices between them."[132]

Perhaps the entire scheme of educational and social welfare policies adopted by many of these countries does, when viewed broadly, reflect such commitment. Unlike our own country, the countries of Western Europe routinely provide resources both to prevent the occurrence of unwanted pregnancies and to create an environment in which it will be easier for a woman to decide to take a pregnancy to term. As Professor Glendon points out, Western European countries almost uniformly provide maternity leaves and benefits, as well as child care, cash grants, and tax benefits to women with dependent children.

One lesson to come from the European experience could well be emulated by those in the United States who oppose abortion: preventing pregnancy works. In Sweden, where the law providing for abortion on request was coupled with a program expanding education about and access to contraceptives, rates of both teenage abortion and teenage

pregnancy have fallen.[133] Further, making childbirth more attractive
seems an obvious route to decreasing the number of abortions. Still,
although this idea is far from new, there is scant evidence of any organized pro-life group in the United States having undertaken to try to
provide for such services.

## *Should We "Import" Europe's Compromise?*

But what of the European laws, viewed narrowly, that directly regulate
abortion? Do those laws offer us a possible solution to the abortion
question in the United States?

Professor Glendon, arguing that they do, focuses in particular on the
French abortion statute first enacted in 1975. "The law guarantees the
respect of every human being from the commencement of life," this
French law asserts. "There shall be no derogation from this principle
except in cases of necessity and under conditions laid down by this law."
The law also states that "[t]he voluntary termination of pregnancy must
under no circumstances constitute a means of birth control."[134]

However, abortions are permitted during the first ten weeks of pregnancy for a woman whose condition, in her own judgment, "place[s]
[her] in a situation of distress." This is one of the statutorily enumerated
"necessities" justifying abortion. The reality, therefore, is that in France
virtually any pregnant woman can get a legal abortion during the first ten
weeks of pregnancy. All abortions must be preceded by a discussion
between the woman and a counselor, "especially with a view toward
enabling her to keep the child." Then, despite the rhetorical disapproval
of abortion in France, social security will cover 70 percent of the cost of
the nonmedically necessary abortion.[135]

Glendon argues that the French law is a "humane, democratic compromise" that shows both compassion for the woman and concern for
the fetus. For Glendon, this statute is valuable in that it goes outside
rights-based rhetoric and *"names* the underlying problem as one involving human life"[136]; she praises the law for its "mode[] of expression."
Indeed, Glendon encourages the adoption in the United States of similar
"life-affirming" legal rhetoric even without specific sanctions designed
to reduce the number of abortions being performed.[137]

Law, of course, can be as important for the message it sends as for the
rules it promulgates. Society may benefit from the incorporation in its
laws of normative statements of principle. Yet the codification of a truly
empty promise, one whose vision is belied by the people's day-to-day
experience, one that is utterly at variance with the substance of the law

in which it is contained, can take an unacceptably high toll on confidence in the rule of law and in the integrity of the legal system as a whole. The French solution, within an Anglo-American legal system that has long insisted that law be composed of *enforceable* norms, seems to teach mostly hypocrisy.

Western European laws, which are designed to encourage childbirth or to offer guidance "with a view toward enabling [the pregnant woman] to keep the child," do represent a less individualistic vision of society than most of us tend to hold, and they may offer a compromise that is workable in some societies. But the fact that *individual rights* provide the primary focus of constitutional law in the United States is no accident. While Glendon applauds the focus in European countries on human life as a collective value, she underestimates the strength and value of the uniquely American ideology of individual worth that has led us to a largely rights-based legal system. A system that permits some government agent—whether bureaucrat, social worker, or physician—to hold such a life-affecting decision as abortion in his or her hands, even if the decision is often made to permit the woman to do what she has requested, disempowers and disrespects women. This, too, would be a serious price to pay for a more tranquil political landscape.

Still worse from the perspective of the integrity of our system of justice is the example of those Western European countries, particularly those with narrower exceptions to the prohibition on abortion, in which the "compromise" that permits most early-term abortions occurs *outside* the text of the governing statute—in a chasm between legislative dictate and real-life practice.

Professor Glendon tells us that even in most of the countries with restrictive abortion laws, it is relatively easy for a pregnant woman to receive what Glendon describes as a "legal" abortion in the first trimester of pregnancy. "For example," she writes, "legal abortions are relatively easy to obtain in Belgium despite the apparent severity of the law there."[138]

But what *is* a "legal" abortion performed in circumstances not permitted by law? What Glendon describes, the product of this version of the European compromise, is in all likelihood not a "legal" abortion at all but at best a safe illegal one.

The United States has had some experience with this type of compromise, and it has not been so benign. In this regard, the Europeans offer us not the solution, but the question out of which the current debate about abortion in the United States arose.

Suppose that it were possible for safe abortions to be obtained anywhere in the United States even when a pregnancy did not fall within a statutory exception because the statute could be stretched far enough by doctors, prosecutors, judges, or juries. Even then, to maintain such a system indefinitely would be incompatible with many of the fundamental values that define our country. The contravention of law with an official wink, in our collective vision, is part of what distinguishes other countries from the United States. An approach that relies upon a strict normative judgment embodied in legislation but dramatically softened in its application by pragmatic concerns is bound, in the long run, to offend American conceptions of equal justice.

In any event, we probably could not expect the kinds of practical results—relative ease in safely terminating first trimester pregnancies—that Glendon describes,[139] whatever the experience of more homogeneous European countries. In the United States the history of the exercise of unfettered governmental discretion is largely a history of unequal treatment based on class, race, and sex.

Furthermore, laws and practices are bound to vary from region to region in the United States on the basis of political and religious views. Indeed, this is the experience in Western Europe, even within individual countries. In Switzerland pregnant women from predominantly Catholic cantons who desire an abortion must travel to Protestant areas, where the exception for a woman's health is given a broad reading. Even more jarring from an American perspective, sometimes those charged with enforcement of the law (particularly doctors, who are not politically accountable) hold views more strict than those that society has chosen to enact. Thus, abortions are actually *harder* to obtain in some regions of West Germany than can be inferred from the relatively liberal language of that country's federal abortion statute.[140]

The availability of abortion by caprice, a regime in which access to a basic source of personal autonomy and self-respect depends upon where one lives, would not conform to the American legal norm of equality. In the United States where, by comparison to Western Europe, distances are greater and the people sometimes poorer and less educated, the hardship imposed by such a system would be remarkable.

It may be that Professor Glendon means only to suggest that as a matter of prudence, some incorporation of pro-life rhetoric in our law might be desirable—that it might be wise for us to denounce abortion in principle while we permit it in practice. This might well cause some people less emotional distress than would the more candid announcement that legal abortion is freely available. To anesthetize through rhetoric those who wish to protect fetal life, though, is a far cry from genuinely protecting fetal life or its value. Merely to affirm in law a sense of responsibility to new life is a far cry from actually treating that life with respect.

Glendon's work also suggests that the *democratic* nature of the European solution might have value in easing the conflict over abortion in the United States. It may be true that if abortion were permitted in this country as a result of democratic choice rather than judicial imposition, both the popular failure of the extreme antiabortion position and the possibility for future legislative reexamination might soften the frustration felt by those who oppose abortion rights.

But the gap between stated principle and actual practice that would be necessary to sustain the European approach would probably make such a solution too costly for us. And of course, urging a democratic solution just begs the question of whether or not the regulation of abortion is properly *for* the legislative arena, a question we will explore at length in the next chapter.

## And Back Again

This survey of approaches to abortion taken by other cultures is not meant to suggest that we replace our own. The views Americans hold about abortion are no less sincere—indeed, they reflect concerns no less *fundamental* to us—because they differ from those held by the Japanese or the Swedes. Yet the rich diversity of views about abortion and the striking variety of the ways in which the question has been settled in different countries and cultures, like the changing face of abortion throughout our own history, show beyond doubt that ideas about abortion and attitudes about its availability are highly culture-specific, reflecting the time and place in which they arise. It seems certain that beneath the abortion debate in America, too, there lurk social and cultural forces of which we are at best dimly aware.

In America the last twenty years have been a time in which the debate about abortion has become fossilized. The arguments we know by heart, arguments that persuade no one, seem immutable—and insoluble. But the faces of the argument about abortion need not be cast, as if by Medusa's gaze, in stone.

# 5

# Finding Abortion Rights in the Constitution

=

Because the abortion question is so difficult and may be approached in so many ways, it should be no surprise that the approach taken by the U.S. Supreme Court generates continuing controversy. It would be foolish to expect any judicial approach to the abortion question to be uncontroversial; if that test were applied, every answer to the question would be wrong. But neither difficulty nor controversy can justify letting the Court's decision in *Roe* escape critical examination. Was that decision legally defensible? We address that issue next, exploring some of the implications of deciding the constitutional question in different ways.

We should be clear at the outset that the abortion issue poses constitutional problems not simply for judges but for every federal, state, or local official who must at some point address the issue. Each such official is required to take an oath to uphold the Constitution of the United States. Even if the Supreme Court were someday to conclude that judges have no business enforcing constitutional limitations in the abortion area, that conclusion would not relieve other public officials of the burden of deciding what they believe those limitations are. In deciding what laws to vote for or against or what enforcement measures to take, public officials cannot properly avoid considering what they believe the Constitution allows or requires them to do.

Those who either defend or attack the constitutional analysis contained in *Roe v. Wade* purely in terms of the role judges should or should not play in our system of government are therefore missing much of what is at stake. Of course, *Roe v. Wade* involved, in part, the question of what the judicial role should be. But that is only part of what it involved. It involved as well the question of what protection, if any, the Constitution, as a document addressed to all officials, extends either to a woman who wishes to terminate her pregnancy or to the fetus, or to both. To say that the abortion question should be resolved, in whole or in part, by officials other than judges tells us nothing about how those officials should resolve it.

In addition, it is an illusion to imagine that all aspects of the abortion issue could possibly be left to officials outside the judicial system. However tempting it might be for judges to throw up their hands and say that the whole matter should be resolved "politically," a little thought should make clear that judges must, at a minimum, set the outer boundaries of political power in this area.

Suppose, for example, that the Constitution is interpreted so as to give each state broad latitude in deciding which abortions to permit and which to prohibit. Judges would still have to decide whether or not a state could pass a law that would force a woman to save a viable fetus when that would require delivery by caesarean section. Judges would still have to decide whether or not a state could constitutionally force a woman to abort one fetus in order to save its twin if the medical circumstances were such that only one could live. Judges would still have to decide whether or not a state could impose financial pressures designed to force a woman on welfare to abort a fetus that would be born with severe genetic defects and whose survival after birth would require a large commitment of public resources.

Whatever a court might conclude about government's power over normal pregnancy, it could hardly avoid determining the limits of government power over an ovum that has been fertilized in a test tube. May the government require that such a fertilized ovum be preserved for future implantation? May the government require that such an ovum be frozen until its fate has been agreed upon? May the sperm donor be given an enforceable veto over the woman's decision to discard the ovum after its test tube fertilization? May the government enforce her promise to have the fertilized ovum implanted in her uterus? May it enforce her promise to have it implanted in another woman? If state officials refuse to enforce such promises, are they violating any rights of the persons to whom those promises were made?

Courts simply cannot avoid deciding, in the multitude of cases spawned by the newest technologies and the oldest human desires, *who* will be permitted to decide *what*: the woman, the man, a doctor, a hospital, or the state?

## Was Roe *Rightly Decided?*

For all the talk of possible future compromises, it must not be forgotten that *Roe* itself represented a compromise. The Supreme Court in *Roe v.*

*Wade* had heard arguments that the woman's right to decide for herself whether, when, and why to terminate a pregnancy is absolute. The Court's conclusion was unequivocal: "With this we do not agree."[1] Thus, the Court in *Roe* and in the decisions that followed it upheld the validity of government regulations requiring that all abortions be performed by licensed physicians, government regulations to protect the health of women in second-trimester abortions and beyond, and government regulations to protect the unborn from abortions that are not needed to protect the woman's life or health once the fetus is "viable" (i.e., can survive outside the woman).

Still, no judicial ruling since segregated public schools were held unconstitutional by *Brown v. Board of Education*[2] has generated anything resembling the degree of criticism and even outright violence triggered by *Roe v. Wade.* Criticism of the decision, and particularly of its result, has led to a revolution in constitutional law that may have profound consequences for all Americans, a revolution touching the full range of our rights. It has already led to a radical transformation in the role of the American judiciary.

## The "Judicial Restraint" Objection

One unexpected consequence of *Roe v. Wade* was the growth of a veritable cottage industry promoting judicial restraint. The epithet "judicial activism," the foe of supposed champions of restraint, is most often used to describe the work of the Supreme Court of the 1950s and 1960s under Chief Justice Earl Warren. But *Roe,* sometimes derided as an example of unparalleled judicial activism, was decided by the Court under the leadership of conservative Chief Justice Warren Burger. Indeed, the decision in *Roe* was written by Nixon appointee Harry Blackmun and was joined by conservative jurists Potter Stewart and Lewis Powell as well as by Chief Justice Burger, who was appointed by President Nixon precisely to fulfill a campaign promise to change the activist complexion of the federal judiciary.

People have undertaken to criticize *Roe,* in every aspect and from every angle, as *illegitimate* judicial activism, and the sheer volume of the attack seems to have lent it legitimacy. Are these criticisms convincing?

## *"Legislators and Not Judges Should Decide"*

The simplest argument against *Roe,* an argument that has gained considerable credence and that has great resonance in a nation devoted to principles of democracy, criticizes *Roe* as antidemocratic. The issue of abortion rights, the reasoning goes, should be returned to Congress and to state and local legislators for decision in a democratic way by the legislative process. How sound is that argument?

Our system of government, of course, neither offers us nor threatens us with *absolute* democracy, in the style, say, of ancient Athens, where it is said that each citizen cast one vote on all matters, or in the style of the New England town meeting. Ours is a republican form of government, in which the votes of citizens are used primarily to select legislatures and executives, which themselves select judges whose role it is to ensure that the government does not violate basic rights or otherwise upset the fundamental agreements underlying our governmental institutions. The whole *point* of an independent judiciary is to be "antidemocratic," to preserve from transient majorities those human rights and other principles to which our legal and political system is committed. Without this role there would be nothing to stop a bare majority of our citizens from deciding tomorrow that the minority should be enslaved or required to give up its belongings for the greater good of the greater number. This elementary civics lesson is forgotten or ignored by those who would leave *every* issue of individual rights that was a matter of moral controversy to be decided *solely* by the legislative and executive branches. And in the end, most of these critics do not seriously attempt to deny that the federal judiciary, and ultimately the Supreme Court of the United States, is empowered to invalidate legislation, although duly enacted by the democratically elected representatives of the people, if it runs afoul of the Constitution.

In particular, the protections of the first eight amendments to the Constitution—the "Bill of Rights" (guaranteeing freedom of speech and of religion, the right to bear arms, and so forth)—and of the Fourteenth Amendment, adopted after the Civil War, which guarantees all persons equal protection of the laws and prohibits deprivations of life, liberty, or property without due process of law, insulate certain aspects of individual behavior from governmental intrusion and provide norms for government action that no legislature can contravene, although the exact bounds of these rights may be open to debate.

Should a legislature, through the democratic process, enact a law that transgresses the guarantees contained in the Constitution, the federal courts have not merely the power but the obligation to strike that law down. Indeed, the Constitution provides for unelected judges, appointed by the President and confirmed by the Senate, who serve for life and whose salary cannot be diminished, precisely to prevent them from making decisions based on the popular will, however formally and democratically expressed.

This power of judicial review and invalidation was first exercised by the Supreme Court to strike down an act of Congress in an opinion written by the great chief justice John Marshall in the case of *Marbury v. Madison* in 1803.[3] There a disappointed office seeker named William Marbury, who had been named to a federal post by President John Adams, sued Secretary of State James Madison for refusing to deliver his commission of office when the administration of President Adams was replaced by that of President Thomas Jefferson. The Supreme Court, after saying that Madison and the new President were acting lawlessly, pronounced itself powerless to award Marbury the judicial relief he sought, explaining that the act of Congress which supposedly empowered it to hear Marbury's suit against Madison violated the Constitution's provision defining the Court's jurisdiction to try cases. Writing for the Court, Chief Justice Marshall held that much as the Court would like to rely on that act of Congress, its duty to obey the Constitution required it to strike that act down. Striking down a law as unconstitutional is "undemocratic," in the sense that no simple majority acting through the legislative process can overcome a ruling of the Supreme Court holding a law invalid. But it is a cornerstone of our system of government.

As Justice Robert Jackson wrote in 1943 in an opinion for the Court holding that children cannot be punished by public authorities for refusing to take part in a school's compulsory flag salute ceremony, the "very purpose of a Bill of Rights was to withdraw certain subjects from the vicissitudes of political controversy, to place them beyond the reach of majorities and officials and to establish them as legal principles to be applied by the courts. One's right to life, liberty, and property, to free speech, a free press, freedom of worship and assembly, and other fundamental rights may not be submitted to vote; they depend on the outcome of no elections."[4]

Every time a court holds that a duly enacted law violates the Constitution, it behaves in what might be described as an antidemocratic way. But this does not make the court's action a usurpation of power. The antidemocratic nature of *Roe* provides no decisive evidence of its illegitimacy—provided we agree, as nearly everyone does, that the Constitution itself has sufficiently democratic roots to count as an enduring basis for a government of, by, and for the people. The question remains, though: Can *Roe* find support in the Constitution?

## *"The Right to Privacy Is Not in the Constitution's Text"*

A second basis for objection to *Roe* is that it protects a right, the right to privacy, that appears nowhere in the text of the Constitution. The Court, it is said, in a naked power grab and on the strength of nothing more than personal disagreement with the outcome of the legislative process, illegitimately carved out an area and put it beyond the reach of the democratic, political branches of government. If true, the charge would be grave indeed; the Supreme Court's only warrant to override the outcome of politically democratic processes is the agreement of "We the People," as the Constitution's preamble calls those in whose name it is ordained.

Judge Robert Bork, in his 1989 book *The Tempting of America,* could find in the Court's opinion "not one line of explanation, not one sentence that qualifies as legal argument."[5] In the years since *Roe,* according to Bork, "no one, however pro-abortion, has ever thought of an argument that even remotely begins to justify *Roe v. Wade* as a constitutional decision. . . . There is no room for argument," writes Bork, "about the conclusion that the decision was the assumption of illegitimate judicial power and usurpation of the democratic authority of the American people."[6]

What may surprise some, given the certitude with which Judge Bork and a number of others pronounce that *Roe v. Wade* was constitutionally illegitimate, is how many lawyers and law professors throughout the country believe the Supreme Court's decision in that case was entirely correct as a legal matter. For example, a friend of the court brief was filed in the *Webster* case "on behalf of 885 American law professors . . . who believe that the right of a woman to choose whether or not to bear a child, as delineated . . . in *Roe v. Wade,* is an essential component of constitutional liberty and privacy commanding reaffirmation by [the Supreme] Court."[7] Similarly, the American Bar Association in February 1990 approved a resolution expressing the ABA's recognition that "the fundamental rights of privacy and equality guaranteed by the United States Constitution" encompass "the decision to terminate [a] pregnancy."[8]

Now, of course, nearly a thousand law professors and the nation's leading organization of lawyers could certainly be wrong on a matter of law. But how plausible is it that all of them would fail to recognize as blatant a legal blunder as some say the Court made in *Roe?* To understand what separates the vast majority of lawyers and legal scholars from those who continue to insist that no honest and professionally competent attorney or academic could possibly agree with *Roe,* we need to look more closely at what *Roe*'s most strident critics claim.

On the most simplistic level, of course, the critics are correct. The word "privacy" is not in the text of the Constitution. But the guarantees of the Constitution are not like itemized deductions. The Constitution contains broad provisions whose meaning requires judicial interpretation. Interpretation, in turn, requires judgment.

One of the most important of these broad provisions, contained in the Fourteenth Amendment, reads: "No State shall . . . deprive any person of life, liberty, or property, without due process of law." It is the guarantee of "liberty" contained in the due process clause, sometimes also called the liberty clause, of the Fourteenth Amendment that provides protection of our rights from infringement by the state governments. And the word "liberty" simply is not self-defining.

## The Meaning of the Liberty Clause

Some commentators believe, or at least argue, that the liberty clause does not give special protection to *any* of our rights. This position has been rejected by every sitting Supreme Court justice and, indeed, by every Supreme Court justice of the last half century, including such conservative jurists as John Marshall Harlan, Felix Frankfurter, William Rehnquist, and Antonin Scalia. Still, it is valuable to understand this argument and to understand why, though touted as "conservative," it is actually revolutionary.

A modern reader of the words of the Fourteenth Amendment might well conclude that they provide only *procedural* protection for "life," "liberty," and "property." Put another way, the amendment appears to authorize deprivations of life, liberty, and property as long as those deprivations are accompanied by "due process" of law. As Judge Bork describes it, the due process clause of the Fourteenth Amendment "was designed *only* to require fair procedures in implementing laws."[9]

And the due process clause *does* provide us with procedural protection for our lives, our liberty, and our property. It has been held by the Supreme Court to mandate hearings and other procedures before a state government can take certain actions that affect a variety of our interests.

However, from its earliest days this clause has also stood for the substantive protection of individual rights from intrusion by the government. During the nineteenth century, and even before, it was widely believed that the people retained certain "natural rights." Legislatures could not enact legislation that intruded upon these rights. Any such attempt would be of no operative effect because it would be outside the sphere of legislative authority. It would not, by definition, be "law."

Consistent with this view, the word "law" in the phrase "due process of law" was employed by courts to limit state legislatures to those areas in which they could *legitimately* operate. As the nineteenth-century Supreme Court explained, "[i]t is not every act, legislative in form, that is law. Law is something more than mere will exerted as an act of power."[10] In a phrase, the Constitution's ideal of "law" rejects the proposition that might makes right. Certain legislative acts that infringed on protected areas of liberty, acts beyond the scope of the legislature's power, therefore were not considered "due process of law." Within a quarter century of the Fourteenth Amendment's adoption in 1868 the Supreme Court began striking down state laws on the basis of that amendment's due process clause because of particular substantive rights those laws infringed.[11] By 1937 the Court had invalidated almost two hundred state laws on this ground.[12]

The most striking aspect of this early foray by the Supreme Court into "substantive due process" was its disastrous result. For the right in whose name the Supreme Court wielded the due process clause was not a right familiar to the law today. It was, rather, an economic right: the "freedom to contract."

During this era—dubbed the *Lochner* era after the 1905 decision in *Lochner v. New York*[13] invalidating New York's sixty-hour limit on a bakery employee's workweek—a majority of the Court imported into the due process clause then-fashionable economic and social theories, most notably the views of Darwin as bastardized by Herbert Spencer in his 1851 book *Social Statics.* It was believed that legislation meant to redress imbalances in economic bargaining power or to redistribute wealth or income was not law enacted for the "general welfare" but power exercised "purely for the promotion of private interests."[14] Such use of government power to readjust the "natural" inequalities arising from the ordinary workings of the common law rules of property and contract was beyond the implicit boundary of legislative authority.

In the name of liberty of contract during this period, social and economic legislation that we now consider routine, even if not always wise, and the enactment of which nearly everyone takes for granted as falling within the legitimate power of legislative bodies, was repeatedly struck down by the Supreme Court. Minimum-wage laws, child labor laws, limitations on the hours of work, laws regulating labor-management relations—indeed, all regulations of the employment relationship except those the Court found to be directly in aid of the *public* health and welfare—were struck down as meddlesome interferences with the worker's liberty to contract and with the employer's freedom to use his property in traditional ways. Any attempt to improve the position of the employee vis-à-vis the employer, or of the buyer vis-à-vis the seller, was invalid. Inequality in bargaining power was, the Court said, "but the normal and inevitable result" of the exercise of the right to contract.[15]

From its inception the doctrine of *Lochner* was criticized. Justice Oliver Wendell Holmes, dissenting in the *Lochner* case, wrote that "a Constitution is not intended to embody a particular economic theory, whether of paternalism and the organic relation of the citizen to the state or of *laissez faire.* It is made for people of fundamentally differing views, and the accident of our finding certain opinions natural and familiar, or novel, and even shocking, ought not to conclude our judgment upon the question whether statutes embodying them conflict with the Constitution of the United States."[16] As he put it most famously, "[t]he 14th Amendment does not enact Mr. Herbert Spencer's Social Statics."

Ultimately the economic realities of the Great Depression graphically undermined *Lochner*'s premise. The belief that the "invisible hand" of economics was functioning both to protect individual rights and to maximize the social good was no longer tenable. The idea of a "natural" economic order that could be restored by striking down the laws that had artificially upset it was no longer believable.

Criticism of the Court grew as the depression deepened and the Court continued to strike down social and economic regulation in the name of what one commentator poignantly described as "the legal right to starve."[17] As Franklin D. Roosevelt's enormously popular New Deal policies were overturned one after another, pressure on the Court increased.

This culminated in Roosevelt's infamous Court-packing plan in 1937. Roosevelt proposed a law to expand the membership of the Supreme Court, a law that would have been most unwise but one that Congress clearly had authority to enact under the Constitution. The bill would have given Roosevelt the right to make six immediate appointments to the Court with which he could easily overcome the already narrow five to four majority that then supported *Lochner* and the liberty to contract.

This state of affairs came to an end only when Justice Owen Roberts, a member of the pro-*Lochner* majority since his appointment to the Court by Herbert Hoover in 1930, in what some saw as a response to the political pressure and the threat to both the prestige and the integrity of the Court, switched his vote in the minimum-wage and maximum-hour case of *West Coast Hotel v. Parrish,* [18] a reversal still described in certain legal circles as "the switch in time that saved nine." [19] Justice Roberts's switch in time was in fact based on a vote he had cast during the Court's confidential deliberations even before FDR's Court-packing scheme had been unveiled. In any event, it laid to rest any residual congressional support for that scheme and permitted the New Deal reforms and, really, most now-familiar state and federal social and economic legislation, to go forward. It also spelled the end of the protection of the liberty of contract from state interference under the due process clause of the Fourteenth Amendment.

The *Lochner* era haunts judges and legal scholars to this day. The damage it did to both Court and country and its invalidation of the democratically enacted will of the people must give us pause. The Court's usurpation of the powers of democratically elected legislatures in the name of the liberty clause animates the concerns of many of the advocates of judicial restraint who oppose judicial protection of abortion rights today. Indeed, it is largely in reaction to *Lochner* that Judge Bork claims that the due process clause is entirely a procedural guarantee.

But the fault with *Lochner* lay not in judicial intervention to protect "liberty"—including the "liberty" of workers and of businesses—but in a misguided understanding of what "liberty" required. The protection of substantive liberties under the Constitution is not, as some have argued, an illegitimate departure from the text. The text of the Fourteenth Amendment, both during and after the *Lochner* era, continues to provide real protection for liberty. The question is how to give this broad guarantee *content.*

### *"Incorporation" of the Bill of Rights*

A simple case proves the point. It may surprise some, but the protections of the Bill of Rights do not apply in any direct way to actions by the state governments. For example, the First Amendment reads: "Congress shall make no law . . . abridging the freedom of speech, or of the press. . . ." *Congress,* not the state legislatures, is prohibited from abridging free speech, perhaps our most cherished freedom.

In a series of decisions beginning as long ago as 1897 but accelerating rapidly in the 1960s, the Supreme Court held that the protection of "liberty" contained in the Fourteenth Amendment's due process clause prevents the states from enacting laws that, if enacted by Congress, would be invalid under the protections of individual rights contained in the Bill of Rights. It is only because of these decisions, decisions that treat the Fourteenth Amendment's liberty clause as protecting substantive rights, that the protections enumerated in the Bill of Rights are relevant to the states at all.

To this day, when we say that a state law violates the First Amendment's protection of free speech or its prohibition on the establishment of religion (the separation of church and state), what we mean is that the state law violates that protection as applied to the states through the liberty clause of the Fourteenth Amendment.

The idea that the liberty clause applies the Bill of Rights to the states, called the doctrine of incorporation of the Bill of Rights into the Fourteenth Amendment, was not fully implemented until the 1960s. Even now the application of the Bill of Rights to the states is not complete. Some of its provisions, for example the Seventh Amendment's guarantee of a jury trial in civil cases, have been held not to apply to the states. Nearly all of the others have been held to apply—for example, the First Amendment freedoms of speech, press, assembly, petition, and free exercise of religion and the prohibition on the establishment of religion; the Fourth Amendment rights to be free of unreasonable search and seizure and to exclude from criminal trials evidence seized illegally; the Fifth Amendment rights to be free of compelled self-incrimination and double jeopardy; the Sixth Amendment rights to counsel, to a speedy and public trial before a jury, to an opportunity to confront opposing witnesses, and to the use of subpoena power for the purpose of obtaining favorable witnesses; the Eighth Amendment right to be free of cruel and unusual punishment. All have been held to be protected from state infringement, based on the due process clause of the Fourteenth Amendment.

The application of the Bill of Rights to the states, although not specifically intended by the framers of the Fourteenth Amendment and although once highly controversial, is now common ground. No sitting justice questions it. History has made it the place from which any discussion of the liberty clause of the Fourteenth Amendment must depart. Indeed, without incorporation of the Bill of Rights, we would have a world in which, although the federal government could not censor an antigovernment newspaper, the state of Illinois could. In which, although the federal government could not take a person's property without providing compensation for it, the state of Kansas could. Or in which, though there could be no official church of the United States, the state of New York could declare Presbyterianism the official state religion, with the governor as its head.

For this reason, the claim that the liberty clause is "entirely" procedural is unsustainable. The liberty clause protects us from infringements of certain rights, although the exact character of these rights is often open to debate.

Judge Bork, one of the few proponents of the claim that the liberty clause has *no* substantive effect, appears to recognize that this position stakes out a Maginot Line. Indeed, in *The Tempting of America* he insists that the clause is purely procedural, *"aside from* incorporating the Bill of Rights."[20] Whether or not there is any basis for limiting the meaning of "liberty" *only* to rights specifically mentioned in the Bill of Rights is therefore plainly the real issue.

### The Question of "Unenumerated" Rights

While the incorporation against the states of the Bill of Rights through the Fourteenth Amendment's liberty clause is now universally accepted, opponents of *Roe v. Wade* argue that the Bill of Rights should be an outer limit to the liberty protected by the Fourteenth Amendment. We are told that only those rights *specifically enumerated* in the Bill of Rights— freedom of speech, the freedom of religion, and so forth—apply against the states so as to create areas in which the states cannot enact laws. We are told that the *Roe* decision erred in defending an "unenumerated" right—namely, the right to privacy. This is hardly a principled objection to the Supreme Court's invalidation of legislative enactments under the broad protection of "liberty" in the Constitution. Indeed, by accepting incorporation, this argument implicitly acknowledges the validity of that judicial enterprise.

Neither is it a principled objection on the grounds of the text of the Constitution. For the text of the Constitution no more explicitly protects, against infringement *by the states,* the right of free speech than it does the right of privacy. Indeed, the very description of this objection is something of a misnomer since *all* individual rights are "unenumerated" with respect to the power of the state governments. The liberty clause of the Fourteenth Amendment simply does not enumerate *any* specific rights.

In any event, the fact that a right is not mentioned in so many words anywhere in the Constitution is not, and cannot be, a decisive objection. For the Constitution tells us that it was not constructed with an exhaustive list of enumerated rights. The Constitution's Ninth Amendment expressly states: "The enumeration in the Constitution, of certain rights, shall not be construed to deny or disparage others retained by the people." That is the one constitutional provision expressly designed to instruct all of us, as readers of the document, how we are *not* to construe, or interpret, what it may fail to list explicitly.

Still, one can formulate an argument, unprincipled though it may be, that only those protections explicitly listed elsewhere in the Constitution apply through the liberty clause of the Fourteenth Amendment. This was the position taken by Justice Hugo Black. This reverse incorporation view, however, never garnered a majority of the votes on the Supreme Court. Indeed, every member of the Court, both in the 1973 *Roe* decision and since, has accepted the Court's role in giving the liberty clause of the Fourteenth Amendment the vitality to protect more than the freedoms expressly listed in the Bill of Rights.

Here is just one example among many of an unenumerated right vindicated by the Supreme Court. Inez Moore lived in East Cleveland, Ohio, with her two grandsons, Dale and John. The boys were not brothers, but cousins; John's mother had died when he was an infant, and he had been raised since then by Mrs. Moore. She lived in a neighborhood that had been zoned for "single family dwelling units." In 1973 she received a notice from the city that since her grandsons were cousins rather than brothers, her household did not meet the city's definition of a "family." She was told that John, who was then ten and had lived with her his whole life, was an "illegal occupant" and that he must be removed. When she refused, East Cleveland fined this sixty-three-year-old grandmother and sentenced her to five days in jail.

The Supreme Court did not let the city of East Cleveland's narrow view of what was an acceptable family interfere with Mrs. Moore's right, her "liberty," to create a household with her grandchildren. This right is nowhere mentioned in the Bill of Rights, yet the Court held that because it is fundamental, it is protected by the liberty clause of the Fourteenth Amendment to the Constitution.[21]

The word "liberty," which appears both in the Fifth Amendment as a limit on federal power and in the Fourteenth Amendment as a limit on state power, does not in any obvious sense mean "those rights specifically listed in the first eight amendments to the Constitution." To limit the meaning of "liberty" only to these listed rights, apart from seeming to violate the command of the Ninth Amendment, would adopt a radical understanding of the Constitution itself. To say that *only* these rights exist is to say that when the framers wrote the Constitution, and the people of the United States ratified it in 1789, they thereby surrendered to government all the fundamental rights they regarded themselves as possessing—the rights that the Revolutionary War had been fought to preserve—with the sole exception of whatever specific rights were to be mentioned in a Bill of Rights that had been promised but that had not yet been written (and was not to be ratified until 1791).

No understanding of the Constitution could be further from the central premises of those who wrote and ratified the Constitution and the Bill of Rights. From the very beginning of our Republic, the Supreme Court has consistently recognized that in adopting the Constitution the people did *not* mean to place the bulk of their hard-won liberty in the hands of government save only for those rights specifically mentioned in the Bill of Rights or elsewhere in the document.

The Supreme Court has, accordingly, never limited the substantive protection of either the Fifth Amendment's or the Fourteenth Amendment's liberty clauses to those rights enumerated in the Bill of Rights. And if the Court were ever to do so, we would live in a nation in which any state or local government would be free to control our lives in innumerable ways, ranging from a federal abolition of birth control to a local imposition of detailed rules like those of East Cleveland about which family members could live together in their grandmother's household.

## Deciding Which Rights Are Specially Protected

If the enumeration of certain rights in the Constitution is not to become an exhaustive list of our protected liberties, the Supreme Court must have some principle for deciding what rights (such as the right to live with one's grandchildren) are fundamental and what rights (such as the right to burn trash in one's backyard) are not.

The Court's duty to protect certain unenumerated rights makes some judicial conservatives anxious. Judge Bork, for example, argues that judges unconstrained by an enumeration of rights in the text of the Constitution will be free simply to invalidate democratically enacted laws "in accordance with their own philosophies."[22]

While it makes sense to proceed with caution, the answer to questions about our liberty simply cannot be found by denying the existence of fundamental rights that are not listed in the Bill of Rights. Nor can there be any precise formula to define fundamental rights because the text of the Constitution offers us only general guidance.

Judges certainly should not feel free simply to import into the Constitution their own personal moral views. They must *interpret* the provisions of the Constitution. Judges, and others sworn to uphold the Constitution, may differ on whether a certain sphere of activity is protected. Indeed, they may differ on what principles should inform that decision.

But interpreting the Constitution is the essential role of the judge in our system of government.

There are also checks on the ability of any single Supreme Court justice to impose upon the country some extremist vision. To begin with, each justice—indeed, every federal judge—must be selected by the President and confirmed by the Senate. History shows that while one cannot predict with certainty a justice's vote in a particular case, the judicial philosophy of a Supreme Court nominee rarely changes drastically after his or her appointment. The President has enormous latitude in his selection of justices, and the Senate has at times exercised a responsibility to satisfy itself about the constitutional vision of a nominee whose name it is sent for confirmation. Indeed, the Senate has rejected almost one out of every five nominees to the Court. Most recently the Senate in 1987 rejected the nomination of Judge Robert Bork, citing objections to his constitutional philosophy.

In addition, no single justice of the Court has the power to transform our nation. The Court is a nine-member body, and the requirement of a majority vote necessarily acts as a restraint on any extreme or outlandish position. For this reason, no one judge's personal philosophy could ever be imposed as the law of the land.

Though some might prefer a system in which the human element, a judge's "temperament," as Judge Bork puts it,[23] would play no role— perhaps a system in which a "justice machine" could predictably resolve constitutional cases—such a world of perfectly defined rights could be achieved only by denying the existence of *any* rights protected from the states under the Fourteenth Amendment.

We are left then with the question of what principles to use to define the content of the Fourteenth Amendment's protection of liberty. What principles should judges use in deciding whether a right is so "fundamental" that it is specially protected by the liberty clause? This is a question about the meaning of America.

The enterprise of answering that question began even as the *Lochner* era crashed to an end. In 1937, the year *Lochner* fell, Justice Benjamin Cardozo wrote for the Court that the due process clause would invalidate legislation that trod upon interests "so rooted in the traditions and conscience of our people as to be ranked as fundamental." As conceived by Justice Cardozo, the interests protected were those "implicit in the concept of ordered liberty."[24]

The hypothetical inquiry Justice Cardozo suggested—could one imagine a civilized system without this or that protection?—was ultimately rejected, and the Court began to define the protection of individual rights less hypothetically and thus more broadly. As it applied more and more of the Bill of Rights to the states in the 1960s, the Court, in an opinion by Justice White, suggested that the rights that are protected are those that are fundamental to the "Anglo-American regime of ordered liberty."[25] More recently the Court explained that it seeks to protect certain areas against state intrusion because they are "deeply rooted in this Nation's history and tradition."[26]

In 1989 Justice Scalia wrote for the four youngest conservative members of the Court (himself, Chief Justice Rehnquist, and Justices O'Connor and Kennedy):

[I]t is an established part of our constitutional jurisprudence that the term "liberty" in the Due Process Clause extends beyond freedom from physical restraint. . . . In an attempt to limit and guide interpretation of the Clause, we have insisted not merely that the interest denominated as a "liberty" be "fundamental" (a concept that, in isolation, is hard to objectify), but also that it be an interest traditionally protected by our society. As we have put it, the Due Process Clause affords only those protections "so rooted in the traditions and conscience of our people as to be ranked as fundamental." Our cases reflect "continual insistence upon respect for the teachings of history [and] solid recognition of the basic values that underlie our society."[27]

## A "Right of Privacy"?

Under such formulations, the Court has protected the constitutional right of privacy, conceived, most famously, in Justice Louis Brandeis's words, as "the right to be let alone—the most comprehensive of rights and the right most valued by civilized men."[28] This right is not some recent invention. It did not spring full-blown like Athena from the head of Justice Harry Blackmun in his opinion in the case of *Roe v. Wade*.

Indeed, the first Supreme Court case decided on this ground came in 1923. In that year the Supreme Court held that the states could not forbid the teaching of modern foreign languages before the eighth grade. Two years later it held that states could not compel all students to attend public schools.

These twin rulings, *Meyer v. Nebraska*[29] and *Pierce v. Society of Sisters,*[30] stand as bulwarks in our legal system. The state law that the Supreme Court struck down in *Meyer* had been passed amid the tension of the nation's struggle with Germany in World War I. It was rooted in suspicion and aimed at suppressing the culture and heritage of Nebraska's German minority. If parents wanted their children to learn German, the Court said, the state had no right to dictate otherwise, even if the United States and Germany were at war. The law that the Court struck down in *Pierce,* which would have shut down both parochial and secular private schools as alternatives to Oregon's public school system, had been aimed at the state's Catholic minority, although it was successfully challenged by the Hill Military Academy as well as by the Society of Sisters. Government has no power, the Court said in these cases, "to standardize its children"[31] or to "foster a homogenous people."[32] Parents have a right to "direct the upbringing and education of children under their control."[33] This, of course, is now beyond challenge. From these now quite ancient roots has developed the "right of privacy," which, Justice Blackmun wrote in *Roe,* is "broad enough to encompass a woman's decision whether or not to terminate her pregnancy." These decisions of the 1920s are immediate ancestors of the very liberty invoked by women when they insist upon a right not to be made mothers against their will.

In 1942 the Court first recognized the fundamental character of decisions concerning reproduction. In the landmark right-of-privacy case of *Skinner v. Oklahoma,* on which the Court later relied in *Roe,* the Court invalidated a state statute providing for the sterilization of persons convicted two or more times of "felonies involving moral turpitude."[34] The Court in *Skinner* characterized the right to reproduce as "one of the basic civil rights of man" and observed, against the implicit background of Nazi policies to eradicate supposedly inferior genetic types, that "[t]he power to sterilize, if exercised . . . [i]n evil or reckless hands . . . can cause races or types which are inimical to the dominant group to wither and disappear."[35] In *Skinner* the Court recognized the grotesque disempowerment that could occur if the choice of whether to beget a child were transferred from the individual to the state.

The privacy right was also found to include decisions about marriage in the aptly named case of *Loving v. Virginia,* in which the Court recognized the fundamental nature of the unenumerated right to marry and struck down Virginia's law against interracial marriage. This added to the list of fundamental rights "the right to choose one's spouse."[36]

In 1965, in *Griswold v. Connecticut,* the Supreme Court recognized that the liberty clause protects the right of a married couple to decide whether or not to use contraceptives. The Court struck down a Connecticut law that made the use of contraceptives by married persons a crime. It overturned the aiding and abetting conviction of someone who had provided a married person with contraceptives and with information regarding their use. In a majority opinion by Justice William O.

Douglas the state's regulation was condemned as invading "the area of protected freedoms," which included "the zone of privacy created by several fundamental constitutional guarantees."[37] Although Justice Byron White was later one of the two dissenters in *Roe,* he wrote a concurring opinion in *Griswold* separately explaining his conclusion that the Connecticut anticontraceptive law failed to serve the purposes the state's lawyers claimed for it (deterring illicit sexual relationships) and impermissibly deprived married persons of "liberty without due process of law."[38]

The Court in 1972 addressed a Massachusetts law that made contraceptives more difficult for unmarried people to obtain than for those who were married. Justice Brennan, writing for the majority, observed that if "the right of privacy means anything, it is the right of the individual, married or single, to be free from unwarranted governmental intrusion into matters so fundamentally affecting a person as the decision whether to bear or beget a child."[39] Again, Justice White concurred in the majority's action in reversing the criminal conviction that was at issue, but his separate opinion, which was joined by Justice Blackmun, did not include anything like the majority's sweeping language about each individual's right of privacy.[40]

Although, in its decision the following year in *Roe,* the Court characterized these contraception decisions as cases about the right not to have to bear and beget children, *that* right could, of course, be vindicated without need for contraception—people could simply refrain from sexual intercourse. What is really protected as a fundamental right in the contraception cases is the right to engage in sexual intercourse without having a child. It was on the basis of these precedents that *Roe* was decided. Interestingly, of the four justices who would apparently vote to overrule *Roe* (Chief Justice Rehnquist and Justices White, Scalia, and Kennedy), none has expressed any disagreement with *Griswold.*

Most people would probably agree that among those liberties that must be deemed "fundamental" in our society, in addition to the freedoms embodied in the Bill of Rights, we must include the right to be free from at least some sorts of state interference in the intimacies of our bedrooms. As Professor Charles Black of Yale Law School put it, describing the Connecticut criminal ban on the use of contraceptives: "If our constitutional law could permit such a thing to happen, then we might almost as well not have any law of constitutional limitations, partly because the thing is so outrageous in itself, and partly because a constitutional law inadequate to deal with such an outrage would be too feeble, in method and doctrine, to deal with a very great amount of equally outrageous material."[41]

When the Court revisited the question of abortion in the *Webster* case in 1989, and when it strongly signaled that it was retreating from the principles of *Roe v. Wade,* Justice Scalia's separate opinion expressed his impatience with most of the other Justices. He thought it too plain to require extended discussion that the constitutional "mansion" of abortion rights that he claimed was "constructed overnight in *Roe v. Wade"* should be dismantled as soon as possible.[42]

He was unclear, however, about just how far the demolition project he had in mind would go. Would it, for example, leave in place the Supreme Court's decisions upholding the right to birth control? Harvard Law Professor Charles Fried, arguing for the Bush administration in *Webster,* went out of his way to emphasize that unlike Judge Robert Bork, he thought the Court had been correct in upholding the birth control right and would not want to see it undone. But if women have no significant "liberty" at stake in the abortion context, how can they possess a fundamental liberty to use birth control? The contradiction becomes clearest when we recognize that some of the most commonly used methods of birth control, such as the IUD and even at times the pill, operate as abortifacients, or abortion-causing agents. That is, they do not invariably prevent conception so much as arrest the embryo's development and implantation in the uterine wall at a very early stage in pregnancy. Although Professor Fried told the Court that *Roe* was merely a "thread" that could be pulled without "unravel[ing]" the "fabric" of the Court's privacy decisions, Frank Sussman, counsel for Reproductive Health Services in the *Webster* case, may have been closer to the mark when he replied, "It has always been my personal experience that when I pull a thread, my sleeve falls off."[43]

The threat of government regulation of these kinds of intimate personal choices cannot lightly be dismissed. At the time of the *Griswold* decision, as recently as 1965, the existence of the law prohibiting the use of contraception had prevented the establishment of family planning clinics in Connecticut. Predictably the poor and uneducated suffered disproportionately.

Even after *Griswold* the state of Massachusetts amended its law to prohibit the distribution of contraceptives to unmarried persons for the prevention of pregnancy.[44] Some have argued that even without the protection of the constitutional right to privacy, laws like this simply would not be enacted. But they have been enacted! Others have described them, dismissively, as "uncommonly silly."[45] Such dismissive remarks only cloud the real point: Those who deny the existence of a constitutionally protected right of privacy would abdicate judicial responsibility in protecting individuals from this threat.

## *Does the Presence of a Fetus Automatically Negate the "Private" Character of the Abortion Decision?*

And so we come to yet another and a considerably more plausible attack on *Roe*. This attack accepts the woman's right of privacy yet argues that the *abortion* right in particular was invented by the justices in *Roe*.

It may seem strange in this regard even to discuss the woman's right to abortion before considering the rights of the fetus. It may seem a case of staging *Hamlet* without the prince. Yet the Supreme Court has had good reasons for its long tradition of asking *first* about the right that is asserted, to see whether it is a fundamental liberty, and only *then* turning to the reasons, such as protection of the fetus's right to life, that might nonetheless justify that liberty's abridgment. Putting the cart before the horse by inquiring from the outset about government's *justifications* for abridging a liberty would leave us without guidance in deciding how strong a justification to demand. Even the right to free speech can be abridged for a reason that is sufficiently compelling—for example, to prevent the publication of the sailing dates of troopships in time of war. But without first assessing how fundamental the liberty of publication is, we would find ourselves at sea.

Justice White in a dissent from a 1986 abortion ruling suggested that because the decision to terminate a pregnancy affects a fetus, the liberty involved is unlike that involved in the question of whether an individual has a right to use contraception. Unlike the latter case, he argued, the woman deciding to end a pregnancy is not "isolated in her privacy." He argued that because of their effect on others, particular *exercises* of otherwise concededly fundamental liberties, "by their very nature, should be viewed as outside the scope of the fundamental liberty interest."[46]

In a more recent case, one dealing with a biological father's alleged right to receive a hearing on issues of paternity and visitation, Justice Scalia has also criticized the Court's traditional method of examining a right in isolation and then seeing what opposing reason the state puts forward to justify its abridgment. Writing for himself and for fellow conservative Justices Rehnquist, O'Connor, and Kennedy in the 1989 case *Michael H. v. Gerald D.*, he said, in language broader than that previously used by Justice White: "We cannot imagine what compels this strange procedure of looking at the act which is assertedly the subject of a liberty interest in isolation from its effect *upon other people*—rather like inquiring whether there is a liberty interest in firing a gun where the case at hand happens to involve its discharge into another person's body."[47]

Although he was writing to explain why he was ruling against the adulterous biological father in a love triangle, Justice Scalia appears to have been talking, indirectly, about abortion. Justice Scalia's immediate objective was to explain why a man who fathers a child through a sexual liaison with another man's wife has no specially protected "liberty" interest in his parental connection with that child despite the existence of parental "liberties" in general. The Scalia approach would link the existence of a parental interest, such as the one urged by this biological father, with an asserted "right" to interfere with a marital relationship and would deny that any such right merits recognition.

In the setting of an abortion case, the method that Justices Scalia and White propose would similarly link the existence of a woman's liberty interest in deciding whether to continue her pregnancy with an asserted "right" to end the fetus's life and would deny the existence of any such right at the threshold. That is, their method would simply deny a woman, in the first instance, even a hard look at the reasons why her ability to choose abortion was being restricted by government. Their method would apparently be to define the *woman*'s liberty in terms of the *fetus*—a great rhetorical advantage, since a "right to kill a fetus" wouldn't be fundamental by anyone's definition—and not in terms of the dignity or autonomy of the woman herself. The state would need no special justification to abridge this right as Justice White and Justice Scalia would define it. Of course, it is in requiring a more serious reason, a "compelling" reason, for a restriction of a fundamental liberty or privacy interest and in closely examining the state law to find such a reason that the Court provides protection against the excesses of a temporary majority.

The approach suggested by Justices Scalia and White, which seems almost tailor-made as a way to overrule *Roe v. Wade*, would do violence to all our rights. If it were applied faithfully, it would give the state nearly absolute power over us all. Take, for example, the state's power of military conscription. Obviously that is a complete restriction on a fundamental right. It completely denies a young person's physical liberty. Yet equally obviously, *some* reasons are sufficiently compelling to permit conscription. Conscription, for example, can be justified by the compelling needs of national security. Other reasons will not be compelling. Conscription surely could not be justified, for example, by the state's desire to have a cadre of youngsters available as chauffeurs for state officials or by its wish to have a crew of garbage collectors or oil-spill fighters.

But Justices White and Scalia, at least as they expressed their views in these two opinions, would define the right in terms of the state's interest. Under this approach, of course, conscription for the military is still permissible since there is surely no fundamental liberty interest in endangering the national security. But neither is there a fundamental liberty interest in inhibiting efficient chauffeur-driven travel by state officials or in preventing the collection of trash or the cleanup of an oil spill. So if the justices' system of analysis were faithfully followed, a state should be as free to conscript a cadre of crack trash collectors or even chauffeurs as it is to draft men for military service in wartime. If we incorporate the state's reason for its regulation into the initial definition of the liberty, in other words, the fundamental nature of that liberty *inevitably vanishes.* We don't even look to the strength of the state's reason for its intrusive action.

If we were to take this approach seriously, then *no right would be fundamental.* And if we do *not* take it at face value—if we assume that Justices White and Scalia would not really have the Court apply so harsh a test in all circumstances—then this method gives judges *more* power to choose whether or not to protect rights than they hold under the Court's current approach. The approach put forward by Justices White and Scalia could not be consistently applied by a majority of the Court without truly radical consequences. So it seems safe to proceed by examining first the asserted liberty—in this case the right of the woman *not to be forced to remain pregnant*—and only then turning to the fetus on the other side of the constitutional equation.

In the context of abortion, the attempt to distinguish the *right not to remain pregnant* from a *right to destroy one's fetus* may seem strange. We must recognize that, in view of today's technology, until the time of fetal "viability" it is (by definition) impossible to perform an abortion— to permit a woman freedom from the sacrifice of pregnancy and child- birth—without killing the fetus from which the woman is separated.

But this is not something that is inherent in nature. One can imagine a time when it will be possible for a woman to decide to terminate her pregnancy but when it will be possible to save the life of the fetus by removing it from the womb and incubating it either in a volunteer "sur- rogate" mother or in some kind of artificial womb. Of course, if such procedures are developed, society will then have to balance the presum- ably higher medical risk for the woman posed by those procedures against the increased chance of fetal survival.

As we shall see, the liberty that is most plainly vindicated by the right to end one's pregnancy is the woman's liberty not to be made unwillingly into a mother, the freedom to say no to the unique sacrifice inherent in the processes of pregnancy and childbirth. A "right" not to have a bio- logical child in existence—the right during pregnancy, for example, to *destroy* one's fetus rather than simply being *unburdened* of it—is analytically distinct, and seems harder to support. No one has such a right *after* a child is born; there is certainly no "right" to commit infanticide. Men certainly have no right to destroy a fetus once pregnancy begins, for while the Constitution protects a man's right to engage in nonprocreative sexual activity, it does not give him the power to insist on abortion of a fetus for which he is partially responsible. While there may be arguments in favor of recognizing a woman's right, early in pregnancy, to destroy the fetus growing within her for the very purpose of preventing a living child of hers from coming into being, this is not the liberty the Court undertook to protect in *Roe.*

Judge Bork says that "the right to abort, whatever one thinks of it, is not to be found in the Constitution."[48] In a sense this is obviously right. Indeed, not one of the words "abortion," "pregnancy," "reproduction," "sex," "privacy," "bodily integrity," and "procreation" appears anywhere in the United States Constitution. But neither do such phrases as "freedom of thought," "rights of parenthood," "liberty of association," "family self-determination," and "freedom of marital choice." Yet nearly everyone supposes that at least some of these dimensions of personal autonomy and independence are aspects of the "liberty" which the Fourteenth Amendment says no state may deny to any person "without due process of law."

The "right to abortion" was first *announced,* it's true, in *Roe v. Wade.* But as we have seen, the "right to privacy," whatever its outer bounds, was suggested as early as 1923 in the case of *Meyer v. Nebraska. Roe* was simply the first case in which the general question of state regulation of abortion was squarely considered by the Supreme Court. To argue that for this reason, the Constitution does not protect the right to abortion, or that it did not do so until January 22, 1973, is no better than to argue that it does not protect the "right to contribute money to a political campaign." Although that right was not *announced* until the Supreme Court's 1976 decision in *Buckley v. Valeo,* [49] it is beyond doubt that this right is, and has long been, a right protected by the free speech guarantee of the First Amendment. For that matter, the Supreme Court has never had occasion to declare that young lovers have a fundamental constitutional right to embrace one another lustily as they dance the night away. But that right, too, is there waiting to be proclaimed against any state or locality so prudish as to insist that the young couple conduct themselves with greater decorum.

## At How Specific a Level Must "Rights" Be Defined?

This, however, is not a completely satisfactory response to Judge Bork's criticism. The question remains: Even if we admit that certain fundamental rights are protected from infringement by the states, how are we to tell what the "right" in question is? By defining the right broadly or narrowly, one can apparently reach whatever result one desires. The "right to abortion" is a narrow way of describing the right protected in *Roe v. Wade.* Its very specificity makes it seem illegitimate.

By contrast, defining it broadly—for example, as "the right to make such intimate decisions as the decision whether to have a child"—makes it sound more like a right whose recognition is consistent with American tradition.

It seems that this may be the judicial battleground in coming years over the right of privacy. It is a question that has captured the attention of Justice Scalia in particular. Addressing this question in the 1989 parental rights case we have discussed, Justice Scalia argued that the proper approach was to "refer to the most specific level at which a relevant tradition protecting, or denying protection to, the asserted right can be identified."[50]

Not surprisingly, Justice Scalia's approach would do away with the right to choose abortion. But quite apart from that result, which some would welcome, his approach presents grave difficulty. To begin with, while Justice Scalia's test has a nice scientific ring to it, it does not tell us upon what axis we are to determine "specificity." In the case of abortion, for example, are we to look to the most specific tradition with regard to reproduction? Or surgery? Or women? Or children? Is the abortion question about a woman's right not to remain pregnant? About a person's right not to have a child? About a fetus's right not to be mistreated by others, as in assaults upon pregnant women? For that matter, why don't we look to see if there are traditions with respect to particular medical techniques? Justice Scalia cannot tell us.

In almost every case, of course, no matter what axis we examine, Justice Scalia's test will mandate a conclusion that there is no tradition protecting the asserted right. There is no more a tradition protecting the *particular* right to nonprocreative heterosexual intercourse or the *particular* right to live with two grandchildren who are not siblings than there is a tradition protecting the *particular* right to choose an abortion. Justice Scalia's formulation of a test to determine whether a right is fundamental would deny protection even to specific examples of the most historically familiar rights.

Most rights for which people seek vindication in the courts are going to be, at their most *specific* level, *new* rights. America has no long tradition of permitting interracial marriage; the history is just the opposite. But because the Court found a tradition protecting the *broader* right to choose whom to marry, it struck down Virginia's antimiscegenation laws in the 1967 case of *Loving v. Virginia.*

It would be a radical transformation indeed if the Constitution were the straitjacket Justice Scalia would make of it—able to protect only those specific practices that existed and were legally approved in the past. The Constitution is, and must be, a living document, not a history book. President Wilson said of the Constitution: "As the life of the nation changes so must the interpretation of the document which contains it change, by a nice adjustment, determined, not by the original intention of those who drew the paper, but by the exigencies and the new aspects of life itself."[51]

Two justices who joined the rest of Justice Scalia's opinion in *Michael H.* (Justices O'Connor and Kennedy) pointedly declined to join him in his strikingly narrow view of the traditions protected by the Constitution. Only Chief Justice Rehnquist agreed completely. Indeed, Justice Scalia's view of the Constitution or at least of its liberty clause drew an emotional dissent from eighty-three-year-old Justice William J. Brennan, Jr., then sitting in his next-to-last term, who had served on the Court for thirty-three years as a jurist universally respected for his intellect and integrity. He wrote:

> The document that the plurality construes today is unfamiliar to me. It is not the living charter that I have taken to be our Constitution; it is instead a stagnant, archaic, hidebound document steeped in the prejudices and superstitions of a time long past. *This* Constitution does not recognize that times change, does not see that sometimes a practice or rule outlives its foundations. I cannot accept an interpretive method that does such violence to the charter that I am bound by oath to uphold.[52]

### Privacy: Who Decides Whether to Terminate a Pregnancy?

So does the right of privacy encompass the right to decide whether to terminate a pregnancy or doesn't it? Is that a fundamental right protected by the Fourteenth Amendment? Is it protected by the tradition and conscience of our people?

Professor Charles Fried, who was solicitor general under President Ronald Reagan, understood that the Supreme Court's line of decisions on the subject of personal privacy rested squarely on "the moral fact that a person belongs to himself and not others nor to society as a whole."[53] In his book *Right and Wrong* Fried acknowledges that to say, "[M]y body can be used," is to say, *"I* can be used."[54] And there can be no doubt that forcing a woman into continued pregnancy does entail using her body. Although the fetus at some point develops an independent identity and eventually even an independent consciousness, it begins as a living part of the woman's body, growing from a single cell supplied by her and sustained solely by nutrients carried to it through her uterine wall. Fetal cells even circulate in the woman's bloodstream as her pregnancy progresses. To say that the fetus might have rights of its own does not demonstrate that it is somehow a being separate and distinct from its mother, at least in the beginning. It is not a lodger or prisoner or guest, nor is its mother a mere home or incubator. The fetus is, after all, her "flesh and blood."

Some people apparently believe that acknowledging the fetus to be part of the woman's body somehow sacrifices any moral claim on its behalf—as though the fetus would be more secure and its value would be enhanced if we were to pretend that it is an entirely separate or alien being. That assumption rests on a strange view of the psychology and morality of women.

It seems a serious mistake to think that a woman who regards a developing fetus as a part of her body will, as a result of that view, feel freer to injure or destroy it than she would if she were to regard the fetus as some sort of intruder temporarily housed within her womb. On the contrary, it is precisely a woman's identification with the fetus as an aspect of herself, her love for the new life within her as flesh of her flesh and blood of her blood, that makes it seem so strange for the law to intervene between her and that life. If the fetus is a part of its mother, it is certainly a unique part, one infinitely more valued by nearly every mother than, say, her arm or her kidney. To recognize the fetus as part of its mother in deciding what her rights are is not to denigrate the moral value of its life or to deny the possibility that it might be entitled to the protection and concern of society as a whole. At the very least, it cannot fairly be denied that telling a woman what to do or not to do with the fetus within her entails telling her what to do or not to do with her own body.

Beyond this basic point about whose body is being used, the privacy cases recognize that the liberty clause of the Fourteenth Amendment guarantees each of us the right not to have the state shackle us with self-defining decisions. It is fundamental that we remain free of the power of total regimentation held invalid more than sixty-five years ago in *Pierce v. Society of Sisters.* This requires a zone that is protected by respect for individual autonomy and reverence for the privacy of intimate human relations. It cannot be denied that this is traditionally central among the values for whose protection the United States, and its Constitution, stands.

The liberty involved in deciding whether to terminate a pregnancy is, in part, the interest in being able to avoid pregnancy without abstaining from sex, the liberty recognized as fundamental in the contraception decisions. But it is much more. Indeed, the right to decide whether to end a pregnancy lies at the very intersection of several liberties that must be deemed fundamental.

Certainly it is a significant restriction of a woman's physical liberty to force her to carry a pregnancy to term. Some have dismissed the burden as mere inconvenience. Whatever the reason some people take that view, it is not sustainable. Pregnancy entails unique physical invasion and risk. As Chief Justice Rehnquist has observed in another context, any pregnancy entails "profound physical, emotional, and psychological consequences."[55]

Over the nine-month term, the size of a pregnant woman's uterus increases five hundred to a thousand times. Her body weight increases by twenty-five pounds or more. Even a healthy pregnancy may be accompanied by frequent urination, water retention, nausea, and vomiting, as well as labored breathing, back pain, and fatigue.[56]

Every pregnancy also entails substantial medical risk. As many as 30 percent of pregnant women have major medical complications, and 60 percent have some kind of medical complication. Labor and vaginal delivery represent unique and painful physical demands that can last for many hours or even days. Caesarean section (required, under current medical practice, in one out of four live births) involves invasive surgery, including an abdominal incision and general anesthesia. Continued pregnancy significantly increases the risk of fatality. Early abortion, of course, is statistically a far safer procedure for a pregnant woman than carrying her pregnancy to term.[57]

Even if one stresses the potential independence of the fetus from the woman's body, forcing her to continue a pregnancy to term and to deliver an unwanted baby obviously intrudes into the integrity of her body far more profoundly than do the other invasions for which the Supreme Court has routinely required extremely strong justification—for example, the stomach pumping for evidence invalidated by the Supreme Court in 1952[58] or the surgical removal of a bullet lodged in a suspect's shoulder invalidated by the Supreme Court in 1985.[59]

Being forced to proceed to childbirth also does extreme and unique psychological violence to a woman. The permanent psychological bond created between mother and child has been well documented. Pregnancy is not in this sense a minor and temporary imposition whose burdens are limited by the availability of adoption. The fact is that in 1986, the most recent year for which data are available, only 3 percent of unwed mothers in the United States, whatever their initial disposition to putting an unwanted child up for adoption, actually did so.[60]

As Dr. Harold Rosen, a psychiatrist, described in his 1967 article about abortion, "A Case Study in Social Hypocrisy," many of his pregnant patients told him the same thing: "Do you think I could give my baby away after carrying it for nine months. . . ? [Y]ou can't turn me into the kind of animal that would give my baby away!"[61] Pregnancy does not merely "inconvenience" the woman for a time; it gradually turns her into a mother and makes her one for all time.

Even more dramatically than laws telling one how to bring up one's children or with which family members one may live or laws saying that one has no right to nonprocreative sex, laws telling a woman she must remain pregnant deprive her of the very core of liberty and privacy. It would be quite unthinkable if a liberty broad enough to encompass intimate decisions about the bearing of children, the formation of a family, and the preservation of one's own body were somehow to *exclude* a woman's decision about whether her body is to carry a baby until she becomes a parent—either a parent who thereafter raises her own child or one who undergoes the trauma of giving it up for adoption.

Attorney Jed Rubenfeld, in a 1989 essay entitled "The Right of Privacy," underscores perhaps the deepest sense in which laws restricting abortion reduce women to "mere instrumentalities of the state."[62] Such laws "take diverse women with every variety of career, life-plan, and so on, and make mothers of them all."[63]

If the constitutional protection of our individual rights and human dignity means much of anything, then the freedom to decide whether or not to endure pregnancy *must* be deemed a fundamental aspect of personal privacy. Even if the introduction of the fetus into the picture makes abortion a close question, the right to decide whether or not to carry a pregnancy to term is not a marginal case in terms of whether or not a fundamental liberty of the woman at least is at stake. Pregnancy is a burden that cannot be imposed by the state without the most serious justification.

## Equality: Abortion Rights and Sex Discrimination

There is a further reason why the decision whether or not to end a pregnancy should not be subject to infringement without a compelling reason. Although the Court in *Roe* relied solely on the liberty clause of the Fourteenth Amendment, any restriction that prohibits women from exercising the right to decide whether to end a pregnancy would, in the absence of a truly compelling justification, deny them the "equal protection of the laws" also guaranteed by the Fourteenth Amendment.

In *Skinner v. Oklahoma,* as we saw earlier, the Court recognized the fundamental nature of the right to control one's own reproduction. It did so in part because, in that case, forced sterilizations were being carried out only against those habitual criminals who were guilty of working-class crimes. The statute at issue applied to those convicted of "felonies involving moral turpitude," but it exempted such white-collar offenses as embezzlement and tax violations. As the Court wrote, "[s]terilization of those who have thrice committed grand larceny with immunity for those who are embezzlers is a clear, pointed, unmistakable discrimination."[64]

Laws restricting abortion so dramatically shape the lives of women, and only of women, that their denial of equality hardly needs detailed elaboration. While men retain the right to sexual and reproductive autonomy, restrictions on abortion deny that autonomy to women. Laws restricting access to abortion thereby place a real and substantial burden on women's ability to participate in society as equals. Even a woman who is not pregnant is inevitably affected by her knowledge of the power relationships created by a ban on abortion.

It is true that not all women are burdened by restrictions on abortion, although certainly all fertile women of childbearing age are. Laws that disadvantage women disproportionately but that also disadvantage many men—laws favoring war veterans, for example—have sometimes been upheld by the Supreme Court without close scrutiny.[65] But laws restricting abortion do not merely burden women disproportionately; they directly burden *women alone.*

A law that discriminates in such a forceful way against an entire group of people and that poses such an obvious danger of majoritarian oppression and enduring subjugation must not be permitted unless it is needed to serve the most compelling public interest. Otherwise its victims are, in the most fundamental sense imaginable, denied the equal protection of the laws. This is the lesson of *Skinner v. Oklahoma.*

## The "Original Understanding" of the Framers

Notwithstanding all this, foes of the right to choose abortion have a further line of attack they advance even before expressly introducing the fetus into the picture. It was put most succinctly by William Rehnquist in his *Roe* dissent: "By the time of the adoption of the Fourteenth Amendment in 1868, there were at least 36 laws enacted by state or territorial legislatures limiting abortion. . . . [Twenty-one] of the laws on the books in 1868 remain in effect today. . . . The only conclusion possible from this history is that the drafters did not intend to have the Fourteenth Amendment withdraw from the States the power to legislate with respect to this matter."[66]

Obviously, in the interpretation of any written document it is important to examine the intention of those who chose the words. So it is with the Constitution. But the suggestion, almost elevated to a fetish by some in the post-*Roe* new wave of conservative legal scholars, that we must look *only* to the understanding of the Framers with regard to each *particular* situation that comes before a court, is outlandish.[67]

To begin with, in a wide variety of circumstances there will be no correct answer. To ask, for example, "What did Thomas Jefferson think (or what would he have thought) about drug testing in the workplace?" is essentially meaningless. The truth is that the framers and the many who voted to ratify the Fourteenth Amendment will have thought and intended many often inconsistent things. In fairness, it must be said that conservatives are frequently as quick to concede all this as liberals and that bogus invocation of "original intent" has by no means been confined to any one part of the ideological spectrum.

We must certainly look at the intent of the framers, but at a much more general level. The Constitution, particularly in its open-ended provisions such as those guaranteeing liberty, equality, and due process, lays down broad principles. It is these principles that courts must apply to particular situations.[68] In the context of the Eighth Amendment's prohibition on cruel and unusual punishments, for example, the Supreme Court has held that what is "cruel" cannot be determined by what practices would have been so considered at the time of the framers. Rather, "[t]he Amendment must draw its meaning from the evolving standards of decency that mark the progress of a maturing society."[69]

As the great chief justice John Marshall put it more generally, "we must never forget that it is a *constitution* we are expounding."[70] Even in situations with which the framers of a particular constitutional provision would have been familiar, therefore, the provisions of the Constitution may have consequences that would have surprised them.

The interpretive method put forward by some of those who view the original understanding as a rigid talisman would plunge our nation into a deep freeze in which, in the absence of a new constitutional amendment for each occasion on which the judiciary has heard a case presenting an arguably new right, only the very rights anticipated in 1791, when the Bill of Rights was ratified, or in 1868, when the Fourteenth Amendment was adopted, would be protected.

For this precise reason one of the principal architects of the Constitution, James Madison, insisted that his notes from the Constitutional Convention not be published until after his death. The United States was not to be bound by the particular vision of the small group of men who, in the late eighteenth century, drafted its fundamental charter. As Madison wrote, "[a]s a guide in expounding and applying the provisions of the Constitution, the debates and incidental decisions of the Convention can have no authoritative character." Indeed, Madison stated that his knowledge of the views expressed by delegates to the Constitutional Convention were a possible source of "bias" in his own interpretation of the Constitution.[71]

A world in which we focused upon the subjective and narrow intent of selected framers in deciding the meaning of various constitutional provisions would be a strange one indeed. For one thing, each constitutional provision has many authors, and there is the problem of which framer's intent should count as decisive. For another thing, constitutional provisions become law not when they are proposed by the authors but when they are duly ratified. Needless to say, the assumptions and intentions of the individuals who vote to ratify a provision may differ from one ratifier to another, and it may be that the ratifiers' intent differs significantly from that of the proposers. However we were to resolve these many differences, the results would be peculiar and often unacceptable. For starters, the Bill of Rights would not apply to protect us from any of the actions of state government, however outrageous.

Or consider this example: If specific "original intent" alone governed, we would live in a world in which although the schools run by the states and their subdivisions (the cities and towns) would have to be racially integrated (this is the command of the equal protection clause of the Fourteenth Amendment as interpreted by the Supreme Court in *Brown v. Board of Education* ), the schools run by the federal government— for example, in the District of Columbia— *could* be segregated by law.

The equal protection clause of the Fourteenth Amendment reads:

"No State shall . . . deny to any person within its jurisdiction the equal protection of the laws." As its words make clear, it applies only to the states. While there is a second due process clause that applies to the federal government, contained in the Bill of Rights, in the Fifth Amendment to the Constitution, there is no textual guarantee that the *federal* government must guarantee *equal protection* of the law. Indeed, the same Congress that adopted the Fourteenth Amendment subsequently operated a segregated school system in the District of Columbia.[72] At this specific level we know that the original understanding of the guarantee of equality in the Fourteenth Amendment must have been that it did *not* prohibit the federal government from running segregated schools in the nation's capital. And on a more general level, it would be hard indeed to attribute to those who wrote or ratified the Fifth Amendment in the late eighteenth century even a broad equality principle that could one day embrace a ban on segregation by race.

Nonetheless, the Supreme Court—on the day in 1954 that it handed down *Brown*—decided in the companion case of *Bolling v. Sharpe*[73] that the public schools of Washington, D.C., must be desegregated. While the Court recognized that the Fourteenth Amendment's equal protection clause does not apply to the federal government, it observed that "[i]n view of our decision that the Constitution prohibits the states from maintaining racially segregated public schools, it would be unthinkable that the same Constitution would impose a lesser duty on the Federal Government."[74] The Court held that the federal law segregating the District's schools violated the due process clause of the Fifth Amendment, which it saw as informed by, and embodying, the equality principle adopted many decades later in the equal protection clause of the Fourteenth.

Strict adherence to a jurisprudence of original intent simply would not have permitted this result. And indeed Judge Bork, who has long been a vocal advocate of "originalism," continues to condemn emphatically the *Bolling* decision that invalidated the school segregation laws of Washington, D.C., as a "clear rewriting of the Constitution by the Warren Court." He calls it "social engineering from the bench."[75] Although Judge Bork often tries to come up with reasons why politically popular decisions that he considers illegitimate should have come out the same way under some different provision of the Constitution—he argues, for example, that *Meyer v. Nebraska* and *Pierce v. Society of Sisters,* the early child-rearing cases, could have been decided the same way under the First Amendment[76]—here he doesn't even try.

## *Judicial Legislation?*

Another criticism of *Roe,* and one that must be addressed because of its apparently powerful hold on many opponents of abortion rights, is that it was an essentially legislative act because the elaborate scheme announced in *Roe,* with its delineation of trimesters and its emphasis on the significance of viability, is not suitably "judicial." This is different from the argument that our democratic system somehow requires that abortion be left to legislatures, but it seems no more convincing.

In *Webster,* Chief Justice Rehnquist wrote that the trimester framework is "hardly consistent with the notion of a Constitution cast in general terms, as ours is. . . . The key elements of the *Roe* framework . . . are not found in the text of the Constitution." He went on to argue that *Roe* has engendered "a web of legal rules that have become increasingly intricate, resembling a code of regulations rather than a body of constitutional doctrine."[77]

This is a remarkable argument for a judge to make. As Justice Blackmun stated powerfully in his *Webster* dissent, much of our constitutional doctrine is made up of judge-made rules that give detailed, operational content to broad constitutional guarantees. For example, the Supreme Court has announced a complicated standard for deciding whether speech is obscene, in order to determine whether it is outside the protective reach of the First Amendment. Even Judge Bork, when sitting on the U.S. Court of Appeals for the District of Columbia Circuit, won praise from free speech advocates when he insisted that First Amendment rules dealing with libel suits must take account of a "rich variety of factors" so that those rules might properly reflect "how the framers' values, defined in the context of the world they knew, apply to the world we know."[78] Equal protection cases, too, are decided by reference to a complex series of judicially created tests whose texts cannot be found in the Constitution.

Neither is the complexity of the rules about what abortion restrictions will and will not pass constitutional muster a hallmark of illegitimately "legislative" judicial decisionmaking. Indeed, it is in areas in which there has been significant adjudication that such lines appear, marking the outer bounds of a well-considered constitutional doctrine. For example, the Fourth Amendment's ban on unreasonable searches and seizures has been held to permit the police, when arresting the driver of a car, to search without a warrant the passenger compartment of the car, any luggage in the car and its glove compartment, but not the car's trunk or any luggage it contains.

The argument that *Roe* is legislative in character retains some vitality and credibility because of the method by which the rules enunciated in *Roe* were handed down. Ordinarily the Court will not, in Justice Brandeis's words, "formulate a rule of constitutional law broader than is required by the precise facts to which it is to be applied."[79] This is a rule of judicial prudence with roots in the policies underlying the constitutional limits on the power of the judiciary, included in Article III of the Constitution, to decide only "cases" or "controversies."

The result of this principle is a system of case-by-case adjudication in which areas of the law evolve gradually as each new situation, with its unique implications, is presented to the Court. The Court can thus consider carefully, in one concrete situation after another, the application of the reasoning of its previous decisions to new circumstances.

*Roe v. Wade,* of course, did far more than that. Rather than simply strike down the Texas statute that prohibited abortion except to save the life of the woman, leaving the exact contours of the constitutional right to privacy for later cases that presented less intrusive abortion regulations, the Court spelled out at one breath much of a complex constitutional doctrine. This obviously was not required by the "precise facts" of the case.

This approach is not necessarily illegitimate. The Court is under no duty to announce Delphic rules or to leave the country guessing about its intentions. On the contrary, it has some responsibility to give lower courts guidance and to permit the American people to order their affairs with confidence in the lay of the legal land and to seek a constitutional amendment if there is overwhelming consensus that the Court is wrong. Indeed, many judges have argued that the general rule about the breadth of constitutional pronouncements should be overridden when good cause exists.

Still, the sensitivity of the abortion question counseled more restraint than the Court exhibited in *Roe.* A gradual enunciation and articulation of the line that separated permissible state laws from laws that violated the constitutional right to privacy might have permitted the nation gradually to become acclimated to each piece of the abortion right and to have understood why each new piece of the framework that protected a woman's right to reproductive choice was put in place. This approach would have been more judicious, and it might also have given those who oppose abortion less of a shock, one that even today informs the arguments of some that *Roe* was a brazen act of judicial fiat.

## What's at Stake?

Why is it so important whether the abortion right, although nowhere mentioned in the Constitution by name, is a fundamental right protected by that document so that any governmental restriction of the right requires special justification? The answer is that much more is at stake in this battle, a battle being fought out in the Supreme Court today, than abortion rights alone.

A world with *only* enumerated rights would be a vastly different one from the world we know today. If women were held not to have a fundamental liberty interest in control over their own bodies simply because that right is not expressly stated in the Constitution, not only could abortion be *prohibited,* but abortion as well as sterilization could be *mandated* by the state. If a person had no specially protected "liberty" interest in privacy or in decisions about reproduction, the state could make a rational decision, for reasons of population control or eugenics, for example, to require abortions in certain circumstances, on pain of criminal punishment or imposition of a tax or other penalty. The courts would be unable to interfere in the name of the Constitution.

But if there *is* a fundamental right to decide whether or not to terminate a pregnancy, then before the Supreme Court could uphold laws of this sort, it would have to decide that the reasons supporting them were exceptionally strong (or, as the Court usually puts it, "compelling"). That is a decision very rarely made. Even if the Court found protection of the fetus a compelling reason for restricting abortions, one would hope it would not find population control a compelling enough reason to abridge reproductive freedom. Thus, the Court could strike down laws requiring abortion or sterilization even while upholding laws banning abortion.

This may seem an unlikely area for concern, but in China, of course, such policies are now in effect. As we saw in the preceding chapter, a policy of forced abortion is utilized by the Chinese government, and has been used by other governments in the past, as a means of population control.

In addition, in the Gansu Province of China, a law mandates that moderately to severely mentally retarded people must be sterilized if they are or plan to become married, even to people of normal intelligence. This law is being strictly enforced. If the woman becomes pregnant anyway, whether she herself is retarded or not, she is forced to have an abortion. An official of the Gansu Province Family Planning Association was quoted in the *New York Times* as saying that the "purpose of the law is to raise the quality of our population and our nation."[80] Similar sentiments animated the policy of Nazi Germany, also described in the preceding chapter. Between 1933 and 1940 more than five hundred thousand people were ordered sterilized against their will by the eugenic health courts in Germany.

Most of us would probably like to believe that such a thing could never happen in the United States. But our states have a long and gruesome history of forced sterilization. Many, many thousands of Americans were sterilized in this century by the states on eugenic grounds. Indeed, the Supreme Court upheld the involuntary sterilization of a woman named Carrie Buck by the state of Virginia in the 1927 case of *Buck v. Bell,* in which Justice Holmes wrote, in words that now seem ominously totalitarian, "society can prevent those who are manifestly unfit from continuing their kind. . . . Three generations of imbeciles are enough."[81]

Stephen J. Gould has written that by today's standards, Carrie Buck, who was sterilized with the Supreme Court's blessing, would not be considered mentally deficient.[82] Under the law upheld by the Supreme Court in 1927, the state of Virginia continued to perform forced, involuntary sterilizations *until 1972.*

This did not violate any right protected by the Bill of Rights. The right to be free of this kind of invasion is nowhere explicitly mentioned in the Constitution. Only the constitutional protection of unenumerated rights under the liberty clause could protect us from a legislative decision to sterilize some of us or to force some of us to have abortions. And if women may be forced to use their bodies to develop and nurture children against their will without even a compelling public justification, who can guess what other bodily invasions and indignities could be imposed upon any of us without any special showing of necessity? The threat of such invasions is as real as the history of the twentieth century.

# 6

# The Equation's Other Side: Does It Matter Whether the Fetus Is a Person?

=

Even if, as we have seen, a fundamental right of a woman is indeed implicated when she decides to end a pregnancy, why shouldn't government be free to prevent abortion out of legitimate concern for the harm each abortion necessarily causes? After all, the Constitution sometimes permits government to limit even the most basic liberties. Many have been conscripted to fight, and even die, in war. Others have been conscripted in situations considerably less cataclysmic. Police, paramedics, and firefighters, for example, will often lawfully order bystanders at an emergency scene to cooperate even at the risk of their lives.

Of course, abortion restrictions might not do much to save fetuses. Such restrictions might instead force desperate women into unsafe back-alley abortions, in which the unborn are not saved and in which more than a few women may die as well. Or abortions may be delayed, with the result that many fetuses that are aborted are more developed than they would have been without abortion restrictions. Or perhaps the restrictions would have no significant effect on conduct, especially considering the growing availability of drugs that induce early abortion without any need for resort to a clinic or hospital. With such modern techniques, abortion restrictions might operate mostly to deny women a symbolic affirmation of their autonomy, while leaving most women quite free to end unwanted fetal life safely.

But efforts might be made to minimize such end runs around the law. If those efforts were made, so that the law served its supposed purpose instead of harming women for no real reason, one might well argue that the burdens the law imposed were justified by the government's interest in enacting it. That seems a genuine possibility. Unlike the more extreme argument explored in the preceding chapter—that the Supreme Court simply invented the existence of a constitutional right on the woman's side of the equation—this argument in support of abortion restrictions hardly requires reducing the freedom of women to a cipher.

Yet considering how much a woman's liberty is burdened when government prevents her from ending her pregnancy if that is her choice, only one of the various "interests" that a state might invoke can plausibly qualify as sufficiently "compelling": the protection of human life. To override a liberty as basic as a woman's freedom not to remain pregnant, not to give birth, and not to become a mother, organized society must surely offer a momentous reason. Only the saving of life would seem to qualify.

Some who argue that a woman has no "right" to an abortion have claimed that even if an early embryo is *not* a "human life," not yet a person, the state may legitimately choose to protect that embryo from deliberate destruction at any point in its development so that it will have an opportunity to *become* a person. Even if the woman was raped, some say, deliberately killing the embryo only creates a second innocent victim.

This argument—that the fetus need not, after all, be considered a person in order to overcome the existence of a woman's "right" to terminate her pregnancy at will—was most famously expressed in an irreverent aside by John Hart Ely, the former dean of Stanford Law School and an esteemed constitutional scholar. In the course of a scathing 1973 attack on *Roe v. Wade,* [1] Ely noted that even though dogs certainly are not persons under the Fourteenth Amendment, a state most assuredly may make it a crime for a demonstrator to kill a dog without thereby impermissibly abridging the demonstrator's First Amendment rights of free speech. Recalling that the Supreme Court had once upheld an act of Congress making it a crime to burn a draft card,[2] Ely remarked, "Come to think of it, draft cards aren't persons either."

The problem with Ely's observation is that a fundamental liberty of protest *need not* entail killing or destroying a dog or anything else. Nobody *has* to kill an animal or mutilate government property in order to exercise the right to engage in freedom of speech. But if a woman's protected liberty includes a right to decide that her body will not be used to incubate and give birth to another, and if a woman is entitled to choose not to develop part of herself into a separate human being, then, in order to exercise *that* right, she unfortunately has to end the life of the fetus she carries within her—as long as she chooses to exercise that right before the fetus develops enough so that it can survive and mature outside her body with the aid of whatever technology exists. If she is to exercise the "liberty" to resist the conscription of her body as a vessel and a vehicle for another life, then, until that other life can as a practical matter be preserved without involuntarily using *her* life to preserve it, she has *no alternative* other than the tragic one of ending the fetus's life.

The right protected by *Roe* is not necessarily a right to end the life of the fetus. That is simply an *outcome* that cannot be avoided prior to fetal viability if the woman is to exercise the right to terminate her pregnancy. It is no answer to suggest that she just wait until the fetus is developed enough to survive after being surgically removed, for that would mean the right the woman claims is an empty one.

## Is the Fetus a Person?

We have seen that the Supreme Court in its contraception decisions has protected the right to have sex without having children. This right is also at stake in the case of abortion. Unless a retreat from *Roe* is to become a retreat from the *Griswold* birth control ruling as well, the Supreme Court will have to draw a constitutionally decisive line between a woman's continuing right to avoid being pregnant through use of birth control and the supposed disintegration of any right to avoid a pregnancy immediately upon the fertilization of an ovum. But as we have just seen, the only plausible basis for drawing such a line, at least in a legal system that takes rights as seriously as ours does, would have to be a belief that the state may legitimately treat *each fertilized ovum* as a bearer of competing, offsetting rights of its own.

The primary argument in support of such a state prerogative is that from the very moment of conception the fetus is a person and is therefore a bearer of human rights. We will later look at some inconsistencies that make it seem unlikely that such a belief really does underlie the views of most people who want to restrict or prohibit abortions. For now, though, let us accept this argument at face value and see where it leads.

The most extreme form of this argument, a form explicitly rejected by the Supreme Court in *Roe v. Wade,* is that when the Constitution uses the word "person," it includes the fetus within that *legal* category. Notice that this is not really an argument in support of a state's power to go either way on the subject of abortion. For under this argument for fetal rights, if a state legislature *permits* abortion, it is licensing others to deprive the fetus of life without due process of law and is denying to the fetus the equal protection of the state's murder laws, in a blatant violation of the Constitution's ban on all such denials.

This is a reflection of what is commonly viewed as the irreducible conflict between the abortion rights position and the right-to-life position. We have what seems to be, at least currently, an insoluble question: When does a person's life begin?

## An Inherently Religious Question?

Those who support a woman's right to choose abortion may object when government officials even pose that question. They may respond that the question of when someone's life begins is inherently a religious one. Justice John Paul Stevens took just such a view in the separate opinion he wrote in the *Webster* case.[3]

But as a matter of constitutional law, a question such as this, having an irreducibly moral dimension, cannot properly be kept out of the political realm merely because many religions and organized religious groups inevitably take strong positions on it. Religious views and groups played prominent roles in opposing slavery in the nineteenth century, urging temperance in the 1920s, and opposing the Vietnam War in the 1960s and 1970s. The participation of religious groups in political dialogue has never been constitutional anathema in the United States. Quite the contrary. The values reflected in the constitutional guarantees of freedom of religion and political expression argue strongly for the inclusion of church and religious groups, and of religious beliefs and arguments, in public life. As Justice Brennan has put it, "[r]eligionists no less than members of any other group enjoy the full measure of protection afforded speech, association and political activity generally."[4] Thus, the theological source of beliefs about the point at which human life begins should not cast a constitutional shadow across whatever laws a state might adopt to restrict abortions that occur beyond that point. And the arguments of pro-choice advocates about the religious nature of attempts to define the beginning of a person's existence as a separate human being really don't answer the question of whether or not abortion must be left to unfettered personal choice. We are left with a clash of deeply held beliefs—and no apparent way to get beyond it.

## Looking for the Answer in Science

Some pro-choice advocates believe that a proper understanding of human biology can somehow rule out the possibility that a fetus is a separate human being. Pro-life advocates commonly invoke our growing

understanding of fetal embryology, particularly the resemblance between fetuses and babies that it is now possible to illustrate through
photographs, in support of their claim that fetuses should be independently respected under the law. Likewise, those who support abortion
rights invoke principles of biology in support of their claim that whatever else it is, a fetus simply *cannot* be a separate "person."

A particularly persuasive form of this argument has been advanced by
Charles A. Gardner, a University of Michigan Medical School doctoral
candidate in the Department of Anatomy and Cell Biology.[5] Gardner
takes as his target the now famous argument of Dr. John Willke of the
National Right to Life Committee that the embryo must be a separate
human person, not simply living tissue, from the moment of conception
since the crucial forty-six chromosomes that determine a person's separate and distinct genetic identity are all present in the fertilized egg.
"Contained within the single cell who I once was," Willke is fond of
saying, "was the totality of everything I am today."

The antiabortion pamphlet *Did You Know?* says to every reader:
"You once were a fertilized ovum. A fertilized ovum? Yes! You were
then everything you are today. Nothing has been added to the fertilized
ovum who you once were except nutrition." A standard pro-choice re-
tort has been that the same is true of the unfertilized ovum and the
sperm, each of which is alive and belongs to no species other than *Homo
sapiens,* and to each of which nothing is added except nutrition and each
other (to the ovum, the sperm; to the sperm, the ovum).

But this response has always been vulnerable to the pro-life rejoinder
that the fusion of sperm and ovum makes all the difference in the world,
for only when this fusion occurs is the genetic identity of a separate, new
person determined and, under many religions, its distinct spiritual identity fixed. Thus, for example, when a Tennessee judge decided in September 1989 that seven frozen embryos over which a divorce battle was
being waged are "human beings," he rested his determination on the
proposition that "upon fertilization, the entire constitution of the man is
clearly, unequivocally spelled-out, including arms, legs, nervous systems and the like."

Gardner quotes this Tennessee judge, as well as Dr. Willke, and responds that a person's constitution is not, in fact, determined by the
genetic material, the DNA, to be found in the fertilized ovum. He explains that there is *not,* in fact, one and only one "path" for the fertilized
egg to travel on its way to full gestation. On the contrary, as cell division
proceeds, the pattern of the embryo's progress toward increasing complexity and differentiation depends not just on the genetic information
contained in the original forty-six chromosomes but, in significant part,

on the pattern of cells and molecules present in the preceding cell division. "The information required to make an eye or a finger does not exist in the fertilized egg," Gardner tells us. "It exists in the positions and interactions of cells and molecules that will be formed only at a later time."[6] As Gardner explains,

> [t]here is no program to specify the fate of each cell. Rather, a cell's behavior is influenced at each stage by its location within the developing body pattern of the embryo. Each stage brings new information, information that will change as the body pattern changes. And each cell will respond to this new information in a somewhat random way. For example, one cell of the sixteen-cell embryo may contribute randomly to the formation of many different organs or structures of the body. . . . With this layering of chance event upon chance event the embryo gradually evolves its form.

Gardner concludes that it is a mix of "chance and planning" that makes each of us a unique person. "Even the distinct pattern of ridges and swirls that make up a fingerprint is not pre-set in the fertilized egg. Identical twins grow from the same egg, have exactly the same DNA and develop in the same maternal environment, yet they have different fingerprints."

As Gardner asks, if a thing as simple as a fingerprint is not genuinely "present" in some programmed sense in the fertilized ovum, how could anything as subtle and unique as the individual human brain or the separate personality or psyche (or soul, though Gardner doesn't speak of souls) be regarded as "present" from the moment of conception? Gardner's dramatic way of putting the point is worth quoting: "The fertilized egg is clearly not a prepackaged human being. There is no body plan, no blueprint, no tiny being pre-formed and waiting to unfold. . . . [T]he particular person that it might become is not yet there."[7]

Indeed, as Gardner points out perhaps even more powerfully, two sibling human embryos sometimes combine into one, yielding a completely normal new "person" at the end of the developmental process. Any particular cell of that baby's body will have the genetic material of one or the other of the original embryos. And the converse is equally telling: A single embryo may split at a very early stage into two or more identical embryos, yielding identical twins or triplets. Was the pretwinning embryo one distinct person or two?

This does seem to demonstrate something that most people must intuitively feel to some degree. A newly fertilized ovum is not fully equivalent to a baby about to be born. Abortion of one does not present the same moral issues as abortion of the other, and the two cases ought not to be treated identically by the law.

Still, the scientific argument does not demonstrate much more than this. The scientific "disproof" of separate embryonic personhood, even if offered in the best of faith, cannot succeed completely. It does not *prove* that the fetus is less a human being than any of us. The particular and distinctive person *you* might become, even today, is "not yet there" either. There is always the path not taken. Many life paths always remain possible; few of us believe that the future is programmed in the present, simply waiting to unfold. Still, it hardly follows that you are not now a human being—a separate person.

Pro-life advocates claim far more than they need to when they assert that the single cell that you once were contained the "totality of everything" you are today. It didn't. But if that were conclusive, then no baby, and no adult, could be a person either.

Cell biologists and experts in the anatomy and physiology of the developing embryo are unable to provide a satisfactory answer to the question of when a separate human life begins. But if that question is being asked in order to decide whether it is right or wrong, in some ultimate moral or theological sense, to destroy an embryo (perhaps an embryo growing in a woman's body or, as in the Tennessee case, an embryo fertilized in a test tube and frozen for storage and possible later implantation), then there is no reason to assume that the answer *ought* to turn on considerations that are susceptible to scientific verification or disproof.

At the same time it's hard to agree with those who insist that this question, simply because it lacks a meaningful scientific or otherwise purely "objective" and incontrovertible answer, can have no "answer" at all. Frances Olsen, a law professor at the University of California at Los Angeles, in a 1989 essay on the Supreme Court's *Webster* decision, argues that since the value of an embryo's life is not "something that can be discovered" but is, instead, "[c]ulturally created," that value "is itself shaped by the answer given to the abortion question . . . a social attribute that arises from the totality of social relations regarding reproduction."[8]

Her conclusion is that "[f]etal life has value when people with power value it." Nicely put, but is it a valid conclusion? The same thing once was said of slaves: the value of black Americans was less than the value of white Americans in the view of people with power. It once was said of women, who were deemed property in the early law of much of Europe, Britain, and some of the colonies. And it once was said of some infants and may be said even today, by some, about the severely deformed.

For most of us, though, it makes overwhelming sense nonetheless to respond: *That doesn't make it right.* The members of these other groups, degraded sometimes by the law, simply *are* human beings even though "people with power" may try to deny it. We must be able to import into the law some moral view from a perspective external to that of those with power, or we will be trapped in a moral world of, by, and for the powerful. Ours is *not* a world in which might makes right.

Nearly everyone, surely, would think it profoundly wrong if "people with power" chose to treat an admittedly "unborn" infant, struggling to push itself through the birth canal during the final minutes of its mother's labor, as not yet a person morally entitled to our protection and love. But would they be wrong if they took that position with respect to a just fertilized, twenty-three-hour-old one-cell embryo or with respect to a more fully developed fetus that has begun to display higher-level neurological activity? We may have no answer, but we cannot deny either that the question is important or that it makes sense to ask it.

## Looking for the Answer in the Constitution

That difficult (and perhaps intractable) moral question is really quite different from the legal question of whether an embryo is a "person" as the Constitution of the United States, the fundamental legal charter of our Republic, uses that word. Even if one were to conclude that the Constitution *ought* to be altered by amendment so as to give embryos the same protection that persons now receive, it would be a matter of no small moment simply to ignore the fact (if it is a fact) that the Constitution as it exists does not currently protect embryos as "persons."

So what has the Constitution to say on the subject? Throughout the text the Constitution uses the word "person" in a way that would not really make sense if fetuses were thought to be included. The Fourteenth Amendment, for example, says that "[a]ll persons *born or naturalized* in the United States . . . are citizens of the United States and of the State wherein they reside." This at least establishes that those who wrote and ratified the Fourteenth Amendment didn't have the unborn in mind when they spoke of "persons." And it also establishes, seemingly, that if fetuses are persons, they most definitely are not "citizens."

But this inference in itself need not be conclusive. It is also true, for example, that the Fifth Amendment says no person may "for the same offence . . . be twice put in jeopardy of life or limb." This provision applies to persons who are not citizens, such as resident aliens. It also implies that those who wrote and ratified that language supposed, back in 1791, that government *could* put people to death and hack off their limbs. But it is possible that *other* parts of the Constitution—such as the Eighth Amendment's ban on "cruel and unusual punishments" or the Fourteenth Amendment's requirements of due process and equal protection—mean that amputation and even execution could now be impermissible under the Constitution, at least in some circumstances.

Apart from how the Constitution uses the word "person," there are serious problems in viewing the body of a woman as the locus of two separate "persons" for purposes of constitutional interpretation. We can explore some of these complications by examining a case in which there undeniably *are* two distinct people within a single, continuous bodily space: the exceptionally rare example of conjoined twins. (Some call these Siamese twins.) We would likely conclude that a conjoined twin who asked to be separated from his brother while his brother slept—so as to spare himself grave physiological injury or severe emotional trauma—and who asked to keep all the organs they shared that were necessary for life knowing that his sleeping twin would never survive such separation, would be asking for our help in committing murder. Such a twin would be asking for something that would have to be denied by a state bound by the Fourteenth Amendment to accord all "persons" the "equal protection of the laws."

If we were *truly* to treat all women, for some significant portion of their lives, as the conjoined locus of two full human beings, extraordinary and perhaps unthinkable implications would follow.

First and foremost, the state would be compelled to treat all abortion as *murder*. But abortion in the Anglo-American tradition has always been considered, if a crime at all, then a lesser crime than murder. No state has ever treated early abortion as the legal equivalent of the murder of a child. Indeed, even in Louisiana, the state that had the harshest abortion law prior to *Roe,* although murder was punishable by death, the punishment for *abortion* was less: ten years' imprisonment at hard labor for the responsible physician.

This no doubt reflects a strong, although not "provable," human intuition. Whatever reaction anyone might have to the pro-life position that a fetus is a human being, nearly everyone is likely to believe, even if they are reluctant to say so openly, that abortion, particularly early in pregnancy, is *not* really the equivalent of killing an already born person and that the woman who chooses such an abortion ought not to be punished as a murderer.

Think next about the principle that a woman must at *least* be permitted to abort a life-threatening pregnancy, a principle that even Chief Justice Rehnquist, one of the original dissenters in *Roe v. Wade,* thought implicit in the "liberty" clause of the Fourteenth Amendment.[9] If an embryo were a person, how could this exception be justified? What basis would we have for deliberately sacrificing one person's life, that of the fetus, to save another's, that of the woman? Especially if the woman initially *chose* to become pregnant, how could we justify securing her survival by destroying her voluntarily conceived child? No claim of self-defense could go this far. We have no established method for balancing the rights of two people in such a situation, no moral or legal calculus for deciding that one person may be killed so that another may live.

If the fetus were a "person," what would we do in the fairly common situation of a pregnancy that subjects a woman to, say, a 10 percent risk of death if she carries to term, but only a 1 percent risk of death if she aborts within the first month? Perhaps 50 percent of such "risky" pregnancies would end in miscarriage if no abortion were allowed. If the embryo were a "person," the state probably could not justify increasing the fetus's risk of death from this 50 percent level to 100 percent by permitting the woman to take an abortion-inducing drug, simply to eliminate her 10 percent risk of death. Nor could a state ever knowingly permit such a woman to travel, in order to obtain an abortion, to another country. For if a fetus were to be seen as a separate "person" in the eyes of the Constitution, letting the mother go elsewhere to abort would deprive the fetus of life in violation of the Fourteenth Amendment.

The implications for women, and for the law, would be staggering. Of course, the traditional immunity of women from prosecution for abortion would be untenable. Any woman who had or sought an abortion would at least be liable to criminal punishment for attempted murder or for aiding and abetting the physician who performed the deed.

What else would follow if we acknowledged the fetus as a person from the moment of conception? One result would likely be the reversal in significant part of the Supreme Court's long line of contraception decisions. Both the IUD and some birth control pills may work to prevent pregnancy *not* by preventing conception but by preventing a newly fertilized ovum from implanting in the wall of the uterus. The liberty to use such abortifacient methods of birth control, long a target of some abortion opponents, would be outweighed by the constitutional requirement that the state not deprive that fertilized ovum (deemed a "person" from the moment of conception) of its "life."

There would be profound problems in administering this rule as well. The line between abortifacient and contraceptive is by no means clear because the discussion of a "moment" of conception is itself misleading. It is especially misleading to object that fetal "viability" does not mark a precise point at which any morally significant event occurs to the fetus, while seizing upon the "moment of conception" as though it does. The Missouri statute at issue in the *Webster* case defines conception as "the fertilization of the ovum by the sperm of the male." Yet modern embryology reveals that fertilization is a *process,* not a moment. Once a sperm has penetrated the outside of an ovum, this process takes roughly twenty-four hours, ending with the intermingling of the chromosomes of the sperm and ovum that produces the forty-six-chromosomes to which many pro-life advocates attach significance.

Is one point in this process the "moment" of conception? Some might argue that a "person" comes into existence only at the point when there is a specific and determined forty-six-chromosome genetic identity. But if this were the case, an easily imaginable pill that interrupted the process of intermingling of paternal and maternal chromosomes before its completion would be a permissible contraceptive. One that worked after the intermingling was complete to prevent normal division of the one-cell zygote would be an impermissible abortifacient.

This kind of line drawing on the basis of ill-bounded microscopic biological developments, particularly on an issue of such importance, seems disturbingly arbitrary. A similar objection may be made to the Supreme Court's use of "viability" in *Roe,* but at least there is no pretense in *Roe* that viability corresponds to a bright line after which the fetus suddenly has full human rights. One might seek to avoid the problem of drawing lines within the process of fertilization by defining personhood as beginning at the "moment" when the sperm enters the inner layer of the ovum, but of course, the arrangement of chromosomes to which right-to-life groups refer is not yet fixed at that point. Indeed, selection of this event as the "moment of conception" would, for example, require prohibition of an imaginable spermicide that would permit a sperm to enter an ovum but would then cause the degeneration both of the sperm's tail, which normally degenerates, and of the sperm's chromosome-containing head. It would be hard to describe such a chemical as an abortifacient.

Perhaps because of the problems inherent in defining fertilization, the American Medical Association has chosen to define "conception" as the *implantation* of the fertilized ovum in the uterus wall. This proposed "moment of conception" is obviously too late for those antiabortion activists who oppose the use of postfertilization, preimplantation methods of birth control. Yet some experts estimate that fully two-thirds of all fertilized ova fail naturally to implant in the uterus. And who among us really believes that we are now faced with a tragedy in which two-thirds of the people who have *ever come into existence* have been lost through this normal feature of human reproduction? Why is there no cry to do more to ensure the successful implantation of fertilized ova?

Use of in vitro fertilization, a process that actually leads to the birth of more babies, might also be impermissible under a regime that regarded all embryos as "people," because the process inevitably results in the accidental but foreseeable destruction of at least some ova that have been fertilized in a glass dish. Indeed, in an episode that sheds light on what some antiabortionists who believe in the "personhood" of embryos have in mind when they describe themselves as "pro-life," it was revealed in late 1989 that the federal Department of Health and Human Services, responding to pressure from some religious groups opposed to abortion, had refused to fund research to help improve in vitro fertilization techniques. As a consequence, the birth of a wanted baby will remain out of reach for countless infertile couples for whom in vitro fertilization offers the only realistic hope.[10]

And what of frozen embryos? If, from the moment of conception, an embryo is a constitutionally protected person, to what lengths would the state be compelled to go to prevent a frozen one-cell or two-cell embryo from being destroyed before it can develop into a baby? The Constitution might well prohibit any state decision to discard a frozen embryo rather than to preserve it for future implantation. For if the state did nothing to ensure eventual placement of a frozen fertilized ovum in a hospitable womb, while caring for persons who are already born but are abandoned by their parents or are orphans, would the state not be denying to "persons within its jurisdiction" (frozen embryos at early stages of cell division) "the equal protection of the laws"?

Even for those who are deeply disturbed by *Roe v. Wade,* the implications of any such view must be disquieting, to say the least. If the Constitution recognized each fertilized ovum as a person, a whole new species of equal protection problem would be born. Each time a state treated a fetus—an "unborn" child—differently from any other child, it would be discriminating against a helpless and manifestly innocent class of people. If a woman's home provided a physical or chemical environment that subjected her children to a 50 percent risk of premature death, the state would surely require those children to be brought up elsewhere. There are uterine environments that are unhealthy for embryos as well. For example, a female fetus developing in the womb of a woman with an arrhenoblastoma (a male hormone-secreting ovarian tumor) may develop abnormal masculine characteristics. If the same fetus developed in another woman's womb, it would develop into a "normal" female child, unburdened by the many difficulties that anyone with hermaphroditic characteristics will confront.[11]

Once the technology was available, it would probably be the state's obligation to require the transfer of a fetus-person to a less hazardous womb, for "foster gestation" by a surrogate mother, under a "best interests of the embryo" standard. If fetuses are persons, the fact that they are very young can hardly be used to justify depriving them of equal protection, and apart from their relative youth, fetus-persons would differ from newborn infants only in being more helpless and dependent. Using their dependent status and relative helplessness to justify giving them less protection would, in turn, set a constitutional precedent terribly dangerous to all children and to adults with various disabilities.

A similar situation might be imagined in which the state would be obliged to require a woman in whose uterus an embryonic "person" faced a 75 percent chance of spontaneous miscarriage and thus premature death to give up her embryo for gestation by a woman in whose uterus the same embryo, once implanted, would face a significantly better chance of surviving to full term. Some have estimated the normal rate of spontaneous abortion of fertilized ova to be as high as 66 percent.[12] Treating the fetus as a person would therefore mean the beginning of the end of the individual woman's right to bear and then give birth to—indeed, to form emotionally important parental bonds with—her own child.

If taking a weekly dose of some new medicine would predictably reduce the rate of spontaneous miscarriage to, say, 5 percent, might not the state force this new fetus-saving miracle drug upon pregnant women? Wouldn't the state be fostering fetus neglect, discriminating against unborn "persons," if it did not make that drug every bit as mandatory as it would make a vaccine designed to protect mothers from becoming hosts to diseases deadly to their newborn infants?

It's no wonder that no Supreme Court justice has ever taken the position that fetuses are constitutional persons. The idea that the Constitution protects fetuses just as if they had already been born seems, on reflection, impossible to maintain without accepting consequences for which no one seems willing to argue.

## Letting Each State Define "Person" for Itself

What, then, of the less extreme suggestion that the Constitution at least *permits* any state to treat embryos as people if that state so chooses?

The crux of the Supreme Court's opinion in *Roe v. Wade* was to deny that any state has such an option. The Court insisted that no state is free, by adopting what the Court called "one theory of life," to cancel out the rights of the pregnant woman that are at stake in the situation.[13] Was the Court correct?

The idea that each state can define "person" differently for purposes of establishing the relevant constitutional protections seems in the end just as difficult to maintain as the idea that each state *must* define fetuses as "persons." When the Constitution speaks of persons, as it does in many places, it quite obviously refers not to fifty different classes of beings, but to *one*. A central purpose of the Fourteenth Amendment was to prevent some states from adopting a narrower view of personhood than others, at least in the context of race. The Fifth Amendment prevents Congress from depriving any "person" of "life, liberty, or property, without due process of law." Which of the fifty concepts of "person" does that amendment embody? Can it possibly embody yet a fifty-first?

Still, could not a state declare a fetus a person for purposes of *state law* even if it were not permitted to decide for itself the meaning of "person" as that word is used in the Constitution? Or could it achieve the same effect by declaring a fetus uniquely valuable without calling it a person? In this way, might not a state avoid many of the unexpected consequences that we saw would result from a Supreme Court declaration of fetal personhood?

Opponents of what the Court did in *Roe v. Wade* argue that the question of when a person comes into being should be decided out in the open by the democratic political process—rather than in the closed chambers of nine judges or by a woman in private consultation with her doctor, her spiritual adviser, and her most intimate friends or relatives.

Some states have already started down this road. Indeed, in the *Webster* case the Supreme Court reviewed a portion of Missouri's law that defined each fetus as a human being. Over the dissents of Justices Blackmun, Brennan, Marshall, and Stevens, the Court concluded that Missouri's declaration that "the life of each human being begins at conception" was permissible because, the Court concluded, it was not being used in the Missouri statute to justify restrictions on abortion. The Court left for another day the question of whether such a declaration could be used to restrict an (already born) person's activities in a concrete way, for example, by prosecuting for manslaughter someone who punched a pregnant woman in the stomach causing her to miscarry.

Without giving each fetus constitutional protection (and thereby barring states from allowing abortion), the Court could still overrule *Roe* and permit states to use a "human life" declaration as a justification for restricting abortion. In states that had such a declaration, the Supreme Court could then find protection of human life to be a sufficient—a "compelling"—reason to restrict abortion rights. This is probably the regime that most of those who oppose *Roe* would like to have in its stead.

But what would such a world look like? What if a woman conceives in a state that regards her fertilized ovum as a person, say, Missouri, but wishes to travel to a state that chooses fetal viability or even birth as the relevant line defining personhood? Can the state in which she conceived forcibly restrain her so that she does not "kidnap" the person that lives inside her en route to the "murder" she plans for it?

The state could probably do just that if the Constitution permitted it to regard the fetus as a baby temporarily trapped inside its mother. Indeed, the possibility is not altogether farfetched. In the years before *Roe* at least one state in fact prosecuted a travel agent for arranging out-of-state trips for women who wanted to have abortions.[14]

If a state were permitted by the Constitution to define every fertilized ovum as a person for the state's own internal purposes and undertook to do so, we would have to accept a variety of "fetal endangerment" prosecutions previously unknown in the law. For if a state could equate the embryo with a captive child, then that state could control the mother's behavior throughout pregnancy in elaborate detail while the state next door would be bound to respect her autonomy in these matters. Indeed, in the wake of *Webster* there have been growing numbers of prosecutions of pregnant women for endangering their fetuses through risky conduct.

A state's declaration of fetal personhood would permit even more invasive state actions to protect every fetus. Women have already been prosecuted for "delivering" drugs to their babies in the womb. Laws designed to punish drug kingpins would be available to restrict the liberty of all women. It is not altogether farfetched to think about the state's prohibiting pregnant women—or even women who only *may* be pregnant, say, those of childbearing age—from smoking or drinking. Pregnant women could be prevented from eating what they choose. A state might be able to force a woman whose ova had been fertilized in a laboratory, or whose ova had been extracted soon after fertilization so that they might be frozen for later use, to incubate those ova, one after the other, especially if any other uterus would provide a more hazardous environment for them.

There could be stranger repercussions still. The Missouri declaration involved in *Webster* is now actually being employed in novel ways, which may themselves eventually be passed upon by the Supreme Court. For example, a lawsuit was brought on behalf of the fetus within a pregnant state prisoner in Missouri. The plaintiff in that suit argued that the fetus (which, of course, committed no crime) was being held in jail in violation of the Constitution.[15] One can imagine further lawsuits in which people claim to be nine months older than their ages calculated from birth, because they were "persons" from the time of conception. A high school student who by ordinary calculations is fifteen years and three months old might argue, for example, that since under Missouri law, life begins at conception, he is already eligible for the driver's license that the state does not want to give him until he is sixteen.

The fetus as chameleon—now it's a person, now it's not—makes the woman less than a full person in some states but not in others. It seems both too totalitarian and too bizarre to contemplate seriously. If the embryo is not a full person in California or Hawaii or New York, then it can't be a full person in Missouri or Utah or Georgia either. The case for the conclusion that an embryo cannot constitutionally be made a person or its legal equivalent in *any* state, and cannot be endowed with rights strong enough to obliterate a pregnant woman's liberty and her very personhood in every state that confers the status of "person" upon all fertilized human ova, thus seems quite strong indeed.

## Taking the Constitution Seriously

If someone thinks the Constitution should be amended to endow all fetuses with the status of persons, there may be no way to convince that individual that such an amendment would be morally wrong because it would subordinate women. But it is vital, morally vital, to see the force of the argument that an *amendment* to our Constitution would be required to achieve that result. For if we allow any fundamental right protected by our Constitution to be taken away in any lesser manner, then truly that charter of liberty will become "only a promise to the ear to be broken to the hope, a teasing illusion like a munificent bequest in a pauper's will."[16]

Of course, the Supreme Court of the United States might disagree; it might continue its retreat from *Roe v. Wade* and conclude that each state is indeed free to decide for itself that an embryo counts as a person. Or the Court might conclude that even *without* regarding a fetus as a person, a state may properly compel some women to remain pregnant whenever state-designated officials are not satisfied with the reasons those women have for wanting to end their pregnancies. Stranger things have happened in the Court's history. But such a decision by the Supreme Court would be indefensible—not necessarily wrong in some ultimate moral sense, but wrong in terms of the Constitution we now have.

This analysis inverts the conclusion reached by many, who feel sure that *Roe*'s result was *morally* correct but who doubt the decision's *constitutional* legitimacy. On the view explained here, the ultimate moral rightness of *Roe*'s result seems considerably less clear than does its defensibility as a constitutional matter. At the very least, the oft-repeated notion that the Supreme Court's decision in *Roe v. Wade* gave women something that *obviously* was not to be found anywhere in the Constitution seems deeply flawed.

## And What If a Fetus Were a Person?

If we were to assume for the sake of discussion that fetuses are separate persons, would it necessarily follow that prohibiting abortion would be a constitutionally acceptable option? Let us see.

Consider the process of physically separating the fetus from the woman. Assume that the procedure is not performed in a manner gratuitously designed to destroy the unwanted fetus, but posit that the fetus still will not survive because no technology yet exists to preserve its life outside the uterus. Should we be able to require the woman to continue with her pregnancy? In answering that question on the premise that the fetus is a person, we must not underestimate the extent of the sacrifice being asked of the woman. It is not merely a nine-month inconvenience. As we have already noted, pregnancy and childbirth are always physically risky activities. More significantly, they produce between woman and child real and life-altering bonds, both psychological and physiological.

In a justly famous 1971 article,[17] MIT philosopher Judith Jarvis Thomson asks each of us to imagine waking up in the morning attached to a famous and accomplished violinist. The violinist has a kidney disorder and, unbeknownst to you, he has been attached to your circulatory system while you were asleep. If he were detached, he could not survive. The violinist need not remain attached to you forever. After nine months or perhaps a bit less (say, twenty-four weeks) he will be able to live on his own. Thereafter, however, you will feel a lifelong attachment to the fellow. But if you reach over to disconnect him before that time, he will surely die.

What are we to say of the act of disconnecting him? No one would doubt that the violinist is a person. But many would doubt that you could legitimately be forced to leave that person attached to you. Indeed, just about everybody would agree with Professor Thomson that no law could justly compel you to take this situation lying down, at least if the violinist were an uninvited intruder—and perhaps even if he had been invited but had overstayed his welcome. If you were to choose to cut the umbilical cord, even knowing that the inevitable result would be the violinist's death, you would be within your rights. This would seem even clearer if, as in the case of mother and fetus, the compelled connection were much more profound and entangling than a merely umbilical link would suggest.

For Thomson, the conclusion is clear: Trying to decide whether an embryo is a person distracts us from the real question of whether the state may force a woman to incubate that embryo, and to serve as its life-support system, against her will. A woman denied the right to decide whether or not to end a pregnancy is not merely being asked to refrain from killing another person but being asked to make an affirmative sacrifice, and a profound one at that, in order to save that person. How coherently does this demand fit within our legal landscape?

## The Good Samaritan

In Anglo-American law there is no general duty to give of yourself to rescue another. That may come as a surprise to many; it certainly surprises many law students when they first confront the principle.

Although the principle may seem heartless and counterintuitive and although it may reinforce aspects of our culture that seem selfish, alienating and anti-communal, we see it in operation all the time. The most famous modern case that highlighted the Good Samaritan question occurred in 1964, when Kitty Genovese was murdered in the borough of Queens in New York City. Thirty-eight neighbors watched and listened to the lengthy attack from inside their homes but did nothing, did not even call the police, until it was too late. One of the reasons this case attracted, and continues to attract, so much attention was that although the neighbors' actions seem morally inexcusable, they violated no law.

Do we not think a person who saves a drowning child to be heroic? If so, does this not reflect a bedrock legal premise upon which our system is built: that our society, whatever its moral aspirations toward altruism and sharing, imposes no routine legal *duty* upon any of its members to rescue another?

This fundamental rule of law has occasioned much philosophical discussion. One of the suppositions that underlies it and that is central to our conception of American society is, as Professor Robert Hale describes it, "that when a government requires a person to act, it is necessarily interfering more seriously with his liberty than when it places limits on his freedom to act—to make a man serve another is to make him a slave, while to forbid him to commit affirmative wrongs is to leave him still essentially a free man."[18] That notion is a "byproduct of the belief that individual autonomy—individual liberty—is a good in itself not explainable in terms of its purported social worth."[19] The philosopher Robert Nozick puts forward an elegant defense of this view in his celebrated book *Anarchy, State, and Utopia.*

The Good Samaritan doctrine has been defended on the ground that even if imperfect, it is at least superior to the alternatives. As long ago as 1908 Professor James Barr Ames suggested that a person should be required to "save another from impending death or great bodily harm, when he might do so with little or no inconvenience to himself."[20] But even this apparently modest rule met with overwhelming opposition. Would one to whom ten dollars meant nothing, it was asked, be under a legal obligation to save the life of a hungry child in a foreign land? Should this be a legal duty or a matter of charity?[21]

No state in the United States has adopted even Ames's suggestion for a modest departure from the common law rule. Only Vermont and Minnesota impose any duty to rescue, and only in the strictest jurisdiction, Vermont, does the average person now have a duty, whenever he knows that another is exposed to grave physical harm, to give reasonable assistance. And even then, he need give assistance only to the extent it "can be rendered without danger or peril to himself or without interference with important duties owed to others."[22] The penalty for failing to give such aid: a fine of not more than one hundred dollars.

We need not celebrate those occasions when people fail to come to each other's assistance. This is an area in which legal dictates have never been congruent with morality. Yet even if the gap between the two ought to be narrowed, it has not been.

There is, in fact, only one place in the law where a really significant and intimate sacrifice has been required of anyone in order to save another: the law of abortion. If you woke up with our hypothetical violinist attached to you, the law—and, probably, the views of morality held by most people—would permit you to free yourself of him. When the law prohibits a woman from freeing herself of the fetus that is inside her, the law appears to work a harsh discrimination against women *even if fetuses count as persons.* [23]

One response is that pregnancy is different from those situations in which we would not ask someone to be a Good Samaritan. The pregnant woman, at least in most cases, "volunteered," in the sense that she chose to have sex and ran the risk of getting pregnant. Thus, she is not in the same position with regard to the fetus as she would have been with regard to the uninvited violinist.

This feeling probably plays a significant role in shaping people's views about abortion rights. What the feeling suggests is not an argument that because the fetus is an "innocent human life," *all* abortion must be prohibited. Rather, it suggests an argument, or at least a sentiment, that, when the woman is "responsible" for the pregnancy, she loses at least her moral right to claim that its continuation interferes with her autonomy.

This sentiment might in turn explain the widespread sense that abortion must be allowed in cases of rape. With rape, of course, the sexual intercourse resulting in pregnancy occurred without the woman's consent. But the same moral view would seem to require an exception from any ban on abortion not only when the pregnancy resulted from a sex act forced upon a woman but also when it resulted from the failure of a conscientiously used, ordinarily effective means of birth control. Yet it is curious that there exists no widespread sentiment, among those who generally oppose abortion rights, that abortion should be allowed when birth control fails. Does this not suggest that such opponents of abortion come to their views about the immorality of abortion not in response to the voluntary nature of the woman's *pregnancy* but in response to the voluntary nature of the *sexual activity* in which she has engaged? And does this not in turn suggest that such antiabortion views are driven less by the innocence of the fetus (which does not turn on how or why the sex occurred *or* the pregnancy began) than by the supposed "guilt" of the woman?

Still, there is some force to the moral argument that the right to choose abortion can be distinguished in cases of voluntary, as opposed to involuntary, pregnancy. To be sure, one powerful strand of feminist legal theory posits that within our society even most nominally "consensual" sex, particularly in cases where the woman does not feel free to use or to suggest the use of birth control, involves coercion. But if one assumes a pregnancy that did not result from any sort of coercion, then perhaps the imposition of continued pregnancy on the woman may not be unjust.

But, however voluntary the *sex* may have been, the woman was, of course, not the sole participant. Yet a ban on abortion imposes truly burdensome duties *only* on women. Such a ban thus places women, by accident of their biology, in a permanently and irrevocably subordinate position to men.

We can too easily imagine this to be the "natural" course of things: Because physiologically a *man* who engages in sex *cannot* be saddled as a consequence with the responsibility of pregnancy, while a woman (at least with current technology) sometimes requires another person—a doctor—to help her achieve equal freedom from pregnancy, it is easy to view the continuation of pregnancy as a natural part of womanhood. It is suspiciously easy to say that women should and must make an enormous sacrifice whenever their sexual activity results in pregnancy, even though men need not.

But even when a man *might* logically be called upon to make a roughly similar sacrifice, after his child is born, our laws do not ever compel him to do so. Although the relationship between a parent and a child carries with it more legal obligation than the relationship between two strangers, nowhere do we require a voluntary parent to make, for an already born child, the kind of sacrifice some would have us impose on the pregnant woman in the name of the fetus. Imagine, for example, a little girl who needs a liver transplant. Even if, because of tissue type, only her father can provide a segment of liver that her body will not reject, our laws have never required any such sacrifice of him.

This is not to say that the gender-specific nature of an abortion ban, in view of the constitutional requirement that the law not discriminate against women, would automatically require striking down *all* restrictions on abortion. Consider, for example, a woman who deliberately became pregnant for the very purpose of having an abortion so that she might sell the resulting fetal tissue for medical experiments or as a source of transplants. Such a sale of fetal tissue, and any act inducing a woman to arrange an abortion for this purpose, could presumably be banned without violating the principle of gender equality contained in the Fourteenth Amendment. The fact that only women are physiologically capable of having and aborting fetuses cannot mean that no such conduct may ever be outlawed. Only men, after all, are physiologically capable of certain sorts of rape, but this does not make laws against such rape instances of impermissible sex discrimination.

In any event, any attempt at legislation based on an analysis in which the morality of an abortion depends upon the circumstances that led to the pregnancy would require us to structure the law of abortion on a basis that consistently distinguished "voluntary" from "involuntary" pregnancy. Doing any such thing would in turn pose enormously difficult, and probably insoluble, problems. What could be more invasive and intrusive than to require a pregnant woman to give various officials her reasons for requesting an abortion rather than having avoided impregnation in the first instance?

The question of proof thus presents problems of its own—problems, indeed, of constitutional dimension. A woman seeking abortion on the "morally acceptable" ground of justifiable birth control failure would be required to expose sexual relationships and personal intimacies to official scrutiny in ways quite incompatible with values of informational privacy that are clearly contained in the Fourth Amendment, which guarantees the "right of the people to be secure in their persons, houses, papers, and effects" and which prohibits "unreasonable searches and seizures."

Indeed, the implications for the rights protected by the Fourth Amendment were among the aspects of the Connecticut ban on contraceptives that most troubled the Supreme Court majority that struck that ban down in *Griswold v. Connecticut.* The Court asked: "Would we allow the police to search the sacred precincts of marital bedrooms for telltale signs of the use of contraceptives?"[24] Some similar procedure would surely be required under a regime in which legal abortions were made available only to those who had conscientiously used contraceptives.

Furthermore, any system that would require approval of a woman's decision to have an abortion, such as the spousal consent requirement struck down by the Supreme Court in the *Danforth* case described earlier, would make an extremely serious statement about our society's willingness to let women control their own lives. The experience that got Kate Michelman, now the executive director of the National Abortion Rights Action League, involved in the movement for abortion rights shows this dramatically.

In 1970 Michelman, then a thirty-year-old mother of three, was pregnant with her fourth child when her husband left her for another woman. Without a husband and without resources to support another child, Michelman, who had hoped to have six children, made a decision she never thought she'd have to make. As she told the story to a newspaper interviewer, "I had no car. I couldn't get credit because I had no husband and I had three children to feed. . . . I understood at that moment the kinds of choices women have to make and how they affect the very fabric of a woman's life."[25]

Michelman decided to get an abortion. But under the pre-*Roe* abortion regime, her request had to be approved by a hospital review board upon application of her physician. She was forced to demonstrate to an all-male hospital panel her inability to be the mother of another child.

When her request was finally granted, she was told, while lying in a hospital bed, that the abortion would not be performed unless her husband, *who had already abandoned her,* would agree *in writing* to the procedure. Michelman told the hospital that it would have to find the man if it wanted his agreement. Ultimately it did, and Michelman had her abortion.

The experience had a powerful and lasting effect. She explained: "I had to go before a panel of four strange men, whose decision was going to impact on the rest of my life, but who would not have to bear the burden of raising four children. I had absolutely no control over my life. Everyone else had control except me, and I had to bear the consequences. It was then I became acutely aware of how desperate the situation is for women."

Society's willingness to impose on women alone the sacrifice required by laws restricting abortion, unique within the landscape of Anglo-American law, may well reflect a deeply held traditional view of the differences in character between the sexes. While we might not impose selfless and virtuous behavior on a man—because it would be futile, perhaps, but more likely because it would demean his capacity for individual choice and independence—some may find it less of a contradiction to impose such virtue on a woman because of the traditional view of her nature.

But to impose virtue on *any* person demeans that person's individual worth. It is no more acceptable when the individual is a woman than a man. There should be no "woman's exception" to our traditional regard for individualism and autonomy. As long as these values remain at the core of our legal system, there is thus a powerful case for the conclusion that laws prohibiting abortion—even if the fetus, no less than Judith Thomson's violinist, is regarded as a person—deny women the equal protection of the laws guaranteed to all by the Fourteenth Amendment. And if this is so, then perhaps the Supreme Court's opinion in *Roe,* by gratuitously insisting that the fetus *cannot* be deemed a "person," needlessly insulted and alienated those for whom the view that the fetus is a person represents a fundamental article of faith or a bedrock personal commitment. Perhaps, as Yale Law School Dean Guido Calabresi has suggested, the *Roe* opinion for no good reason said to a large and politically active group, "[y]our metaphysics are not part of *our* Constitution."[26] The Court could instead have said: Even if the fetus *is* a person, our Constitution forbids compelling a woman to carry it for nine months and become a mother.

## Roe's Vision

Calmly assessed, *Roe v. Wade* does not seem to represent a blatant power grab by the Supreme Court, an exercise in fiat rather than in constitutional interpretation. A difficult decision, yes; an indefensible decision, no. Indeed, *Roe* at its core rests on a vision that seems compatible, in broad outline, with the views of most Americans about abortion. Most Americans who look at the abortion issue see both a fetus and a pregnant woman. Too often, when activists on either side present their picture of the abortion issue, they leave room for only the fetus *or* the pregnant woman.

Those who oppose abortion often use a process of visualization to stir people's emotions. Yet what they ask us to visualize is an isolated picture of a fetus. Where is the person who develops, nurtures, and sustains the fetus we are looking at? Where is the woman? In this vision, she is insignificant, devalued. When a woman does somehow momentarily enter our view, she is rendered translucent, a ghost of a real person.

In the congressional debates about the ban on Medicaid funding for abortion, women disappear in this way before our very eyes. The members of Congress debated for months whether there should be an exception for women's lives or whether the health exception should incude "severe *or* long lasting physical health damage" or "severe *and* long lasting physical health damage." Did they see in the picture a real woman, a mother or wife or sister or friend?

One strains to imagine any of the male legislators who voted against these exceptions truly believing that the government should not help his wife or sister or daughter to have an abortion just because her chance of blindness was only 40 percent, or chance of death 15 percent, or because she would suffer an injury that would be excruciating painful for only a few years instead of a few decades, or because the permanent injury she would suffer was not quite disabling enough to be labeled severe.

The very narrowness of the few exceptions that antiabortion lawmakers, and indeed many of us, have tended to identify as posing hardship cases suggests that we are seeing far less than a full picture of a whole woman with a real life, real hopes and real pain. Many seem genuinely to believe that abortions sought in the most tragic circumstances are merely desired for convenience. But is an abortion a matter of mere convenience for impoverished single mothers who can barely support their current children? For teenage girls who believe a pregnancy would ruin their future and cause them shame in their communities? For women who find themselves pregnant after their husbands have left them or died?

Whether or not people believe abortions in these situations should be legal, the law should let no one hide from the real woman or her suffering. In movies we often shed tears when a person is devastated by a ruined marriage, by sudden poverty, or by the breakup of a family. Yet in the abortion context these harsh life experiences are often dismissed as "inconvenience," so that we are not truly required to see two full parties in the picture. In his dissent in *Roe v. Wade,* for example, Justice White wrote dismissively that "at the heart" of the controversy were those pregnancies that are "unwanted for any one or more of a variety of reasons—convenience, family planning, economics, dislike of children, the embarrassment of illegitimacy, etc."[27]

Recently the National Right to Life Committee (NRLC) and others have tried to appeal more to the undecided middle, by discussing less-than-absolute restrictions on abortion. Yet nearly every one of the "moderate" regulations being considered trivializes women.

A twenty-four-hour waiting period, for example, seems to reflect an assumption that a woman making this decision is misguided and is likely to be acting rashly. The state apparently should not trust a woman to be mature or rational. Could Justice Scalia have been guilty of a similar mistrust when he went out of his way in *Webster* to accuse Justice O'Connor of being "irrational" and to say that her approach "cannot be taken seriously"?

In a similar vein, the NRLC has offered a proposal, to which it is giving great emphasis, to outlaw abortions for reasons of "sex selection." Indeed, in late 1989 such a provision was enacted in Pennsylvania. But there is no proof that this is a problem that requires legislative resolution. So far, at least, it rarely happens in the United States. Why would someone who truly cares about preserving fetal life stress such a limited proposal? The goal of the proposal may well be to advertise the implied message that women who have abortions do so for inconsequential or even morally despicable reasons and to begin a process of forcing all women to explain publicly their decisions for exercising this fundamental right. But the real risks to their lives and health undertaken by the one million women who had illegal abortions each year prior to *Roe* suggests that they were motivated by weightier considerations.

Those who support abortion rights have at times also been guilty of pretending that there was only one party in the picture. Some in the women's movement, like the lawyers in *Roe v. Wade,* have argued that abortion should be legal on the ground that a woman has an absolute right to control her own body. Some of them have described the fetus as just tissue, a morally insignificant part of the woman unless and until she chooses to value it as an independent being. But most of us see much more in the fetus than that. And most rights must, at least to some degree, be balanced against other societal and moral considerations. Even the freedom of speech, surely a key "liberty," may be curtailed by government if the reason is compelling enough.

The problem with declaring that a pregnant woman's right to control her body is absolute is that it also requires us to see only one party in the picture—in this case, the pregnant woman. Many Americans, probably most, are willing up to a point to see the picture this way. But as pregnancy progresses, the fetus's value becomes ever harder to deny. To most of us, the more the fetus is like a baby, the more we must admit that the moral picture reveals two beings. Even someone who is strongly pro-choice but who has seen an ultrasound picture of a fetus may be offended by any suggestion that only one human life is at stake.

Despite all the criticism of *Roe v. Wade,* it is a decision that sees abortion much the way that most Americans see it: with moral and legal consideration both for the woman and for the fetus.

## The Lines Drawn

*Roe* did not just announce broad principles. It drew lines, and this has led to much of the criticism of the opinion. But the decision drew lines precisely because the Court recognized what most people recognize: that the picture must include both the interest of the fetus and the interest of the pregnant woman.

Yes, the Court could have written a clearer and more resolute opinion in *Roe.* It could have simply found either that women have an absolute right to control their bodies or that a state's interest in the fetus completely trumps a woman's liberty in all circumstances. But how many of us who do not hold the extreme positions of the most vocal participants in the abortion debate would have been content with either result?

In *Roe,* Justice Blackmun interpreted the Constitution in a way that recognized both the woman and the fetus. He was unwilling to turn either being into a ghost. Justice Blackmun's opinion acknowledged that the state *always* has an "interest" in the fetus but that this interest grows as pregnancy progresses. He concluded, ultimately, that this interest becomes compelling enough to trump a woman's right to make a basic life-altering decision only at the point when the fetus really can exist without the woman in the picture, the point of viability. *Roe* reflects the widely shared sense that we should erase neither the fetus *nor* the woman from the picture our law presents. As an interpretation of the Constitution *Roe* will remain controversial. But it has much to commend it and cannot fairly be dismissed as indefensible or flatly wrong.

# 7

# The Politics of Abortion: From a New Right to the "New Right"

*Roe v. Wade* was decided on the same day that Lyndon Baines Johnson died. But even the death of a former President could not bury a story that would so powerfully affect American politics. Major newspapers like the *New York Times* and the *Washington Post* still made room for the story on the front page.[1] It is not clear, however, that the media immediately understood the full weight of the ruling. The *Washington Post,* for example, did not run an editorial on it until eight days after the decision.[2]

The reaction of the Roman Catholic Church to the decision, though, was immediate and intense. Terence Cardinal Cooke of New York instantly called the decision "horrifying" while Philadelphia's John Cardinal Krol called it an "unspeakable tragedy."[3] The Society for the Christian Commonwealth called for the excommunication of Justice Brennan, the Court's only Catholic and a member of the majority in *Roe,* as a "symbolic gesture," while Justice Blackmun, the decision's author, found himself the target of pickets and hate mail.[4]

The reaction among non-Catholic religious leaders was divided and generally less extreme. The Reverend Dr. Howard Spragg, executive vice-president for Homeland Ministries of the United Church of Christ, called the opinion "historic not only in terms of women's individual rights, but also in terms of the relationships of church and state."[5] Bishop William Cannon of the United Methodist Church, on the other hand, stated that "[i]f this leads to promiscuity and to taking the creation of life lightly, then it is a step backwards."[6]

## The Effects of Roe

The actual effects of the ruling on women seeking to terminate pregnancies were profound. While four states had repealed abortion restrictions for at least the first trimester, and many others had moved toward liberalization, only New York seemed to be unaffected by the ruling. Residency requirements such as those in effect in the other three "repeal" states (Hawaii, Washington, and Alaska) were found unconstitutional in *Roe*'s less well-known companion case, *Doe v. Bolton*, [7] which spelled out some of the implications of the Court's ruling in *Roe*, holding that states cannot outlaw abortions simply because the women who seek them are nonresidents, and that states can neither require abortions to be performed in specially accredited hospitals nor mandate that they be approved by hospital committees or by other physicians second-guessing the performing physician's judgment.

What was an expensive and often brutal black market for abortion services sought by up to one million women each year would be transformed by *Roe* into a widely available, legal, and basically safe and simple medical procedure. While widespread access to abortion has not been uniformly achieved, partly because of antiabortionists' success at enacting restrictions less severe than those expressly invalidated in *Roe* and *Doe*, legalization has increased safety substantially. Within only a few years of *Roe* the death rate for women undergoing legal abortions was ten times lower than that for women who had illegal abortions and five times lower than that for women who went through childbirth.[8]

Prior to *Roe* both the right-to-life and the abortion rights movements had developed considerable momentum in articulating coherent philosophies and in organizing their respective forces for political impact. While the ruling fueled the progress of each side in developing a public message, it had a vastly different effect on their respective political and organizational efforts.

Although, as we saw earlier, the initial impetus for the movement to repeal abortion laws had come largely from the doctors, clergy, and public health advocates who saw that reform laws were not effective, the repeal initiatives tapped into a far broader and more powerful force: feminism. Feminists did not base their support for abortion repeal on any specific findings of how abortion reform laws were working. Access to abortion was a corollary of the underlying philosophy of the movement. Criminal abortion laws were anathema to those who believed that women, no less than men, should be able to control their bodies and their lives. While the passage of New York's 1970 repeal law seems to

have been the first occasion when the question of abortion gained prominence in political debate as a matter of women's rights (indeed, Governor Nelson Rockefeller credited women's groups for the success of the
bill[9]), this approach to the abortion issue gained predominance among
women at an accelerated pace in the early 1970s.

*Roe* helped legitimize the belief that a personal reproductive decision
made by a woman, even one that involves the kind of stigma often
associated with unwanted pregnancy, should be understood as a matter
of individual right. Justice Blackmun had not rested the Court's decision
on women's equality. But by recognizing that the decision of whether or
not to terminate a pregnancy was constitutionally protected in the same
way as other, less intimate decisions (like the parental right to decide
whether or not to send a child to a private school), the Court no doubt
helped women see that the power to make such a decision could be
considered a right. This could be so even if the decision itself appeared
at odds with what was traditionally regarded as the "proper role" of
women.

While *Roe* was a dramatic loss for those who opposed abortion, it
gave their message attention and urgency. Flush from John Willke's
successful efforts in Michigan to defeat that state's abortion reform
referendum, the serious pro-life advocates had an unequivocal message:
Abortion is murder. The successful pre-*Roe* battles had also given the
budding pro-life movement confidence that if it could get people to pay
attention both to its pictures of the fetus and to its arguments, it could
win their support.

Willke's *Handbook on Abortion* was very influential.[10] With grisly
color pictures of aborted fetuses, this pamphlet was geared, like Willke's
other literature, to make people visualize a fetus as a baby. In Willke's
pamphlet *Four Ways to Kill a Baby,* for example, a picture of a nine-
week-old baby was placed side by side with an enlarged picture of a
dismembered ten-week-old fetus.[11] Although the total length of the actual fetus was only two inches, the display conveyed the impression
that no physical difference existed between the two. Further, Willke
instructed pro-life advocates always to show pictures or slides
of fetal development in reverse order.[12] This way audiences would
be shown pictures of a fetus only after seeing pictures of a newborn
infant.

*Roe* made concrete for the right-to-life movement the evil its adherents sought to combat. They portrayed legalized abortion as govern-
ment-sponsored mass killing. In right-to-life literature, comparisons to
the Holocaust abound.

Because of America's large Catholic population and because of the still-existing moral disapproval of nonprocreative sex, the pro-life message did not so much need legitimation to be effective as it needed attention. *Roe* in a sense gave both sides in the abortion debate what each needed most for its message: It gave legitimacy to the pro-choice position and attention to the more traditional pro-life view.

## Pro-Choice Reaction to Roe

In terms of political organization and intensity, the *Roe* decision had different effects on the two competing movements. Some feminists found *Roe* too weak because it accepted the principle that in some circumstances the government could intrude on a woman's autonomy on behalf of a fetus she carried. On this belief, for example, thirty New York State legislators pushed a bill to make abortion completely a private decision at any stage of pregnancy.[13] But most who were active in the movement for abortion rights regarded *Roe* as adequate and shifted their posture from one of aggressive activism to one of implementation and defense.

One main pro-choice concern about implementation was that although *Roe* stated a principle under which state abortion laws could be struck down, the Court did not mandate a remedy that would make abortion safe and accessible. Planned Parenthood and NARAL sought to give the right meaning by ensuring both that newly legal abortion would be accessible and that women seeking abortions would not be victimized by inflated prices or untrained doctors performing unsafe office abortions.[14]

Planned Parenthood set out to open clinics nationwide not only to provide safe and low-cost abortions but in the hope of driving unethical abortion providers out of the market. Since New York City had developed a remarkable safety record for abortions since the repeal of its restrictive abortion law (there had not been a single death resulting from a legal abortion since July 1971), Planned Parenthood together with NARAL held nationwide seminars on how to set up clinics of the type used in New York City.[15]

Despite the success of these groups in developing a nationwide network of low-cost, safe abortion clinics to complement the services provided by hospitals, many women who lived far away from urban centers or in areas with mostly Catholic hospitals still had trouble obtaining abortions. As recently as 1975 an estimated 770,000 women—mostly poor, rural, or young—did not have practical access to abortion, while another 500,000 were faced with travelling out of state to obtain one.[16] With the legality of abortion removed from the uncertainties of the political process, the pro-choice movement worked to increase the availability of safe, low-cost abortion services.

## Pro-Life Reaction to Roe

At the same time, the pro-life movement was preparing for war. *Roe* precipitated the real rise in the Catholic right-to-life movement. In the spirit of the statements released by Cardinal Cooke and Cardinal Krol, some archbishops called for sermons on the first Sunday following *Roe* to stress that the views of the church had not changed—that abortion was still evil, still murder.[17] The Roman Catholic archbishop of Washington, D.C., called on all the archdioceses in the Washington area to deliver such sermons, although conspicuously abortion was not mentioned that week in the annual Red Mass for the legal profession, where Attorney General Richard Kleindienst and former Chief Justice Earl Warren were in attendance.[18]

The Catholic hierarchy attacked *Roe.* Within one month of the opinion it had called for civil disobedience against the Court's abortion decisions and for the excommunication of any Catholic having an abortion or assisting one in any way.[19] One priest, Joseph O'Rourke, was suspended for baptizing the child of a woman, Carole Morreal, simply because during a local dispute over a planned abortion clinic, she had been quoted in the newspaper as supporting the right to choose. Several other priests had refused her request for the baptism.[20]

In California Bishop Leo T. Maher of San Diego announced that no one in his 512,000-member diocese who admitted publicly to membership in any organization promoting abortion rights, including the National Organization for Women (NOW), could receive the eucharist or serve as a lay reader. This move, which included conditioning communion to all NOW members on the basis of their answers to questions about abortion, was apparently directed at one particular parish member: Jan Gleason, who was the national head of an organization called Catholics for Free Choice. When Gleason heard of Bishop Maher's actions after returning from a trip to Vietnam, where she had been bringing back orphans to the United States as part of the "baby lift" that accompanied Saigon's fall, she remarked simply: "I like the Bishop very much, but he's never been pregnant."[21]

Politically the antiabortion forces launched a two-tiered attack. They would work toward the overthrow of *Roe,* which was their ultimate objective, while waging a war of attrition by erecting barriers that would hinder the exercise of the right announced in that decision.

In search of complete vindication, they sought an all-or-nothing solution to the problem created by *Roe:* a constitutional amendment that would overturn *Roe* and either criminalize abortion permanently or, at the very least, permit the matter to be decided by state legislatures. *Roe* had hardly come down when constitutional amendments were proposed by conservative Senators James L. Buckley of New York and Jesse Helms of North Carolina.[22] This go-for-broke strategy paid low dividends in the early years after the *Roe* decision. Democratic Congressman Don Edwards, chairman of the subcommittee of the House Judiciary Committee with jurisdiction over constitutional amendments, refused to hold hearings. His counterpart in the Senate, Indiana Democrat Birch Bayh, did hold sixteen days of hearings on a proposed constitutional amendment in 1974 and 1975, but the amendment never achieved the majority needed to be reported out of the subcommittee.

In the war of attrition fought primarily at the state level, right-to-life strategists sought to construct as many barriers as possible to inhibit exercise of the newly declared right to choose abortion. They sought to enact restrictions on abortion in the gray zone of constitutionality. Most of these restrictions are still kicking around today: twenty-four-hour waiting periods, bans on using Medicaid funds, record-keeping requirements, restrictions on facilities, requirements of various medical tests, and regulations that require women to gain the consent of the men responsible for their pregnancies or, if the woman is a minor, the consent of her parents. As we have seen, most of these types of restrictions were struck down by the Supreme Court in the years following *Roe* because they were not necessary to protect either the pregnant woman's health or the life of a viable fetus. Yet every ruling created a new gray area of constitutionality, and new legislation to block abortion that skated as close to the zone of known unconstitutionality as possible, and that often went over the line, was continually introduced.

The battles in this war of attrition at the national level were designed mostly to chip away at abortion rights—partly by displaying the political muscle of the hardest core right-to-life position. The right-to-life movement learned early that politicians were impressed with shows of political might. Certainly many took notice when, in August 1973, the United States Catholic Conference's lobbying efforts were able to convince thirty-eight CBS affiliates not to air reruns of two episodes of the television comedy *Maude* in which the main character decides to have an abortion.[23]

There is an interesting political tale about the genesis of the story idea for these *Maude* episodes. Two top officials with the United States Catholic Conference claimed that the idea originated at a luncheon meeting between network executives and three guests. Two of them are well-known advocates of the pro-choice position, Senator Robert Packwood of Oregon and John D. Rockefeller III, chairman of the President's Commission on Population Growth and the American Future. The third guest, who is not now known for his position in favor of the right to choose to end a pregnancy, was George Bush, whom the Population Institute described as, "in 1970, a principal sponsor in Congress of the landmark family planning and contraceptive research bill."[24]

The year 1973 also saw the right-to-life movement's first success in an area in which it was to make its greatest impact during the sixteen years following *Roe:* the denial of otherwise available federal funds that would facilitate abortions. Bills were passed in 1973 forbidding any federal money provided to the Legal Services Corporation or spent for foreign aid to be used in any way to fund, or assist the procurement of, an abortion. Furthermore, Congress passed a "conscience clause" bill—one that was to be replicated by many states—which permitted any individual or hospital opposed to abortion to refuse to perform the procedure.

The conscience clause for individuals was largely uncontroversial.[25] Yet the availability of the clause to entire *hospitals* seriously threatened access to abortions in places where there was only one hospital in a large geographic area. This institutional conscience clause was at least partly responsible for the low percentage of hospitals performing abortions in 1975—only 17 percent of public hospitals and 28 percent of private, non-Catholic hospitals.[26] Of course, in Catholic hospitals the numbers were lower still.

Throughout the 1973–1975 period the Catholic Church continued its assault on *Roe.* In March 1974 four American cardinals (John Cardinal Krol, Humberto Cardinal Medeiros, John Cardinal Cody, and Timothy Cardinal Manning) testified in favor of a pro-life constitutional amendment before Birch Bayh's Senate Judiciary Subcommittee on Constitutional Amendments. No Catholic cardinal had ever before testified at a congressional hearing.[27]

In addition to such widely publicized actions, the Catholic Church spent massive amounts of money to foster and organize new or expanded political groups to pursue the pro-life political fight. Subpoenaed records show that in 1973 alone the Catholic Church spent four million dollars on lobbying Congress. This figure, of course, does not include additional money spent on state activities that year or on national initiatives such as the *Maude* boycott.

While the church constantly employed separate organizational structures to avoid losing its tax-exempt status, it is widely believed that the

Catholic Church either supported or quietly ran most right-to-life organizations during the years immediately following *Roe.* Indeed, Roy White, executive director of the National Right to Life Committee, said in 1975: "The only reason we have a pro-life movement in this country is because of the Catholic people and the Catholic Church."[28] The NRLC, even now the largest of the pro-life organizations, received its initial support from the United States Catholic Conference's Family Life Division. While the NRLC cut its ties to the Catholic Church in 1973 in order to allow the church to maintain its tax exemption, there is documentary evidence that officials of the Family Life Division continued to try to provide financial support for the NRLC.[29]

Despite occasional shows of pro-life political force in the first two years following *Roe,* victory for pro-life conservatives in the post-Watergate 1974 elections proved elusive. After refusing to hold hearings on a constitutional amendment, Congressman Edwards of California was picketed by pro-lifers every day[30] and targeted by them for defeat in his bid for reelection. Yet he won by a large margin. Worse for the right-to-life side was the defeat of several of its most aggressive leaders in the House of Representatives in 1974.[31] Although abortion was an issue in a special election won by pro-life Democrat Tom Lukens over his pro-choice opponent, Republican candidate William Gradison, in a mostly Catholic district in Ohio, a Peter Hart poll showed that fewer than 5 percent of the voters said the abortion issue was relevant to their choice of candidate.[32]

The pro-life movement's lack of political success and its apparent inability to persuade the general public, or even most Catholics, that abortion should be illegal did not go unnoticed by a Catholic hierarchy that had already given the movement both resources and prestige. Exactly one year before the 1976 presidential election, the National Conference of Catholic Bishops made clear, in dramatic fashion, that it was prepared to increase its efforts.[33]

The Catholic bishops announced a comprehensive pastoral plan for pro-life activities. The pastoral plan was an extraordinary organizational blueprint for political action. Coordinating committees, including representatives of the bishops, were to be formed in each state to coordinate the political efforts of various dioceses and congressional districts while monitoring the "political trends in the state and their implications for the abortion effort."[34] Within each diocese, and even within each parish, pro-life committees were to be formed to advocate "a constitutional amendment to protect the unborn child."[35] Perhaps most controversially, the plan encouraged the establishment of an "identifiable, tightly-knit and well-organized pro-life unit" in each congressional district that would, among other things, keep track of the abortion-related record of every elected official and potential candidate and organize a telephone network for instant mobilization.[36]

This was a blueprint for the type of nationwide organization that even the most sophisticated presidential campaign could only dream about. Yet there was one significant difference: While a presidential campaign would have to build offices district by district, the Catholic Church had in its parishes a ready-made, nationwide political infrastructure. The bishops had their sights set on 1976.

## The 1976 Election: The Roots of Single-Issue Politics

It quickly became apparent that 1976 would be an extraordinarily tumultuous year at the intersection of abortion and politics. In January, in recognition of the third anniversary of the *Roe* decision, the Catholic hierarchy instructed its priests to encourage pro-life political efforts. On the anniversary of the decision, sixty-five thousand pro-life supporters braved the bitter cold to join a Washington pro-life rally. And in mid-February the Administrative Board of the United States Catholic Conference issued a statement entitled "Political Responsibility: Reflections on an Election Year," which sought to justify the active political involvement of the church on issues about which it cared deeply.[37]

Before this point political activists knew that abortion was controversial and that it generated intense feelings, but few thought it could be used as a potent issue in a presidential campaign. By February, however, *Newsweek* declared abortion "1976's sleeper issue," concluding that those who failed to see its importance, or who had guessed that political concern about abortion would not be long-lived, were wrong.[38]

Abortion made its appearance early in the Iowa caucuses. Democratic candidate Birch Bayh, who had maintained silence on the issue during the two years in which he had held hearings in the Senate on a constitutional amendment to overturn *Roe,* became a target of fundamentalist fury when he announced his opposition to a constitutional amendment. Religious opposition to abortion had never been exclusively Catholic, but the Protestant fundamentalist strands had earlier been less visible. By 1976 opposition to abortion was on its way to becoming a main vehicle for the rise in political influence of Protestant fundamentalism in the United States. In Iowa the pro-life side was further disappointed when two other Democratic candidates, Frank Church, principal supporter of the conscience clause bills, and Sargent Shriver, a practicing Roman Catholic, also came out against a constitutional amendment.

With pro-life Democrats casting about for a candidate, Jimmy Carter, a born-again Christian, fudged his position on a constitutional amendment and won a stunning Iowa victory, while publicly disputing any suggestion that he had purposely created confusion about his position on the issue. His strategy was certainly politically effective; he garnered a high percentage of pro-life Iowa Democrats.

Among conservatives, both Democrat George Wallace and Republican Ronald Reagan came out for a constitutional amendment that would essentially ban abortions. Reagan successfully played down the significance of his refusal to veto California's 1967 Therapeutic Abortion Act and became the darling of the pro-life groups. Also, Ellen McCormack, a New York housewife and the leader of New York's Right to Life party, ran in several Democratic presidential primaries on a single-issue pro-life plank and, despite a complete lack of experience in elective office, won 2 percent of the vote.[39]

On the Republican side the general prominence of the abortion issue, along with Reagan's strong pro-life stance, put President Gerald Ford in a tight situation. His wife, Betty, had already expressed her support for *Roe,* stating that she was "glad to see that abortion had been taken out of the backwoods and has been brought into the hospital."[40] Ford came out with a vague statement only in late winter, saying that he supported abortion only in narrow circumstances—cases of rape and where necessary to save the life of the pregnant woman—and that he favored a constitutional amendment that would permit the abortion issue to be decided by the state legislatures.

Ford's position highlights what was, and still is, a major split in the pro-life movement. The pragmatists in the movement have seen a political advantage in trying to amend the Constitution to return the issue to the states, rather than trying to secure passage of an amendment that would prohibit all or most abortions. The states' rights option has always had a greater chance of success.

The states' rights position was more politically palatable to many members of Congress not strongly committed to either side in the abortion debate. These politicians apparently thought they could avoid taking a substantive position on the question by simply saying that the issue was best left to the states. The states' rights approach allowed politicians to support an amendment on the basis of general opposition to "judicial activism." When put this way, the issue seems to involve not whether one supports or opposes abortion rights, but whether one thinks the decision should be made by nine unelected judges in Washington or by the people of each state through their elected representatives.

The states' rights approach also played into an anti-Supreme Court populism that was strong at that time. President Nixon had run and won twice on a platform including an anti-Warren Court plank. Disputes over busing had intensified the anti-Court feeling among those working class white Democrats who were considered swing voters. The states' rights approach also found support among conservative opinion leaders and legal scholars who thought that the *Roe* Court was simply wrong to conclude that the decision whether or not to carry a pregnancy to term was a fundamental right.

Although Ford won the Republican nomination, Reagan's supporters actively pushed a more conservative Republican platform, winning a plank that supported those who sought "a constitutional amendment to restore the protection of the right to life for unborn children."[41] By contrast, the pro-choice plank of the Democratic party platform was less adamant, stating merely that it was "undesirable to attempt to amend the U.S. Constitution to overturn [*Roe*]."[42]

Some Republican women (including members of the Republican Women's Task Force) were upset by their party's pro-life plank and organized to try to strike it from the platform, although some feminists in the Republican party were concerned that this fight might distract from their defense of a pro-Equal Rights Amendment plank. The efforts of these pro-choice Republicans were futile, but this dispute foreshadowed a split in the Republican party that only surfaced fully after *Webster* was decided in 1989.

Ultimately, despite its importance in the primary campaigns, abortion did not play a significant role in the 1976 national presidential election. It became largely a special-interest Catholic issue. Both campaigns believed that the Catholic vote could be critical in populous northeastern states. Democratic nominee Jimmy Carter therefore arranged a meeting with six Catholic bishops to stress that although he had not yet seen a constitutional amendment banning abortion that he could support, he nonetheless opposed abortion and "would never try to block" an amendment prohibiting it. The bishops would not be placated, and Carter's meeting with them only proved embarrassing.[43]

Republican nominee Gerald Ford set up his own meeting with the bishops in the hope that their frustration with Carter might make them more receptive to his less than absolute position in favor of a constitutional amendment to leave the issue to the states. His approach seemed to work. The bishops, showing some flexibility, stated that while they were not "totally satisfied," they were "encouraged" by Ford and that "support for the concept" of an amendment to overturn *Roe* was more important at that juncture than the "specific kind of amendment."[44] The bishops' willingness to consider Ford's states' rights plan seemed to indicate a pragmatic approach to the political possibilities in 1976.

In the end the victorious Carter received 54 percent of the Catholic vote, less than the percentage Democrats traditionally had had to win to be elected, but 10 percent more than Senator George McGovern had received as the Democratic nominee in 1972.[45] Still, notwithstanding the preelection maneuvering and early interest in the issue, abortion seems not to have been a significant factor in the outcome of the election. Voters asked to rank the importance of fifteen issues ranked abortion fifteenth.

That abortion could have a real impact on political strategy when most Americans did not consider it a major issue is a testament both to the organization and prominence of the Catholic Church and, from the politicians' viewpoint, to the power of a visible, vocal, and intensely active minority. Longtime pro-choice champion Senator Robert Packwood commented in 1977 that pro-lifers were a "very significant force" and that "[t]o politicians, they are a frightening force. They are people who are with you 99 percent of the time, but if you vote against them on this issue it doesn't matter what else you stand for."[46]

## *A Change in Approach: A Constitutional Convention?*

Generally, in their war of attrition the pro-lifers' main strategy had been to try to chip away at abortion rights through state legislative restrictions while hoping that a constitutional amendment might allow them to achieve their ultimate goal. In the late 1970s there appears to have been a slight shift in this strategy. Those who opposed abortion rights had enjoyed some success at the state level, achieving the passage of some state restrictions designed to block access to abortion. But the movement suffered a setback in this effort in 1976, when the Supreme Court struck down as unconstitutional a number of such restrictions in the case of *Planned Parenthood v. Danforth.* [47]

At the same time it was increasingly apparent that although Congress was willing to cut off federal funds in areas related to abortion, passage of a constitutional amendment restricting or prohibiting abortion was unlikely. Thus pro-life forces, aware of their increasing strength in state legislatures, started looking for their big victory—a constitutional amendment—in the states while Congress became a more important focus of their war of attrition.

The Constitution is explicit on the subject of how to achieve an amendment without congressional approval. Article V provides the method: A constitutional convention for the purpose of proposing amendments for ratification by the states *must* be called by the Congress upon the application of two-thirds of the state legislatures—the legislatures of thirty-four of our fifty states. Although no amendment to the Constitution has ever originated in this fashion (perhaps because of a justified fear that once called, a constitutional convention might run wild, proposing radical revision of our fundamental charter), by 1978, as an expression of antiabortion sentiment, thirteen state legislatures had called for convening such a convention to amend the Constitution so as to overturn *Roe.*

### Restrictions in Congress: Abortion Funding

Meanwhile, in Congress antiabortion energies were focused on what turned out to be the most severe restriction that would pass constitutional muster in the Court until *Webster*: the ban on Medicaid funding for abortion. Before 1976 nearly three hundred thousand abortions annually—33 percent of all legal abortions—were funded by Medicaid. The idea of banning federal funding for abortion was not new. In 1974 the Senate had voted to keep debate alive on just such an amendment by a vote of fifty to thirty-four, an indication of the support behind the effort. Yet two years later, when the amendment's author, Republican Dewey Bartlett, a Catholic and the former governor of Oklahoma, was taken on by another prominent Catholic, pro-choice Senator Edward Kennedy, a vote to end consideration of the amendment had passed the Senate fifty-four to thirty-six.[48]

In 1976, however, the measure gained a new champion in the House of Representatives: Henry Hyde, a Republican from Illinois who was to become so closely identified with the movement to restrict Medicaid funding for abortions that such restrictions at the federal level are now generically referred to as Hyde Amendments.

Medicaid is a cooperative federal-state program, and by 1976 some states had already passed measures to ban the use of Medicaid for almost all abortions. Hyde sought to ban the use of all federal funds throughout the country. The large number of Medicaid-funded abortions gave each side in the abortion debate a large stake in the outcome. For opponents of abortion, a ban on all Medicaid-funded abortions was thought to represent one of the most effective means of reducing the number of abortions short of overturning *Roe.* It would constitute an important moral statement by the federal government and provide a means of showing politicians that the pro-life movement could flex its muscle in Congress on an issue of substance.

The abortion rights side also had reason to view this as a battle of profound importance. First, for many of those who supported a woman's right to choose an abortion, it would seem a farce to recognize a constitutional right to choose abortion but then to allow the government to discriminate in funding so as to make it nearly impossible for poor women to exercise that choice. Second, many women in the abortion rights movement were sensitive to the charge that women's liberation in general, and abortion rights activism in particular, were dominated by and geared only toward the interests of middle-class white women. For the leaders of this movement, vigorous opposition to a law so directly affecting poor and minority women was necessary to demonstrate the moral legitimacy of the entire effort.

Finally, and most important, the abortion rights side feared the consequences the right-to-life side so desired: that many of the three hundred thousand poor women would be unable to afford abortions. While those who were against letting women choose abortion thought this would mean saving the lives of many of the unborn, for those who favored leaving the matter in the woman's hands it threatened a return to the pre-*Roe* days.

Despite the profound questions of life and death that were debated by such senators as Packwood and Bayh, who opposed the cutoff of funds, and Helms and Buckley, who supported the cutoff, in the climate of the times many politicians seemed to believe that the public would not see this simply as an abortion issue. In particular, the issue of Medicaid funding for abortions seemed to touch on several emerging sentiments of large segments of the American public: the backlash against the omnipresence of big federal government, the resentment toward welfare recipients, and the concern that society had grown morally lax on issues related to family and sex. Some politicians believed that they could not afford to be seen as "soft" on these sensitive issues.

Lobbyists at NARAL and the Religious Coalition for Abortion Rights (RCAR) tried to counter the impression that support of abortion rights was the less religious or less moral stance by showing members of Congress a list of clergy and non-Catholic religious organizations that supported the right to choose abortion. This was a defensive tactic. The goal was less to win converts than to hold on to the votes of known abortion rights members of Congress by letting them know that their stance could be defended on the ground that they were respecting the diversity of religious beliefs within their districts.

The right-to-life movement succeeded in shifting the Medicaid funding debate from the merits of pro-life and pro-choice arguments to the role of government in encouraging or discouraging abortion. In addition to allowing politicians to show their toughness about limiting the welfare state, opposition to Medicaid funding gave some politicians a way of taking what they perceived as a middle ground on abortion. Although this approach had not satisfied the Catholic hierarchy, Jimmy Carter always championed it: oppose both a constitutional amendment and Medicaid funding on the basis that government should be kept out of the decision entirely and certainly should not act to encourage abortion.

This argument, of course, purposefully ignored the government's role in discouraging abortion by continuing to fund the costs of pregnancy and childbirth for poor women. Some opponents of the Hyde Amendment seemed to regard the pro-*Roe* antifunding position as a totally unprincipled compromise—more deplorable than support for the Hyde Amendment on absolute right-to-life grounds. Its sterile, theoretical approach to the problem seemed to make a mockery of the compassion for women one might suppose to have underlain support for *Roe* in the first place. The "moderate" Democrats and Republicans who supported Hyde were seen by this group as cowardly hypocrites willing to sacrifice the rights and health of the most weak and vulnerable women to buy off a very intense and uncompromising lobby.

When Henry Hyde, as a freshman congressman in 1976, tacked the Hyde Amendment on to a budget proposal for the Department of Labor (and eventually on to the budget for the Department of Health, Education, and Welfare (HEW)) as a test of pro-life sentiment in the House of Representatives, he did not expect it to gain the support of a majority of the members of Congress.[49] Yet the Hyde Amendment passed in the House, 207 to 167, even though it included no explicit exceptions for funding abortions when pregnancy and childbirth endangered a woman's life and even though a similar but weaker restriction had failed two years earlier by a vote of 247 to 123.

Though the Senate at first rejected the amendment, with the new visibility the abortion issue had gained during the 1976 election year many members of Congress found it hard to oppose, especially when they could argue that it would probably be struck down by the courts anyway. Debate in the Senate focused primarily on the absence of an explicit exception for cases in which the pregnant woman's life was at stake and not so much on the larger question of whether it was appropriate to deny Medicaid funding for abortions in general. The House-Senate conference committee designed to achieve compromise between the wishes of the two chambers added an explicit exception for situations "where the life of the mother would be endangered," and the Senate passed the bill.

The members of Congress who had hoped the Court would take this issue out of the political system were immediately, although temporarily, vindicated. The day after the Hyde Amendment was finally passed, the law was challenged by Cora McRae, a twenty-five-year-old pregnant woman from Brooklyn.[50] After ordering McRae's abortion to be funded, federal Judge John Dooling allowed the case to continue as a class action and found the law unconstitutional.

Before the Supreme Court could review Judge Dooling's rulings in the case of *Harris v. McRae,* it handed down its decision in *Maher v. Roe,* holding that it was permissible for states to deny funding for non-therapeutic abortions for poor women. Although the *Maher* decision dealt only with *state* aid, the basis of the Court's ruling appeared equally applicable to the restriction on *federal* funding contained in the Hyde Amendment. As a result, the Supreme Court set aside the injunction issued by Judge Dooling and sent the case back for him to reconsider in light of the *Maher* opinion.

The ban on Medicaid funding had to be reenacted every year, and in 1977 one might have expected a serious debate. The *Maher* decision suggested that the impact of voting for a funding cutoff would be real and significant, and the political climate for debate might be better since it was no longer an election year. But the Hyde Amendment was not particularly controversial, perhaps because it already seemed to be a settled policy.

The Hyde Amendment also received a boost from the new Democratic President, who made it clear that he intended to act upon his campaign promise to keep federal funds from encouraging any abortions. Speaking at his confirmation hearings in January 1977, Carter's nominee for secretary of HEW, Joseph Califano, who personally opposed abortion, indicated that the new administration would support a continued ban on the use of federal funds to finance abortion. Califano's statement accorded with President Carter's position on the issue.[51]

Carter saw his stance on Medicaid funding of abortion as a way to demonstrate that he was a Democrat who understood the limits of the role of Big Government. For example, when asked whether the Supreme Court's ruling in *Maher* was fair, Carter replied that "there are many things in life that are not fair, that wealthy people can afford and poor people can't. But I don't believe that the Federal Government should take action to try to make these opportunities exactly equal, particularly when there is a moral factor involved."[52]

The White House activism on the issue may have made a difference. Although President Ford had not favored federal funding, he never stressed the issue, nor had he sought to initiate a funding cutoff. By sending approving signals on the Hyde Amendment, the Supreme Court and the Carter White House together did much to legitimize what had not previously been established as a legitimate political position. In a very short time the political landscape had been altered. In 1977 a Democrat who wished to oppose the Hyde Amendment had to oppose not only a growing antiwelfare sentiment and a vocal pro-life lobby, but also a Democratic President.

Even before *Maher* had been decided, Carter and Califano had already included language in the HEW appropriations bill that would have denied Medicaid funding for any abortion that was not necessary to save the pregnant woman's life.[53] When a vote on the measure came up in the House, however, pro-choice members realized that the exception for an abortion where the pregnant woman's life was in danger could not be included in the appropriations bill because that would impermissibly impose a new substantive duty—namely, a duty to fund lifesaving abortions—in a mere appropriations measure. Democrats who actively favored federal funding for all lawful abortions by women eligible for Medicare ironically raised this technical objection to the insertion of an exception for the pregnant woman's life.

This parliamentary maneuver meant that the 1977 version of the Hyde Amendment either had to be dropped or had to go through with no exceptions at all. The purpose of the maneuver, explained then Congresswoman Elizabeth Holtzman of New York, was to show that the right-to-life forces were such "extremists" that they would be "willing to sacrifice the lives of mothers" for their bill.[54] Their fight could thus be portrayed as more selective than principled: they wanted to defend not human life as such but *fetal* life, even when women would die as a result.

In one of the most striking moments in the post-*Roe* political debate, this version of the Hyde Amendment, with no exception for the funding of an abortion to save the life of the pregnant woman, passed in the House by a solid 201 to 155 vote. Commented Republican Congresswoman Millicent Fenwick of New Jersey: "Those who are helpless are condemned."[55] Black members of Congress embittered by the House action stated that the vote marked the "process of establishing a second post-Reconstruction period in this country."[56]

In the Senate lawmakers who favored abortion rights began looking for compromise solutions. The Senate thus passed the Hyde provision with an amendment added by Republican Edward Brooke of Massachusetts that allowed Medicaid funding for abortions where there was a "medical necessity." Brooke and Senator Packwood apparently hoped that the medical necessity language would remain in the bill and that courts would interpret "medical necessity" broadly. Many other senators, however, apparently considered the medical necessity provision a bargaining chip in negotiations with the House over the final wording of the bill. There is little evidence that it was ever taken seriously again.

The exception from the funding ban included in the final bill that emerged from the conference committee and that was eventually enacted into law was narrow: It allowed for Medicaid funding of abortion when the woman's life was endangered, when a pregnancy resulted from rape or incest (provided the rape had been "reported promptly"), and when "severe and long-lasting physical health damage to the mother would result if the pregnancy were carried to term when so determined by two physicians."[57]

The battle in 1977 over the precise wording of the Hyde Amendment was typical of the remarkably prolonged and intense debates that took place in the late 1970s on the floors of the House and Senate over exactly how abused or sick or endangered a Medicaid recipient had to be if she were to receive funding for an abortion.

Right-to-life forces battled fiercely against any health exception. Some held an absolute view that no external condition could justify the destruction of a fetus—an unborn child—that obviously was not to blame. And certainly pro-lifers had a justifiable fear that an extremely broad health exception would eviscerate the Hyde Amendment. Yet the fights over exceptions to the Hyde Amendment also became the main political arena in which those who were pro-life could flex political muscle and exhibit the fierce absolutism of their cause by "deciding," as one commentator put it, "precisely how much suffering and danger a poor woman must face before Medicaid will pay for her to have an abortion."[58]

In 1977, for example, opponents of abortion refused to budge on the health exception as pro-choice advocates in the Senate kept offering "a bit more pain and suffering, a slightly higher likelihood of permanent damage."[59] Even the wording "severe or long-lasting physical health damage" was deemed unsatisfactory; it was altered to "severe *and* long-lasting physical health damage as determined by *two* physicians" before it was passed. Even this was vigorously objected to, in that and every year since, by those who saw themselves as pro-life. It was considered a major victory for the right-to-life movement when this narrow restriction was finally dropped in the 1980 appropriations bill for the Department of Health and Human Services (HHS), the successor to

HEW, so that even an indigent woman whose pregnancy would cause her severe and long-lasting physical health damage could not get federal funds for an abortion.

The apparent disregard of those who said they were pro-life for the suffering of these women was highlighted in an approach suggested by Senator Helms of North Carolina. During the debate on the first Hyde Amendment, Helms argued that it was unnecessary to write an exception into the law for cases in which a woman's life was in danger because "the doctrine of self-defense is also applicable here." In the abortion context the doctrine of self-defense is usually invoked in discussions of proposed constitutional amendments that would prohibit abortion even in a case that threatens the pregnant woman's life. The idea is that an otherwise illegal abortion might be performed—in "self-defense"—to save a woman's life. But this would require both the woman and her doctor to subject themselves to arrest under the clear language of the statute by deliberately killing the fetus. Then, at a criminal trial, the woman or doctor could raise the defense that the act was justifiable and therefore not murder.

This seems a strange argument for right-to-life advocates to make. It portrays the fetus not as an innocent life but as an aggressor that threatens to kill the pregnant woman. In any case the self-defense argument is nonsensical in the context of Medicaid funding. For, as Senator Bayh pointed out at the time, "[t]he self-defense doctrine does not say that you can have federal funds for self defense."[60]

Abortion-rights advocates were unable to mount a successful counterattack in the case of Medicaid funding. One reason was that politicians saw support for Hyde as a means to pacify not only right-to-lifers but the increasingly influential political right. Some politicians clearly thought that accepting these restrictions was simply the price that had to be paid for maintaining a generally pro-choice position. Yet even beyond the political obstacles, the abortion-rights forces, now using the label "pro-choice," faced several difficulties in trying to craft a response to those who supported the Hyde Amendment.

First, it was often difficult to deal head-on with the welfare question. Pro-choice activists knew that many people looked at Medicaid funding of abortion as simply another handout to welfare recipients. And as the 1980s dawned, welfare programs were not in favor. Hyde's opponents countered with the argument that the Hyde Amendment would increase both welfare costs and welfare dependency by keeping single mothers from breaking the welfare cycle. Unwanted new children in a single-parent household might well force the family further into poverty, and into welfare eligibility. A major problem for the pro-choice groups was that in advancing such arguments, they opened themselves up to the accusation that they were advocating a difficult moral outcome on the basis of a crude analysis of costs and benefits.

Also facing opponents of the Hyde Amendment was a problem with stressing the unfairness of the provision. Certainly they had a powerful argument that whatever one thought of *Roe,* it was wrong and even cruel deliberately to put a judicially recognized constitutional right beyond the economic reach of every poor woman. Yet the more the fairness issue was stressed, the more the issue looked like another social welfare question and the less it looked like a threat to the rights of a broad constituency. With a six to three majority on the Court still in favor of *Roe,* and with Justice Powell straining in his opinion in *Maher v. Roe*[61] to demonstrate that there had been no retreat from the 1973 *Roe* decision, pro-choice activists were already having great difficulty convincing the public that the congressional and judicial approval of Hyde-like legislation constituted a general threat to every woman's right to privacy.

Finally, some liberal activists and members of Congress who were predisposed to a pro-choice position may have been less vocal on the issue of federal funding because only a few years earlier they had relied on essentially the same argument, that taxpayers shouldn't have to pay for government activity that they find deeply immoral, in the context of the Vietnam War. Of course, the hypocrisy cut both ways, and as Birch Bayh reminded conservative senators who had opposed a right to avoid payment for the Vietnam War but now found a right to avoid funding abortion, this type of rationale could easily lead to chaos:

> This argument is very closely related to an argument that I found great sympathy with. Why should my tax dollars be used to dump napalm on defenseless civilians in Vietnam? I am opposed to the war so why should I not be able to opt out? Once we make that exception, I do not know where it stops. Maybe I do not want a highway going someplace because of environmental problems. Should I be given the option to determine where my tax dollars are going to be spent?[62]

The day after the Supreme Court finally decided *Harris v. McRae*—holding that the Hyde Amendment did not unconstitutionally impinge on the right recognized in *Roe* to choose whether or not to end a pregnancy—a twenty-five-year-old single New York mother of four, including eleven-month-old twin girls, nervously asked whether she could still get Medicaid funding for an abortion she had scheduled for that day. She was told that because the Court's decision would not immediately take effect she would remain eligible for at least the next twenty-five days. When a reporter asked her how she would have found the money had the Medicaid funding not been available, she replied: "My family doesn't have it, so I probably would have used my welfare check and then eaten from house to house. I couldn't have managed. I love the four children I have, but sometimes I don't have enough milk and diapers for them. So I couldn't clothe another baby. I could barely try to feed it and I wouldn't want to see another child suffer."[63]

## Fundamentalist Christians, Catholics, and the New Right

Opposition to abortion gained much of its political potency in the late 1970s and early 1980s from being interwoven with various other issues that were important to an increasingly vocal political right that included organized fundamentalist Christians. The antiabortion plank in the 1976 Republican platform, for example, was pushed by a group that promoted this position as part of a larger agenda, one that included support for voluntary school prayer and opposition to the Equal Rights Amendment. While the degree to which the general public moved in a conservative direction in the late 1970s remains in dispute, there can be no question that the rise of conservative political action committees and politically active fundamentalist Christian organizations had many politicians hearing what Alan Crawford called the "thunder on the right."[64]

As this New Right became increasingly powerful and influential in helping its favorite candidates—most particularly Ronald Reagan—it also became a powerful ally of the more single-issue-minded pro-life forces. While this was not much of a problem for groups like the National Right to Life Committee that held conservative views on most issues, it was a source of some unease within parts of the Catholic Church. Unlike most other voices in the pro-life movement, elements within the Catholic Church were far from uniformly conservative on questions of social policy. In 1986, for example, they were to issue a pastoral letter on social justice that sounded more like Jesse Jackson than like Jesse Helms. While the Catholic bishops supported significant funding increases in programs for the poor, powerful New Right organizations like Terry Dolan's National Conservative Political Action Committee (NCPAC) were fighting to eliminate food stamps.[65]

The tension in this uneasy alliance surfaced as early as 1976, when the bishops found that the only political element willing to support their cause was the far right of the Republican party. The possibility of a coalition with this group raised an outcry from many priests. The executive board of the National Federation of Priests' Councils, perhaps the most representative body of Catholic priests in the country, wrote a letter to Cardinal Cooke of New York, stressing its concern that the fight against abortion was crowding out all other issues about which the Catholic priests cared deeply. The priests maintained their support of the hierarchy's right-to-life position but expressed "deep concern . . . that this one issue is being stressed by the U.S. hierarchy to the neglect particularly of other important issues stressed by the National Conference of Catholic Bishops."[66]

In *Priests-USA,* the monthly newspaper of the National Federation of Priests' Councils, the Reverend Marty Peter of Indianapolis, a vice-president of the priests' federation, commented editorially on the matter: "Some who became impassioned about abortion are the same ones who are philosophically on the opposite side of some of us on the other life issues. . . . They were opposed to conscientious objectors to the Vietnam war, in favor of capital punishment and not very impassioned on the need for equal rights for blacks and Chicanos or the need for equal and integrated housing."[67] The *National Catholic Reporter* was even harsher in its headline describing the 1976 Republican platform: CONSERVATIVE GOP CONVENTION DEFENDS RIGHTS SELECTIVELY—FETUSES HAVE THEM, HUNGRY DON'T.[68]

Despite the intensity of these complaints, the Catholic hierarchy never seriously considered altering its strategy with regard to what it identified as pro-life causes or candidates because of disagreement on other social issues with other parts of the pro-life movement. If there was to be any hope of a constitutional amendment to overturn *Roe,* something for which the bishops were willing to make almost any sacrifice, the church would have to work with the New Right.

# 8

# The Politics of Abortion: The Pro-Life Advocates in Power

Roe, as we have seen, had an electrifying effect on the right-to-life movement. The target it provided was broad and clearly visible. Those politicians who would not commit themselves unequivocally to protecting the unborn to whatever degree Roe v. Wade still permitted, and ultimately to overturning Roe itself, could be opposed as enemies of life, whatever their positions on other issues might be. It was not until 1980, however, that this implacable commitment was to bear fruit in the form of a major shift in nationwide political power.

### The 1980 Election: The Reagan Era

The 1980 election and, more generally, the ascendancy of the New Right were major steps in the pro-life campaign for federal action to reverse Roe v. Wade. Not only did the pro-life movement have an avowed believer in the White House, but the defeat of several Democratic senators, including Birch Bayh of Iowa, Frank Church of Idaho, and George McGovern of South Dakota, had led to Republican control of the Senate. For the first time since Roe had been decided, those who opposed abortion rights could look forward to a Senate Judiciary Committee sympathetic to their cause and willing to regard them as *pro*-something rather than *anti*-something. Those who opposed the pro-choice position saw their chance and, not wanting to risk a Democratic recapture of the Senate in 1982 or 1984, sought to take immediate action. With a Republican-controlled Senate, the pro-lifers looked not to Henry Hyde in the House but to Orrin Hatch and Jesse Helms in the Senate to champion their cause.

The two pro-life proposals that were to dominate debate in the Senate for the next two years were the Helms Human Life Statute (the Helms Bill) and the Hatch Human Life Federalism Amendment (the Hatch Amendment). As the Reagan era was to make clear with some frequency, verbal and visual packaging could be vital; it was no accident that these provisions bore "human life" rather than "antiabortion" or "antichoice" labels.

Because Senator Helms recognized the low prospects for winning the two-thirds majority of both houses of Congress necessary to submit a constitutional amendment to ban abortion to the states for ratification, he sought to achieve the elimination of abortion indirectly through a statute that would require only a majority vote in Congress. The vehicle by which the Helms Bill sought to bypass the constitutional amendment process was a statute that would have defined "person" to include an embryo from the moment of conception. Again, political positions were made to pivot on labels. He who has the power to name may exercise control. And naming every fetus a person, it was argued, would have the same effect as a constitutional amendment extending constitutional protection to fetuses.

Even as strong an opponent of *Roe* as John Hart Ely, the noted constitutional scholar and later dean of the Stanford Law School, thought this a fatally flawed idea.[1] In an essay he coauthored with me in the *New York Times,* he argued that the Human Life Statute was in fundamental conflict with our very structure of government. The idea underlying the statute was that any constitutional doctrine could be overturned, not by constitutional amendment, as the Constitution itself provides and as the framers clearly intended, but by a mere majority vote in Congress to change the meaning of such constitutional terms as "speech," "religion," and "property." Indeed, if such a law were upheld, the essay pointed out, we could "skip all the bother and just let Congress redefine 'due process of law' to include 'any law Congress or a state legislature approves.' "[2]

Even conservative Republican Senator Orrin Hatch of Utah seemed inclined to agree. Fear that the potential constitutional obstacles would limit support for the Helms Bill, coupled with concern that a majority in Congress might not support an outright ban on abortions, led many in the pro-life movement to seek an alternative with a greater chance of success. Senator Hatch provided that alternative.

His proposed constitutional amendment, like Helms's bill, sought to overturn *Roe.* The difference was that while Helms sought effectively to take away the constitutional protection of a woman's right to choose by imposing a federal statutory ban on all abortions, the Hatch Amendment sought to override *Roe* by a constitutional amendment that would let the states or Congress decide whether or not abortion should be outlawed.

Senator Hatch's amendment had various political advantages over Helms's bill. First, simply because of the Helms alternative, Hatch could try—although ultimately he was unsuccessful—to portray his attempt to overturn *Roe* as moderate. Second, Hatch's amendment resonated with the popular states' rights, anti-Big-Government theme; it carried an appealing "spin" of local autonomy. Shouldn't the people themselves, not nine appointed-for-life judges at the federal level, decide such important issues? Third, unlike the Helms Bill, the Hatch Amendment did not require members of Congress to state affirmatively that they would outlaw abortion; they simply had to say that they thought a different decisionmaker should make the final choice.

Despite these advantages, the Hatch Amendment caused the same rift within the right-to-life community that had always plagued attempts to pass a constitutional amendment. To those most deeply committed to the protection of the unborn, an amendment that merely sent the issue to the states was heresy; it was a declaration that what was at stake was more a matter of preserving legislative choice than a question of preventing the mass murder of unborn children on an unprecedented scale. It was not tenable to argue both that the fetus was in all relevant respects a full human life and that national policy toward abortion had to be balanced with democratic values and political concerns. Furthermore, some who opposed abortion rights also feared that the Hatch Amendment would sap political energy that could be used on a Helms-like provision. "The Hatch Amendment doesn't save any lives, so it's a waste of time," stated Paul Brown, executive director for the Life Amendment Political Action Committee. "And if Hatch thinks he can get the country to pass two Constitutional amendments on abortion, he's talking pie in the sky."[3]

This absolutist position was severely undermined in November 1981, when the United States Catholic Conference of Bishops voted overwhelmingly to support the Hatch Amendment. The Reverend Edward Bryce, director of the Bishops' Committee for Prolife Activities, defended this decision, noting that in light of the mood of Congress and other pragmatic considerations, an absolutist position had to be balanced against "the Christian's responsibility . . . to advocate the improvement of such laws at every stage of the legislative process."[4] Furthermore, Bryce said, the Hatch Amendment could be portrayed popularly as a moderate measure. It also would not engender more tortuous debate over whether there should be life, health, rape, or incest exceptions.

One implication of Bryce's comments was that mutually destructive bickering was damaging the movement's effectiveness. This point had been made many times before,[5] but it was of particular concern throughout this period because President Reagan was widely known to be frustrated with the pro-life movement's inability to unify behind one measure.[6]

In March 1982 the Hatch Amendment was reported favorably for debate on the floor of the Senate by a ten to seven vote in the Senate Judiciary Committee. It was the first time a constitutional amendment to overturn *Roe* had been approved by a full congressional committee.[7]

While Helms was never able to obtain a vote on his bill that would have effected an outright abortion ban, nicknamed "pure Helms,"[8] he was able to bring to the Senate floor a less ambitious bill—"adulterated Helms"—to prevent any federal funds from being used for any abortion-related service and to put on record a congressional statement that "life begins at conception." While this bill failed by one vote (forty-seven to forty-six), pro-life activists were delighted that President Reagan both had taken a personal role in lobbying for the bill and, according to National Pro-Life Political Action Committee executive director Peter B. Gemma, had "even got George Bush, of all people, involved."[9]

Bush, who had come under criticism by pro-life groups for his earlier stand in favor of *Roe v. Wade,* was even sent a bouquet of red roses, the pro-life movement's traditional thank-you gesture, for his last-minute lobbying.[10] And although some White House staffers were known to be less than enthusiastic about the pro-life cause, with the economy in recession and with an eye on the 1984 elections White House strategists were recommending that Reagan again stress his social policy agenda, of which support for school prayer and opposition to abortion were the central components.

When the Hatch Amendment finally came up for a vote in the Senate, it failed to reach not only the necessary two-thirds margin (sixty-seven votes) but even a bare majority, going down to defeat by a vote of fifty to forty-nine. While the forty-nine votes it received represented an impressive showing for the pro-life movement, the failure, after the pro-lifers had come so far, was disheartening.

One of the dangers of any go-for-broke strategy is that, after one marshals the resources and expectations that are needed to go for total victory, failure makes it difficult to raise interest again among the public, the media, and the politicians. Having finally received a vote in a Republican-controlled Senate and having failed, the pro-life movement could not easily generate enthusiasm soon for another fight over a constitutional amendment.

Besides, despite the fairly impressive forty-nine votes Senator Hatch was able to garner, that number had to be seen in the light of certain mitigating political realities. First, some economically conservative voters were not comfortable with the social agenda in which opposition to abortion was a major theme. There was little evidence that abortion had helped pro-life members of Congress in the 1982 election. Indeed, several pro-life leaders in the House had been soundly defeated. Second, those who were pro-life had to recognize the possibility that pro-choice sentiment could gain intensity when faced with a serious threat. Patricia Gavett, director of the Religious Coalition for Abortion Rights, noted in 1982 that with the threat of the Helms and Hatch proposals, supporters of abortion rights had begun to become more vocal. "For years we've been fighting the perception of strength rather than strength itself," said Gavett. "Now we're hearing that pro-choice mail to the Congress is running at least fifty-fifty and in some cases ten to two"[11] against pro-life mail. Finally, those who were pro-life learned the hard way that they could not count on solid Republican support. Thirteen Republican Senators had crossed over to oppose the Hatch Amendment. They included Arizona's Barry Goldwater, the father of the modern conservative wing of the Republican party, California's Pete Wilson, Kansan Nancy Kassebaum, Texan John Tower, and Wyoming's Alan Simpson.

## The 1984 Campaign: Attacking the Church-State "Wall of Separation"

In the 1984 presidential campaign the issue of abortion was enveloped in a broader debate over religion and politics. President Reagan had made support for school prayer and opposition to abortion the twin cornerstones of his social agenda, and some thought he was seeking to weaken the wall separating church and state when he said that those on the other side of the school prayer debate were "intolerant of religion." The religion debate intensified when Democratic vice presidential nominee Geraldine Ferraro commented on television that it was not clear that Reagan's position showed him to be a "good Christian."

The abortion issue soon found its way into this dispute after two Catholic New Yorkers, Ferraro and Governor Mario Cuomo, were criticized for their views on abortion by New York's Archbishop John J. O'Connor. O'Connor lambasted both Cuomo and Ferarro for saying that while they were personally opposed to abortion, they did not support the use of the power of government to impose this view on others.

Bishop James W. Malone, president of the National Conference of Catholic Bishops, added to Archbishop O'Connor's criticism by rejecting as "simply not logically tenable" the notion that Catholic politicians' "personal views should not influence their policy decisions." The debate continued for weeks and focused on whether or not the bishops had meant that "good" Catholics could not vote for a candidate who was not pro-life.

Some Catholics, and others who supported the pro-life position, found this debate between the Catholic Church and Cuomo and Ferraro peculiarly uncomfortable. For years many people, including such religious pro-choice organizations as the Religious Coalition for Abortion Rights and Catholics for Free Choice, had argued that leaving the abortion choice in private hands represented the best solution in a religiously pluralistic society committed to separating secular from theological authority.

While the support of organized religion for a moral viewpoint should never make its enactment into law constitutionally impermissible, or even suspect, the idea of the Catholic hierarchy's dictating the position that Catholic voters and politicians *must* take on a divisive public issue strengthened the hand of those who argued that laws against abortion represented the imposition by secular law of an absolute religious doctrine. If the general public was left with this impression, some even feared that this would undermine the gains John F. Kennedy had made in convincing the country that a Catholic politician, and in particular a Catholic President, would answer first to the American people and the U.S. Constitution—not to the hierarchy of the church.

In September 1984 Senator Edward Kennedy spoke to defend Cuomo and Ferraro from the Catholic hierarchy's attack. When the senator invoked President John Kennedy's words, he seemed to be deliberately reminding the Catholic Church of the risks for all Catholics, and for the country, that the church would incur if it sided with those who held such an apparently intolerant position:

> One of the clearest warnings of history, a warning that led our founders to the First Amendment, is that if religious differences become central to society, they too easily become religious wars. Great Britain persecuted Quakers, Puritans, Catholics. . . .
>
> We need to hear [President Kennedy's] words once again: "I believe in an America that is officially neither Catholic, Protestant, nor Jewish, where no religious body seeks to impose its will upon the general populace and where religious liberty is so indivisible that an act against one church is treated as an act against all."[12]

There can be no doubt that our constitutional commitment to religious liberty leaves any church free to tell its members (if it chooses to do so) how they must act, as citizens or as public officials, if they are to remain in good standing with that church. It would not be surprising, however, if many voters were in turn to respond by opposing office seekers who seem likely to follow church dictates rather than their own views of what the public interest and the Constitution require. The cost for our system, and for religious tolerance and mutual forbearance, could be incalculable.

## The Judiciary: The Real "Reagan Revolution"

By 1984 it was increasingly apparent to all involved in the abortion debate that the most promising route for overturning *Roe* was through the judicial appointments President Reagan could make, particularly if he were to be elected to a second term. And indeed, by the time Reagan did leave office he had appointed one-third of the members of the Supreme Court and more than half of the lower federal judiciary.[13]

Reagan's first Supreme Court appointment was not a source of great comfort to the pro-life groups. As an Arizona legislator, nominee Sandra Day O'Connor had cast some arguably pro-choice votes. Most Republican senators were nonetheless convinced she would be an opponent of *Roe.* But when she refused at her confirmation hearings to disclose her views about that case—on the ground that she had an obligation to remain impartial because if confirmed she would soon hear abortion cases—pro-life groups asked that her nomination be withdrawn.[14] Yet these pro-life efforts suffered a devastating setback when Arizona's Senator Barry Goldwater was asked what he thought of Jerry Falwell's claim that all good Christians should ask their senators to vote against O'Connor's confirmation. With characteristic candor, Goldwater replied that "all good Christians should kick Jerry Falwell in the ass."[15]

Justice O'Connor was confirmed by a ninety-nine to zero vote. Despite the fears of those who opposed abortion, O'Connor delivered a relatively strong criticism of *Roe* in her 1983 dissent in the *Akron* case, the first abortion case on which she sat. Those who were pro-life began to see Justice O'Connor as friend and not foe.

In 1986 the election returns suggested some concern among the public about how abortion rights might be affected by an increasingly conservative judiciary. The Democrats regained control of the Senate, with several of the prevailing Democratic candidates stressing the importance of a Democrat-controlled Senate in checking future conservative Supreme Court nominations.

Chief Justice Warren Burger had stepped down prior to the 1986 elections, and President Reagan had promoted the Court's leading conservative, Justice William Rehnquist, to the chief justiceship, nominating U.S. Court of Appeals Judge Antonin Scalia to fill the open seat on the Court. Although several pro-choice groups were among those that put up a serious challenge to the Rehnquist nomination—he was confirmed by the narrowest majority of any nominee in the Court's history—the likable Antonin Scalia coasted through his confirmation hearings even though his constitutional outlook countenanced only a narrow view of the constitutional protection afforded women and suggested an almost sure vote to overturn *Roe*. Chief Justice Burger, whose vote Scalia's would replace, no longer seemed a strong ally of the right to choose; his 1973 opinion in support of *Roe* had by 1986 become an agreement that the Court "should reexamine *Roe*."[16] Even counting Scalia among those prepared to abandon *Roe* in whole or in part, his appointment to the Court still left a bare majority of five justices (Brennan, Marshall, Blackmun, Powell, Stevens) protecting *Roe*. The idea that *Roe* could be in real danger had not caught the attention of the public.

When Justice Lewis Powell, one of the five remaining justices supporting abortion rights, retired in the summer of 1987, it was plain that the justice who replaced him would likely be the decisive vote in a number of sensitive constitutional areas, including the question of abortion rights. It was this reality that caused the scrutiny of President Reagan's proposed replacement for Justice Powell, U.S. Court of Appeals Judge Robert Bork, to be so intense and immediate.

The issue, even initially, was not whether Bork standing alone was qualified to be on the Supreme Court, but the effect such an extremely conservative appointment could have as the decisive vote on issues like abortion. Although there remain strong differences of opinion on many aspects of the Bork confirmation process, there isn't much dissent from the proposition that the Senate Judiciary Committee hearings on the Bork nomination provided an extraordinary public dialogue on the role of the right to privacy in our Constitution and in our national life. The emotional public response to what many saw as Bork's threat to privacy rights, as well as to civil rights generally, provided lessons for pro-choice strategists to use in the battles to come.

Justice Blackmun, as we have seen, had based his opinion in *Roe* on the notion that the fundamental right to privacy that protected such activities as using contraceptives or sending one's children to private schools was broad enough to encompass the decision whether to continue or to terminate a pregnancy. Yet outside legal circles, abortion was not generally discussed in terms of a constitutional right to privacy. Even the idea that a woman should be able to control her own body was usually cast in terms of sexual equality rather than as a privacy or autonomy right.

Judge Bork's jurisprudence, however, clearly required a public discussion of the privacy issue. For while many of *Roe*'s opponents based their opposition to that decision on the ground that the Court had simply overextended the right to privacy, Judge Bork had long argued that the very *notion* of a fundamental right to privacy under the U.S. Constitution is illegitimate. Indeed, he had for years been one of the most prominent critics of *Griswold v. Connecticut,* the 1965 case that decided that the constitutional right to privacy protects the use of contraceptives by married couples. Because Bork's views about abortion implicated the right to privacy in general, the Bork confirmation hearings probably did more than any other event since *Roe* was decided in 1973 to focus national attention on the proposition that the constitutional right to choose to have an abortion, as protected by *Roe,* was part of a broader constitutional doctrine recognizing a fundamental right to personal privacy.

The widespread negative reaction to Bork's claim that *no* general constitutional right to privacy existed because it could not be found listed in the Bill of Rights or in the "original intent" of the framers of the Constitution powerfully displayed how deeply entrenched was the belief among the American people that there had to be such a right. The Bork hearings showed that belief that the Constitution protected such a right to privacy cut across political lines. Liberals saw it as a matter of basic civil rights, while conservatives and libertarians saw it as a question of limiting the scope of permissible government interference in our lives. Although it was inaccurate and unfair to suggest, as some pro-choice publicists did at the time, that Robert Bork was personally opposed to privacy or that he supported, as a matter of proper national policy, police searches of people's bedrooms, or that he personally favored forced sterilization, the fact is that Bork did not, and does not, believe that the *Constitution* protects against such intrusions if they are duly authorized by state or local legislatures.

Of course, Supreme Court justices do not command armies or run police departments. What is at stake when a justice is nominated is what he or she would allow others, who do hold such immediate power over people's lives, to do. Thus, whatever inaccurate or unfair remarks were made by some during Bork's confirmation process about the policies he might personally desire, it was entirely appropriate for senators and the public to take note of the fact that Bork did not construe the United States Constitution to provide a check against what they regarded as outrageous state intrusions on personal privacy.

## The 1988 Election: Kinder and Gentler?

Considering the intense controversy and speculation over the abortion views of Judge Bork and, after Bork's rejection by the Senate, over the abortion views of the nominee who was eventually confirmed to replace Justice Powell, Anthony Kennedy, it was perhaps surprising that abortion played such a minor role in the 1988 presidential election. The Democratic nominee, Massachusetts Governor Michael Dukakis, was apparently neither helped nor hurt in the primaries by the fact that he was one of the few candidates who supported both *Roe* and Medicaid funding of abortion. And in the general election, both campaigns at first shied away from the issue.

After defeating strong pro-lifers Jack Kemp and former television evangelist Pat Robertson in the Republican primaries, Vice President Bush may have sought to play the issue in a low-key way to avoid alienating Republican women and other likely supporters who might have been less than enthusiastic about the unflinching right-to-life position that Bush had espoused since the day he accepted the vice presidential spot on Ronald Reagan's 1980 Republican ticket, a position that was not evident in the 1960s or 1970s or when Bush responded to a question about *Roe v. Wade* without equivocation during the 1980 campaign for the Republican presidential nomination, stating, "I happen to think it was right."[17] Dukakis, on the other hand, apparently believed at first that campaigning on the effect future Supreme Court nominations might have on *Roe* might backfire by focusing attention on issues that would hurt him with the conservative Democrats he needed to win, issues like busing, which he favored, and capital punishment, which he opposed.

After the first presidential debate, however, the Dukakis campaign staff realized that his campaign organization had underestimated the potential power of this issue. When Bush said on TV that he hadn't "sorted out" what the penalties should be for women who had abortions, Dukakis successfully suggested that "the vice-president is saying that he's prepared to brand a woman a criminal for making this decision."[18] Bush's lack of preparation on this issue not only was embarrassing, it exposed a political weakness in the pro-life position: Whatever people's views on abortion, few thought of women who chose abortion as criminals. Perhaps too many Americans knew someone who had had an abortion, someone they surely didn't think of as having committed a crime. It was powerful testimony to how shaken the Bush campaign was by this issue that the next morning, in lieu of the usual postdebate attempts to control the spin that the press gave the face-off, campaign manager James Baker called a press conference to make it clear that Bush did not intend to jail women who had abortions.

Even in Dukakis's tortured second debate performance, it was an abortion question to which he gave his best answer, and, in a performance otherwise marked by its absence of emotion, it was certainly his most passionate moment. When abortion came up in this second debate, Bush first suggested, apparently in reference to abortions justified by fetal abnormality, that even though he and his wife, Barbara, had lost a child in infancy he was not in favor of abortion. After mentioning that he and his wife, Kitty, had lost a child, too, Dukakis responded: "But isn't the real question that we have to answer not how many exceptions we make, because the vice-president himself is prepared to make exceptions? It's who makes this decision, who makes this very difficult, very wrenching decision. And I think it has to be the woman, in the exercise of her own conscience and religious beliefs, that makes that decision."[19]

Despite the relative success for Dukakis of the abortion issue during the debates, some enthusiastic responses when he made pro-choice speeches, and the insistence from pro-choice groups that polling data showed the issue could move voters, the Dukakis campaign never successfully seized the issue in its efforts to catch up with Bush.

## Operation Rescue

Perhaps the most interesting abortion-related phenomenon that arose by the time of the 1988 presidential election was the development by pro-life groups of more aggressive methods to try to stop legal abortion. Their tactics have included picketing clinics and the homes of clinic staffs, shouting at women who seek abortions, pelting pregnant teenagers with plastic replicas of fetuses, harassing clinic employees, chaining themselves to doors, and lying motionless in streets and driveways. Some have sought to intimidate women seeking abortions by setting up sham pregnancy "counseling" centers. These centers, rather than provide the counseling they advertise, have traumatized unsuspecting pregnant women with films of abortions and with pro-life literature graphically depicting aborted fetuses. Such centers have been known to counsel women falsely that abortion often leads to death, disease, insanity, and sterility.[20]

More ominously, some antiabortion activists have vandalized and even bombed abortion facilities. There has been a remarkable, although not much-remarked-upon, rise in the incidence of such antiabortion violence. Since 1977 extremists in the United States have bombed or set fire to at least 117 clinics and threatened 250 others. They have invaded some 231 clinics and vandalized 224 others.[21]

In the late 1980s the most visible manifestation of the antiabortion movement's offensive has been Operation Rescue, a national group headquartered in Binghamton, New York, that first attracted widespread attention when its supporters mounted a blockade of Atlanta abortion clinics during the 1988 Democratic National Convention. Its carefully chosen name again illustrates the power that many ascribe to labels. Operation Rescue members have often sought arrest and then refused to provide their names to authorities, preventing them from formally charging the protesters. Operation Rescue protesters are willing to spend time in jail, and many of them have. Since the action in Atlanta, Operation Rescue has used similar civil disobedience tactics to blockade clinics throughout the United States, resulting in more than twenty thousand arrests in 1989.[22] These tactics take a form reminiscent of the civil rights protests of the 1960s, however different the goals.

For many women and teenage girls, Operation Rescue's blockades have turned the experience of seeking an abortion into a nightmare of jeering demonstrators, a spectacle that in turn attracts the added horror of media coverage of this intensely personal decision. Pro-choice advocates, including NARAL, have responded by providing escort services and support for women who seek to enter abortion clinics. Clinics have also countered by filing lawsuits against Operation Rescue, some of them successful, but these actions have thus far been foiled by the refusal of the movement's organizers to pay out on adverse court judgments and by the success of the organizers so far in concealing their financial assets.[23] In the name of life, clinics continue to be firebombed and terrified pregnant women continue to be assaulted.

## *The Coming of* Webster

Despite the failure of the 1988 presidential campaign to demonstrate any widespread outpouring of public concern about the right to choose, some pro-choice advocates still believed that if the public perceived an immediate threat to *Roe,* a pro-choice reaction would occur. This possibility created a strategic problem for pro-choice groups. They had to decide whether publicly to portray the 1988 challenge to *Roe* that came before the Supreme Court in *Webster v. Reproductive Health Services* as a case in which the Court would be likely to overturn *Roe.*

As we saw earlier, the *Webster* case itself really did not *require* the Court to reconsider *Roe* at all. Missouri Attorney General William Webster had taken the position that the one legislative provision that *seemed* to conflict directly with *Roe*—the law's preamble, stating that "[t]he life of each human being begins at conception"[24]—was simply a policy statement with no substantive effect on abortion rights. Yet it was also true that with four justices potentially eager to overturn *Roe* and a fifth (Justice O'Connor) who had written two opinions sharply criticizing the Court's analysis in *Roe,* it was not an exaggeration to say that *Roe* hung by a thread.

At the same time the pro-choice forces believed that there was a danger in framing the public issue in terms of whether or not *Roe* would be *explicitly* overturned. *Roe* was just as likely to die with a whimper as with a bang. It was quite likely that the justices would simply chip away at *Roe* until it was nothing more than a hollow shell, never admitting that they had in essence overturned the Court's original 1973 decision.

Because pro-choice voters seemed to be concerned with abortion only when they sensed that women were on the verge of losing the right to choose, it would be valuable for the pro-choice movement to portray the Supreme Court as likely to overturn *Roe* in *Webster.* On the other hand, if the issue was framed this way, there was a real likelihood that those who were pro-choice would mistakenly think they had won a victory in *Webster,* and would go back to political sleep, if *Roe* were not explicitly overturned, even if the decision was, in fact, quite damaging to the pro-choice cause.

Kate Michelman, NARAL's executive director, decided early in 1989 that NARAL had to launch a major campaign to let pro-choice supporters know that if they stayed asleep much longer, they would wake up to find that they no longer possessed the right to choose. Working with the other major pro-choice organizations, NARAL designed a two-part strategy. The first part of the strategy was to use the possibility that *Roe* would be overturned in *Webster* as a vehicle to tell pro-choice voters that the moment of truth for abortion rights had arrived. After delivering this initial message, a "wake-up call," the second part of the strategy was to try to educate the general public to understand that even if *Roe* were not overturned, a defeat in *Webster* would be a major setback that would signify that the Supreme Court would no longer preserve a woman's right to decide whether to end a pregnancy. In that circumstance the only recourse for those who were pro-choice would be through political activism aimed primarily at state legislatures.

There would be costs to the second part of the strategy even if it were successful. Maximizing instead of minimizing the cost of a loss in *Webster* might limit the extent to which some state legislators could oppose new restrictions on abortion on the ground that they were unconstitutional. It might also encourage lower court judges to see a decision in *Webster* narrowly upholding the Missouri abortion regulations as giving courts broad power to uphold other restrictions on the right to decide whether or not to end a pregnancy.

NARAL held a press conference early in 1989, on the day the Supreme Court announced it would hear *Webster.* Michelman released a book of letters by women describing their experiences with both legal and illegal abortions, announced a campaign to get one million Americans to sign a pledge to work to support *Roe,* and issued a warning that by Independence Day 1989 women might lose one of their most important liberties.

Two weeks later, on the sixteenth anniversary of the decision in *Roe,* NARAL placed in newspapers across the country a full-page ad displaying a coat hanger. The ad said: "For most of our daughters this looks like a coat-hanger. Let's keep it that way." While the coat hanger ad ran the risk of attracting accusations of extremism, NARAL believed that it had to start its campaign in a way that would grab people's attention. During early 1989 there were signs that the long-awaited pro-choice backlash might be emerging. Membership in pro-choice groups soared and when NOW and pro-choice groups sponsored a March for Women's Lives in Washington in April, an enormous crowd of about half a million pro-choice marchers responded.

As part of its campaign, NARAL settled on a clear and simple message: "Who decides?" Previously the pro-choice movement had always spoken of a woman's right to choose and to control her own body, and the message had always been a mixture of women's rights, freedom of religion and conscience, health concerns, and libertarian philosophy. "Who decides?" was apparently the right message for the right moment. First, as *Time* magazine documented, even though women favored women's rights and the women's movement, many did not like to see the issue described in strident terms. As Betty Friedan said about younger women, "[i]t's the 'I'm not a feminist, I just want to be an astronaut' syndrome."[25]

Interestingly, the "Who decides?" message took command of a stage set largely by the pro-life movement's oft-repeated states' rights message. For at least a decade the pro-life movement had scored political points by attacking *Roe* through an antijudicial, anti-federal government message. In essence the pro-life movement asked people whether they thought the Supreme Court or the state legislatures should be the decision maker on this sensitive issue. This message worked well as long as the "choice" presented was between the Supreme Court and the elected state legislatures. Yet in framing the debate in this way, the pro-life movement unwittingly invited the pro-choice side to "out-antigovernment" them. When Judge Bork or Senator Hatch asked, "Who decides?," the choice was between governmental units: big government, in the form of the Supreme Court, or state and local government. NARAL was able to adopt the same question with a more powerful distinction: Who decides: you—the individual—or them—the politicians? As polling data have regularly demonstrated, this formulation of the abortion issue as a question about who decides is the one that receives the most sympathetic pro-choice response from the American people.

With its newly crafted message, NARAL poured unprecedented resources into a nationwide paid media campaign, which for the first time ever included pro-choice television commercials warning of the dangers of returning to the days of illegal abortions. In one such commercial a doctor recounted his memories of working before *Roe* in a hospital ward where women were treated for injuries following botched abortions. Another ad followed a woman walking through a dark alley and up an unlit staircase to an illegal abortionist. Finally, one commercial showed snapshots of a girl growing up. The pictures stopped when she was a young woman, and the narrator said: "She grew up in the '50s and died in the '60s, a victim of an illegal abortion." NARAL was the target of criticism for its use of such high-priced media spots, in addition to well-paid consultants and pollsters. But after sixteen years of being outspent and outlobbied while going from defeat to defeat at the hands of the pro-life movement, NARAL was anything but dismayed to hear the "criticism" that it had become too slickly political.

As public attention focused on the impending decision in *Webster,* NARAL and other pro-choice groups sought to shift attention away from whether or not *Roe* would be overturned. They wanted to drive home the idea that *any* loss would signal that women could no longer rely on the Supreme Court to uphold the right to choose and that any restriction would amount to an absolute obstacle to abortion for some women.

The Supreme Court does not announce when it will hand down its decisions, and by the middle of May 1989 members of the national media were making daily pilgrimages to the steps of the Supreme Court in order to be able to announce and analyze the decision "live" within minutes of its announcement. Like many such vigils, it was a long wait. The *Webster* decision was announced only on July 3, 1989, the last day of the Court's 1988–89 term, when most Americans were enjoying a long July Fourth weekend.

For the umpteenth time John Willke, president of the National Right to Life Committee, and Faye Wattleton, head of Planned Parenthood, stood poised on the Supreme Court steps while NARAL's Michelman and others sat in national network news television studios ready to give comments. When the *Webster* opinion came down, it was close to what many observers had expected: *Roe* was left standing—barely—but restrictions on the provision of abortions in public hospitals were upheld, as were the provisions for testing fetal viability. There was no majority opinion, and four justices suggested their desire to overturn completely the fundamental privacy right to choose an abortion established in *Roe.*

For the pro-choice leaders the message they wanted to communicate was that this was a serious setback, that the Supreme Court could no longer be relied upon to protect the right to choose, and that from now on the only way to protect a woman's right to choose would be to hold politicians—particularly state legislators and governors—accountable. "The Court has left a woman's right to privacy hanging by a thread and passed the scissors to the state legislatures," warned NARAL's Michelman. On the day of the *Webster* decision this pro-choice message got a tremendous boost from an unlikely source: the leadership of the pro-life movement. After contested partisan political events, each side normally seeks to place its own spin on what has happened in an attempt to influence popular and media interpretation of the event. Yet on this July 3 morning something unusual occurred. The pro-life leaders were giving out almost exactly the same political message as those who supported abortion rights: *Webster* was a great victory for the pro-life movement, *Roe* hung by a thread, and a pro-life victory was imminent in the state legislatures.

This was a political blunder. With both sides interpreting the case in the same way, the message that those who supported abortion rights had to act immediately or lose their rights came through loudly, clearly, and without confusion. After sixteen years of battle in a war of attrition in which every win had to be blown up to inspire followers and to impress the media and politicians, the pro-life movement's victory declaration was almost reflexive. Yet it was ironic that a movement built in reaction to the victories of the other side should, after all these years, help galvanize support for their opponents by their own victory declaration.

## *After* Webster: *The Pro-Choice Backlash*

When the pro-life movement's campaign to transform the American judiciary finally succeeded with the *Webster* decision in 1989, the constellation of calculations that seemed firmly fixed in the domestic political firmament began to shift in a more sudden and fundamental way than at any other point in the half century since Franklin Roosevelt's rise to power. The tumultuous, intense, and geographically varied reaction to the decision reflected the political reality that *Webster* had placed the abortion issue in the hands of the state legislatures. If the fragmented five-opinion decision in *Webster* was a discordant symphony, the immediate nationwide reaction was political rock and roll.

Those who were pro-choice launched demonstrations all over the country in the two days following the decision. Pro-life groups quickly began organizing their own demonstrations and, of course, each demonstration spurred an immediate counterdemonstration. In Boston, when a pro-choice rally overflowed with an unexpected three thousand marchers, there were shoving matches with local police officers. A few days after *Webster,* mounted police and canine patrols in Denver arrested sixty antiabortion demonstrators trying to close down a Planned Parenthood clinic, while another sixty were arrested in Milwaukee.[26]

At the national level each side proceeded as if the momentum were in its favor. With the *Webster* ruling giving state legislators a constitutional green light to try drafting abortion restrictions previously thought unconstitutional, the National Right to Life Committee announced immediately that although it would utilize specific strategies based on the politics of each state, it would propose restrictions in four categories: (1) laws requiring women to be informed of alternatives to abortion; (2) parental consent or notification laws; (3) laws giving the man involved with the pregnancy some rights; and (4) laws prohibiting abortions sought for specific reasons, such as sex selection or birth control.[27] Later in the fall the NRLC announced a strategy aimed at the incremental removal of the remaining protections offered by the *Roe* decision. The strategy added as additional goals limitations on public funding for provision of abortion services, funding of agencies that provide alternatives to abortion, and the dissemination of public information stressing the sanctity of life beginning at conception.[28]

Although most of these proposals were not novel, they were advocated in a new way that reflected the reality of political control over the question of abortion. Previously the pro-life movement had tried to enact the strictest restrictions allowed in the space left open by the most recent Supreme Court decision. Now the movement proposed restrictions that might appear moderate and mainstream in order to attract political support.

This political strategy required many pro-lifers to walk a tightrope. In one breath they had to claim that they sought only moderate restrictions, while in the next breath they had to admit that they continued to believe that all abortion is murder. Furthermore, even if the NRLC was willing to try to cultivate a more moderate image, it still had to contend with the fact that many people could not distinguish it from the militant Operation Rescue.

Of course, those who advocated abortion rights faced a similar problem. Many commentators noted that NOW President Molly Yard's strident tone and language sometimes drowned out the more moderate, libertarian messages being delivered by Wattleton of Planned Parenthood and Michelman of NARAL. And while the pro-choice movement did not have within it an organized arm like Operation Rescue whose purpose was disruption, pro-choice groups also saw that they would have little means to prevent random acts of pro-choice violence carried out by determined protesters. Such acts could disturb otherwise solid support for the movement for abortion rights.

The pro-choice groups were quicker to go on the offensive than those who opposed abortion. NARAL, Planned Parenthood, NOW, the ACLU, and the Fund for the Feminist Majority were among two dozen pro-choice groups that met in the first few days following *Webster* to establish task forces and devise a comprehensive strategy aimed primarily at state legislatures. Most of the major groups also began meeting with the staffs of pro-choice members of Congress for regular sessions on potential federal legislation. NARAL held a nationwide teleconference with all its affiliates in which pro-choice congressional leaders Les AuCoin and Robert Packwood gave pep talks. NOW's Molly Yard called for another major march on Washington, and Wattleton and Planned Parenthood made clear, in new full-page ads, that they were ready to combat Operation Rescue's efforts in every way possible.

One source of pro-choice concern was the composition of the nation's state legislatures when *Webster* was handed down. Through single-issue voting, the pro-life movement had built up legislative majorities in many states. A NARAL study found that despite strong public support for keeping the abortion decision private, in only nine states were both houses of the legislature in favor of protecting the abortion right, while in twenty-four states both houses favored prohibiting abortions.[29] Thus, in many states, pro-choice groups had to hope that *Webster* had created a new political accountability in which politicians were forced to pay close attention to the views of their pro-choice constituents.

It had been the conventional political wisdom in the years between *Roe* and *Webster* that voters who were pro-life held politicians accountable for their votes in a way that those who were pro-choice didn't. Whatever their views might be on other issues, politicians who weren't pro-life wouldn't get pro-life votes. Voters who were pro-choice, on the other hand, had tended not to use politicians' stands on abortion as a litmus test. In Pennsylvania, for example, in 1986, pro-choice advocates were unable to convince the predominantly pro-choice Democratic voters not to nominate pro-life candidate—and later Governor—Robert Casey. But the pro-life single-issue approach had helped elect local officials who shared only one trait: opposition to abortion.

The question now for pro-choice activists was twofold. First, could they convince state politicians that there was such a new single-mindedness among those who supported abortion rights that the politicians should refigure their political calculations before voting for restrictions on abortion? And second, if this were not successful, could they deliver on what NARAL's Michelman called the "Take our rights, lose your job" threat by turning out of office those who voted to restrict abortion? Both sides waited for the legislative challenge that would shed light on the first question or the electoral contest that would shed light on the second. The first test cases came quickly.

As both sides in the abortion debate awaited major electoral contests in Florida, Virginia, New Jersey, and New York City in October and November 1989, each—but particularly the pro-choice side—yearned to show that it had political momentum by winning in special elections held during the summer and early fall.

The California Abortion Rights Action League (CARAL) declared that a special election for a state legislative seat in California's Seventy-sixth District would be "a test case in a new climate on the abortion issue." CARAL poured time and resources into supporting Republican Patricia Hunter, a registered nurse in favor of abortion rights. The campaign manager for her main opponent, Richard Lyles, a Republican who opposed abortion in most circumstances, complained that the pro-choice forces were outspending him two to one, and soon pro-life groups declared that they had no choice but to respond with "more effort ourselves."[30]

In August Hunter finished first in a field of eight, and in October she won a runoff election. In September another pro-choice Republican, Holly Cork, the only pro-choice candidate in a field of eight, won a special election for a seat in the House of Representatives of the South Carolina General Assembly. While pro-life groups claimed that pro-life candidates had also won special elections since *Webster,* pro-choice candidates appeared to be winning the contests in which abortion was an important issue and the candidates held opposing views.

With all the posturing over which side was winning and which way the political wind was blowing, the first pro-choice victory to grab national attention came somewhat unexpectedly—not in a state race but in the national legislature. In August the U.S. House of Representatives reviewed the part of the funding measure for the District of Columbia for fiscal 1990 that dealt with abortion. Because the District of Columbia is not a state, its people are ultimately ruled by the national politicians in the Congress. It had become almost a reflex for Congress each year to add a restriction to the budget of the strongly pro-choice District of Columbia to prevent the District from using its own local tax dollars on abortion, even in cases of rape or incest. Yet when California Republican Congressman Robert Dornan offered such an amendment in the wake of *Webster,* it was defeated, 222 to 186, even though the same restriction had passed in the House the year before by a vote of 219 to 186.

This was the first time since September 1980—two months *before* Ronald Reagan was first elected President—that an abortion spending restriction had been defeated in the House.[31] Perhaps even more portentous, twenty-two members of Congress had changed their votes from the previous year. While a few members sought to explain their votes by arguing that an exception for the pregnant woman's life could not be added until the House-Senate conference committee met, the bill that was defeated was essentially the same as the bill that had passed the year before. What had changed was the mood of constituents, or at least of politicians, in the wake of *Webster.*

Any thought that the District of Columbia appropriations vote was a fluke vanished when, in October 1989, the House again reversed course by voting to allow Medicaid funding of abortion in cases of rape and incest. When President Bush threatened to veto the Medicaid bill because it would have provided funds for such abortions, a public debate erupted within the Republican party. While the pro-life position had been a solid part of the foundation that had made the party ascendant in the 1980s, the return of the issue to the states—the chance that a pro-life position might make a practical difference to the availability of abortion—made party regulars question whether abortion mightn't become the party's Achilles' heel.

To begin with, some of these restrictions seemed cold and inhumane. Many believed, with American Enterprise Institute scholar William

Schneider, that a veto of abortion funding for impoverished rape and incest victims fell into the category of actions that a politician can never totally explain to constituents. "It will be his Willie Horton," said Schneider, referring to the convict whom President Bush had used to destroy the reputation of his 1988 opponent, Massachusetts Governor Dukakis, after Horton had committed a rape while furloughed from a Massachusetts prison.

It was true that this heartless Medicaid measure had been routinely passed for years, but that was before *Webster*. *Webster* had put abortion under a media magnifying glass, and many previously unnoticed issues were taking on new importance. Furthermore, Bush did not even have a principled pro-life basis for his position. Bush *supported* rape and incest exceptions to strict antiabortion laws; he merely opposed giving this abortion option to poor women who needed public help. While he suggested that this was because there was no way to verify that a rape had actually occurred, he never spelled out whether he thought the problem of lying about rape was more common among poor women, whether he believed no women could be trusted to tell the truth about such a serious and traumatic event, or what.

In the fall of 1989 public sentiment did not seem as warm to the Bush view on such a rigid restriction on Medicaid funding as it had been a decade earlier. George Bush himself realized during the 1988 presidential campaign that American attitudes toward the poor had somewhat altered since the late 1970s and early 1980s. The visible crisis of homelessness and a feeling that President Reagan had sought to go too far in cutting social welfare funding were part of a more sympathetic attitude toward the poor. No presidential candidate in 1988 treated poverty in quite the cavalier way that Ronald Reagan had in 1980.

Moreover, *Webster* had done for the pro-choice movement what all its work had been unable to achieve for more than a decade. It persuaded a large segment of the population that a vote for any abortion restriction was a real threat to the right to choose whether or not to terminate a pregnancy. This meant that more people saw the Medicaid votes not as votes about welfare but as votes about abortion. If a member of Congress could support such a harsh measure, he or she might not be trustworthy to those who opposed other restrictions on abortion rights.

All these factors played a role in shaping the way people visualized the poor woman who sought an abortion. With less national hostility toward the poor, people now saw the funding question primarily as one about the right to choose an abortion—especially in the case of a rape. This view permitted people to visualize the reality of a woman, a real rape victim, being forced to carry to term a pregnancy that was violently forced upon her. Indeed, on the House floor Republican Nancy Johnson of Connecticut delivered a speech to her colleagues more impassioned than most that chamber has heard: "Will you be part of denying that 14 or 15-year old welfare mother, with one young baby, who is trying desperately to succeed in school that opportunity? If she is raped by the drug addict next door, if she is invaded by her God-damned alcoholic father, will you deny her the medical care your wife or daughter has access to?"

For most Republican strategists, the party's stand on abortion was problematic not merely because it appeared callous. There was a more pragmatic concern. Polling data showed a majority in support of abortion rights, particularly in cases of rape and incest. While the data were sensitive to wording, and while a majority also opposed abortion "on demand," a strong majority of the population said that a pregnant woman should have the right to decide whether or not to have an abortion.

Among those who were pro-choice, one could identify a group of voters who held conservative views on fiscal matters but who were "liberal" on social issues, particularly abortion. These voters, primarily young urban professionals and Republican women, had been a mainstay of Republican growth and success in the presidential elections of 1980, 1984, and 1988. Many Republican party regulars warned President Bush and other party leaders that if the Republicans didn't reconsider their stance on abortion, it could cost them dearly in 1990 and 1992—not to mention 1989.

While opposition among some Republican women to the pro-life tack taken by the Republican party dated back at least to the 1976 Republican party platform fight, the single-issue intensity of pro-life sentiment among fundamentalists and the members of the strictly conservative New Right—so-called movement conservatives—had previously kept the pro-choice voices within the Republican party from asking for anything more than mere tolerance of their views. As the pro-choice position gained its own single-issue constituency, Republican women, such as Congresswomen Nancy Johnson and Maine's Olympia Snowe, could make a case that it was the pro-*choice* view that was politically sound and that maintaining the party's unyielding pro-life position would threaten its national base of support.

Aware of these pressures, President Bush at first sent out signals that he might be willing to compromise on the rape and incest exception to the Medicaid funding bill if there were strict reporting requirements—for example, a proviso that women would qualify for the exception only if they had reported the rape or incest within a few days of its occurrence. This did nothing to placate those who supported funding of these abortions. They argued not only that rape victims frequently don't report rapes immediately but that, for completely understandable reasons—including fear of violence at the hands of the perpetrator and fear of exposing themselves to further shame and degradation at the hands of police, prosecutors, and defense attorneys—victims, who, of course, can't know at first whether they will become pregnant, often don't report instances of rape or incest at all.

Some supporters of women's rights, such as Brooklyn's Democratic District Attorney Elizabeth Holtzman, were furious that Bush, by suggesting that funding for abortions be linked to a time limitation on rape reporting, was moving public attitudes backward, implying that women could not be trusted truthfully to report rape and other acts of sexual violence. Others in both political parties simply found it telling that in the midst of multibillion-dollar scandals involving the savings and loan industry and the Department of Housing and Urban Development, the government was suggesting that the place to crack down on deceit and corruption was among poor pregnant women claiming to have been raped.

The limited practical value of a prompt reporting requirement was probably clearest in the most urgent case, that of incest. Part of the tragedy of incest, of course, is that the victim is usually in an ongoing relationship of dependency from which she cannot escape. It is unrealistic to imagine that truthful incest allegations could be separated from false ones by requiring a child who does not yet know she is pregnant to report her father or uncle to the police within seventy-two hours of having been forced to have sex with him.

In the end President Bush simply vetoed the Medicaid funding bill. High White House sources were surprisingly candid in admitting that the reason for this veto was that after having failed to act decisively in October 1989 to assist a coup attempt to unseat Panamanian dictator Manuel Noriega (who was finally ousted several months later following American military action in that country), Bush and his advisers were concerned that any capitulation or compromise on the abortion issue might raise the impression that the President was a "wimp," an image against which he had worked hard during the 1988 election campaign. A few days after the Medicaid veto President Bush also vetoed the District of Columbia appropriations bill.

Those within the pro-choice movement and the Republican party who believed that *Webster* had altered the political landscape found significant support for their view in the final months of 1989. The Republican governor of Florida, Robert Martinez, had announced immediately after *Webster* that he planned to call a special session for the Florida legislature to consider new restrictions on abortion.[32]

Governor Martinez's call for a special legislative session turned out to be a political miscalculation of the highest magnitude. No sooner had Martinez thrust himself into the national abortion spotlight than public opinion polls in Florida showed him being hurt by his strong antiabortion position.[33] He received criticism not only from Democrats opposed to the idea of a special session but from many Republican lawmakers in his state who were "disappointed" and left "scratching [their] heads" over his move.[34] Significantly, this controversy was not even about criminalizing abortion; Martinez made clear that he sought the special session only to implement provisions similar to those approved by the Supreme Court in *Webster* as well as to enact stiffer restrictions on clinics that provided abortion services.[35]

Days before the special session was to take place, Martinez received a major blow when the Florida Supreme Court ruled six to one in a parental consent case that whatever the United States Supreme Court might say about the protection of abortion rights by the United States Constitution, the right to privacy in the Florida Constitution protects "a woman's decision of whether or not to continue her pregnancy." The Florida Supreme Court stated that "[w]e can conceive of few more personal or private decisions concerning one's body that one can make in a lifetime, except perhaps the decision of the terminally ill in their choice of whether or not to discontinue necessary medical treatment."[36]

While pro-choice groups had lobbied vigorously for weeks in Florida, the night before the special session pro-lifers staged an impressive and emotional eight-thousand-person rally in which Martinez asked the crowd to remember that "[w]e're talking about an unborn baby who's seeking life. It's a heartbeat, a heartbeat that must be heard and seen."[37] Despite this showing of support, by the evening of the first day of the special session three of Martinez's six proposed restrictions on abortion had been defeated in committee in the state senate by votes of nine to three.[38] By lunchtime the next day the state senate's Health Care Committee had defeated all three of the remaining proposals, the bills to restrict abortion clinics. Every bill proposed by Martinez—bills that were intended to be debated during a four-day special session—had been gunned down by high noon on the second day. The pro-choice win in Florida suggested the national mood. Martinez had gone out on a limb; other politicians would have to consider his embarrassment before they decided to move quickly or boldly to restrict abortion.

Two gubernatorial races and the New York City mayoral race also became major tests of the politics of abortion in 1989. NARAL declared that it intended to spend big money in the New Jersey gubernatorial race between pro-life Republican Representative James Courter and Democratic pro-choice Representative James Florio. In Virginia, the other 1989 gubernatorial battleground, the Republican candidate, Marshall Coleman, had once supported *Roe v. Wade* but had later reversed himself, opposing abortion even in cases of rape or incest. The Democratic nominee, Lieutenant Governor Douglas Wilder, was pro-choice but had supported parental consent laws. He was warned publicly by Grace Sparks, the executive director of the Virginia League for Planned Parenthood, that if he remained "vague" on the abortion issue, it would cost him the election.[39]

Even in states where no gubernatorial election would be held until 1990, the abortion issue reared its head. Only two days after *Webster* Governor Mario Cuomo of New York announced he would oppose any further restrictions on abortion in his state. The political message was that this was an issue that even a governor as popular as Cuomo felt the need to deal with quickly.

The impact of *Webster* was also felt early in the Massachusetts gubernatorial race, in which the election was more than a year away. Lieutenant Governor Evelyn Murphy, looking for an issue to spark her campaign and to divert attention from the state's grave budget deficit problems, spoke at a rally days after the *Webster* decision to proclaim her intention to make herself the candidate of choice for pro-choice voters. Another candidate, former Massachusetts Attorney General Francis Bellotti, a Catholic father of twelve who helped bring to the U.S. Supreme Court two cases bearing his name in attempts to uphold state parental consent laws, countered by proposing a state constitutional amendment that, on the state level, was designed to preserve the protections of *Roe*.

No less interesting was widespread speculation that *Webster* was at the heart of the initial reluctance by Boston's generally liberal but pro-life Mayor Raymond Flynn to run for governor. Flynn had been an early favorite to replace outgoing Governor Michael Dukakis. While there is no direct evidence of how the abortion issue influenced his decision about running, much of Flynn's traditional support came from voters who were pro-choice, and polls in late 1989 showed that of the voters who initially said they would support him, nearly 50 percent said they would not support him when they were informed of his stance on abortion. By February 1990 statewide polls were beginning to show that fewer pro-choice voters in Massachusetts said they would automatically vote against pro-life candidates. As the state's fiscal paralysis persisted and as the state's bond rating maintained its pathetic place as fiftieth in the nation, likely Massachusetts voters displayed what would probably become a nationwide pattern. The force of the abortion issue as a decider of elections, especially above the local level, would wax and wane with the emergence of alternative focal points for electoral politics, and pro-choice groups in particular might confront great difficulty in defeating statewide right-to-life candidates who convinced the electorate that they would be the most likely to deliver a state from some other, more widely perceived and pervasive threat. Even so, it was becoming clear that *Webster* had significantly strengthened the political hand of pro-choice activists around the country.

Abortion found its way, for instance, into the contest for the 1990 Democratic gubernatorial nomination in California, where considerable controversy arose when Attorney General John Van de Kamp opposed a portion of a Crime Victims' Justice Reform Initiative that stated that defendants' rights of privacy under state law "shall not be construed" to provide greater protection than that provided by the United States Constitution.[40] While this provision was meant to limit expansive procedural protections for criminal suspects under the California constitution, Van de Kamp noted that the provision's language might jeopardize abortion rights in the state if *Roe* were overridden.[41] Van de Kamp took a significant risk in voicing that concern. In the political climate of the late 1980s his opposition to a new drug and crime initiative could readily be misinterpreted to make him seem "soft on crime." Another pro-choice politician, former San Francisco Mayor Dianne Feinstein, opted to downplay this issue despite her strong pro-choice record.

Meanwhile, abortion took on new political importance as the November 1989 election races entered the home stretch. In New Jersey the Republican candidate, James Courter, apparently assumed from the start that even in that state, where the citizenry is 50 percent Catholic, his pro-life stance would be a political liability in the election. For most of the race Courter tried to fudge his stand on the abortion issue with the result that he alienated many of his pro-life supporters without making any significant gains among those who were pro-choice. As early as August Courter sought to play down his personal views by stating that he would follow the lead of the New Jersey legislature. This position won him few supporters. Courter, a congressman, also undermined the credibility of his pledge of deference by voting in Congress against allowing the District of Columbia to decide whether to use its own tax dollars to fund abortions in cases of rape and incest. Perhaps more embarrassing, his own campaign chair, Republican New Jersey Representative Dean Gallo, voted the other way.[42] Courter's difficulty in finessing the abortion issue was painfully clear during the campaign.[43]

Courter's conspicuous waffling on abortion put the National Right to Life Committee in a difficult position. NARAL and NOW had made the New Jersey race a test case on abortion and had promised substantial resources to help elect Democrat Florio. NARAL had announced plans to target fifty thousand pro-choice voters, and NOW undertook its own independent grass-roots drive and media campaign.[44] The NRLC thus faced a choice between getting involved in support of a candidate who waffled in his support of the pro-life position and who was behind in the polls and doing nothing while risking a big loss by Courter that would be perceived as a major pro-choice victory. It decided to stay away from the New Jersey race and to downplay the importance of the election. "The abortion groups have really duped the press," said Sandy Faucher, head of the National Right to Life Political Action Committee. "If you want a test on abortion, take a state where both sides are even and both sides are involved."[45] Still, the fact that Courter felt the need to hide his pro-life position, coupled with considerable anecdotal evidence of pro-choice energy, seemed to ensure that fairly or not, a strong Florio showing would be perceived as a strong victory for the pro-choice position.

Another candidate who found himself trying to comfort pro-choice voters despite a pro-life record was former U.S. Attorney Rudolph Giuliani, the Republican nominee for the mayoralty of New York. Before Giuliani had secured the Republican nomination, he and his advisers recognized that in liberal New York City he would lose many voters with a pro-life position.[46] While Giuliani had implied from the start that he might be willing as mayor to implement pro-choice policies despite personal opposition to abortion, exactly one month after *Webster* he made a firm statement that he not only supported a woman's right to choose but opposed any attempt to end or reduce the city's extremely liberal policy of funding abortions for poor women.[47] While Giuliani was initially hit with a round of accusations that he had flip-flopped, unlike Courter, he had at least come out with an unequivocal statement. His task for the remainder of the campaign was to convince pro-choice voters that he could be trusted and pro-life voters that he was still a better option for them than pro-choice Democratic nominee David Dinkins or a wasted vote for the New York Right-to-Life party candidate.

The nationally watched contest that ultimately presented the truest test case on abortion was the Virginia governor's race. With local Washington news shows covering the race in detail, and the *Washington Post* covering the election as both a national and a local story, this race was also where most members of Congress, congressional staffers, and the army of national political reporters in Washington got their closest look at the new politics of abortion.

After an initial post-*Webster* shyness about his pro-choice stance, Wilder had come to the conclusion that abortion could help him. This was not as obvious as it may seem in hindsight. Wilder and Florio were probably the first gubernatorial candidates ever to use a pro-choice position as an offensive weapon in a closely contested statewide campaign. Wilder may have been encouraged by the possibility of emphasizing the conservative values inherent in a pro-choice position. NARAL had already shown that many key voters were favorably affected by the libertarian "Who decides? You or the politicians?" message. Virginia's Democratic nominee for lieutenant governor, Donald S. Beyer, Jr., had shown that this message could be blended with Virginia's heritage in a powerful post-*Webster* statement that asserted the need for "firm conservative leadership at the state level. Thomas Jefferson wrote extensively about the requirement for separating church and state in a democracy. George Mason incorporated the right to privacy in the Bill of Rights. . . . I will take the conservative position to keep government out of the most personal decision an individual may ever have to make."[48]

Wilder hired Frank Greer, NARAL's media consultant, to design a media strategy on abortion. In September Wilder released television ads depicting Thomas Jefferson and the American flag. The narrator told viewers that only Wilder supported Virginia's tradition of a right to choose[49] and that his opponent, Republican Marshall Coleman, "wants to take away your right to choose and give it to the politicians."[50] Wilder's efforts were bolstered by a $350,000 media campaign launched on his behalf by NARAL. This time, however, the National Right to Life Committee decided to retaliate; it spent at least $150,000 on behalf of Coleman.[51]

Coleman retreated from the position he had taken during the Republican primary, in which he had expressed support for a constitutional amendment that would outlaw abortion, with no exceptions for cases of rape or incest. In the first debate during the general election campaign, Coleman said he would not propose laws to ban abortions in cases of rape or incest because they were not politically viable. Toward the end of the campaign he went further, suggesting that his was a passive pro-life stance and that he would not initiate legislation that would conflict with the wishes of the people of Virginia. Polls and news stories showed Coleman being hurt by the abortion issue, and ultimately he chose to employ a negative media campaign of character attacks against

Wilder specifically designed to deflect attention away from the abortion issue.

In Virginia, New Jersey, and New York the pro-choice candidates proved victorious. In New York City Dinkins won the mayoral race narrowly over Giuliani, although the closeness of that race and the fact that Giuliani had come out with a clear pro-choice stance made it hard to determine the significance of the abortion issue for the voters in New York City's general election.

There was less question about the importance of abortion in the two gubernatorial races. In New Jersey, where Florio won in a landslide, a CBS poll found that 22 percent of the voters considered abortion the "most important" issue in the campaign and that these voters supported Florio by a margin of two to one.[52] In Virginia the election result was surprisingly close compared with preelection polls, with Wilder becoming the first elected black governor in the nation's history by fewer than 7,000 votes out of almost 1,800,000 votes cast. Most attributed the unexpected closeness of the Virginia election to opposition to Wilder on the basis of race, opposition some voters apparently hid from preelection pollsters. Wilder's victory, however, was apparently due in large measure to his position on abortion. When voters were asked about abortion, 71 percent called it somewhat or very important to them, and 62 percent of these were for Wilder.

Of all the November electoral contests, however, perhaps the most telling was the race for lieutenant governor of Virginia. There, relatively inexperienced pro-choice Democrat Don Beyer was taking on a pro-life Republican, the former first lady of Virginia, State Senator Edwina "Eddy" Dalton. Because the results of this race could reflect no hidden racial bias, it was an even better test of the electoral power of the abortion issue than the Virginia governor's race. Beyer maintained a strong pro-choice position throughout the election, and he won by a wide margin, crediting his position on abortion rights as a major reason for his surprising success.

The Democratic sweep heightened the urgency of the debate about abortion within the Republican party. Pro-choice Republicans in Congress as well as other leading party members, like outgoing New Jersey Governor Thomas Kean, argued that these elections were proof that in the world built by *Webster,* the Republican party's firm pro-life stand meant political suicide. Yet others, including Susan Smith of the National Right to Life Committee, argued that these elections were merely proof of poorly run campaigns in which pro-life candidates were hurt by showing that they did not have the courage of their convictions. Considering the traditional American disapproval of indecisiveness among our leaders, there is probably something to this view. Yet there is little proof that even a well-articulated, consistently held pro-life stance would have been a political asset in any of these races.

A subsequent special election in California suggested that zealotry in opposition to abortion rights could well backfire. San Diego Bishop Leo Maher, who had tried to deny NOW members communion in 1975, now denied communion to California Assemblywoman Lucy Killea, a pro-choice candidate for the California Senate running for a seat representing conservative San Diego County. Objection to the bishop's action probably provided Killea with her razor-thin margin of victory (she got 50.97 percent of the votes), tipping the balance in the state legislature in favor of abortion rights.[53]

After all these elections, evidence continued to mount that an increasing number of candidates believed they could not win elections without modulating or abandoning their pro-life positions. By October forty-one members of Congress had switched sides in votes on rape and incest exceptions.[54] A Massachusetts state representative, Robert Ambler, who had been an opponent of abortion rights for a quarter of a century, abandoned his position before announcing his candidacy for state senate, arguing that this would enable him to be a "consensus-type legislator."[55] In perhaps the most surprising of the many conversions from the position opposing abortion rights, the longtime pro-life Ohio attorney general, Anthony Celebrezze, who once had publicly called abortion "murder," to the horror of pro-life groups defected to the pro-choice side days before announcing his candidacy for governor in 1990.[56]

The most immediately significant change of heart involved Illinois Attorney General Neil Hartigan. Illinois regulations that would have closed down 80 percent of that state's abortion clinics (by requiring them to have facilities more like those of hospitals) were struck down by the United States Court of Appeals, and Hartigan had succeeded in his request that the Supreme Court review the decision. After *Webster* the case appeared to be the most likely vehicle for the further erosion, or, indeed, the complete overturning, of *Roe v. Wade*. But Hartigan, who was seeking the Democratic nomination for governor in 1990, now saw his defense of the restrictions on abortion clinics as a potentially fatal political liability in a contest against pro-choice Republican Jim Edgar. After weeks of negotiation with his opposing counsel from the ACLU, Hartigan announced on the day before Thanksgiving 1989, two weeks before oral argument was to be heard by the Supreme Court, that the two sides had settled the case. He had in essence agreed to most of the demands of pro-choice groups. NARAL's Michelman triumphantly declared that Hartigan had learned that "you can't travel the road to public office by forcing women to detour to the back alleys for health care."

## A New Role for Congress:
## Post-Webster *Freedom of Choice Legislation*

While most of the legislative action was in the states, the federal government was not completely out of the picture. In Congress a bill to protect abortion rights that was introduced with 23 cosponsors in the Senate and 113 in the House actually reached the House floor. The bill, whose chief sponsor in the House was California Democrat Don Edwards, was entitled the Freedom of Choice Act of 1989. The bill was designed essentially to preserve the protections of *Roe v. Wade* through federal statutory law, by prohibiting the states from imposing restrictions on previability abortions or on later abortions necessary to protect the life or health of the pregnant woman.

While there has been much talk about a reversal of *Roe* "returning the issue to the states," the Constitution leaves no doubt that *federal* law is the "supreme Law of the Land." Opponents of abortion and of the Freedom of Choice Act argued that the federal government, a government whose powers are limited to those enumerated in the Constitution, would be beyond its authority in enacting a law limiting state power to restrict abortion. However, even apart from Congress's power to regulate interstate commerce (a broad power under which a statute similar to the Freedom of Choice Act could probably be enacted), Section 5 of the Fourteenth Amendment expressly states that Congress "shall have power to enforce, by appropriate legislation," that amendment's provisions. The Supreme Court has held that Section 5 "is a positive grant of legislative power authorizing Congress to exercise its discretion in determining whether and what legislation is needed to secure the guarantees of the Fourteenth Amendment."[57]

Under this power, even if the Supreme Court were to conclude that the Fourteenth Amendment does not itself require that women be given *any* of the protections outlined in *Roe,* Congress could still pass a statute such as the Freedom of Choice Act so as to make the "liberty" and "equality" of women more secure by providing such protections purely as a matter of federal statutory law. This would not be the first time Congress had moved ahead of the Court in protecting the freedom of a group of citizens. For example, in *Katzenbach v. Morgan*[58] the Supreme Court upheld the authority of Congress, exercising the power granted it by Section 5 of the Fourteenth Amendment, to pass a law enabling Puerto Ricans in New York to vote despite their failure to meet English literacy requirements. The fact that the Court itself had previously *upheld* these very literacy requirements against a direct constitutional challenge[59] did not lead the Court to doubt Congress's authority to conclude that extending the franchise to educated Puerto Rican citizens notwithstanding their limited ability to speak, read, or write English would be a reasonable means of protecting them from being unfairly treated by state or local officials in matters other than voting. So long as the Supreme Court does not conclude that the fetus is a "person" whose rights Congress is bound to respect, even a decision overruling *Roe v. Wade* would leave Congress with the latitude to protect women more fully than the Fourteenth Amendment alone does. While the Freedom of Choice Act was given little chance of becoming law when first introduced (in light of President Bush's veto pen), the existence of congressional power under Section 5 leaves open a continuing possibility of future involvement by Congress in any political resolution of the abortion issue.

## The Political Landscape in the 1990s

Despite these pro-choice victories, as the 1980s ended, the political war over abortion had reached a new stage. Notwithstanding the fact that those who support abortion rights were now willing at times to vote on this basis, many state legislatures still contained pro-life majorities as the decade of the 1990s began. The political success of abortion rights would require a demonstration of the electoral power to unseat pro-life legislators. In 1989 this political fact of life was most evident in Pennsylvania, where previously elected pro-life forces controlled the state legislature and the governor's office. Even amid the year's pro-choice victories and polls showing Pennsylvanians to be pro-choice, the Pennsylvania legislature in the wake of *Webster* enacted one of the most restrictive abortion laws in the country in an action that seems to have met with fairly wide public approval. The Pennsylvania law contains significant restrictions on the abortion right, including a requirement of spousal notification and a twenty-four-hour waiting period.

Those who oppose abortion rights may also regain momentum by moderating their absolutist stance. If the pro-life side can focus attention on the problems of teenage misbehavior and promiscuity and can stress particular restrictions (such as parental consent laws) that have wide support rather than pressing opposition to *all* abortion, the upshot may be political victories for the antiabortion position.

The pro-choice movement might be expected to respond to this strategy in a variety of ways. One would be to stress that the avowed purpose of groups like the NRLC is not to be "moderate" but to outlaw *all* abortion as murder. Pro-choice advocates might also try to shift attention to the devastating consequences on individual women of even these supposedly moderate restrictions. Polling data suggest that if the pro-choice movement is to maintain its momentum, it cannot let the pro-life side shift the debate to *why* a woman wants any given abortion. The movement's current popular appeal clearly depends on keeping the question focused on *who* will make the decision.

## The Effects of Roe—Revisited

Whatever the outcome of the political battles about abortion in the coming months and years, the early polls and contests that followed the Supreme Court's *Webster* decision reveal something important about the effect both of the passage of time and of the sixteen-year reign of *Roe v. Wade*.

The power to decide whether or not to end a pregnancy is now widely viewed as an individual right. The success of the right-to-life reaction to *Roe* does not appear to reflect an enduring popular view about the illegitimacy of abortion rights. The strength and commitment of pro-choice voting appear to be far greater now than before *Roe*. Remember that at the time *Roe* was handed down, only four states had repealed their abortion laws. And even in some of those states there was real contention. Indeed, the state with the most permissive abortion law prior to *Roe*, New York, had voted to reinstate harsh restrictions on abortion just two years after lifting them. Abortion rights in New York were preserved only by Governor Rockefeller's veto.

Under *Roe*'s protection, abortion rights appear to have taken root and flourished. The pro-choice political movement is in this sense among *Roe*'s progeny. Prior to *Roe* a woman's most vital liberty and equality interests were all but invisible to the Constitution. The choice necessary for reproductive freedom and equality in controlling one's life was more a dirty secret than a constitutional right. *Roe* proclaimed government protection of such private and personal interests to be legitimate precisely because they are so personal and private.

*Roe* also taught a lesson about the first-class citizenship of women.

Even women who oppose abortion rights because of a belief that human life begins at conception are becoming familiar with the idea that the constitutional right to choose also ensures that no one can ever force a woman to have an abortion. Affluent professional women who would probably be able to obtain safe abortions even if the procedure were criminalized now see access to abortion not merely as a question of a *service* that can be bought elsewhere if it is unavailable in the current manner but as a *right* women must have if they are to achieve equal respect and an equal capacity to control their own destinies. These were not widely held views in the United States at the beginning of 1973. *Webster* was able to alter the political landscape in 1989 only because sixteen years earlier, *Roe* had altered so much more.

## *Does the Reaction to* Webster *Indirectly Safeguard Choice?*

It is striking that by early 1990 both President Bush and Republican National Committee Chairman Lee Atwater, while reaffirming that they were still pro-life in their views, were pleading with the Republican rank and file to define the party broadly enough to embrace pro-choice Republicans as well. That plea plainly dramatized the assessment of savvy and seasoned politicians that the pendulum of public pressure had swung so far from the pro-life pole that right-to-life purity would be unacceptably costly to the Republicans.

How are we to assess this shift, and the political victories for abortion rights in the months following *Webster*? What are we to make of the claim that since it appears that abortion rights may well be protected for many in the legislative arena, there is nothing to be feared from *Webster* or from the further dismantling of *Roe*?

The question of whether women received something constitutionally *illegitimate* in *Roe v. Wade* still counts for a great deal in this equation. If they did, then taking it away from them, as the Supreme Court began to do in *Webster,* would be justifiable, and making them fight for their reproductive freedom and autonomy in the political arena would be justifiable as well. But if women received nothing that was not their constitutional due in *Roe v. Wade,* then what the Court began to do in the *Webster* case was simply wrong. If women have a *constitutional right* to reproductive autonomy, then making them fight for their reproductive liberty in the arena of politics, even if they do manage to win much of it back, is wrong—both morally and under our Constitution.

When something belongs to you as a matter of right, making you spend political chips in order to hold on to it is deeply inconsistent with our system of constitutional government. So it is not enough to say that if they fight hard and long, women will end up with pretty much the same rights after *Webster* that they had under *Roe.* Even if the rights were to end up looking the same—and it is far from certain that they will—what is crucial is that women may now be forced to sacrifice a great deal in order to vindicate those rights. Women who might otherwise have poured their energy and their resources into the fight for better child care, or higher wages for women's work, or improved environmental quality will instead have been required to put that energy and those resources into the fight to win back what the Constitution, if *Roe* read that document correctly, already promised them.

Nor is the point limited to women with a "liberal" agenda. What about the Republican women in the suburbs of Virginia who believed they had to vote for Douglas Wilder in order to preserve their reproductive freedom and who, on most other grounds, would have preferred Marshall Coleman as their governor? Whether you are a Republican or a Democrat, you should not view with indifference the sacrifices these women were required to make in order to secure what, if *Roe v. Wade* was right, the Constitution already assured them.

Those who are eager to see *Roe* dismantled and are quick to predict that the political process will offer reasonable protection to the reproductive freedom of women are already saying, "I told you so," as they scan the landscape and observe one pro-choice political victory after another—from the Florida legislature to the floor of the U.S. House and Senate, from the gubernatorial race in Virginia to that in New Jersey, and in a number of mayoral elections besides. Although some politicians, like Neil Hartigan of Illinois, may abandon challenges to *Roe* in light of their electoral aspirations, the push to continue dismantling the legal structure erected in *Roe v. Wade* may be expected to gain force from the illusion that when the dust has cleared, women will have lost little or nothing after the first phase of the demolition has been completed.

We are in danger of being seduced by that illusion. For if *Roe v. Wade* was a more defensible interpretation of the current Constitution than *Roe*'s critics insist, then adherence to constitutional processes and respect for the rights they secure should make even pro-life advocates dubious about what women are being required to give up and about how hard they will be forced to run just to stay in place.

This is not to say that women do not derive major benefits from winning the battle for abortion rights in the legislatures of the nation. They surely do. One significant downside of the protection provided by *Roe* was the apathy it apparently engendered among those who just now are coming out of their political sleep. Another was the illusion *Roe* fostered that rights, once wrested from the political process by judicial decree, need no further political defense. In a representative democracy such as ours, the last word *always* belongs to the people; those elites that prevail in the courts, sometimes feeling an unwarranted contempt for the less well-educated groups they have outflanked, can only lose in the long run if they take the justice of their cause for granted and discount the significance of views they think less "enlightened" than their own.

Because of its importance to many people, interest in the abortion issue may ultimately trigger a political realignment in the United States and the rise of new and powerful coalitions in other areas of American politics. It may make the face of American politics more truly representative of the views of the American people. Perhaps most important, working to win recognition of equal rights in the legislature, rather than have them protected by judicial pronouncement, may give women in American politics greater self-respect and greater knowledge of their own potential political power. That in turn may, more than anything before it, help advance the cause of equality, a cause that, in the long run, may do more than abortion restrictions ever could to advance a genuine reverence for life and a true respect for all humanity.

# 9

# In Search of Compromise

Because neither the pro-life nor the pro-choice advocates are likely soon to win a consensus among the public that their views are entirely correct, it seems fruitful to explore the grounds for a political compromise *other* than the one reached in *Roe* itself, a compromise that has seemed unsatisfactory to many.

After *Webster* the state legislatures have an expanded power to enact legislation that regulates abortion. On issues as subtle as these, nobody can plausibly maintain that the Constitution, or morality, requires every state, every community to arrive at an absolutely identical solution. *Roe*, like whatever principles might plausibly come to replace it, necessarily acknowledged some room for local variation—for example, on matters of funding and in deciding which postviability abortions, among those that are not strictly required by the pregnant woman's health and survival, to prohibit. But many who have long urged that states and localities be given more options than *Roe* left them, particularly in the direction of greater protection for the unborn, have depicted *Roe* as reflecting a "pro-abortion" extreme that must give way to a more "pro-life" resolution.

Yet examining some of the supposedly "moderate" legislative solutions that have been put forward, solutions falling somewhere between *Roe* and a total prohibition on all abortions from conception onward, exposes some uncomfortable truths about these compromises. In general, although the compromises are designed to sound reasonable, they would sacrifice much more than they would accomplish.

## Consent Requirements

A commonly offered type of compromise legislation is the consent requirement. This type of law would require the consent of the pregnant woman's husband or of the man who shares responsibility for the pregnancy before a woman seeking an abortion could legally be provided one. States have also enacted laws that require pregnant women who have not reached the age of majority to obtain the consent of one or both parents before a desired abortion procedure can be performed.

Although a spousal consent requirement no doubt has some intuitive appeal—why should one partner be able to end a pregnancy caused by both?—in practical operation the consent requirement would be relevant only when the husband wanted to veto an abortion sought by his wife. Of course, it would be ideal if both parties concurred in an abortion decision, but when the woman is unwilling to continue the pregnancy, a requirement of consent from the man would not facilitate *consensus*. It would simply transfer the power to decide from the woman, who has decided on an abortion, to the man, who has decided to stop her. Only one party can prevail in such a situation. Since the abortion at issue is one that would be legal if the man had no objection, the interest in the life of the fetus cannot justify ruling for the man. Thus the Supreme Court, in the 1976 case of *Planned Parenthood v. Danforth,* held that the woman's interest in the consequences of her pregnancy outweighed the man's and invalidated this type of consent requirement. The alternative—to say that the man's interest trumps the woman's—seems on its face indefensible. Once we have decided that the law should not intervene to protect the fetus unless the woman chooses to remain pregnant, conditioning her power to choose upon some formal role for the man neither protects life in a consistent way nor encourages genuine mutuality.

The situation is obviously different when it is a parent, not the man involved, who seeks a role. Even before *Webster* the Supreme Court upheld parental consent requirements, but only those that provide for the alternative of judicial approval when a pregnant minor can demonstrate that she is sufficiently mature to decide for herself whether to terminate her pregnancy or that there is a good reason for not seeking parental approval and it is in her best interest to have an abortion. A new push is on in the wake of *Webster* to impose consent requirements that have no such bypass provision but that leave the minor's fate (and that of the fetus) entirely in the hands of the pregnant minor's parents. Polls show that most Americans support such legislation.[1]

As Yale Medical School Professor Angela Holder has pointed out, however, such requirements might have some unintended and frightful consequences. As the law has addressed the question of when adolescents may consent for themselves to various forms of medical care, a rule has emerged that a minor too young to consent to a particular form of treatment is also too young to refuse such treatment when a parent insists upon the minor's receiving it. After all, immaturity is a factor that cuts both ways.

Accordingly, in the context of abortion, parents have frequently insisted that physicians terminate the pregnancies of their unwilling teenage daughters. In the past in the absence of a court order physicians have told such parents no, and no court has ruled in a reported case that a parent may force a pregnant child to have an abortion against her will. But if a state is permitted by the Supreme Court to treat all its minor women and girls as too immature to make this momentous a decision for themselves, physicians and courts might well accede to the decision of a parent who believes an abortion is in his or her daughter's best interest—"just as parents have the unquestioned authority to force their unwilling adolescent to have an appendectomy or enter a drug treatment facility."[2] This suggests that parental consent requirements, whatever might be said for them as a matter of parental authority generally, cannot plausibly be defended as part of a "pro-life" compromise since the premises on which such consent requirements rest equally support parentally *compelled* abortions.

## Notification Provisions

In 1990 the Supreme Court considered the latest variant of the legislative attempt to mandate parental involvement: the parental notification law. Two cases decided by the Supreme Court presented challenges to such laws. These two cases, *Hodgson v. Minnesota*[3] and *Ohio v. Akron Center for Reproductive Health,*[4] also represent the first tests of the status of abortion law in the Supreme Court since its 1989 decision in the *Webster* case.

Under the Minnesota law at issue in *Hodgson,* a pregnant minor was *required* to allow notification of *both* her parents forty-eight hours before she could obtain an abortion. The statute made no exception for the children of divorced or unmarried parents who do not have custody, nor for children who live with only one parent. It also made no exception for situations in which parents may react abusively (whether psychologically, physically, or sexually) unless the pregnant girl was willing to declare herself the victim of sexual or physical abuse. Although such a declaration would result in state intervention within the family and would virtually insure that the abusive parent would find out that the girl was having an abortion, the statute offered the pregnant minor no alternative course of action. A second provision in the Minnesota law was to take effect if this first provision was enjoined by a court. Rather than *absolutely* requiring notification of both parents, this "backstop" provision created an exception permitting the pregnant minor to get a court order authorizing her abortion either on the ground that she was mature enough to give consent or on the ground that an abortion without notice to both parents would be in her best interests.

The companion case to *Hodgson,* a lawsuit filed by the Akron Center for Reproductive Health, presented a challenge to a similar law, although a law in which only one parent had to be notified. In *Akron Center for Reproductive Health v. Ohio,* the United States Court of Appeals struck down the Ohio law because it found, among other reasons, that the judicial bypass mechanism was insufficient to meet the requirements for such provisions in parental consent laws first set out by four justices in *Bellotti v. Baird* in 1979 and then adopted by a Court majority in *Akron v. Akron Center for Reproductive Health* in 1983. The Ohio law permitted a pregnant minor to seek a court order authorizing an abortion on three grounds: her maturity, her best interests, or a pattern of sexual, physical, or emotional abuse against her by one of her parents. The judicial bypass system in the Ohio law, however, contained a complex maze of pleading requirements. If a girl alleged only that notification was not in her best interests (on grounds of abuse or otherwise), the court was not empowered to grant her request on grounds of maturity, and vice versa. Although a girl could allege both that she was sufficiently mature and that notification was not in her best interests, and could appeal if the court were to dismiss her complaint because she had failed to ask for judicial approval on the proper ground, the procedures set out in the Ohio law would be difficult for any nonlawyer to maneuver around. In addition the law placed an unusual hurdle in the pregnant minor's path by requiring those women seeking court approval to prove maturity, best interests, or a pattern of abuse by "clear and convincing" evidence.

These cases presented the questions of whether a two-parent notice requirement is constitutional and of whether parental notification laws require a judicial bypass mechanism such as that required since before *Webster* in cases of parental consent laws.

At oral argument in the cases, held before the Supreme Court in November 1989, tempers flared between Justices O'Connor and Scalia in a verbal replay of the previous summer's *Webster* opinion. When the decision was handed down in June 1990, the Court was again grievously splintered.

In *Hodgson,* the Court, by a five-to-four vote, struck down the Minnesota two-parent notification requirement but at the same time, also by a five-to-four vote, upheld that portion of the Minnesota law which coupled the two-parent notice requirement with a judicial bypass system. Only Justice O'Connor was in both majorities. While she did vote to strike down the harshest two-parent notification provision, she appeared to do so not on the ground that the abortion right recognized in *Roe* was unduly burdened, but rather on the ground that two-parent notification in many circumstances would not actually serve the state's articulated goals of helping the pregnant minor and her family. Indeed, after joining a discussion by Justice Stevens of the way in which the two-parent provision would intrude upon the right of an individual parent to make decisions regarding the welfare of a child, Justice O'Connor specifically concluded that "Minnesota has offered no sufficient justification for its interference with the family's decisionmaking processes created by . . . two-parent notification."[5]

While it is undeniable that Justice O'Connor in *Hodgson* for the first time demonstrated some willingness to hold a regulation of abortion unconstitutional, the decision raises as many questions as it answers. For example, does it mean that Justice O'Connor would vote to uphold any abortion regulation so long as it permits a judge to issue an order authorizing an abortion? Does this not undermine the idea that the right in question belongs to the pregnant woman? Will Justice O'Connor vote to strike down abortion regulations in other areas where there can be no argument that they pose a risk to the best interests of minors?

In the *Ohio* case, the Court avoided reaching the question whether a parental notice statute *requires* a judicial bypass mechanism simply by concluding that the judicial bypass provided in the statute—by far the most complicated such procedure with which the Court has ever been faced—was sufficient to pass constitutional muster, even under the Court's earlier parental consent decisions. Again, the Court upheld an abortion regulation that would in all likelihood have been struck down before *Webster.*

Taken together, the Court's 1990 decisions thus renew *Webster*'s invitation for states to enact strict abortion regulations, and one can predict that many of these laws, though not necessarily all, will in turn be upheld by the Supreme Court. A further wild card of course was dealt those who oppose abortion regulation with the 1990 replacement of liberal Justice William Brennan with Justice David Souter. With four solid votes to uphold the constitutionality of almost all abortion regulation, any time Justice Souter votes to uphold an abortion restriction that Justice O'Connor would find unconstitutional, her objection will be unavailing.

Whether or not the Court does ultimately vote to uphold the most stringent regulations on a minor's abortion right, it seems clear that parental consent laws and notification requirements share a common problem. All such laws, while perhaps intended in part to foster communication within families, may only compound desperate situations where communication just is not possible. In families whose children feel free to discuss such things with a parent, neither consent laws nor notification requirements are necessary. And even if one could as a general matter legislate intrafamily communication, something that seems most unlikely, there are some circumstances in which the consequences of the attempt would surely be devastating.

Abortion rights advocates point to the case of a young woman who was advised by a doctor not to tell her father of her pregnancy because of the threat that he might have a stroke. Another pregnant girl did not want to tell her mother because she was a recovering alcoholic who the girl feared would return to drink.[6]

Perhaps the saddest of these stories is the one of Becky Bell, a seventeen-year-old girl from Indiana, whose story was first reported in the newspapers in late 1989. When Becky discovered that she was pregnant, she sought an abortion, but Indiana law required that she have parental approval. Her best friend says Becky, a blond, blue-eyed former cheerleader, loved her parents "so much, she couldn't bear telling them."[7] Becky thought about having the baby and thought about going out of state for an abortion. What she did in the end remains unclear. It seems that she made plans to have an abortion "performed on a Saturday in Kentucky" but that "in the interim, desperate, she tried a home remedy."[8] She became unbearably sick; it later turned out she had been suffering from pneumonia caused by an infection in her uterus. She got sicker but refused to see the doctor because he would discover her pregnancy and tell her parents. She soon began to hemorrhage. She told her mother that her period had started. Once she began bleeding, she agreed to see a doctor. At the hospital, the day before she had been scheduled to go to Kentucky, Becky died. Only then did her parents learn of their daughter's pregnancy from a doctor at the hospital.[9]

Becky's "grieving father is crusading against consent laws that, he believes, cost Becky her life."[10] "If you had a beautiful daughter and she was lying in a graveyard, what would you do?" her mother asks.[11]

Consent and notification also present a different danger—the real danger of parental violence. Spring Adams was a thirteen-year-old Idaho girl made pregnant by her own father. In 1989, after learning she was pregnant with his child, her father killed her with a rifle.[12]

In sum, parental consent and notice requirements may sound like moderate recognitions of the parents' central role in family life but are likely in practice to achieve little and to cause great grief.

## Waiting Periods

Another popular legislative approach to the question of abortion has been the mandatory waiting period. In 1983, in the first parental consent case from Akron, the Supreme Court also struck down that city's twenty-four-hour waiting period. The Court held that Akron's waiting period law lacked any medical basis, added financial burdens of extra travel, and increased the medical risks associated with delay by causing scheduling difficulties. In 1989 the Pennsylvania legislature nonetheless enacted a waiting period provision. A federal district court early in 1990 ordered that the provision not be enforced pending outcome of a suit that was filed immediately upon enactment to challenge the law.[13]

As we have seen, these laws suggest, and are probably *meant* to suggest, that women routinely make grave decisions about abortion rashly and that they will think better of the idea if only they are sent away from the clinic and told to sleep on it. Apart from their value as propaganda, laws imposing such waiting periods seem to be written in the belief that they may pass constitutional muster where an outright prohibition would not, while at the same time they will act as an absolute obstacle for at least some women who might otherwise obtain legal abortions. For example, in Minnesota, where abortion services are available in just five of the state's eighty-seven counties and where women may have to drive seven hours to obtain abortion services, a court found that a forty-eight-hour waiting period after parental notification by the physician might require a young woman seeking an abortion to travel to an abortion provider twice or to spend up to three additional days in a city far from her home.[14] This is bound to lead at least some rural women either to abandon hope of getting abortions or to seek unsafe, illegal alternatives closer to where they live.

At least in the American context, these laws won't in any event serve their ostensible purpose of fostering consideration of the gravity of a decision to abort a pregnancy. What woman who would take lightly the decision to have an abortion will rethink it more seriously simply because a law says she has to wait a day before having the procedure? By contrast, some of the many women who have considered the decision carefully will be among those for whom the legal requirement presents an absolute obstacle.

## Limiting the Reasons for Which Abortion Will Be Allowed

A new post-*Webster* twist on legislative compromise is the regime that purports to examine the reason a woman seeks an abortion. The new incarnation of this type of law—hospital review boards are, of course, the traditional version—was first enacted in Pennsylvania, which in the wake of *Webster* outlawed abortion for purposes of sex selection.[15] And a bill that its sponsors say would ban the use of abortion as a means of birth control was recently introduced in Alabama.[16] Legislators in Idaho, Minnesota, and Utah have followed suit with similar proposals.[17]

The idea of permitting abortion only for certain approved reasons probably appeals to many. For although a strong majority of the American population, almost 70 percent, believes that the decision on whether or not to have an abortion should not be subject to government interference,[18] an equally strong majority believes that abortion should not be used, for example, as a method of birth control.[19]

The fear that women are using abortion frivolously—say, to avoid the bother of inserting a diaphragm—appears to be widespread. In fact, half of all abortion patients used some form of contraception during the month in which they became pregnant.[20] Anyone who reflects even briefly on the way things are will not be surprised to learn that abortion is not a principal means of birth control in this country (unlike the Soviet Union, as we saw in Chapter 2). After all, a sexually active woman relying on abortion as her primary means of avoiding conception might be expected to have thirty or more abortions during her lifetime. But 84 percent of women who seek abortions here have never had an abortion before or have had only one.[21]

There is further evidence that women simply do not have abortions for frivolous reasons. Those who brought the challenge that resulted in the federal injunction against Pennsylvania's waiting-period law did not even attack the sex-selection provision because they believe it will have no practical effect on women.[22] Thus, it appears that those who draft such legislation are simply trying to exploit the widespread opposition to certain uses of abortion as a back-door path to their goal of outlawing abortion altogether. They obviously hope to appeal to those voters who imagine women as impulsive and irrational, as preferring the risk of surgery to the regular and disciplined use of basic contraceptives.[23]

But the Alabama bill, for example, is not really about "birth control" abortions at all. Notwithstanding the description given it by its supporters, the bill's text reveals a blanket prohibition on abortion, with only narrow exceptions for cases of rape and incest, abortion to save the pregnant woman's life, and cases in which the fetus is so deformed that it would not survive. It is as harsh an antiabortion measure as any pro-life advocate could hope to enact. It is false advertising to describe it as a modest compromise.

Nor is it clear how Pennsylvania intends to enforce *its* law. As we have already seen, enforcement presents serious problems of invading privacy that, in any effective scheme, would rise to the level of constitutional violation. Indeed, even the Alabama law with the exception for rape would require an inquiry not merely into whether the woman was raped but whether it is the rapist's child that she is carrying. For example, under a California law in the years before *Roe v. Wade* that made an exception to its prohibition on abortion in cases of rape, a woman who was raped was denied an abortion because she was unable to prove that she had not been impregnated by her husband.[24]

## Abortion Funding

Another restriction, one long approved by the Supreme Court as constitutional, is the restriction on public funding of abortion. In the *Webster* case the Court permitted Missouri to prohibit the use of any public facilities for, or the participation by any public employee in, performing or assisting any nontherapeutic abortion. The Supreme Court's conclusion that the Constitution permits government to cut off such public support does not embody any decision by the Court that such a resolution is a wise or a moral one, only that the woman's right to choose includes no right to public funding or to the use of public facilities. Because the Court in *Roe v. Wade* based the woman's constitutional right on a purely *negative* notion of privacy grounded in the right to be "left alone" rather than in a broader and more *positive* concept of maternal "liberty" informed by ideals of gender equality, it may be unsurprising that the Court later held that government has no constitutional duty to help women exercise that right.[25]

Although withholding public funds from the private abortion choice may have some intuitive appeal—each individual is free to choose, but no one who objects has to pay for it—it is, within the context of a system that provides governmental assistance for medical services and particularly for childbirth, perhaps the most peculiar of all the legislative compromises on the question of abortion.

To begin with, it is odd to suggest that any individual has a "right" not to pay for those governmental programs with which he or she morally disagrees. Recall former Senator Birch Bayh's comparison with the Vietnam War: We certainly had a right, as a matter of collective will, to stop that war altogether, but while the war went on, no citizen had a right on moral grounds to keep his or her tax dollars from being used in its prosecution. Our system of government could hardly function if the law were otherwise.

Besides, any supposed right not to help pay for abortions would in a sense be frustrated so long as *any* public money contributes to that end. For public money spent on abortions in, say, California or New York is public money not available to meet the other needs of those states, some of which will then be met through federal taxes collected from everyone, including taxpayers in, say, Missouri. And anybody who believes in an imagined right to withhold his tax support from abortion could have no quarrel with a possible system in which the dollars spent on abortion would come only from individuals who affirmatively agreed to allow their taxes to be used in this manner, perhaps by a tax return checkoff like that for presidential campaign funds. Thus, the withholding of *all* public support is either largely pointless or a form of overkill from the perspective of any supposed right of objecting taxpayers.

Nor is there any other perspective from which it makes genuine sense. For the collective decision to end funding for abortion is not at all like a collective decision to end a war. Insofar as abortion itself remains legal, denying public funds for abortion is simply a collective decision that abortion be available only to the rich and that abortion should remain, as Mary Ann Glendon has put it, not just the woman's prerogative but the woman's problem. The denial to some women of the right to choose to terminate a pregnancy, while others can exercise that right freely, is really no compromise at all and seems particularly immoral when the line between the two groups is based on something as unrelated to the situation of the pregnancy or to any right of the unborn, and as frequently beyond a woman's control, as personal wealth.

## Restricting Clinics

Another type of restriction that states have placed on abortion directly limits the provision of abortion services. Laws of this type regulate abortion clinics and the procedures that must be used to perform abortions. But the simplicity of the procedure early in pregnancy and the extraordinary safety record of abortion clinics in the years of legal abortion in America (fewer than 10 of the 1,600,000 women undergoing legal abortions each year now die as a result of the procedure[26]) suggest that these restrictions simply represent another indirect way of placing obstacles in the path of women who would choose abortion.

Consider, for example, the regulations adopted by Illinois that were challenged in the lawsuit settled in November 1989, just before the case was to be argued in the Supreme Court. These regulations, which covered early abortions, were really medically appropriate only to procedures requiring a general anesthetic or a surgical incision. While the regulations would have added significant costs to the provision of abortion services—driving some abortion clinics out of business or greatly raising the price of an abortion for a woman seeking one—none was medically justified, and some (for example, a requirement of a large procedure room) were apparently medically unwise.[27]

### Earlier Cutoff Dates

It seems probable that one last, increasingly popular kind of "compromise" proposal will involve the selection of a brief, fixed period—somewhere between four weeks and fourteen weeks from conception, probably—within which legal abortions, perhaps even with public funds in some instances, will be generally available. Under such proposals there would be a rigorously enforced ban on all abortions past that initial fixed period except for those few later abortions that hospital panels certify are necessary to avoid a substantial likelihood of the women's deaths.

Although such proposals have more to commend them than the other cutbacks on *Roe* we have considered, they seem less defensible than *Roe* itself. No one who objects to *Roe* on the basis that every embryo is an unborn baby from the moment of conception can find much comfort in a rule that routinely sacrifices unborn babies under the age of two or three months in order to save some of those who are older (and who escape the back-alley abortionist's knife). And no one who firmly believes in a woman's right to self-determination can be much appeased by a rule that arbitrarily denies such self-determination in a fairly blatant exercise in vote trading. Any time limit is inherently arbitrary to some degree, but at least *Roe*'s focus on fetal viability—when the fetus, given current technology, can survive independently—reflects the special concern that a woman not be forced to use her body to bring a new life to the point where *it* can lead a separate existence but *she* no longer can.

Agreements to disagree, and to cut things down the middle in the name of civil peace, have undoubted appeal—which is why some such previability cutoff dates may be expected to pass—but the appeal is a necessarily limited one when it buys only a little peace and when the "things" that are being cut down the middle are not things at all but people or at least beings that many will continue to regard as people.

## Cruel Compromises

The overarching problem with all these purported compromises is that they are not compromises at all. Many of the laws put forward to stake out what is supposedly a middle ground in the abortion debate, rather than meaningfully protecting either life or choice, randomly frustrate both and do not move us closer to a society of caring, responsible people.

In the case of any given woman, these laws will either act as an absolute obstacle to abortion or will not stand in the way. To the extent that women have abortions despite such laws, most of their proponents will be dissatisfied. To the extent that women are stopped from having abortions, we will still be faced with the disruptions of life, and the unwanted children, that those who oppose the restrictions want to prevent. Indeed, it seems obvious that most of these solutions are unsatisfactory in that they promise abortion rights in principle but deny them in practice to those who are least able to bear the burden of motherhood—particularly the young, the uneducated, the rural, and the nonwhite.

Other measures are not real compromises because they don't even serve the purpose of decreasing the number of abortions. They are bizarre and irrational because they seem to have *only* unintended consequences.

The clearest example, the example on which we have the best data, is the parental notification and consent law. Statistically these laws do not appear to cause any gross decrease in the number of abortions performed on teenagers. For example, in Minnesota, where the parental notification law was in operation for six years between 1981 and 1986, changes in the rates of pregnancy, abortion, and childbirth among teenagers covered by the law during the time it was in effect were little different from the changes in those rates among eighteen- and nineteen-year-olds whom the law did not cover.[28]

Parental notification or consent laws *will* at least force some minors to go out of state to get abortions. The number of Massachusetts minors getting abortions in Maine, for example, rose from zero before a consent law went into effect in 1981 to 219 in 1987.[29] Yet of the 3,573 petitions for judicial bypass of the notification requirement during the first four and a half years of the Minnesota statute's operation, only *nine* were denied.

In practice, the effects of parental consent or notification laws appear to be much more complex than the simple deterrence of abortion. It appears that these laws take their toll primarily in terms of severe emotional stress for the pregnant girl at a time of trauma in her life and of abuse of the girl by parents who would not otherwise have been informed. In families where real communication goes on, such laws are redundant or insulting. And in families where communication has broken down, such laws are unlikely to facilitate respectful dialogue between children in crisis and their parents. Perhaps a statute could successfully legislate a "right" for parents to control a daughter's decision and to force an unwilling child to carry a fetus to term or, when the parent refuses to become a grandparent, to force an abortion on a daughter who wants to become a mother. But no statute could realistically hope to legislate love or communication between parents and children. Besides, as we have seen, this type of statute can cause horrible consequences in isolated cases, not cases that anyone supporting the law would have had any reason to single out for such tragic results, but cases in which unpredictable intrafamily dynamics trigger disaster. The result will be unintended, and the destruction frighteningly random, striking like lightning.

No Solomon would have decreed splitting the baby *this* way. Indeed, this is a good time to remember that the essence of Solomon's wisdom lay not in splitting the baby but in using that suggestion as a way to discover the truth and to create a world that would be better for all concerned.[30]

## Humane Options

If the clash of absolutes is a clash between life (the life of a fetus) on the one hand, and liberty (that of a woman) on the other, solutions that split the difference—denying some fetuses life and some women liberty—hardly offer a solution.

To the extent that we think of the fetus as an unborn human child, a number of the philosophical and moral arguments in favor of letting women choose for themselves may leave us emotionally cold. For example, while it is easy to say that even parents have no *legal* duty today to rescue a child who needs their aid, many will feel that parents have a *moral* duty to do just that and that our legal system ought to move toward an imposition of enforceable obligations and responsibilities to-

ward those who are in need of help. Those who have such feelings need
to ask themselves, though, whether those feelings run more strongly
toward a pregnant woman than, say, toward a man whose daughter
needs one of his kidneys or a section of his liver to survive. Are you
more willing to legislate *mothers'* duties as a first step toward a more
duty-based legal order than you are to legislate duties whose burdens
fall equally on men? If the answer is yes, that may well signal a sexist
distinction between the role of a mother and the role of a father. Still,
many a father *would* willingly donate a kidney to save his child's life. And
some would be prepared to force a father to make just such a sacrifice.

Although one can argue that in having an abortion, the woman doesn't
necessarily want to *kill* the fetus but only to be free of it, many will feel
that the very act of abortion, given current technology, represents a
decision to kill and not simply a refusal to help or an unwillingness to
sacrifice.

So let us address those feelings in opposition to letting women
choose that genuinely reflect not a sexist view of a woman's "place" but
a humane concern for the fetus as an unborn baby, as a helpless member
of the human family but a family member nonetheless. From the perspective of such concern, can anyone who truly cares about human life
be indifferent to the suffering of unwanted children? Not even someone
who regards every abortion as wrong is likely to think it just doesn't
matter whether children whose mothers do not want them are born. For
many of these children, adoption is an unrealistic alternative in our society, either because of birth defects, or because of the child's race, or
because after giving birth, the mother cannot bring herself to give up her
child even though she does not welcome it as hers. The compassionate
impulse that leads everyone to agree that the plight of such unwanted
children *does* matter no doubt plays an important part in the decisions of
many women not to have children, to use contraception, and, if they
have become pregnant, reluctantly to choose abortion.

Women who make that choice to end a pregnancy ordinarily recognize the gravity of what they are doing. "Compromises" that pretend
otherwise, that treat each woman as a stranger to her fetus and pit the
two against one another, are lacking in human understanding and are not
plausible moves toward a world in which people reach out to each other.

## Postnatal Care

The most obvious thing all of this suggests about how we might best find our way around the conflict between the woman's liberty and the fetus's life is that we must reduce the number of situations in which women are pregnant but do not want to be.

The ways to do this are far from novel, but the truth is that we in the United States have never really tried them. First, we could encourage people to *want* children by making it easier for them to care for infants once they are born. Affordable postnatal health care and mandatory maternity and paternity leaves would be a beginning. The provision of other postnatal services—especially good child care and flexible time arrangements in the workplace—might go a long way toward reducing the crushing financial burden that a child can impose, particularly in an age when families need two incomes just to get by.

In Europe, as Professor Mary Ann Glendon has noted, measures like these are routine. The public health services in most Western European countries provide much broader care in general than that provided by public health services in the United States. In addition, a majority of the countries of Western Europe mandate a paid six-month maternity leave. In Sweden the leave time is nine months, and it may be divided between the infant's parents. Some European countries provide as much as one full year of additional unpaid leave, with protection of the woman's job and benefits. And most Western European countries provide day care for youngsters between three and five as part of the system of public education.[31]

This same approach can also prevent one of the major life dislocations, having to give up working, that motherhood has traditionally imposed on women—one of the dislocations that has led women to demand control of their reproductive freedom in the first place. The promise, and the hard-won reality, of equality will remain empty for a pregnant woman who wants to have a baby but for whom motherhood means a loss of social and economic liberty because it forces her into a frustrating life at home when she would prefer work outside—or, painfully, into a working life with a latchkey child, a life in which she cannot ensure that her child has the guidance, direction, and support that the child needs and that the mother desperately wants to give.

## Birth Control Education and the Provision of Contraceptives

A second familiar but still-underutilized approach to reducing the number of situations in which women are pregnant and don't want to be is, of course, to prevent pregnancy through the only proven means for doing so: sex education and the wide availability of birth control. Some will no doubt think that the only moral means of pregnancy prevention is abstention from sex. But it doesn't work as policy because people don't abstain. This is the lesson of human history.

In addition, equality for women must mean the same ability to express human sexuality without the burden of pregnancy and childbirth that has always been, by accident of biology, available to men. With technology that is no longer even new, this equality is within reach. And indeed, sex education and birth control work. In Sweden a law was enacted in 1974 that was designed to increase the use of birth control in order to reduce the rate of abortion. This law put into place an aggressive program of birth control education and provided for reductions in the cost of contraceptives. The result has been a sharp decrease in the rate of both teenage pregnancy and abortion in Sweden.[32]

Of course, some of those who view abortion as the taking of a human life, an absolute wrong, also object to a progressive sex education policy perhaps because they believe that it condones premarital or nonprocreative or irresponsible sexuality, which they regard as immoral. But anyone with such an objection must remember the hierarchy of values in which she or he believes. If one truly believes that abortion is *murder,* preventing it through sex education is surely a lesser of two evils. To the extent that a person is willing to do just about anything to stop abortion *except* prevent pregnancy, much is revealed about that person's *true* values and his or her reasons for opposing abortion, as we will see later in this chapter.

## Using Technology to Circumvent Destiny: Better Contraceptive Techniques

Other paths around the clash of absolutes lie in science and technology. Technological developments could resolve, or at least reorient, the abortion question in three ways.

First, it would make sense to pour significant sums of research and development money into new forms of contraception that will be safer or will feel less awkward or unnatural to use than currently available methods.[33] Condoms are imperfect because men don't like the way they reduce sensitivity. Diaphragms are at times neglected in passion, or are left in the drawer because their use may interfere with the spontaneity people want to associate with their sexual relationships, or are rejected by women who are led to think that "good girls" resist sex. The current generation of birth control pills present medical risks to some women and may have unpleasant side effects: weight gain, swollen, painful breasts, headaches, and mood changes, to name a few, and which for many are understandable disincentives to their use.

An absolutely safe, highly effective, nonintrusive contraceptive could prevent an enormous number of unwanted pregnancies. Even slightly improved contraceptives would reduce the demand for abortions.

Several alternatives to available contraceptive technologies are in effective use in some parts of Europe or are at least being examined seriously. For women these include: contraceptive implants placed under the skin; injectable microspheres and microcapsules that provide a constant dose of a contraceptive hormone over several months; monthly injectables; vaginal rings that release hormones; nasal sprays that prevent ovulation; and, apparently, intracervical implants to neutralize sperm by using an electrical current to deter migration across the cervix and toward the fallopian tubes.[34]

It is also easy to envision new contraceptives in which the focus is not exclusively upon the *woman*'s reproductive system. For men the alternatives being studied include: a long-lasting insertion that blocks a man's vas deferens, the internal sperm delivery tube, and lowers its level of acidity, in turn limiting the mobility of sperm that might make their way through an incomplete blockade; ultrasound treatments to suppress sperm production; gossypol, a chemical found in cottonseed oil that may have the same effect; and hormones that disrupt sperm development without decreasing sex drive.[35]

Perhaps most promising are proposed long-lasting but reversible contraceptives, either mechanical or chemical, that will require an affirmative act above and beyond sexual intercourse if one is to begin a pregnancy. Many of the alternatives now being studied, both male and female, would use drugs or surgical procedures that create a temporary, reversible infertility. The development of such technologies has potential for dramatically shifting our conception of what is "natural."[36] Human beings obviously aren't "hard-wired" for birth control. Perhaps males may even be biologically programmed to distribute their genes as widely as possible. Thus these biomedical developments might be resisted almost instinctively by many. But we weren't "programmed" for aviation or television either, and it would be shortsighted to doom the debate about abortion to the fairly dismal set of options our ancestors had to face.

Of course, despite their promise, these technologies alone could not entirely eliminate the demand for abortions. First, no known contraceptive is 100 percent effective, nor is any future one likely to be. Second, even if a fully effective technology were found, people would still have to have the opportunity to use it and would have to choose in the first instance to do so—unless it were placed in the water like fluoride, an option raising its own difficulties.

Lastly, the failure to use contraceptives and contraceptive failure when some method is used, are obviously not the only reasons women have abortions. Sometimes women choose abortions because the fetuses they carry have severe genetic or medical abnormalities. And there will always be some pregnancies that *become* unwanted when a woman's circumstances change in ways that make it extremely difficult for her to give a new child her love and support without neglecting other deeply felt obligations, often to other children.

### Newer Technologies: RU-486

A second and more novel technological route around the dilemma is the development of an abortion pill. While some regimes of oral contraception, taken daily, may operate as abortifacients because they may prevent a fertilized ovum from becoming implanted in the uterine wall, until recently there was no effective pill that a woman could safely take on a one-time basis, after discovering she was pregnant, to induce an abortion. The first version of such a pill, called RU-486, has been developed in France and is already widely used there. Indeed, it is currently being used to perform almost one-quarter of all French abortions.[37]

Studies have shown RU-486, which is not now approved for use in the United States, to be more than 95 percent effective as an abortifacient when used within seven weeks of the last menstrual period.[38] It is extremely effective in causing shedding of the fertilized embryo after implantation in the uterine wall.[39] It is taken in conjunction with the hormone prostaglandin, which causes uterine contractions. The wide availability of RU-486 could bring truly revolutionary results. A large percentage of surgical abortions are now sought early in pregnancy, at a time when RU-486 might be effective. Fully half of all abortions in the United States currently take place within the first eight weeks of pregnancy.[40]

In France a pregnant woman can get RU-486 at a clinic. She returns forty-eight hours later to receive a prostaglandin injection. She stays for three hours, since prostaglandin may cause nausea, vomiting, and, in a small number of cases, heavy bleeding.[41] Each day more than a hundred women in France take RU-486. More than ten thousand French women have already taken the drug, while four thousand women in the United States, Britain, China, and other countries have participated in studies in which they have taken it.[42]

In a sense, of course, neither RU-486 nor any other abortifacient pill really solves, or even circumvents, the problem of abortion. Although the fact that these abortifacients can be effective at an earlier stage of pregnancy than can either the vacuum aspiration or suction techniques may make them less objectionable to some than these currently-used methods of abortion, those who oppose abortion from the moment of conception may well oppose it just as vehemently when it is performed with a simple pill. Indeed, some opponents of letting women choose for themselves whether or not to end a pregnancy find upsetting the way in which they believe a drug like RU-486 might both conceal from the woman the reality of what she is destroying and withhold from the public its current methods of exerting control over that choice.

One unique aspect of the abortion problem is that the woman's exercise of her liberty to choose not to continue a pregnancy generally requires another person, typically a doctor, for its exercise. Making abortion an essentially self-administered procedure that can be performed safely and completely outside a clinic or hospital would change this forever. Many of the arguments, and to some extent the laws, about abortion would be made largely irrelevant by a widely available abortion pill.[43] The traditional publicly regulated nexus, the doctor-patient relationship, would virtually vanish, although a pharmacist-consumer relationship might entail similar opportunities for public oversight.

Thus, what RU-486 would at minimum do is transform the abortion debate by making abortion a truly private decision and by ending the stigma and social opprobrium that still attach, almost everywhere, to those doctors who perform surgical abortions.[44]

## Marketing the Drug

Proponents of RU-486 argue that it is a medical development that cannot be denied to women. And considering both the safety of RU-486 for women when compared with surgical abortion and the consistently high number of abortions performed in the United States, it is hard from the perspective of medical safety to deny the force of this argument.

Already, however, the advocates of RU-486 foresee difficulty bringing the drug to market in the United States. To begin with, there is the threat of boycott from groups that oppose abortion. Indeed, this was the strategy adopted by French antiabortion groups that opposed RU-486. The threat of boycott succeeded in intimidating the drug's developer, Groupe Roussel Uclaf, from manufacturing the drug. Significantly, Roussel's majority shareholder, the West German concern Hoechst A.G., put pressure on Roussel not to market RU-486 in France, in part out of concern about a boycott by far more militant American pro-life groups against its United States subsidiary, which has six billion dollars in annual sales. Ultimately the French government, which owned a 36.25 percent stake in Roussel, stepped in, declared the drug "the moral property of women," and ordered Roussel to make the drug available.[45]

An American boycott might be ineffectual for a number of reasons. First, in light of the potential market, it is unlikely that a boycott would be financially effective. Even if Roussel is intimidated by the threat of boycott, other companies might not be. The West German corporation Schering, for example, has developed a drug similar to RU-486. Even if Schering retreats, other companies are working on similar drugs.[46] Indeed, some financial experts have suggested that in the face of a threatened boycott, a small company is more likely than a large one to choose to market RU-486 because a smaller company is likely to face smaller risks and relatively greater potential benefits than a large company.[47]

Even if private companies are intimidated into refusing to distribute RU-486, nonprofit organizations have shown an interest in doing so. Roussel has conducted discussions with nonprofit organizations in Britain, Sweden, and the United States, all of which wish to purchase the drug at minimum cost and distribute it in their home countries. Under other suggested distribution schemes, China (where RU-486 has been approved for use) or the World Health Organization would buy the RU-486 patent and manufacture the pill for the entire world. Roussel is reluctant to relinquish its patent, however, because the drug shows great promise in treating certain ovarian, prostate, and breast cancers, glaucoma, and endometriosis (which causes infertility) and in dilating the cervix so as to ease difficult or prolonged labor.[48]

The story of the introduction of the birth control pill may be suggestive of how the new abortifacient pill will become available. While fear of a similar boycott initially caused many U.S. drug companies to defer production of oral contraceptives, the G. D. Searle Company ignored the threat and, in the late 1950s, began their manufacture.[49]

Although the pill had already been approved by the Food and Drug

Administration (FDA) as a treatment for menstrual disorders,[50] other drug companies refused to pursue its contraceptive possibilities. In 1959 Searle alone applied to the FDA to license the pill as a contraceptive, a decision later described as "going out on the longest limb in pharmaceutical history."[51] The president of Parke, Davis & Company telephoned John Searle to warn him that "a birth control pill was 'crazy' business,"[52] and Parke, Davis stated publicly that "[i]ts policy is to keep out of the contraceptive field, and it will never recommend, nor even test, [the drug] for contraceptive purposes—only as a therapeutic agent for disorders of the female reproductive system."[53] Indeed, Parke, Davis waited until 1964, four years after the FDA had approved use of the pill as an oral contraceptive, to reverse its decision. The Ortho Division of Johnson & Johnson was also interested in marketing the pill, but it was not until 1962 that it brought its product, Ortho-Novum, to the U.S. market.[54]

Searle's choice to pursue the contraceptive uses of the pill turned out to be a wise business decision. According to Dr. Pasquale DeFelice, the FDA official who licensed the pill as a contraceptive, "I knew what was going to happen once we licensed it. I knew that birth control pills would be flying out the windows. Everybody and her sister would be taking it. . . . I was stupid. I should be a millionaire. I should have bought Searle stock, but I didn't. Somehow I thought I shouldn't since I was the person who approved it. But I have often wondered why I never got an award for okaying the pill. It changed the whole economy of the United States."[55]

The threatened boycott never materialized. And although right-to-life groups, which are much better organized than anti-birth-control forces were in the early 1960s, may indeed boycott a company that chooses to produce RU-486, there is reason to think that defying such a boycott would prove even wiser from a business standpoint, considering the changes that have occurred in women's attitudes toward control of reproduction since the pill was first released.

## FDA Approval

If some company or group does seek FDA approval to distribute RU-486 in the United States, the regulatory process will present another hurdle. The FDA might, for political reasons, choose not to approve the drug for use.

It is not clear where the Bush administration stands on RU-486. The President might be pleased to have the drug approved, especially if a "neutral" panel, rather than any identifiable Bush administration official, could be seen to make the decision. Approval of RU-486 might reduce the current political furor over abortion and thereby spare the Republican party one of the worst dilemmas it has ever confronted.

Even if the President were a strong advocate of suppressing the drug, he would not necessarily succeed. The FDA approval process is, at least nominally, run by a panel of medical experts. Although the panel could be stacked with known foes of abortion, those experts might not be able to come up with appropriate evidence to suppress RU-486 under the scientific criteria set up for drug approval. Moreover, Congress has oversight and appropriations authority over the FDA. Thus, just as they did when AIDS drugs faced bureaucratic barriers at the FDA during the Reagan administration,[56] members of Congress could exert pressure to accelerate the RU-486 approval process. The likelihood of that increases every time a pro-choice position is shown to have electoral appeal.

If RU-486 were not approved as an abortifacient, it might nonetheless gain availability through FDA approval for some other use. As we have seen, RU-486 has shown promise as a treatment for a number of medical problems. Once a drug is approved for one purpose by the FDA, there is normally nothing to prevent its dispensation by medical prescription for another purpose. Although this path to a drug's introduction is far from ideal and entails obvious risks of adverse side-effects associated with the drug's use in an unauthorized context, it certainly represents one possible option.

Indeed, this is how the birth control pill originally became available. Searle initially asked for FDA approval of the drug for treating only menstrual disorders, even though the company was aware of its contraceptive effects. Searle conducted extensive additional testing before applying for permission to market the pill as a contraceptive.[57] The FDA first licensed oral contraceptives solely to treat menstrual disorders and required a "warning" on the package that women taking the drug would not ovulate. In 1959, to nobody's surprise, "many women suddenly had menstrual disorders requiring treatment with the pill, women who had never seemed to have menstrual problems before."[58]

Nor is RU-486 the only known abortifacient drug. One drug already licensed by the FDA for prevention of stomach ulcers in patients who take large doses of anti-inflammatory drugs for arthritis, misoprostol, is known to cause changes in the muscle tone of the uterus that trigger miscarriages.[59] Misoprostol is currently being marketed by Searle. The FDA requires that women of childbearing age to whom physicians prescribe misoprostol be tested for pregnancy and warned not to become pregnant while taking the drug.[60] However, historical evidence suggests that some physicians will assist women in obtaining relief from unwanted pregnancies by prescribing an effective abortifacient drug. Because misoprostol was not developed specifically as an abortifacient, its optimum dose and effectiveness in producing abortions are not now known.[61]

In addition, although the FDA "has not approved post-coital contraceptive methods, physicians in the United States have used post-coital methods of contraception for at least the past eight years, particularly to treat rape victims."[62] It seems that some doctors currently prescribe high doses of a widely available birth control pill, Ovral, following an unprotected act of sexual intercourse. This procedure has been found to prevent pregnancy when the pills are taken within three days after intercourse. Because the procedure operates on the fertilized ovum, it may be viewed as an abortifacient.[63]

In any event, if RU-486 remains unavailable or if it is available but not approved for use in inducing abortion, the incentives to flout the law and to use RU-486 (or another abortifacient pill) will grow as other forms of abortion become subject to greater degrees of state regulation. If the Supreme Court continues to cut back on *Roe v. Wade,* giving the states increasing latitude to restrict abortion, some states will choose to regulate abortion more closely, and we may find RU-486 an illegal drug in great demand, particularly because ending a pregnancy with RU-486 is far less expensive than a surgical abortion,[64] and because its relative safety and ease of use may make it a highly attractive alternative.

Needless to say, America has an unhappy history with illegal drugs, substances that, unlike RU-486, cannot even be legitimately *produced* because they serve no legal purpose. Regulating the transaction between a seller and a purchaser of a single dose of an illegal drug is vastly more difficult than regulating the provision by a doctor of surgical services to pregnant women. And the demand for RU-486, particularly when the alternative is a back-alley surgical abortion, will come from all strata of society. Demand is likely to be strongest from the powerful middle class: the rate of abortion among women from families with incomes over twenty-five thousand dollars is said to be dramatically higher than that for women from families with lower incomes.[65] Considering the ease of travel to Europe, a black market in the drug is almost certain. If President Bush's War on Drugs is an uphill battle, if Prohibition was unwinnable, a ban on RU-486 will be a lost cause.

### The More Distant Future: An Artificial Womb

A third technological development that would drastically alter the clash over abortion lies in the more remote future but is worth thinking about even now. It would be the development of an artificial womb or placenta. In theory, at least, such a womb might be either freestanding or incorporated into a human host, who might even be male. Even though the idea of a laboratory-based fetal "incubator" still seems quite fantastic, and the vision of a "pregnant" man even more so, neither possibility can be ruled out. In any case, even if such technology never actually becomes available, we might find it instructive to dwell on how it would reshape the abortion question if it were available.

One effect of any such technology would be to accelerate the time of fetal "viability," the time at which the fetus can survive outside the original mother's uterus, although with artificial support. An earlier point of viability based on advances in medical technology has long been predicted. Indeed, that prediction, along with improvements for pregnant women in the safety of abortion procedures, led Justice O'Connor to say in 1983 that the trimester approach of *Roe v. Wade* was "on a collision course with itself."[66]

But in the almost twenty years since *Roe* the hypothesized advance has not arrived. Indeed, some who support the right to choose abortion have suggested that further developments toward an earlier point of fetal viability are not likely. They have argued that given the underdevelopment of fetal organs, viability is simply not possible much before twenty-four weeks of gestational age, a "biological threshold"[67] for fetal survival outside the womb. The American Medical Association and other organizations of health care professionals have taken the position that the development of fetal lung capacity in particular precludes fetal survival independent of the woman before about twenty-three to twenty-four weeks of gestation.[68] And a task force report commissioned by the governor of New York State concludes that the development of technology to permit extrauterine survival "between a three-day embryo culture and the 24th week of gestation"[69] is not possible in the foreseeable future, leading Justice Blackmun to conclude that "the threshold of fetal viability is, and will remain, no different from what it was at the time *Roe* was decided."[70]

Maybe so, but maybe not. Predictions of inflexible technological roadblocks have been notoriously inaccurate in modern times. This prophecy may be no exception. A fetus in its mother's womb, after all, receives oxygen through its umbilical cord, notwithstanding the immaturity of the fetal lungs. There is no intrinsic reason why the source of oxygen and nutrition for the fetus must be the woman who supplied the ovum or in whose uterus the ovum was first implanted.

Long before the twenty-third week of gestation, cell differentiation occurs "under the concerted control of numerous biological signal substances—including hormones and regulatory molecules—that are either produced by the fetus, the woman's organs, or the placenta."[71] The fetus's bodily functions are in effect performed by the womb. While research concerning these processes has not gone beyond its most elementary stages, there need be no theoretical barrier to the development of an environment outside the mother to permit the independent survival and continued development of the fetus at ever earlier stages of gestation. A fetus brought to term in an artificial womb, without the myriad developmental influences of the mother, with her complex emotional and intellectual life, may well be different in important respects from a healthy baby brought to term the "natural" way. Whether computers controlling biochemical processes could ever successfully simulate human gestation is a question much like that of whether computers will ever be able to "think" and "feel."[72] And however faithfully any such development might mimic human processes, some may object to it on moral or theological grounds.

Less troublesome philosophically and more immediately accessible technically is the removal of an embryo from one woman for gestation in the uterus of another, a voluntary surrogate mother. As the New York State Task Force on Life and Law's reference to a "three-day embryo culture" suggests, *every* embryo is, at least at the outset, theoretically viable, in the sense that if it is removed from its natural mother not just after twenty-four weeks of gestation but during the first five days after fertilization, it can still develop into a human child. Human embryos have, in this sense, not one point of viability, but two. Indeed, children have already been born to women other than those in whom they were conceived, after a process called "uterine lavage and embryo transfer," or surrogate embryo transfer (SET).[73]

In the SET procedure a fertilized embryo is removed from one woman's uterus by washing the uterine wall with saline solution. The embryo is then transferred directly to a recipient woman's uterus by use of a uterine catheter.[74] This procedure can be performed "some five days after fertilization."[75] One commentator has accordingly observed that the "technique of cryopreservation" (embryo freezing) "coupled with the method of embryo transfer and uterine lavage, may extend the moment of viability back to the very moment of conception."[76]

One can quite readily imagine the development of techniques for the transfer of embryos and, later, fetuses, from one woman to another at later and later stages of pregnancy. Ultimately the two points of fetal viability, now set at about five days and at about twenty-four weeks of gestation, might well converge.

Either the development of an artificial womb or the perfection of embryo transfer technology beyond the first few days of pregnancy would in practical reality separate the two analytically distinct questions raised by the debate about abortion that have heretofore remained practically inseparable—the question of the imposition on a woman's liberty, and the question of the destruction of a fetus for which one is responsible. Of course, we can imagine situations even today in which these two aspects are in tension. This may now occur, for example, when a woman who has agreed to carry a couple's embryo to term (a surrogate mother) seeks an abortion that the biological parents oppose or, more tellingly, when she refuses to have an abortion that the biological parents seek. Until now, the act of abortion has included both the removal of the fetus from the woman's uterus, thus ending its imposition upon her liberty, and the fetus's destruction. That knot may come untied sooner than some suppose.

What would we make of the ability to save the life of a fetus with no continuing imposition on a woman's liberty? If a technology were developed that permitted resolution of the abortion question without loss of life *or* liberty, society would have to deal with the trade-off between the increased risk to the pregnant woman (from requiring removal of the embryo or fetus) and the increased chance of the fetus's survival (from requiring its placement in a surrogate mother or in an artificial womb). And society would also have to address the entire strategy of seeking to replicate, outside women, something that has always seemed special and indeed miraculous about womanhood. Some may well believe that the very notion is a perversion of how technology should be put to human use. Still, the prospect offers, at least in theory, one end run around the current clash of absolutes.

### Shedding New Light on Old Attitudes: Splitting the Woman's Right in Two

Such a technological development would force us to reexamine the beliefs that underlie whatever support we may feel for a pregnant woman's right to choose abortion. Indeed, even the prospect of such a development alters the picture considerably, for we can use the very *idea* to perform a revealing thought experiment.

Many would find the solution offered by an artificial womb—"abortion" without the destruction of the fetus—unsatisfactory or profoundly offensive. Why? One reason may be that part of the intuitive appeal of recognizing a woman's right to choose abortion is that it affirms the special value of motherhood by firmly locating the decision to become a mother in the woman whose body, mind, and genetic material are at stake. It permits her to control her own procreation, to prevent the unconsented-to use of her genetic material in the creation of another human being. The idea of having a child alive somewhere in the world, a child to whom one is a stranger, is deeply unsettling for many. Most of us may intuitively feel that the continued survival of an unwanted fetus, its development into a child by governmental command, is an invasion of the personality from which each of us has a right to be protected.

We may think, in particular, that the state should have no greater authority to preserve the life of a fetus when the woman doesn't want a child than to take a woman's ovum (or, for that matter, a man's sperm) and make an embryo of it. Surely the state must be forbidden from "kidnapping" our chromosomes for its own purposes, from saying, "If you do not choose to breed, the state will breed for you by confiscating part of you." Recognizing each individual's "right" to control his or her own genetic material may be vital in decentralizing control over genetic material, in order to prevent an all-powerful state from making eugenic decisions (as in Nazi Germany), and vital, as well, in affirming the dignity and particularity of human reproduction and human relations. Yet when such a "right" entails destroying another human life, we must surely pause.

After all, any imagined "right" to control the fate of one's genetic material apart from one's right to choose whether or not to remain pregnant is a right that no one has in many circumstances today. One obviously has no right, for example, to kill one's offspring. If someone with a baby doesn't wish to have it, he or she can give the youngster up for adoption, but most assuredly the parent cannot *kill* the child. None of us has a right to a life free of the burden of knowing that, somewhere, one of our children lives. In this sense, an artificial womb or placenta, or the perfection of SET technology, could be said simply to hasten the point in time at which a "child" that can live outside its mother's womb, and over whose existence she has no control, will come into being.

Similarly, men do not now have any right to choose not to have a baby once they have impregnated a woman. Because women certainly have the right to decide *not* to terminate a pregnancy, we will not empower a man to force a woman to end the pregnancy for which he is partly responsible; thus any man's "right" to control the destiny of his genetic material necessarily ends when his sperm fertilizes an ovum. Viewed in this way, the development of an artificial womb would place women in the same position with regard to pregnancy as men. Given the possibility of an artificial womb, women would no longer be subjected to the extreme imposition on liberty that pregnancy entails. And they would be no more able than men are today, once pregnancy occurs, to insist that the life of the fetus be terminated.

Most people no doubt feel intuitively that a fetus occupies some middle ground between sperm and ova, on the one hand, and a newborn infant, on the other. Of course, a fetus, at least after it is firmly implanted in the wall of a uterus, unlike any given sperm or ovum, will—whether it is at that particular moment a person or not—at least develop into a person with the passage of time (unless it is among those that miscarry). Nonetheless it may be that, particularly early in pregnancy, a woman's liberty not merely to avoid pregnancy but to decide not to *have a child,* and in that sense to control her genetic material, should be deemed fundamental. It may be that the state, even if it could keep the fetus alive, has no interest strong enough to permit it to interfere with a woman's decision to abort, and to destroy, a fetus before some intermediate and important point of fetal development—such as the time of higher brain functioning.

It may be thought, too, that it would violate a woman's rights to offer her equality only by rendering her womanhood inconsequential and marginalizing her distinctiveness as a woman. This is the tradeoff offered by any prospect, such as an artificial womb or improved SET technology, that would vindicate a woman's right to be free of the burden of pregnancy but *not* her right to control the use of her genetic material in the creation of a child.

Still, a woman's moral claim that she has a right to choose a fetus-destroying abortion would be weakened if the fetus could be saved without the sustained imposition on liberty that is involved whenever a woman is forced to carry a pregnancy to term. If, on reflection, one's pro-choice views rest on a sense that a woman should be allowed to prevent her fetus from becoming a child even if it could become one without the woman's having to undergo a prolonged pregnancy, then perhaps, in a technologically transformed world, those views would have to yield to the claim to life of all but the most undeveloped fetus. When one fights for the abortion right in the name of something less than the liberty not to be molded physically and psychologically into a mother, one stands on shaky ground.

If an embryo could be extracted from a pregnant woman at any stage of its development without damaging it, in a procedure as safe and easy as the abortion that the woman might prefer, whether or not the state could then *require* the mother to extract the embryo alive rather than destroy it in such an abortion remains a profoundly difficult question. But the reason the question is so difficult is not that the mother necessarily has an individual right to destroy the embryo but, rather, that society might be justified in resisting the dehumanization—and the devaluation of women—that could follow if such state power were to be approved.

These are questions that we shall, no doubt, have to face before too long. A Louisiana law, as yet untested in the courts, forbids a couple to destroy their own frozen embryos.[77] It is just a matter of time before state power over one's genetic destiny is passed upon in some judicial challenge.

## Still More Light: How Technology Can Force Us to Confront the Unexamined Costs We Have Imposed on Women

Anyone who resists a woman's freedom to choose abortion in the belief that such resistance protects human life must come to grips with a further question. If the extensive exploration of technologies to improve fetal survivability seems unappealing, might one reason be an underlying attitude that, by comparison with any technological alternative, women represent cheap "baby machines"? Is that an attitude people can maintain without growing discomfort? The current system of nurturing fetuses to term seems inexpensive largely because people tend to think of pregnancy as a natural phenomenon with no economic costs. Most American jurisdictions indeed treat pregnancy as a wholly costless process and do not even acknowledge, let alone attempt to quantify, its economic price. This position differs from that of many other developed countries, which, for example, provide special support for mothers around the time of childbirth.[78] This treatment of pregnancy as economically valueless is, no doubt, related to the widely maintained failure to value other services traditionally performed by women.[79]

But embryo transfer simply could not be treated as a costless process, regardless of whether embryos were transferred into other women or into machines. The only remotely similar procedure currently available, in vitro fertilization and embryo implantation, can cost more than forty thousand dollars.[80]

If the state chose to forbid the destruction of any fetus that a woman did not wish to carry to term and required that it be incubated either in an artificial womb or in the body of a surrogate mother, the state would *have* to face the costs of enacting that choice into law. Indeed, former presidential counsel Lloyd Cutler has perceptively suggested that any time a woman is prevented by some government action or policy from ending a pregnancy that she does not want to continue, her body is in a sense being "taken" for the public's purposes.[81] This is a "taking" at least as surely as one's home might be taken for public use in order to build a hospital or to provide shelter for a homeless person. Just as that could not be done, under the Fifth Amendment to our Constitution, without "just compensation," so a woman's body should not be subject to conscription without payment—at least in the form of financial support for the health and welfare of the woman and her child.[82]

It is a curious feature of our legal system that we think it necessary for the government to compensate people when taking their *property* for public use but not when restricting their *liberty* for public purposes. But surely that anomaly would not lead us to tolerate governmental decisions to extract blood, or kidneys, or liver tissue without compensation, however clear and compelling the public need. Just as our law has been quicker to protect women's physical possessions from being taken when they say no than to protect their bodies from rape (how often do people think "no" means "yes" in the context of a theft prosecution, as Professor Susan Estrich has so insightfully asked?[83]), so it might be quite some time until Cutler's notion is translated into legal doctrine. But simply contemplating the development of techniques for saving a fetus after extracting it from a woman who decides not to continue her pregnancy makes the cost of "incubation" impossible to hide, impossible any longer to impose haphazardly on the female who conveniently happens to be the first carrier of the unborn life.

Even without new incubation devices, there would, of course, be significant costs associated with persuading women to choose to act as surrogates, particularly in light of the restrictions on liberty that, as we have seen, pregnancy and childbirth entail. It is imaginable that women who regard themselves as pro-life would voluntarily donate their services in order to preserve the life of an unborn fetus. But if they did not, the public would have to pay for a service often obtained for free prior to *Roe v. Wade*.

Artificial wombs would certainly be even more costly. The only figures that might even remotely reflect the price of such incubation are the costs of treating extremely premature infants. Embryo transfers to artificial wombs might be similar to the treatment of these infants, who cannot survive in the absence of placement in life-support systems.

At present, premature babies require extremely expensive care, including placement in life-support systems, which can cost two to three thousand dollars per day. Of course, artificial wombs may utilize some totally unrelated technology; thus, it is difficult to move from this figure to any confident estimate of the cost of artificial wombs. But it is safe to say that such an alternative would be far from costless.

The prospect of artificial wombs also raises justified fears about a Brave New World of state-run baby farms, including the specter of state control over the disposition of fetuses that are not wanted by their biological parents but that develop under state command into viable infants, some of them perhaps badly handicapped. In one sense, these issues are already with us, posed by the systems of foster care and adoption that are currently used to deal with abandoned, orphaned, or abused children. With 1,600,000 abortions now performed annually in the United States, bringing to term a substantial number of fetuses that would otherwise have been destroyed by abortion—rather than creating an environment in which these fetuses would be *wanted* by their mothers—would represent an increase on a massive scale in the number of unwanted children in America.

How the overloaded, and largely unsuccessful, American system of foster care and placement could be maintained under the weight is anyone's guess. What seems clear, though, is that we need not await any new technology to recognize that any system for requiring fetuses to be brought to term when their mothers will not raise them separates the gestation of children from their upbringing in ways that are difficult to square with our traditions of family life.

## Toward Common Ground

The traditions that divide us and the myriad difficulties that plague all attempts at compromise in matters touching the absolutes of life and liberty, and lying at the crossroads of power and sex, may seem overwhelming. But we should not let them obscure the common ground on which we all can stand.

If advocates on both sides of the abortion debate would just pause, they would recognize at least one broadly shared interest, that of working toward a world of only wanted pregnancies. Better education, the provision of contraception, indeed the creation of a society in which the burden of raising a child is lighter, are all achievable goals that are lost in the shouting about abortion. For while, as we shall see, solving the puzzle of the abortion dispute will take a journey of self-discovery, nearly all of us already agree that we should strive for a society in which every child a woman conceives is wanted and in which every child born has someone to love and nurture it.

# 10
# Beyond the Clash of Absolutes

Whatever compromises we might achieve in our struggle with abortion, it should be clear by now that the debate itself—if we allow ourselves to listen closely to its arguments—may shed valuable light on many of the things we believe, and why.

## *Looking Inward: What Our Views Of Abortion Can Teach Us About Ourselves*

Most of us are torn by the abortion question. There is something deeply misleading about discussing the abortion debate solely in terms of a clash between pro-life "groups" and pro-choice "groups," as though each of us could properly be labeled as belonging to one camp or the other. For nearly everyone, the deepest truth is that the clash is an internal one. Few people who really permit themselves to feel all of what is at stake in the abortion issue can avoid a profound sense of internal division. Whatever someone's "bottom line"—whether it is that the choice must belong to the woman or that she must be prevented from killing the fetus—it is hard not to feel deeply the tug of the opposing view.

A story told in a recent newspaper interview by Dr. Warren Hern, director of the Boulder Abortion Clinic in Colorado, demonstrates this well. Dr. Hern recounts calling one of his closest friends, a "strongly pro-choice" physician who had "done abortions himself." When Dr. Hern told his friend that he was at work at his office, his friend asked, "Still killing babies this late in the afternoon?" Dr. Hern recalls: "It was like a knife in my gut . . . it really upset me. What it conveys is that no matter how supportive people may be, there is still a horror at what I do."[1]

Something akin to horror must be felt by everyone involved in the question of abortion who has not become anesthetized to the reality of what is at stake. This feeling may be less intense with abortions performed in the very beginning stages of pregnancy, when the embryo is a tiny, visually undifferentiated, multicelled growth without discernibly human features. But certainly by some point in pregnancy, as soon as abortion involves a fetus that is recognizably human in form, or when it involves a fetus that one might imagine feeling pain, few of us can avoid the sense of tragic choice that each abortion entails.

The "absolutes" described in this book are the fetus's right to life and the woman's right to liberty. We have seen, though, that neither "absolute" is really that. We have seen that whatever right a woman might have to choose abortion would be undermined if the fetus could be saved without sacrificing the woman's freedom to end her pregnancy. Most would intuitively sense the force of any such fetus's claim to life.

But that claim to life, as we have also seen, must in turn be offset by the potential evils, real, even if ill defined, of state-run fetus factories. Examining closely the source of our unease at such government involvement in the extraction and incubation of fertilized embryos suggests that the underlying conflict would not pit life against liberty, the unborn against their mothers, so much as it would pit life against the avoidance of government intrusion into life's mysteries, life against the avoidance of potentially monstrous state intervention into processes we intuitively feel should be beyond government's reach.

### From the Right to Life to the Right to Die

Not surprisingly, the question of when life ends, like the one of when it begins, has found its way to the nation's highest court. On the day it decided *Webster,* the Supreme Court announced that it would take up the case of Nancy Cruzan, a woman whom a car accident reduced to what doctors call a persistent vegetative state, a state of unconsciousness and unresponsiveness from which she will never recover. Nancy Cruzan's parents are battling the state of Missouri to establish the right to withdraw Nancy's feeding tube so that she may die.

By the time the *Cruzan* case was argued in the Supreme Court in December 1989, Court watchers had already linked the fate of Nancy Cruzan with that of "Jane Roe." The oral argument was carefully observed for clues not only about where the Court was leaning on the right to die issue itself, but also about where the Court was leaning on the broader issues of personal liberty and privacy that surface most dramatically in the abortion context.

The logic of the right-to-die controversy will not necessarily have any close encounter with the logic of the abortion debate. Yet much like arguments over abortion, right-to-die disputes may, in the end, pit the value of preserving life against the value of avoiding grotesque technological intrusions. At bottom there is a similarity between the state's decision to lay hands on the intimate and delicate matter of life's reproduction and the state's decision to have the last word on the personal and subtle matter of life's termination. A woman's right to decide if and how to give birth thus shares a common root with the right to avoid the demeaning tangle of state-mandated technology that has become death's least human face.

Thus, it may be that the right-to-life impulse and the pro-choice impulse may yet find common cause—in the desire to avoid government manipulation of technologies to save or preserve life, but only at the expense of sacrificing what we sense to be most natural.

Yet we must concede that reverence for what seems natural and aversion to what seems to alter nature's plan can all too easily become a mask for the desire to preserve the power that some of us wield over others, that men in particular wield over women. For some pro-life believers, though not for all, confronting that mask squarely may be a source of great discomfort, a first step toward deciding to remove the mask and perceive the world anew.

## Separating the Strands Underlying Pro-Life Sentiment

One way to explore that possibility is to take a hard look at a phenomenon that we have noted from time to time: Most of those who regard abortion as, at best, a necessary evil would nonetheless make an exception permitting abortion in cases of rape and incest. (This exception is really about rape. Most cases of incest probably involve an older relative and a young child, and so in most people's experience, incest is really a particular kind of rape.) Although polling numbers on abortion are notoriously sensitive to the wording of the questions (the *New York Times* has observed that "one of every six Americans says simultaneously that abortion is murder and that it is sometimes the best course"[2]), the polls do reveal this truth quite starkly.

One nationwide poll, for example, showed that 40 percent of the American public oppose abortion when it is sought because "the mother

is an unmarried teenager whose future life might be seriously affected."
Yet 81 percent favor abortion "if the woman became pregnant because
of rape or incest." Only 17 percent oppose abortion in such cases. This
suggests that almost 60 percent of those who oppose abortion for the
unmarried teenager would support it in cases of rape or incest.[3]

Regional polls corroborate the hypothesis that people who generally
oppose abortion would nonetheless permit it in cases of rape and incest.
For example, polls in Florida in the weeks after the *Webster* decision
showed that although 59 percent of the registered voters said they
agreed that during the first trimester of pregnancy the decision to have
an abortion "should be left entirely to a woman and her doctor,"[4] 53
percent of those polled said that abortion should be "illegal" when
sought because the woman's family "has a very low income and cannot
afford to have any more children," and 60 percent said that abortion
should not be permitted where sought because "the pregnancy would
interfere with the mother's work or education."[5] Still, 78 percent of
those polled thought abortion should be available in cases where the
pregnancy resulted from rape or incest. Only 13 percent said it should
not. This suggests that more than 75 percent of the people who oppose
abortion in circumstances of economic or personal hardship may well
accept it in cases of rape and incest.

A similar poll in Utah found that, although 58 percent of the adult
population thought abortion should not be available "to women who
choose it in the first trimester" and 68 percent thought it should not be
available to women who choose it in the second trimester, prior to
viability, again an overwhelming majority (81 percent) agreed that abortion should be available in cases of rape and incest.[6] Only 11 percent
disagreed. This suggests that up to 80 percent of Utah residents who
oppose abortion on request in the first trimester of pregnancy may
nonetheless support the availability of abortion in cases of rape and
incest.

Support of a rape exception makes plain that most people's opposition
to abortion, unlike their opposition to murder, *can* be overridden. It
therefore suggests that antiabortion sentiment is not *entirely* rooted in a
belief that abortion constitutes the killing of an innocent human being. It
is hard to see how any such justification for limiting abortion could plausibly be put forward by anyone who thinks that abortion should be permitted in cases of rape. A fetus conceived as a result of a violent rape is no
less innocent than one conceived in a mutually desired act of love. The
fetus obviously is not responsible for the circumstances surrounding its
conception. Yet the vast majority of people who oppose abortion would

permit such a fetus to be destroyed, even if they were rewriting from scratch the constitutional rules governing this thorny topic.

## Exploring the Rape and Incest Exception

If support for a rape and incest exception suggests that most opposition to abortion is *not* entirely about the destruction of innocent human life it might also reveal something about the views, conscious or unconscious, that lie at the heart of the belief that in general, access to abortion should be restricted.

Surely there should be nothing abhorrent about the *particular* fetuses that are the products of rapes. It is true that a position in favor of denying criminals the right to reproduce has at times been expressed in the United States—for example in the Oklahoma law struck down in the 1940s by the Supreme Court in *Skinner v. Oklahoma,* a law that provided for the sterilization of anyone previously found guilty two or more times of "felonies involving moral turpitude."[7] But a desire to deny the rapist his child could hardly explain a willingness to make abortion available to women who have been raped. And any notion that the fetus itself is tainted by a kind of "original sin" seems most implausible. After all, when the woman who has been raped *chooses* to give birth to the rapist's child rather than to abort, she is commended, not condemned.

Right-to-life advocates who would allow abortion for a woman who becomes pregnant after a rape are probably reacting out of compassion for the woman; they don't think she should have to live through having her rapist's child develop within her. But the only thing to distinguish that from any other unwanted pregnancy is the nature of the sexual activity out of which the pregnancy arose. A fetus resulting from rape or (in most cases) from incest is the product of a sex act to which the woman did not consent. It is only the *nonconsensual nature of the sex* that led to her pregnancy that could make abortion in the case of rape seem justified to someone who would condemn all other abortions not needed to save the pregnant woman's life.

This in turn suggests that one's opposition to such *other* abortions reflects a sense that continued pregnancy is simply the price women must pay for engaging in *consensual sex.* The lack of sympathy toward women who have experienced contraceptive failure suggests that many of us have no discomfort at the idea that women who choose to have sex simply cannot be allowed to avoid *some* risk of a pregnancy that they will just have to carry to term.

As we have seen, this feeling may be partly rooted in the belief that in general, this is the way of nature. In this view, opposition to abortion may reflect an ambivalence about the use of technology in general, in this case medical technology, to overcome that which always before seemed "natural": that sex would lead to pregnancy and pregnancy to childbirth.[8]

But notice how often this feeling about abortion is held by people who generally welcome the energetic uses of new technologies. Especially if such people regard nervousness about nuclear reactors or computers or other "unnatural" developments as silly or childish, their aversion to abortion rights would seem to reflect a deeply held *sexual* morality, in which pregnancy and childbirth are seen as a punishment that women in particular must endure for engaging in consensual sex. The fact that opposition to abortion rights may in large part be about sexual morality is reflected, too, in the attitude, noted earlier, of those who oppose abortion and seem willing to do almost anything to stop it—*except* take the effective pregnancy-reducing step of providing birth control education and better contraceptives.

At least to *these* "pro-life" activists, it seems to be more important to prevent the marginal increase in sexual activity that they believe will follow from sex education and the availability of birth control than to lower the number of abortions being performed. Theirs is thus a position in which sexual morality is primary, with any claim of a fetus's right to life taking a very distant backseat.

### Frozen Embryos

Some other thought experiments may help clarify the extent to which objections to permitting abortion may reflect a deeply held view not that an embryo is already a child but that the only natural course is that an embryo inside a woman should develop into one.

Let us consider, for example, the Tennessee frozen embryo case. Junior Davis and Mary Sue Davis were a Tennessee couple who, after five tubal pregnancies (a type of pregnancy that occurs in the fallopian tube rather than the uterus and that cannot lead to a live birth) turned to in vitro fertilization. As a result, they produced a number of embryos in a laboratory and had those embryos frozen. Later, without having successfully had a child, the Davises sought a divorce. As part of the divorce settlement, Mrs. Davis sought the right to implant in her womb the seven frozen embryos produced with her ova and Mr. Davis's sperm. Mr. Davis sought to prevent their implantation. A Tennessee judge, relying in large measure on the argument that an embryo is a unique human being at the moment of conception, ruled that the embryos were "persons"—they were *already* the Davises' "children"—and granted "custody" of them to Mrs. Davis.[9]

Many right-to-life advocates seem as unsure as others about the troubling issues raised by the judge's decision—about whether the frozen embryos should have been treated as though they were microscopic babies. Yet if one of those same embryos had been conceived in the usual fashion and was still inside Mrs. Davis, these same people would quickly insist that the embryo be brought to term. Why?

The answer must lie not in their views about the embryo as such but in their views about nature in general, "natural" sex roles and sexual morality. It is the natural fate of an embryo *inside a woman* to come to term, making her a mother.[10] The "natural" fate of an embryo created in a petri dish and stored in a freezer is far less clear.

## Fetal Endangerment: Child Abuse?

Like opposition to abortion, fetal endangerment suits, which have proliferated since the Court's *Webster* ruling,[11] are said to reflect a desire to protect the unborn. For example, a Massachusetts woman was charged in the months after *Webster* with vehicular homicide when her fetus was delivered stillborn after she got into a car accident.[12] But we must ask: Was the prosecutor's zeal an indication of concern for fetal life or a reflection of an attitude toward the responsibilities and roles of women?

It is striking how much more energetically some would combat fetal endangerment than they would child abuse. Not long ago the Supreme Court considered the case of a four-year-old boy, Joshua DeShaney. As the Court described him, he was beaten "so severely that he fell into a life threatening coma. Emergency brain surgery revealed a series of hemorrhages caused by traumatic injuries to the head inflicted over a long period of time. Joshua did not die, but he suffered brain damage so severe that he is expected to spend the rest of his life confined to an institution for the profoundly retarded."[13]

Wisconsin state officials had received several reports over a period of more than two years that suggested that Joshua was a victim of child abuse. During a six-month period prior to the beating that left Joshua in a coma, a Department of Social Services caseworker "made monthly visits to the home, during which she observed a number of suspicious injuries on Joshua's head. . . . The caseworker dutifully recorded these incidents in her files, along with her continuing suspicions that someone in the DeShaney household was physically abusing Joshua." On the case-worker's final two visits to the DeShaney home before Joshua's final beating, "she was told that Joshua was too ill to see her."[14] Yet neither she nor any other state official took any action to protect the child. Would we be surprised to find a caseworker eagerly reporting a pregnant woman for substance abuse?

Chief Justice Rehnquist, writing for a six-justice majority of the Supreme Court that happened to include the Court's four anti-*Roe* members and Justice O'Connor, declined to impose any liability on the state of Wisconsin or its officials for a violation of Joshua's constitutional right under the Fourteenth Amendment not to be deprived of liberty (here, Joshua's right to physical well-being) by the state "without due process of law." If the state officials had *themselves* beaten Joshua, the Court, under long-established principles of law, would have imposed such liability. But, the chief justice wrote, "[w]hile the State may have been aware of the dangers that Joshua faced in the free world, it played no part in their creation, nor did it do anything to render him any more vulnerable to them."[15]

This exposition about the "free world" in which this four-year-old victim of child abuse supposedly lived vividly captures the ideology of self-reliant individualism that is quintessentially American. It expresses a persistent unwillingness to impose on government the responsibility to intervene in the "private" relationships between "free" individuals and particularly to intervene in an intrafamilial setting, as between a parent and his or her minor child.

That reluctance stands in revealing contrast to the willingness of some to intervene in the setting of a woman's relationship with the fetus she is carrying. For example, a 1988 decision by a California court held that the use of drugs during pregnancy was sufficient to give the court jurisdiction in a proceeding to have the child declared dependent and taken away from his or her parents.[16] While such decisions may of course be motivated in part by a justifiable desire to address the horrible plight of addicted babies (just one side effect of the massive problem of illegal drugs in the United States), it is noteworthy that the California court suggested that a woman's conduct *during pregnancy* may result in her loss of custody of her child *after it is born*. The California court stated that "a living child must be afforded the protection of the Juvenile Court even though he is at risk because of his mother's actions before his birth."[17]

What can explain the growing interest in protection of the fetus at a time when child abuse prosecutions are still undertaken only in the most extreme and unusual circumstances and when the already born child is left to fend for itself in the "free world"? What is the meaning of this fixation on the responsibility of the pregnant woman? Part of the explanation may well be that society is not really treating pregnant women as "parents" of "unborn" children but rather is trying to exert a kind of power over women who happen to be pregnant that it does not wish to exert over parents in general.

## Absolutes or Contingents?

These examples reinforce the suspicion that resistance to a woman's freedom to choose to terminate a pregnancy is more complex than any reverence for life, for nature, or for children could manage to explain. Rather than center entirely on the protection of "unborn children" or on the preservation of the "natural," the feeling that abortion should be blocked by government may grow, at least in part, out of a reflexive willingness to enforce traditional sex roles upon women and to impose upon them an unequal and harsh sexual morality.

When viewed in this light, the comments of those "absolute" foes of abortion rights who would make no exception even to save the life of the pregnant woman and who would leave her, if she could find someone to perform her abortion safely, to argue in court that she killed her fetus in "self-defense" are more understandable. In this vision the fetus is not an innocent child but an unwanted intruder who can be justifiably killed only to save one's own life.

This hypothesis is corroborated by Kristin Luker's study revealing that in general, right-to-life activists believe that men and women are different by nature and that they have intrinsically different roles to play in society. Luker found a fear among many such activists that the incorporation of women into traditionally male roles in the workplace threatens to strip women of the role that is uniquely and properly theirs.[18] Believing that an important and natural function of women is the bearing of children, such right-to-life activists (themselves often women) evidently believe that abortion and, indeed, all methods of fertility control subordinate the special value of pregnancy and the uniqueness of the woman's natural place.[19] These activists accordingly oppose artificial means of contraception that interfere with the unpredictable possibility of pregnancy. Many of them also believe that nonprocreative sexuality departs from the "natural," that is, the procreative, purpose of the sexual experience.[20]

Indeed, those who most violently oppose the pro-choice position make an explicit connection between such opposition and their desire that women be put back in their traditional roles. Randall Terry, the originator of the militant Operation Rescue, sees the logic behind abortion rights as a force that would destroy "the traditional family unit" and "motherhood."[21] But whether Terry sees the economic and social freedom of women as the root cause behind abortion or sees abortion rights as freeing women to lead lives as full participants in the economy and in public life, his avowed goal is to put the genie of equality back in the bottle. Whether in the name of traditional sex roles or in the name of a traditional sexual morality, much opposition to abortion seems really to be about the control of women. Again, the depth of the division between the pro-choice and pro-life tendencies appears to reflect not simply different perspectives on the value of fetal life but different orientations toward matters of tradition, change, sex, and power.[22] Such differences in turn reflect class and culture in ways that cut across the divide between Democrats and Republicans in our political life.

## How We See and Talk to One Another

It is an uncomfortable truth that the pro-choice movement draws its support disproportionately from various privileged elites, the "upper echelons" of American society: scientists, intellectuals both inside and outside universities and other academic institutions, high-earning corporate executives, other highly educated men and women, the working press, much of the publishing industry, and all those "pointy-headed" types whom George Wallace loved to hate. Those who are pro-choice as a group tend to earn more than those who are pro-life; they have enjoyed more of modern society's ostensible benefits, from more advanced education to more exposure to travel; and they are more likely to live along the nation's coastline (with a gap in the Southeast) than in the heartland or in the South.[23] The pro-life movement, in turn, draws disproportionately from the remaining groups, those "distanced from elite culture by their membership in relatively recent immigrant groups and in lower-status religious groups."[24]

It has been remarked that in the last century and in the early years of this century, the upper middle class tended to impose social restrictions on lower-middle-class groups, many of them representing various ethnic minorities, whereas the situation has been reversed in recent decades, with a lower-middle-class tendency to favor the retention of social restrictions that the upper middle class seeks to escape.[25] One need not subscribe to any particular view of how concepts of "class" should be discussed in contemporary postindustrial society to see that at a minimum, the attitudes about the competing "absolutes" at stake in the abortion issue are not distributed evenly or randomly throughout the United States. In particular, there is a pervasive sense of mutual distrust that arises from the conspicuously different social positioning and cultural orientation of the combatants in the abortion war.

Thus, pro-life adherents are quick to denounce those who favor choice as morally blind, deceived by their supposed sophistication into equating license with liberty and into rationalizing the murder of the helpless as a way to preserve the "quality of life." But at least those who hold such contemptuous views of the pro-choice position rarely claim to be especially tolerant of diversity, to be distinctively broad-minded, to be uniquely open to competing moral perspectives.

Pro-choice advocates, for their part, tend to denounce the hypocrisy of pro-lifers and stress their supposed insensitivity to life in other settings (military adventurism, gun control, the death penalty) and their supposed lack of concern for babies and toddlers in such contexts as infant nutrition, day care, and aid to families with dependent children. At the same time—and this is richly ironic in light of the pro-choicers' charge of pro-life hypocrisy—pro-choice advocates *are* quick to boast of their own broad-mindedness and respect for others, their devotion to democracy and to egalitarian values.

Where are those fine qualities, one might ask, when pro-choicers sometimes talk as though pro-life advocates are nasty and brutish types whose opinions don't deserve to be taken all that seriously? More than a few of the pro-choice advocates who boast of their equal respect for all can barely suppress the sentiment that some are just a bit more "equal" than others, that it must surely be a lack of education and of cultural exposure that accounts for the moral certitude of many pro-lifers that theirs is the right position. Some pro-choice "true believers" can barely conceal their contempt for what they regard as the prejudiced, superstitious, backward views of pro-life groups. Indeed, some in the pro-choice camp embrace, at least implicitly, a doctrine of "false consciousness" that permits them to dismiss pro-life *women* in particular as benighted victims of social conditioning that prevents their views from authentically reflecting their own genuine needs and deepest beliefs.

Needless to say, anyone who is dismissed in this way has a hard time listening with sympathy to the arguments of those who look down on her with such contempt while professing a philosophy of tolerance and mutual respect. Yet counterproductive though they are, such contemptuous attitudes are common among the educated elites that tend to favor a cluster of positions including abortion rights, more vigorous enforcement of laws protecting racial minorities, unrestricted speech and artistic expression, tighter control of police brutality, opposition to the death penalty, stronger environmental protection, stricter gun control, gay rights, and so forth.[26] The very fact that both this listing and its mirror image are so familiar and so predictable suggests either that a remarkable moral logic ties all these views together or, far more plausibly, that much of what *each* of us believes about all these matters says more about who we are and where we come from than about our depth of vision or about the ultimate truth.[27]

For both sides, therefore, a greater measure of humility seems in order. If we genuinely believe in the democratic principle of one person, one vote, then each of us will have to treat the votes, and hear the voices, of our "opponents" as being no less worthy or meaningful than our own.

On both sides of the abortion debate, this will require an unaccustomed and in some ways almost unnatural forbearance. Right-to-life advocates are inclined to respond to pleas for tolerance by insisting that the exclusion of the fetus from the processes of voting and debate distorts the discussion profoundly from the outset, for reasons that bear no proper relation to a moral or just outcome. That the fetus is voiceless and voteless, they may say, follows from its biological condition but is irrelevant to how society is morally bound to behave.

And pro-choice advocates are inclined to react to pleas for mutual respect by insisting, no less vehemently, that it begs the question to attribute legitimacy to the views of those who would tell women how to lead their lives and what to do with their bodies. To submit a woman's fate to a popular referendum, they may insist, already *assumes* that the matter is properly one to be resolved by voting.

In the end, the answer to both sides is the same: *In a democracy, voting and persuasion are all we have.* Not even the Constitution is beyond amendment. And since we must therefore persuade one another even about which "rights" the Constitution ought to place beyond the reach of any temporary voting majority, *nothing,* neither life nor liberty, can be regarded as immune to politics writ large. Either some of the views expressed in the political arena are to be privileged and untouchable from the start or all views are to count equally, those of the supposedly less sophisticated no less than those of the self-professedly more tolerant elite.

But this implies nothing about whether any particular contested "right"—either a woman's alleged right to end her pregnancy or a fetus's alleged right to life—should be subjected to control by majority vote or should instead be placed by the Constitution, as interpreted by the judiciary, beyond the reach of all except the sort of *super*majority it takes to amend the Constitution. It's true that judges tend to be drawn from the same elite groups that are often guilty of arrogantly dismissing pro-life views as primitive and unenlightened, although the federal judiciary under President Reagan was selected with an arguably offsetting bias. But it is a massive non sequitur to argue that *because* treating an alleged right as entitled to special constitutional protection might make "the elite" more confident and "the rest" more embittered, it follows that the alleged right ought to be included in the list of interests that are subject to ordinary logrolling and electoral politics.[28] The lesson to be drawn from the arrogance of many pro-choice people who profess humility and mutuality is not that they should prove their democratic bona fides by sacrificing what they believe are fundamental rights, but that they should never take the rightness of their fundamental views as self-evident or think of their opponents as unworthy of engaging in serious, respectful debate.

In sum, none of this should deter believers in abortion rights from urging that theirs is indeed the better view, any more than it should deter adherents of the pro-life position from responding that the pro-choice position is wrong and indeed immoral. There is a profound difference between recognizing that persuasion in a dialogue of mutual respect is all we have and suggesting that there are no moral truths, that once the votes have been fairly tallied, nothing worth saying remains.

Even when they concede that their view is entitled to no special presumption of correctness, pro-choice advocates may nonetheless conclude as the debate unfolds that *all* rights may be jeopardized—those of the unborn, too, in the long run—if the pro-life position is imposed by force of law rather than embodied solely in moral argument. To the pro-life advocate, it may become clear in the end that at a deep level, the opposition to women's having the right to choose to end a pregnancy is more about the control of women than about the sanctity of life or of nature. If this is so, then opposition to a right to choose seeks to restrict the liberty of unwilling women in the name of something less than the "absolute" of the protection of human life. And if this is the case, then even the pro-life advocate may conclude that the objection to abortion rights ought to yield, as a matter of morality, to the claim of the woman to her liberty and equality. To conscript a woman to save a *life* might be one thing. To conscript her to save a *way* of life, one in which she is relegated to a second-class role, is another thing entirely.

For right-to-life advocates who remain unpersuaded, then, the challenge becomes one of persuading others, including the women whose liberty they would restrict, that it is indeed the value of life, not the subordination of women, that their commitment reflects. The more such advocates are willing to support women in their struggles, to sustain them in their choices rather than to condemn them for their sexuality, the more likely they will be to succeed in this challenge.

Neither side's moral claims are without flaws. Both may agree that dangers lurk in government usurpation of natural processes, that mothers are often the safest guardians of their young, and that the unborn deserve our care. And both may agree, too, that sex as a servant of love should triumph over sex as a tool of power.

So it is that a close look at the clash of absolutes may in the end reveal a sliver of light in a world of shadow. For if, in a moment of honesty with ourselves, we recognize—on either side of the question—that what is at stake is not really the absolute in whose name the battle has been fought, then we may get beyond our once intractable dispute about the question of abortion.

# Notes

## Chapter 1: Approaching Abortion Anew

1. *United States v. Nixon,* 418 U.S. 693 (1974).
2. *Roe v. Wade,* 410 U.S. 113 (1973). *See* Mark Tushnet, "The Name of the Rose," *Constitutional Commentary* (1989), 215, 216, discussing a point made by Professor Martha Minow.
3. 410 U.S. 179 (1973).
4. Newman, "Daughter of Woman in Abortion Case Takes a Pro-Choice Stand," *Los Angeles Times,* November 11, 1989, B1.

## Chapter 2: *From* Roe *to* Webster

1. 410 U.S. 113 (1973).
2. Ibid., 117–18.
3. Ibid., 162.
4. Ibid., 172 (Rehnquist, J., dissenting).
5. Ibid., 221 (White, J., dissenting).
6. Ibid., 165.
7. *City of Akron v. Akron Center for Reproductive Health, Inc.,* 462 U.S. 416, 419 (1973).
8. Richard Fallon, "A Tribute to Justice Lewis F. Powell, Jr.," *Harvard Law Review* 101 (1987), 395, 399.
9. 428 U.S. 52 (1976).
10. 462 U.S. 416, 439–40 (1983).
11. *Bellotti v. Baird,* 443 U.S. 622, 644 (1979) (plurality opinion).
12. *Planned Parenthood v. Danforth,* 428 U.S. 52, 65–67 (1976).
13. *Akron,* 444.
14. Ibid., 450.
15. *Doe v. Bolton,* 410 U.S., 179, 194–95, 195–98, 198–200 (1973); *Danforth,* 75–79.
16. *Thornburgh v. American College of Obstetricians and Gynecologists,* 476 U.S. 747, 765–68 (1986).
17. Ibid., 769.
18. *Planned Parenthood v. Ashcroft,* 462 U.S. 476, 482–86, 485 n. 8 (1983).
19. 432 U.S. 464 (1977).
20. 432 U.S. 519 (1977).
21. 448 U.S. 297 (1980).
22. See Herman Schwartz, *Packing the Courts* (1988), 42, 60–62, 64–66, 78, 84–85, 87–88, 100–01.

23. 109 S. Ct. 3040 (1989).
24. Linda Greenhouse, "A Seemingly Routine Missouri Case Takes Abortion Issue to High Court," *New York Times,* April 16, 1989, 28.
25. *Missouri Revised Statutes,* §188.029 (emphasis added).
26. *Webster,* 851 F.2d 1071, 1075 n.5 (8th Cir., 1988).
27. 109 S. Ct. 3055 (plurality opinion).
28. Ibid., 3055–58.
29. Ibid., 3058.
30. Ronald Dworkin, "The Future of Abortion," *New York Review of Books* (September 28, 1989), 47.
31. 109 S. Ct., 3064–67 (Scalia, J., concurring).
32. Ibid.
33. Ibid., 3064.
34. Ibid., 3064–65.
35. Ibid., 3066 n.*.
36. Ibid., 3067.
37. *Hodgson v. Minnesota,* 110 S. Ct. 2926 (1990).
38. *Ohio v. Akron Center for Reproductive Health,* 110 S. Ct. 2972 (1990).
39. Ibid., 2949–50 (O'Connor, J., concurring in part and concurring in the judgment).
40. Ibid., 2950.
41. See "Federal Court Refuses to Reinstate Louisiana Antiabortion Law," *Washington Post,* January 27, 1990, A3.

## Chapter 3:   Two Centuries of Abortion in America

1. See James Mohr, *Abortion in America: The Origins and Evolution of National Policy, 1800–1900* (1978), 4–6; see generally Brief of 281 American Historians as Amici Curiae Supporting Appellees in *Webster v. Reproductive Health Services,* 109 S. Ct. 3040 (1989) (No. 85-605), the point of departure for much of this chapter. This brief is hereafter referred to as Historians' Brief.
2. Mohr, 128.
3. Michael Gordon, *The American Family: Past, Present, and Future* (1978), 173.
4. Michael Grossberg, *Governing the Hearth: Law and Family in Nineteenth-Century America* (1985), 159.
5. Historians' Brief, 7.
6. Mohr, 21.
7. Ibid., 22.
8. Faye Ginsburg, *Contested Lives: The Abortion Debate in an American Community* (1989), 27.
9. Ibid., 26. See also Carl Degler, *At Odds: Women and the Family in America from the Revolution to the Present* (1980), 230.
10. Ginsburg, 26 and n. 4.
11. Mohr, 33.
12. See generally Paul Starr, "A Sovereign Profession: The Rise of Medical Authority and the Shaping of the Medical System," in *The Social Transformation of American Medicine,* ed. Paul Starr (1982).
13. Mohr, 36–37.
14. Ibid., 36.
15. Ginsburg, 25.
16. Rosalind P. Petchesky, *Abortion and Woman's Choice: The State, Sexuality, and Reproductive Freedom* (1984), 79.
17. Mohr, 165.
18. John Noonan, "An Almost Absolute Value in History," in *The Morality of Abortion: Legal and Historical Perspectives,* ed. John Noonan (1970), 36, 38.

19. Ibid., 39.
20. Ibid., 33.
21. Mohr, 167.
22. Ibid., 86.
23. Degler, 134.
24. Horatio Storer, "The Criminality and Physical Evils of Forced Abortions," *Transactions of the American Medical Association* 16 (1865), 736.
25. A. Kinney, *The Conquest of Death,* quoted in Linda Gordon, *Woman's Body, Woman's Right: A Social History of Birth Control in America* (1974), 138.
26. Degler, 229.
27. Quoted in Historians' Brief, 17–18. See also Atlee and O'Donnell, "Report of the Committee on Criminal Abortion," *Transactions of the American Medical Association* 22 (1871), 241, quoted in C. Smith-Rosenberg, *Disorderly Conduct* (1985), 236–37.
28. Kristin Luker, *Abortion and the Politics of Motherhood* (1984), 32.
29. Ibid., 49.
30. Ginsburg, 32.
31. Luker, 33.
32. Ibid., 53.
33. Ginsburg, 34.
34. Luker, 56, 61.
35. Eva Rubin, *Abortion, Politics and the Courts* (2d ed., 1987), 18.
36. Emily Moore-Cavar, *International Inventory of Information on Induced Abortions* (1974), 502 (Table 7.9).
37. Lawrence Lader, *Abortion II: Making the Revolution* (1973)(hereinafter Lader, *Abortion II).*
38. Luker, 62–65.
39. Rubin, 23.
40. Ibid.
41. "Jane Hodgson's Odyssey," *U.S. News & World Report* (December 4, 1989), 26.
42. Luker, 77.
43. Petchesky, 124.
44. Colin Francome, *Abortion Freedom: A Worldwide Movement* (1984), 107.
45. Ginsburg, 36, n. 19.
46. Petchesky, 107, 115.
47. Luker, 115.
48. Petchesky, 104 (Figure 3-1).
49. Luker, 117–18.
50. Lader, *Abortion II,* 30.
51. Marcia Cohen, *The Sisterhood: The True Story of the Women Who Changed the World* (1988), 175–77.
52. Ibid., 104–08.
53. Gloria Steinem, *Outrageous Acts and Everyday Rebellions* (1983), 17.
54. Clayton Knowles, "Clergymen Offer Abortion Advice," *New York Times,* May 22, 1967, 1.
55. Lader, *Abortion II,* 42–55.
56. Ibid., 49.
57. Mohr, 254.
58. Nanette Davis, *From Crime to Choice: The Transformation of Abortion in America* (1985), 102.
59. Ibid., 21–23.
60. Rubin, 27.
61. Ibid., 23.
62. Graham, "The Law: Review of Abortion," *New York Times,* September 10, 1967, E11.
63. Rubin, 28.
64. See *Doe v. Bolton,* 410 U.S. 179, 202–05 (1973).
65. Ibid.

66. Richard Lyons, "Colorado Abortion Reform Assessed," *New York Times,* December 8, 1969, 1.
67. Graham, E11.
68. Lader, *Abortion II,* 85.
69. Monroe, "How California's Abortion Law Isn't Working," *New York Times Magazine,* December 29, 1968, 10.
70. Ibid.
71. See Council of Economic Advisers, *Economic Indicators,* December 1989, 23, and *Economic Indicators,* December 1984, 23.
72. Monroe, 18.
73. Rubin, 26.
74. Lader, *Abortion II,* 30.
75. Luker, 107–08.
76. This personal account is recorded in Luker, 107.
77. Cohen, 177.
78. Ibid., 177–78.
79. Rubin, 23–24.
80. See David Kennedy, *Birth Control in America: The Career of Margaret Sanger* (1970).
81. Quoted in Lader, *Abortion II,* 36.
82. Betty Friedan, *The Feminine Mystique* (1963), 261.
83. Rubin, 25.
84. Ibid. See also Lader, *Abortion II,* 37.
85. Luker, 121.
86. Ginsburg, 39–40.
87. See Lader, *Abortion II,* 88–97.
88. Ibid., 81–82.
89. Francome, 113.
90. Ibid.
91. Ginsburg, 40; Luker, 122–23.
92. Petchesky, 122–24.
93. See Patricia Steinhoff and Milton Diamond, *Abortion Politics: The Hawaii Experience* (1977), vii.
94. Ibid., 25–27; see also Francome, 113–15.
95. Steinhoff and Diamond, 26.
96. Francome, 116.
97. Lader, *Abortion II,* 122–23; Francome, 117.
98. Lader, *Abortion II,* 123–24.
99. Ibid., 137–38.
100. Ibid., 137.
101. Ibid., 144–45.
102. Ibid., 145.
103. Bill Kovach, "Abortion Reform Is Voted by the Assembly," *New York Times,* April 10, 1970, 1.
104. "Man Who Cast Key Vote on Abortion Is Rebuffed," *New York Times,* April 20, 1970, 63.
105. Bill Kovach, "Two Key Backers of Abortion Reform in the Legislature Are Defeated Upstate," *New York Times,* June 24, 1970, 35.
106. Lader, *Abortion II,* 143.
107. Clines, "Pressures on Assemblymen over Abortion Were Personal and Powerful: Lobbies Included Wives and Clergy," *New York Times,* April 11, 1970, 17.
108. Mary Ann Glendon, *Abortion and Divorce in Western Law* (1987).
109. Interview with Mary Ann Glendon in Bill Moyers, *A World of Ideas* (1989), 478.
110. Lader, *Abortion II,* 202–07.
111. Francome, 112.
112. Leismer, "Abortion Reform—Election's Most Emotional Issue," *Detroit News,* November 6, 1972, 3A.

113. Ibid.
114. See Laurence Tribe, *American Constitutional Law* (1978), 930. See also Ronald Dworkin, "The Future of Abortion," *New York Review of Books* (September 28, 1989), 47.


## Chapter 4:    *Locating Abortion on the World Map*

1. George Devereux, "A Typological Study of Abortion in 350 Primitive, Ancient and Pre-Industrial Societies," in *Abortion in America,* ed. Harold Rosen (1967).
2. Ibid., 144–45.
3. Ibid., 133.
4. Ibid., 106–07.
5. Ibid., 133–34.
6. Frank Sussman, "Child Transport, Family Size, and Increase in Human Population During the Neolithic," *Current Anthropology* 13 (1972), 258, 259.
7. Devereux, 114; Saucier, "Correlates of the Long Postpartum Taboo: A Cross-Cultural Study," *Current Anthropology* 13 (1972), 238–40.
8. Devereux, 114.
9. Hawkinson, "Abortion: An Anthropological Overview," in *Liberalization of Abortion Laws: Implications,* ed. Abdel Omran (1976), 126.
10. Ibid., 110.
11. Ford, "Control of Conception in Cross-Cultural Perspective," *Annals of the New York Academy of Sciences* 54 (1951), 763, 767.
12. Douglas, "Population Control in Primitive Groups," *British Journal of Sociology* (1966), 263, 270.
13. Devereux, 145.
14. Ibid., 108.
15. Ibid., 112–13.
16. Ibid., 113, 116.
17. Ibid., 111–14, 146, 148–51.
18. Ibid., 146.
19. Alan Guttmacher, "The Legal Status of Therapeutic Abortions," in *Abortion in America,* 176, citing W. E. H. Lecky, *History of European Morals* 11 (1890), 22.
20. Millar, "Human Abortion," *Human Biology* 6 (1934), 271, 274; Guttmacher, 175.
21. Frederick Joseph Taussig, *Abortion Spontaneous and Induced: Medical and Social Aspects* (1936), 32.
22. Guttmacher, 175, 176, citing Lecky, 22.
23. Guttmacher, 176.
24. See, for example, "Poland's Hard Life Finds More Women Choosing Abortion," *New York Times,* May 23, 1983, B12.
25. Mark Savage, "The Law of Abortion in the Union of Soviet Socialist Republics and the People's Republic of China: Women's Rights in Two Socialist Countries," *Stanford Law Review* 40 (1988), 1028, 1063 (student note).
26. See 1987 *Abortion Research News,* 1; Savage, 1053–57.
27. Savage, 1037–38.
28. Donald Meyer, *Sex and Power* (1987), 220–29; Savage, 1036–42.
29. Meyer, 149–61.
30. Farnsworth, "Bolshevik Alternatives and the Soviet Family: The 1926 Marriage Law Debate," in *Women in Russia,* ed. D. Atkinson, A. Dallin, and G. Lapidus (1977), 161.
31. See Savage, 1038, quoting A. Kollantai, *Trudzehnshchin v Evoluitsii Khoziaistua* (The Labor of Women in the Evolution of the Economy); see generally Savage, 1036–53.
32. Meyer, 220–30; Francome, *Abortion Freedom,* 63.
33. Meyer, 226.
34. Savage, 1048–53.

35. Savage, 1059, citing H. David, "Soviet Union," in *Abortion Research: International Experience,* ed. H. David (1974), 209, 211.

36. Savage, 1061–62.

37. Savage, 1062–63.

38. See, for example, Klinger, "Hungary," in *International Handbook on Abortion,* ed. P. Sachdev (1988), 218–19 (hereinafter *International Handbook*). Okolski, "Poland," in *International Handbook,* 387.

39. Cowell, "Full Blooded Candor Is Restored, and Evils Not of Dracula Unfold," *New York Times,* January 9, 1990, A12.

40. Bishop, "Abortions on Demand Will Cost Only £2," *Daily Telegraph,* January 4, 1990, 10.

41. Cowell, A12.

42. *World News Tonight,* January 3, 1990 (ABC television broadcast).

43. Mary Ann Glendon, *Abortion and Divorce in Western Law* (1987), 59–60.

44. Burke, "Ceausescu's Main Victims: Women and Children," *New York Times,* January 10, 1990, A27.

45. Ibid.

46. Bohlen, "Rumanians Moving to Abolish Worst of Repressive Era," *New York Times,* December 28, 1989, A1. See also "The Voice of the New Romania," *Financial Times,* December 29, 1989, 11.

47. Tagliabue, "Abortion Issue in Poland Splits the Opposition," *New York Times,* May 29, 1989, A1.

48. Savage, 1063–64, n. 191.

49. Claudia Koonz, *Mothers in the Fatherland: Women, the Family, and Nazi Politics* (1987), 267.

50. Ibid., 185–87, 197, 306.

51. Jill Stephenson, *Women in Nazi Society* (1975), 5–6, 61–62, 69.

52. Ibid., 63–71.

53. Ibid., 62; Koonz, 186–87.

54. Stephenson, 68–69.

55. Koonz, 150.

56. Clifford Kirkpatrick, *Nazi Germany: Its Women and Family Life* (1938), 182–83.

57. Stephenson, 62.

58. Koonz, 186–87.

59. See, for example, Marten, "Abortion Is Not an Issue in Japan," United Press International, May 12, 1989 (BC cycle); Jain, "Family Traditions, Banning of Pill Help Make Abortion Accepted Practice in Japan," *Los Angeles Times,* April 23, 1989, part 1, 12.

60. Samuel Coleman, *Family Planning in Japanese Society* (1983), 60.

61. David, "Abortion Policies," in *Abortion and Sterilization,* ed. Jane Hodgson (1981), 4.

62. Sripati Chandrasekhar, *Abortion in a Crowded World* (1974), 110.

63. Ibid., 111.

64. See Jain.

65. K. van Wolferen, *The Enigma of Japanese Power* (1989), 368.

66. Coleman, 58–73.

67. Minoru Muramatsu, "Japan," in *International Handbook,* 295.

68. Coleman, 58–66.

69. Ibid., 59.

70. Ibid., 61–62; Okabe, "Japanese Temple Enshrines Children Lost to Abortion," United Press International, October 20, 1982 (BC cycle).

71. Coleman, 62.

72. Ibid., 63–64.

73. Ibid., 75.

74. David, 4.

75. Savage, 1072–73.

76. Ibid., 1078.

77. Basheda, "An End of Fear," *Los Angeles Times,* July 27, 1989, part 1, 3; Savage, 1089, 1091–92.

78. See Basheda.

79. Croll, "Fertility Norms and Family Size in China," in *China's One-Child Family Policy,* ed. Elisabeth Croll, Delia Davin, and Penny Kaye (1985), 3, 11, 17.

80. Ibid., 3.

81. "China Warned of Threat from Infanticide," *Daily Telegraph,* September 8, 1989, 12.

82. Chandrasekhar, 106–07 and n. 4.

83. Ibid., 89, 92, 93.

84. Ibid., 42, 44.

85. Ibid., 42.

86. Basim Musallam, *Sex and Society in Islam* (1983), 14–16.

87. Ibid., 47; Tahir Mahmood, *Family Planning: The Muslim Viewpoint* (1979), 34.

88. Chandrasekhar, 47–48.

89. Ibid., 48.

90. Ibid., 47–48, Ragab, "Islam and the Unwanted Pregnancy," in *Abortion and Sterilization,* 509; Musallam, 57–58.

91. Qur'an 17:31.

92. Ibid.; Mahmood, 66–69.

93. See, for example, Barbara Daly, *Perfecting Women: Maulana Ashraf Ali Thanawi's Bihisthti Zevar: A Partial Translation with Commentary* (1990).

94. See, for example, Heise, "The Global War Against Women," *Washington Post,* April 9, 1989, B1.

95. Ibid.

96. See, for example, Weisman, "No More Guarantees of a Son's Birth," *New York Times,* July 20, 1988, A1; "Saving the Daughters of India," *Christian Science Monitor,* July 27, 1988, 13; Roger Crabb, "Tradition Means Many Asians Still Don't Want Baby Girls," Reuters, September 9, 1986 (BC cycle).

97. Pandya, "Prenatal Attack on Women," *Christian Science Monitor,* March 10, 1988, 23.

98. Ibid.

99. See Weisman.

100. Stuart Auerbach, "Birth Test Said to Help Indians Abort Females," *Washington Post,* August 25, 1982, A24.

101. See Weisman.

102. Victoria Greenwood and Jock Young, *Abortion in Demand* (1976), 19.

103. Colin Francome, "United Kingdom," in *International Handbook,* 458 (hereinafter Francome, *International Handbook*).

104. Ibid.

105. Ibid., 459

106. Colin Francome, *Abortion Freedom: A Worldwide Movement* (1984), 30 (hereinafter Francome, *Abortion Freedom*).

107. Greenwood and Young, 20.

108. Ibid., 21.

109. Ibid.

110. Francome, *Abortion Freedom,* 78–85.

111. Karen DeYoung, "Limit of Abortions Passed in London," *Washington Post,* January 23, 1988, A12.

112. Pallot, "Record Number of Abortions for Teenagers," *Daily Telegraph,* December 5, 1989, 8.

113. Francome, *International Handbook,* 965, 971.

114. Simons, "Abortion Fight Has New Front in Eastern Europe," *New York Times,* June 28, 1989, A1.

115. Francome, *Abortion Freedom,* 90–99, 158–83; DeYoung.

116. See generally Anthony Fisher and Jane Buckingham, *Abortion in Australia* (1985), 150.

117. Francome, *Abortion Freedom,* 151.

118. "Judge Allows Abortion," Reuters, July 12, 1989 (PM cycle).
119. *Morgentaler v. Regina,* 1 S.C.R. 30, 172 (Can. 1988) (Wilson, J.) (citation omitted).
120. "Court in Canada Rules on Abortion," *New York Times,* January 29, 1988, A1.
121. See Mary Ann Glendon, *Abortion and Divorce in Western Law* (paperback ed., 1989), 145.
122. *Tremblay v. Daigle,* 1989 S.C.J. Q.L. 79 (November 16, 1989).
123. Blinch, "Canadian Court Finds Fetus Not Protected Under Quebec Charter," Reuters, November 16, 1989 (AM cycle).
124. Glendon, 11.
125. Francome, *International Handbook,* 461.
126. Glendon, 149.
127. Ibid., 15.
128. Ibid., 21, 146–48; Rademakers, "The Netherlands," in *International Handbook,* 333, 335.
129. Glendon, 22–23.
130. Ibid., 18, 40.
131. Ibid., 20
132. Ibid., 18.
133. Ibid., 23.
134. Law No. 75-17 of 17 January 1975, relating to the voluntary termination of pregnancy, Art. L 162-1 (J.O. January 18, 1975, p. 739), reenacted and amended by Law. No. 79-1204 of 31 December 1979 (J.O. January 1, 1980, p. 3).
135. Glendon, 16–17.
136. Ibid., 19 (emphasis in original).
137. Ibid., 61.
138. Ibid., 13–15.
139. Ibid., 13.
140. Ibid., 15.

## Chapter 5:    Finding Abortion Rights in the Constitution

1. 410 U.S. 113, 153 (1973).
2. 349 U.S. 294 (1954).
3. 5 U.S. (1 Cranch) 137 (1803).
4. *West Virginia State Board of Education v. Barnette,* 319 U.S. 624, 638 (1943).
5. Robert Bork, *The Tempting of America* (1989), 112.
6. Ibid., 115–16.
7. Brief for a Group of American Law Professors as Amicus Curiae Supporting Appellees in *Webster v. Reproductive Health Services,* 109 S. Ct. 3040 (1989) (No. 85-605), 1.
8. "A.B.A. Policy Group Backs Right of Women to Decide on Abortion," *New York Times,* Feb. 14, 1990, A23. The vote in the ABA's House of Delegates was 238 to 106.
9. Bork, 43 (emphasis added).
10. *Hurtado v. California,* 110 U.S. 516, 535–36 (1884).
11. See *Allgeyer v. Louisiana,* 165 U.S. 578 (1897).
12. See Benjamin Wright, *The Growth of American Constitutional Law* (1942), 154, 175–76, and n. 96.
13. 198 U.S. 45 (1905).
14. Thomas Cooley, *A Treatise on the Constitutional Limitations Which Rest upon the Legislative Power of the States of the American Union* (8th ed., 1927), 1227–28 n. 2.
15. *Coppage v. Kansas,* 236 U.S. 1, 17–18 (1915).
16. 198 U.S. 45, 75–76 (Holmes, J., dissenting).
17. "The Legal Right to Starve," *New Republic* 34 (May 2, 1923), 254.
18. 300 U.S. 379 (1937).
19. See Wright, 202; Leo Pfeffer, *This Honorable Court* (1965), 295–320.
20. Bork, 236 (emphasis added).

21. *Moore v. City of East Cleveland,* 431 U.S. 494 (1977).
22. Bork, 220.
23. Ibid.
24. *Palko v. Connecticut,* 302 U.S. 319, 325 (1937).
25. *Duncan v. Louisiana,* 391 U.S. 145, 150 n. 14 (1968).
26. *Moore,* 431 U.S., 503 (plurality opinion).
27. *Michael H. v. Gerald D.,* 109 S. Ct. 2333, 2341 (1989) (citations omitted).
28. *Olmstead v. United States,* 277 U.S. 438, 478 (1928) (Brandeis, J., dissenting).
29. 262 U.S. 390 (1923).
30. 268 U.S. 510 (1925).
31. *Pierce,* 268 U.S., 535.
32. *Meyer,* 262 U.S., 402.
33. *Pierce,* 268 U.S., 534–35.
34. 316 U.S. 535, 536 (1942).
35. Ibid., 541.
36. See *Turner v. Safley,* 482 U.S. 78 (1987); *Zablocki v. Redhail,* 434 U.S. 374 (1978); *Loving v. Virginia,* 388 U.S. 1 (1967).
37. 381 U.S. 479, 485 (1965).
38. Ibid., 507 (concurring opinion).
39. *Eisenstadt v. Baird,* 405 U.S. 438, 453 (1972).
40. Ibid., 460–65 (concurring opinion).
41. Charles Black, "The Unfinished Business of the Warren Court," *Washington Law Review* 46 (1970), 3, 32.
42. 109 S. Ct., 3069 (Scalia, J., dissenting).
43. "Transcript of Oral Arguments Before Court on Abortion Case," *New York Times,* April 27, 1989, B12.
44. Mass. G.L. c. 272 §21 (1966).
45. *Griswold v. Connecticut,* 382 U.S., 527 (Stewart, J., dissenting).
46. *Thornburgh v. American College of Obstetricians and Gynecologists,* 476 U.S. 747, 792 n. 2 (1986) (White, J., dissenting).
47. *Michael H.,* 109 S. Ct., 2341 n. 4 (plurality opinion) (emphasis added).
48. Bork, 112.
49. 424 U.S. 1 (1976) (per curiam).
50. 109 S. Ct., 2344 n. 6 (plurality opinion).
51. Woodrow Wilson, *Constitutional Government in the United States* (1908), 192, quoted in Kammen, *Sovereignty and Liberty* (1988), 141.
52. 109 S. Ct., 2351 (Brennan, J., dissenting) (emphasis in original).
53. Correspondence, *Philosophy & Public Affairs* 6 (1977), 288.
54. Charles Fried, *Right and Wrong* (1978), 121 n.* (emphasis in original).
55. *Michael M. v. Superior Court of Sonoma County,* 450 U.S. 464, 471 (1981).
56. See Susan Estrich and Kathleen Sullivan, "Abortion Politics: Writing for an Audience of One," *University of Pennsylvania Law Review* 138 (1989), 119, 126–27.
57. Ibid.
58. *Rochin v. California,* 342 U.S. 165 (1952).
59. *Winston v. Lee,* 470 U.S. 753 (1985).
60. McNamara, "Choice Wasn't Abortion: Maternity Homes a Refuge for Some," *Boston Globe,* November 26, 1989, Metro/Region, 1.
61. Harold Rosen, "A Case Study in Social Hypocrisy," in *Abortion in America,* ed. Harold Rosen (1967), 310.
62. Jed Rubenfeld, "The Right of Privacy," *Harvard Law Review* 102 (1989), 737, 790.
63. Ibid., 788.
64. *Skinner,* 316 U.S., 541.
65. *Personnel Adm'r of Massachusetts v. Feeney,* 442 U.S. 256 (1979).
66. *Roe v. Wade,* 410 U.S., 174–77 (1973) (Rehnquist, J., dissenting).

67. See Ronald Dworkin, *A Matter of Principle* (1985), 33–71.

68. See Ronald Dworkin, *Law's Empire* (1986), 70–72, 355–99.

69. *Trop v. Dulles,* 356 U.S. 86, 101 (1958) (plurality opinion).

70. *McCulloch v. Maryland,* 17 U.S. (4 Wheat) 316, 407 (1819) (emphasis in original).

71. Powell, "The Original Understanding of Original Intent," *Harvard Law Review* 98 (1985), 885, 936, quoting *Letters and Other Writings of James Madison* 3 (1865), 53, 54, 228.

72. Brief for Respondents in *Bolling v. Sharpe,* 347 U.S. 497 (1954), 12–13.

73. 347 U.S. 497 (1954).

74. Ibid., 500.

75. Bork, 83, 84.

76. Ibid., 47–49.

77. 109 S. Ct., 3057 (plurality opinion).

78. *Ollman v. Evans,* 750 F.2d 970, 993–95 (D.C. Cir. 1984) (concurring opinion), *cert. denied* 471 U.S. 1127 (1985).

79. *Ashwander v. TVA,* 297 U.S. 288, 347 (1936) (Brandeis, J., concurring), quoting *Liverpool & Philadelphia Steamship Co. v. Commissioner of Emigration,* 113 U.S. 33, 39 (1885).

80. Nicholas Kristof, "Chinese Region Uses New Law to Sterilize Mentally Retarded," *New York Times,* November 21, 1989, A1.

81. *Buck v. Bell,* 274 U.S. 200, 207 (1927).

82. Stephen J. Gould, *The Mismeasure of Man* (paperback ed. 1981), 336.

#### Chapter 6: The Equation's Other Side: Does It Matter Whether the Fetus Is a Person?

1. John Hart Ely, "The Wages of Crying Wolf: A Comment on *Roe v. Wade,*" *Yale Law Journal* 82 (1973), 920, 926.

2. *United States v. O'Brien,* 391 U.S. 367 (1968).

3. I, too, once took the position that *any* political resolution of the abortion issue necessarily involves an impermissible degree of governmental entanglement with religion, but some years ago I came to reject that view, for the reasons explained here.

4. *McDaniel v. Paty,* 435 U.S. 618, 641 (1978) (Brennan, J., concurring).

5. Charles A. Gardner, "Is an Embryo a Person," *Nation* (November 13, 1989), 557.

6. Ibid., 557.

7. Ibid., 558.

8. Frances Olsen, "Comment—Unraveling Compromise," *Harvard Law Review* 103 (1989) 105, 128.

9. 410 U.S., 113, 173 (1973) (Rehnquist, J., dissenting).

10. "A Tragic Side Effect," *Time* (December 4, 1989), 44.

11. Keith L. Moore, *The Developing Human* (3d ed., 1982), 286.

12. Andrea Bonnicksen, *In Vitro Fertilization* (1989), 150.

13. 410 U.S. 113, 162 (1973).

14. See Brief of 608 State Legislators from 32 States as Amicus Curiae in Support of Appellees in *Webster v. Reproductive Health Services,* 109 S. Ct. 3040 (1989) (no. 88-605), citing *New York Times,* January 26, 1970, 20; February 3, 1970, 40; and April 3, 1970, 24.

15. "Missouri Fetus Unlawfully Jailed, Suit Says," *New York Times,* August 11, 1989, B5.

16. *Edwards v. California,* 314 U.S. 160, 186 (1941) (Jackson, J., concurring).

17. Judith Jarvis Thomson, "A Defense of Abortion," *Journal of Philosophy and Public Affairs* 1 (1971), 47.

18. Robert Hale, "Prima Facie Torts, Combination and Non-Feasance," *Columbia Law Review* 46 (1946), 196, 214 (emphasis omitted).

19. Epstein, "A Theory of Strict Liability," *Journal of Legal Studies* 1 (1973), 151, 198.

20. James Barr Ames, "Law and Morals," *Harvard Law Review* 22 (1908), 97, 112.

21. See Epstein.

22. 12 Vermont Stat. §519 (1973).

23. See also D. Regan, "Rewriting *Roe v. Wade,*" *Michigan Law Review* 77 (1979), 1569.

24. *Griswold v. Connecticut,* 381 U.S. 479, 485–86 (1965).

25. Jubera, "Kate's Choice," *Atlanta Journal and Constitution,* October 4, 1988, 1D.

26. See Guido Calabresi, *Ideals, Beliefs, Attitudes and the Law: Private Law Perspectives on a Public Law Problem* (1985), 95–96.

27. 410 U.S., 221 (White, J., dissenting).

## Chapter 7:   *The Politics of Abortion: From a New Right to the "New Right"*

1. See, e.g., "High Court Rules Abortions Legal the First Three Months," *New York Times,* January 23, 1973, 1; MacKenzie, "Supreme Court Allows Early-Stage Abortions," *Washington Post,* January 23, 1973, A1.

2. "Abortion: Out of the 19th Century," *Washington Post,* January 31, 1973, A18.

3. "Statement by 2 Cardinals," *New York Times,* January 23, 1973, 20.

4. "Catholic Group Hits Justice Brennan," *Washington Post,* January 26, 1973, A12; "Blackmun Defends Abortion Decision," *Washington Post,* January 26, 1973, A2.

5. Van Gelder, "Cardinals Shocked—Reaction Mixed," *New York Times,* January 23, 1973, 1.

6. "A Stunning Approval for Abortion," *Time* (February 5, 1973), 50; see also Wright, "Protestants Split on Abortion Edict," *Washington Post,* January 26, 1973, B7.

7. 410 U.S. 179 (1973).

8. Schultz, "Though Legal, Abortions Are Not Always Available," *New York Times,* January 2, 1977, 4, 8.

9. Kovach, "Rockefeller, Signing Abortion Bill, Credits Women's Groups," *New York Times,* April 12, 1970, A47.

10. Joseph Scheidler, *Closed: 99 Ways to Stop Abortion* (1985), 307.

11. Sanders, "Enemies of Abortion," *Harper's* (March 1974), 26, 28.

12. Ibid.

13. Farber, "Abortions at Any Time Sought in State," *New York Times,* January 24, 1973, 13.

14. See "A Stunning Approval for Abortion," 50–51.

15. "Abortion: What Happens Now?" *Newsweek* (February 5, 1973), 66.

16. See Schultz.

17. Hyer, "Cardinal Boyle Asks Pastors to Preach Against the Abortion Rule," *Washington Post,* January 25, 1973, B1.

18. Hyer and Elsen, "Ruling on Abortions Criticized in Sermons," *Washington Post,* January 29, 1973, C1.

19. Hyer, "Catholic Bishops Urged Defiance of Any Law Requiring Abortion," *Washington Post,* February 14, 1973, A17.

20. Connie Paige, *The Right to Lifers* (1983), 59–60.

21. "Saying No to NOW," *Time* (April 28, 1975), 75–76.

22. Russell, "Anti-Abortion Measures Grow," *Washington Post,* June 1, 1973, A4; David Broder, "Hill Fears Abortion Issue," *Washington Post,* May 6, 1974, A1.

23. Beuss and Shaw, "Maude's Abortion: Spontaneous or Induced?," *America* (November 3, 1973), 324.

24. Ibid., 325.

25. K. Mulhauser, "Congressional Activities," in *Abortion in the Seventies,* ed. W. Hern and B. Andrikopoulos (1977), 225.

26. Komisar, "Sellout on Abortion," *Newsweek* (June 9, 1975), 11.

27. Eva Rubin, *Abortion, Politics and the Courts* (2d ed., 1987), 154; Hyer, "Senators Hear 4 Cardinals Argue for Strict Abortion Ban," *Washington Post,* March 6, 1974, A2.

28. Paige, 51.

29. Ibid., 56–57.

30. Broder.

31. Rubin, 91.
32. Broder.
33. Rubin, 92.
34. Weber, "Bishops in Politics: The Big Plunge," *America* (March 20, 1976), 220 (citing pastoral plan), quoted in Rubin, 92.
35. Ibid.
36. Ibid. See also Castelli, "Anti-Abortion, the Bishops and the Crusaders," *America* (May 22, 1976), 442–44.
37. Weber, 220.
38. "1976's Sleeper Issue," *Newsweek* (February 9, 1976), 21.
39. "The Right-to-Life Candidate," *Newsweek* (February 9, 1976), 23; Rubin, 99–101; Pamela Conover and Virginia Gray, *Feminism and the New Right* (1983), 92.
40. Rubin, 97.
41. "G.O.P. Panel Backs Anti-Abortion Plank," *New York Times,* August 11, 1976, 14; Rubin, 98.
42. Rubin, 100.
43. Joseph Califano, *Governing America* (1981), 51; Charles Mohr, "Abortion Stand by Carter Vexes Catholic Bishops," *New York Times,* September 1, 1976, A1.
44. McNaughton, "Bishops 'Encouraged' by Ford on Abortion," *New York Times,* September 11, 1976, A1.
45. Rubin, 106.
46. Tolchin, "Senators Elucidate Shift on Abortions," *New York Times,* July 1, 1977, A24.
47. 428 U.S. 52 (1976).
48. Robert Drinan, "Abortions on Medicaid?" *Commonweal* (May 9, 1975), 102.
49. Hunter, "The Man Behind the Anti-Abortion Amendment," *New York Times,* July 1, 1980, B8.
50. See *Harris v. McRae,* 448 U.S. 297, 353, n. 5 (1980).
51. Califano, 55–63.
52. "Transcript of the President's News Conference on Domestic and Foreign Affairs," *New York Times,* July 13, 1977, A10.
53. "Mr. Carter's Cruel Abortion Plan," *New York Times,* June 13, 1977, A28.
54. Tolchin, "House Bars Medicaid Abortions and Funds for Enforcing Quotas," *New York Times,* June 18, 1977, 1.
55. Ibid., 7.
56. Ibid.
57. Continuing Appropriations Act, Public Law No. 95-205, 91 Stat. 1460 (1977).
58. Becker, "Mr. Hyde," *New Republic* (November 17, 1979), 10.
59. Michael Kinsley, "Danse Macabre," *New Republic* (November 19, 1977), 15.
60. *Congressional Record,* S 27674 (daily ed., August 25, 1977), 122.
61. 432 U.S. 464, 475–77 (1977).
62. *Congressional Record,* S 27674, (daily ed., August 25, 1977), 122.
63. Brozan, "High Court's Abortion Ruling Stirs New Worries and Confusion," *New York Times,* July 4, 1980, A10.
64. Alan Crawford, *Thunder on the Right* (1980).
65. MacPherson, "The New Right Brigade," *Washington Post,* August 10, 1980, F1, F2.
66. Hyer, "Some Catholics Lament Bishops' Abortion Stress," *Washington Post,* September 11, 1976, A4.
67. Ibid.
68. Ibid.

*Chapter 8:    The Politics of Abortion: The Pro-Life Advocates in Power*

1. John Hart Ely and Laurence Tribe, "Let There Be Life," *New York Times,* March 17, 1981, A17.
2. Ibid.

3. Wohl, "The New Danger: A Three Step Abortion Plan," *Ms.* (February 2, 1982), 87.

4. Edward Bryce, "Abortion and the Hatch Amendment," *America* (March 6, 1982), 166, 167.

5. See, e.g., Lynch, " 'Abortion' and 1976 Politics," *America* (March 6, 1976), 177, 178.

6. Clines, "Abortion Foes, Hailing Reagan Efforts, Plan to Renew Stalled Drive," *New York Times,* September 17, 1982, A19.

7. Weinraub, "Abortion Curbs Endorsed, 10–7, by Senate Panel," *New York Times,* March 11, 1982, A1.

8. "Abortion: The Debate Begins," *Newsweek* (August 30, 1982), 29.

9. Clines.

10. Ibid.

11. Wohl, 87, 88.

12. "Excerpts from Kennedy's Remarks on Religion," *New York Times,* September 11, 1984, A26.

13. See Herman Schwartz, *Packing the Courts* (1988).

14. Sperling, "Justice in the Middle," *Atlantic Monthly* (March 1988), 26.

15. Pamela Conover and Virginia Gray, *Feminism and the New Right* (1983), 96.

16. *Thornburgh,* 476 U.S. 747, 785 (1986) (Burger, C.J., dissenting).

17. McQueen, "Bush's Vacillating Statements on Abortion Issue Lead to Criticism from Both Sides," *Wall Street Journal,* October 25, 1989, A20.

18. Boyd, "Bush Camp Offers a Clarified Stand About Abortion," *New York Times,* September 27, 1989, A1.

19. "Transcript of the Second Debate Between Bush and Dukakis," *New York Times,* October 14, 1988, A14, A15.

20. Faludi, "Where Did Randy Go Wrong?," *Mother Jones* (November 1989), 22, 61.

21. Ibid., 25.

22. Ibid., 22, 24.

23. Ibid., 27–28.

24. *Missouri Revised Statutes,* §1.205 (1) (1986).

25. Speech at NARAL Twentieth Anniversary Celebration, October 14, 1989, Washington, D.C.

26. "More Than 180 Are Arrested in Abortion Demonstrations," *New York Times,* July 9, 1989, 19.

27. Balz, "Abortion-Rights Groups Map Strategy to Protect Access," *Washington Post,* July 8, 1989, A2.

28. Marshall, "Pennsylvania Abortion Bill Attacks *Roe."* *USA Today,* October 4, 1989, 3A.

29. Dionne, "On Both Sides, Advocates Predict a 50 State Battle," *New York Times,* July 4, 1989, A1.

30. Mydans, "For Abortion Rights Groups, Small Contest Is a Big Test," *New York Times,* August 7, 1989, A8.

31. Rouner, "In Debate on Abortion Funding, Only the Dynamics Are New," *Congressional Quarterly* (November 11, 1989), 3063, 3064.

32. Reid and Yost, "Florida Plans Speedy Abortion Review," *Washington Post,* July 6, 1989, A10; Schmalz, "Florida Lawmakers Are Asked to Meet on Abortion," *New York Times,* July 6, 1989, A16.

33. "Martinez Scores Low in Poll," *Miami Herald,* July 28, 1989, A1.

34. O'Neal, "Abortion Strains Ties That Bind," *Orlando Sentinel,* July 29, 1989, A1.

35. Balz, "Governor at Risk on Abortion Issue: Public Opinion in Florida Opposes Martinez Plan for Restrictions," *Washington Post,* August 1, 1989, A3.

36. Lewis, "Florida Court Rules Against Abortion Curbs," *New York Times,* October 11, 1989, A1.

37. Schmalz, "Lawmakers Spurn Curbs on Abortion in Florida Session," *New York Times,* October 11, 1989, A1.

38. Ibid., A22.

39. Baker and Melton, "Abortion Debate Heats Up Va. Gubernatorial Race," *Washington Post,* July 8, 1989, B5.

40. "Privacy Right Emerges as Issue in Race for Governor," *Los Angeles Times,* August 7, 1989, part 1, 3.
41. Ibid.
42. Cohen, "Courter, Campaign Chief Split on Abortion Issue," *Sunday Star-Ledger*, August 6, 1989, 46.
43. Phillips, "Courter Position on Abortion Still Murky," *Morristown Daily Record,* July 13, 1989, A1.
44. Schwartz, "New Jersey Contest Targeted by Backers of Abortion Rights," *Washington Post,* August 27, 1989, A18; Sullivan, "Abortion Rights Are Pressed in Jersey," *New York Times,* August 24, 1989, B5.
45. Freivogel, "Abortion Key in New Jersey Race," *St. Louis Post-Dispatch,* September 18, 1989, B1.
46. "Giuliani's 'Gender Gap,' " *Newsday,* August 4, 1989, 3.
47. Frank Lynn, "Giuliani Changes His Stance to Accept Right to Abortion," *New York Times,* August 4, 1989, B3.
48. See Baker and Melton.
49. Bowman, "Abortion Made an Issue in Virginia Gov's Race," *USA Today,* September 21, 1989, 3A.
50. Melton, "Wilder TV Ad Flays Coleman on Abortion," *Washington Post,* September 20, 1989, B4.
51. Howard, "Abortion Debate Enters as Third Force in Va. Governor's Race," *Washington Post,* October 13, 1989, B1.
52. "Abortion: The Critical Public Opinion Shift," *American Political Report,* XIX, 5.
53. "Democrat Penalized by Church in Abortion Stand Wins Election," *New York Times,* December 7, 1989, B25.
54. Shribman, "Celebrezze's Switch on Abortion Propels Issue to Center of 1990 Ohio Gubernatorial Battle," *Wall Street Journal,* December 12, 1989, A22.
55. Ibid.
56. Ibid.
57. *Katzenbach v. Morgan,* 384 U.S. 641, 651 (1966).
58. Ibid.
59. See *Lassiter v. Northampton County Board of Elections,* 360 U.S. 45 (1959).

### Chapter 9:    *In Search of Compromise*

1. See, e.g., *New York Times*/CBS News Poll: "Weighing Abortion Restrictions," *New York Times,* September 29, 1989, A13.
2. Letter to the editor from Angela R. Holder, clinical professor of pediatrics (law), Yale School of Medicine, *New York Times,* November 27, 1989, A18.
3. *Hodgson v. Minnesota,* 110 S. Ct. 2926 (1990).
4. *Ohio v. Akron Center for Reproductive Health,* 110 S. Ct. 2972 (1990).
5. *Hodgson,* 110 S. Ct. 2950 (O'Connor, J., concurring in part and concurring in the judgment in part).
6. Shribman, "Parental Notification and Consent Emerge as Key Abortion Issues," *Wall Street Journal,* November 29, 1989, A10.
7. Sharpe, "Abortion Law: Fatal Effect?," Gannett News Service, November 22, 1989.
8. "Teenagers and Abortion," *Newsweek* (January 8, 1990), 32.
9. See Sharpe.
10. See "Teenagers and Abortion."
11. See Sharpe.
12. Boule, "An American Tragedy," *Portland Oregonian,* August 27, 1989.
13. "Federal Judge Blocks a New Anti-Abortion Law in Pennsylvania," *New York Times,* January 12, 1990, A18.
14. *Hodgson,* 648 F. Suppl., 779.

15. "Pennsylvania Abortion Limits Become Law," *New York Times,* November 19, 1989, 38.
16. "Alabama May Ban 'Birth Control' Abortions," *USA Today,* December 14, 1989, A3.
17. Gene Sperling and Walter Dellinger, "Anti-Abortionists' Semantic Scam," *New York Times,* February 7, 1990, A25.
18. *New York Times*/CBS Poll, *New York Times,* September 29, 1989, A13, and August 3, 1989, A18.
19. Lake, "Abortion: A New Era," *Polling Report,* May 22, 1989, 7 (KRC/*Boston Globe* Poll, March 1989).
20. National Abortion Federation Fact Sheet, "Women Who Have Abortions," November 1989.
21. Ibid.
22. *New York Times,* January 12, 1990, A18.
23. Sperling and Dellinger, A25.
24. Ibid.
25. See *Harris v. McRae,* 448 U.S. 297 (1980).
26. Specter, "Not Letting the Numbers Speak for Themselves," *Washington Post Review,* December 18–24, 1989.
27. *Ragsdale v. Turnock,* 841 F.2d 1358, 1402 (7th Cir., 1988).
28. "When Pregnant Girls Face Mom and Dad," *U.S. News & World Report* (December 4, 1989), 25–26.
29. See Shribman.
30. Martha Minow, "The Judgment of Solomon and the Experience of Justice," in *The Structure of Procedure,* ed. R. Cover and O. Fiss (1979), 447.
31. Mary Ann Glendon, *Abortion and Divorce in Western Law* (1987), 53–58.
32. Ibid., 23.
33. Hilts, "U.S. Is Decades Behind Europe In Contraceptives, Experts Report," *New York Times,* February 15, 1990, A1.
34. Robert A. Hatcher, et al., *Contraceptive Technology* (14th ed., 1988), 431–33 (citations omitted).
35. Ibid., 433 (citations omitted).
36. See Laurence Tribe, *Constitutional Choices* (1985), 244.
37. Greenhouse, "Fears Confine Abortion Pill to France," *New York Times,* March 26, 1989, §4, 18.
38. Ibid.
39. Hatcher et al., 378 (citations omitted).
40. See National Abortion Federation Fact Sheet.
41. Greenhouse, "Fears Confine Abortion Pill to France," March 26, 1989, §4, 18.
42. Ibid.
43. See Cole, "Abortion Will Be Moot Soon," *New York Times,* October 9, 1989, A7.
44. "Abortion, Harassment and RU-486," *New York Times,* January 1, 1990, A26.
45. Greenhouse, "A New Pill, a Fierce Battle," *New York Times Magazine,* February 12, 1989, 23.
46. Greenhouse, "Fears Confine Abortion Pill to France," 18.
47. Greenhouse, "A New Pill, a Fierce Battle," 23.
48. Ibid.; letter to the editor from Diana M. Gurieva, president, Planned Parenthood, New York City, *Wall Street Journal,* November 28, 1989, A19.
49. McLaughlin, *The Pill, John Rock, and the Church* (1982), 133–45.
50. Ibid., 132.
51. Ibid., 140.
52. Ibid. 136.
53. Ibid., 136–37 (quoting a *Detroit Free Press* report).
54. Ibid., 137.
55. Ibid., 143–44.
56. Randy Shilts, *And the Band Played On* (1987), 598.
57. See McLaughlin, 108–46.
58. Ibid., 139.

59. William Stevens, "Drug Approved to Prevent Ulcers in Arthritis Sufferers," *New York Times*, December 28, 1988, A12.
60. Ibid.
61. Ibid.
62. Hatcher et al., 374.
63. Ibid.
64. Greenhouse, "A New Pill, a Fierce Battle," 23.
65. National Abortion Federation Fact Sheet.
66. *City of Akron v. Akron Center for Reproductive Health,* 462 U.S. 416, 458 (1983) (O'Connor, J., dissenting).
67. Brief for a Group of American Law Professors as Amicus Curiae in Support of Appellees in *Webster v. Reproductive Health Services,* 109 S. Ct. 3040 (1989) (No. 88-605), 23 (hereinafter Law Professors' Brief).
68. Ibid.
69. *Fetal Extrauterine Survivability,* Report to the New York State Task Force on Life and Law (1988), 10.
70. *Webster,* 109 S. Ct. 3076 n. 9 (Blackmun, J., concurring in part and dissenting in part).
71. Law Professors' Brief, 24 n. 43, citing J. R. Pasqualini and F. Kincl, *Hormones and the Fetus* (1985).
72. See Exchange of articles by J. R. Searle and by P. M. Churchland, and P. S. Churchland, "Artificial Intelligence: A Debate," *Scientific American* 262 (January 1990), 25–37; Roger Penrose, *The Emperor's New Mind* (1989).
73. Bustillo, Buster, Cohen, Hamilton, Thorneycroft, Simon, Rodi, Boyers, Marshall, Louw, Seed, and Seed, "Delivery of a Healthy Infant Following Nonsurgical Ovum Transfer," *Journal of the American Medical Association,* 251 (1984) 889.
74. Kaplan, "Fetal Research Statutes, Procreative Rights, and the 'New Biology': Living in the Interstices of the Law," *Suffolk University Law Review* 21 (1987), 723, 728–29.
75. Burch, "Ethical Considerations in the Patenting of Medical Processes," *Texas Law Review* 65 (1987), 1139 n. 1.
76. Kaplan, 753–54, n. 157.
77. McAuliffe, "The New Rules of Reproduction," *U.S. News & World Report* (April 18, 1988), 67.
78. Glendon, 54–55.
79. Note, "Redefining Mother: A Legal Matrix for New Reproductive Technologies," *Yale Law Journal* 96 (1986), 187, 200 n. 51.
80. Deborah Rhode, *Justice and Gender* (1989), 223.
81. Lloyd Cutler, "Pro-Life? Then Pay Up," *New York Times,* July 7, 1989, A29.
82. Ibid.
83. Susan Estrich, *Real Rape* (1987), 70.

## Chapter 10:    Beyond the Clash of Absolutes

1. Kolata, "Under Pressures and Stigma, More Doctors Shun Abortion," *New York Times*, January 8, 1990, A1.
2. Dionne, "Poll on Abortion Finds the Nation Is Sharply Divided," *New York Times,* April 26, 1989, A1.
3. Harris Poll, January 29, 1989, 2.
4. Mason-Dixon Opinion Research for WCIX, WTSP, *Miami Herald, Tampa Tribune,* et al., reprinted in *Polling Report,* August 14, 1989, 4.
5. *New York Times* Regional Newspaper Group, "Florida Opinion Poll," reprinted in *Polling Report,* September 4, 1989, 7.
6. University of Utah State Research Center poll, reprinted in *Polling Report,* August 14, 1989, 4.
7. 316 U.S. 535, 536 (1942).
8. Compare Kristin Luker, *Abortion and the Politics of Motherhood* (1984), 165–66.

9. *Davis v. Davis,* 1989 Tenn. App. LEXIS 641 (September 21, 1989).
10. Compare Luker, 205.
11. McNamara, "Fetal Endangerment Cases on the Rise," *Boston Globe,* October 3, 1989, 1.
12. Ibid.
13. *DeShaney v. Winnebago County,* 109 S. Ct. 998 1002 (1989).
14. Ibid., 1001–02.
15. Ibid., 1006.
16. *In Re Troy D.,* 89 Daily Journal D.A.R. 13866 (Cal. Ct. App., Fourth App. Dist., Div. One, November 15, 1989).
17. Ibid., 13867. See generally Martha Field, "Controlling the Woman to Protect the Fetus," *L. Med. & Health Care* 17 (1989), 114.
18. Luker, 159–60.
19. Ibid., 204.
20. Ibid., 164.
21. Faludi, "The Antiabortion Crusade of Randy Terry," *Washington Post,* December 23, 1989, C1.
22. See Luker, 192–215.
23. See generally Gallup Poll, *Public Opinion 1984* (1985), 240–41; Schneider, "State-Interest Analysis in Fourteenth Amendment 'Privacy' Law: An Essay on the Constitutionalization of Social Issues," *Law & Contemporary Problems* 79 (Winter 1988), 108–10.
24. Schneider, 109.
25. Ibid.
26. See, e.g., Herbert McCloskey and Alida Brill, *Dimensions of Tolerance: What Americans Believe About Civil Liberties* (1983); Skerry, "The Class Conflict over Abortion," *Public Interest* 52 (1978), 69.
27. Rodes, "Greatness Thrust upon Them: Class Biases in American Law," *American Journal of Jurisprudence* 28 (1983), 1.
28. See, e.g., Schneider, 110 and n. 121.

# Abortion Case Law

=

### Roe v. Wade
#### 410 U.S. 113 (1973)*

MR. JUSTICE BLACKMUN delivered the opinion of the Court.

This Texas federal appeal and its Georgia companion, *Doe v. Bolton,* present constitutional challenges to state criminal abortion legislation. The Texas statutes under attack here are typical of those that have been in effect in many States for approximately a century. The Georgia statutes, in contrast, have a modern cast and are a legislative product that, to an extent at least, obviously reflects the influences of recent attitudinal change, of advancing medical knowledge and techniques, and of new thinking about an old issue. . . .

The Texas statutes [make procuring an abortion a crime except] "by medical advice for the purpose of saving the life of the mother." . . .

[The district court held the Texas abortion statutes unconstitutional but denied the injunctive relief requested. Roe appealed.]

. . . [R]estrictive criminal abortion laws in effect in a majority of States today . . . derive from statutory changes effected, for the most part, in the latter half of the 19th century. . . . at common law, at the time of the adoption of our Constitution, and throughout the major portion of the 19th century, . . . [a] woman enjoyed a substantially broader right to terminate a pregnancy than she does in most States today. . . .

Three reasons have been advanced to explain historically the enactment of criminal abortion laws in the 19th century and to justify their continued existence.

It has been argued occasionally that these laws were the product of a Victorian social concern to discourage illicit sexual conduct. Texas, however, does not advance this justification in the present case, and it appears that no court or commentator has taken the argument seriously. . . .

A second reason is concerned with abortion as a medical procedure. When most criminal abortion laws were first enacted, the procedure was a hazardous one for the woman. . . .

Modern . . . medical data indicat[es] that abortion in early pregnancy, that is, prior to the end of the first trimester, although not without its risk, is now relatively safe. . . . Moreover, the risk to the woman increases as her pregnancy continues. Thus, the State

*Citations and footnotes contained within the text of the cases in this Appendix are omitted without notation. Where footnotes do appear, the original numbering has been retained.

retains a definite interest in protecting the woman's own health and safety when an abortion is proposed at a late stage of pregnancy.

The third reason is the State's interest—some phrase it in terms of duty—in protecting prenatal life. . . . Logically, of course, a legitimate state interest in this area need not stand or fall on acceptance of the belief that life begins at conception or at some other point prior to live birth. In assessing the State's interest, recognition may be given to the less rigid claim that as long as at least *potential* life is involved, the State may assert interests beyond the protection of the pregnant woman alone. . . .

It is with these interests, and the weight to be attached to them, that this case is concerned.

The Constitution does not explicitly mention any right of privacy. . . . [But] the Court has recognized that a right of personal privacy, or a guarantee of certain areas or zones of privacy, does exist under the Constitution. In varying contexts, the Court or individual Justices have, indeed, found at least the roots of that right in the First Amendment; in the Fourth and Fifth Amendments; in the penumbras of the Bill of Rights, *Griswold v. Connecticut;* in the Ninth Amendment; or in the concept of liberty guaranteed by the first section of the Fourteenth Amendment. These decisions make it clear that only personal rights that can be deemed "fundamental" or "implicit in the concept of ordered liberty" are included in this guarantee of personal privacy. They also make it clear that the right has some extension to activities relating to marriage; procreation; contraception; family relationships; and child rearing and education.

This right of privacy, whether it be founded in the Fourteenth Amendment's concept of personal liberty and restrictions upon state action, as we feel it is, or . . . in the Ninth Amendment's reservation of rights to the people, is broad enough to encompass a woman's decision whether or not to terminate her pregnancy. The detriment that the State would impose upon the pregnant woman by denying this choice altogether is apparent. Specific and direct harm medically diagnosable even in early pregnancy may be involved. Maternity, or additional offspring, may force upon the woman a distressful life and future. Psychological harm may be imminent. Mental and physical health may be taxed by child care. There is also the distress, for all concerned, associated with the unwanted child, and there is the problem of bringing a child into a family already unable, psychologically and otherwise, to care for it. In other cases, as in this one, the . . . stigma of unwed motherhood may be involved. All these are factors the woman and her responsible physician necessarily will consider in consultation.

On the basis of elements such as these, appellant and some *amici* argue that the woman's right is absolute and that she is entitled to terminate her pregnancy at whatever time, in whatever way, and for whatever reason she alone chooses. With this we do not agree. . . . The Court's decisions recognizing a right of privacy also acknowledge that some state regulation in areas protected by that right is appropriate. . . . [A] state may properly assert important interests in safeguarding health, in maintaining medical standards, and in protecting potential life. At some point in pregnancy, these respective interests become sufficiently compelling to sustain regulation of the factors that govern the abortion decision. . . .

Where certain "fundamental rights" are involved, the Court has held that regulation limiting these rights may be justified only by a "compelling state interest," and that legislative enactments must be narrowly drawn to express only the legitimate state interests at stake. . . .

. . . Appellee argues that the State's determination to recognize and protect prenatal life from and after conception constitutes a compelling state interest. . . .

The appellee and certain *amici* argue that the fetus is a "person" within the language and meaning of the Fourteenth Amendment. . . . If this suggestion of personhood is established, the appellant's case, of course, collapses, for the fetus' right to life would then be guaranteed specifically by the Amendment. . . .

The Constitution does not define "person" in so many words. [But none of its uses of the word] indicates, with any assurance, that it has any possible prenatal application.

All this, together with our observation that throughout the major portion of the 19th century prevailing legal abortion practices were far freer than they are today, persuades us that the word "person," as used in the Fourteenth Amendment, does not include the unborn. . . .

The pregnant woman cannot be isolated in her privacy. She carries an embryo and, later, a fetus . . . [I]t is reasonable and appropriate for a State to decide that at some point in time another interest, that of health of the mother or that of potential human life, becomes significantly involved. . . .

Texas urges that, apart from the Fourteenth Amendment, life begins at conception and is present throughout pregnancy, and that, therefore, the State has a compelling interest in protecting that life from and after conception. We need not resolve the difficult question of when life begins. When those trained in the respective disciplines of medicine, philosophy, and theology are unable to arrive at any consensus, the judiciary . . . is not in a position to speculate as to the answer. . . .

. . . [W]e do not agree that, by adopting one theory of life, Texas may override the rights of the pregnant woman that are at stake. We repeat, however, that the State does have an important and legitimate interest in preserving and protecting the health of the pregnant woman, . . . and that it has still *another* important and legitimate interest in protecting the potentiality of human life. These interests are separate and distinct. Each grows in substantiality as the woman approaches term and, at a point during pregnancy, each becomes "compelling."

With respect to the . . . interest in the health of the mother, the "compelling" point, in the light of present medical knowledge, is at approximately the end of the first trimester. This is so because of the now-established medical fact that until the end of the first trimester mortality in abortion may be less than mortality in normal childbirth. It follows that, from and after this point, a State may regulate the abortion procedure to the extent that the regulation reasonably relates to the preservation and protection of maternal health. . . .

This means, on the other hand, that, for the period of pregnancy prior to this "compelling" point, the attending physician, in consultation with his patient, is free to determine, without regulation by the State, that, in his medical judgment, the patient's pregnancy should be terminated. If that decision is reached, the judgment may be effectuated by an abortion free of interference by the State.

With respect to the . . . interest in potential life, the "compelling" point is at viability. This is so because the fetus then presumably has the capability of meaningful life outside the mother's womb. . . . If the State is interested in protecting fetal life after viability, it may go so far as to proscribe abortion during that period, except when it is necessary to preserve the life or health of the mother.

Measured against these standards, [the Texas statute] . . . sweeps too broadly . . . [and] therefore, cannot survive the constitutional attack made upon it here. . . .

Mr. Justice Stewart, concurring.

In 1963, this Court, in *Ferguson v. Skrupa,* purported to sound the death knell for the doctrine of substantive due process, a doctrine under which many state laws had in the past been held to violate the Fourteenth Amendment. As Mr. Justice Black's opinion for the Court in *Skrupa* put it: "We have returned to the original constitutional proposition that courts do not substitute their social and economic beliefs for the judgment of legislative bodies, who are elected to pass laws."

Barely two years later, in *Griswold v. Connecticut,* the Court held a Connecticut birth control law unconstitutional. . . . [I]t was clear to me then, and it is equally clear to me now, that the *Griswold* decision can be rationally understood only as a holding that the

Connecticut statute substantively invaded the "liberty" that is protected by the Due Process Clause of the Fourteenth Amendment. As so understood, *Griswold* stands as one in a long line of pre-*Skrupa* cases decided under the doctrine of substantive due process, and I now accept it as such. . . .

. . . The Constitution nowhere mentions a specific right of personal choice in matters of marriage and family life, but the "liberty" protected by the Due Process Clause of the Fourteenth Amendment covers more than those freedoms explicitly named in the Bill of Rights.

[I]n *Eisenstadt v. Baird*, we recognized "the right of the *individual*, married or single, to be free from unwarranted governmental intrusion into matters so fundamentally affecting a person as the decision whether to bear or beget a child." That right necessarily includes the right of a woman to decide whether or not to terminate her pregnancy. . . .


Mr. Justice Rehnquist, dissenting.


. . . I have difficulty in concluding, as the Court does, that the right of "privacy" is involved in this case. Texas . . . bars the performance of a medical abortion by a licensed physician on a plaintiff such as Roe. A transaction resulting in an operation such as this is not "private" in the ordinary usage of that word. Nor is the "privacy" that the Court finds here even a distant relative of the freedom from searches and seizures protected by the Fourth Amendment. . . .

If the Court means by the term "privacy" no more than that the claim of a person to be free from unwanted state regulation of consensual transactions may be a form of "liberty" protected by the Fourteenth Amendment, there is no doubt that similar claims have been upheld in our earlier decisions on the basis of that liberty. I agree with the statement of Mr. Justice Stewart in his concurring opinion that the "liberty," against deprivation of which without due process the Fourteenth Amendment protects, embraces more than the rights found in the Bill of Rights. But that liberty is not guaranteed absolutely against deprivation, only against deprivation without due process of law. The test traditionally applied in the area of social and economic legislation is whether or not a law . . . has a rational relation to a valid state objective. . . . If the Texas statute were to prohibit an abortion even where the mother's life is in jeopardy, I have little doubt that such a statute would lack a rational relation to a valid state objective . . .

The Court eschews the history of the Fourteenth Amendment in its reliance on the "compelling state interest" test. . . .

. . . [T]he adoption of the compelling state interest standard will inevitably require this Court to examine the legislative policies and pass on the wisdom of these policies in the very process of deciding whether a particular state interest put forward may or may not be "compelling." The decision here to break pregnancy into three distinct terms and to outline the permissible restrictions the State may impose in each one, for example, partakes more of judicial legislation than it does of a determination of the intent of the drafters of the Fourteenth Amendment.

The fact that a majority of the States . . . have had restrictions on abortions for at least a century is a strong indication, it seems to me, that the asserted right to an abortion is not "so rooted in the traditions and conscience of our people as to be ranked as fundamental." Even today, when society's views on abortion are changing, the very existence of the debate is evidence that the "right" to an abortion is not so universally accepted as the appellant would have us believe.

. . . By the time of the adoption of the Fourteenth Amendment in 1868, there were at least 36 laws enacted by state or territorial legislatures limiting abortion. . . .

. . . The only conclusion possible from this history is that the drafters did not intend to have the Fourteenth Amendment withdraw from the States the power to legislate with respect to this matter.

M<small>R</small>. J<small>USTICE</small> W<small>HITE</small>, with whom M<small>R</small>. J<small>USTICE</small> R<small>EHNQUIST</small> joins, dissenting [in *Roe* and *Doe*].

At the heart of the controversy in these cases are those recurring pregnancies that pose no danger whatsoever to the life or health of the mother but are, nevertheless, unwanted for any one or more of a variety of reasons—convenience, family planning, economics, dislike of children, the embarrassment of illegitimacy, etc. The common claim before us is that for any one of such reasons, or for no reason at all, . . . any woman is entitled to an abortion at her request if she is able to find a medical advisor willing to undertake the procedure.

The Court for the most part sustains this position: During the period prior to the time the fetus becomes viable, the Constitution of the United States values the convenience, whim, or caprice of the pregnant woman more than the life or potential life of the fetus. . . .

. . . I find nothing in the language or history of the Constitution to support the Court's judgments. The Court simply fashions and announces a new constitutional right for pregnant women and, with scarcely any reason or authority for its action, invests that right with sufficient substance to override most existing state abortion statutes. . . . As an exercise of raw judicial power, the Court perhaps has authority to do what it does today; but in my view its judgment is an improvident and extravagant exercise of the power of judicial review . . .

The Court apparently values the convenience of the pregnant woman more than the continued existence and development of the life or potential life that she carries. Whether or not I might agree with that marshaling of values, I can in no event join the Court's judgment because I find no constitutional warrant for imposing such an order of priorities on the people and legislatures of the States. In a sensitive area such as this, involving as it does issues over which reasonable men may easily and heatedly differ, I cannot accept the Court's exercise of its clear power of choice by interposing a constitutional barrier to state efforts to protect human life and by investing women and doctors with the constitutionally protected right to exterminate it. This issue, for the most part, should be left with the people and to the political processes the people have devised to govern their affairs.

## *Akron v. Akron Center for Reproductive Health*
### 462 U.S. 416 (1983)

J<small>USTICE</small> P<small>OWELL</small> delivered the opinion of the Court.

. . . [This case] come[s] to us a decade after we held in *Roe v. Wade* that the right of privacy . . . encompasses a woman's right to decide whether to terminate her pregnancy. . . . [A]rguments continue to be made . . . that we erred in interpreting the Constitution. Nonetheless, the doctrine of *stare decisis,* while perhaps never entirely persuasive on a constitutional question, is a doctrine that demands respect in a society governed by the rule of law. We respect it today, and reaffirm *Roe v. Wade.* . . .

J<small>USTICE</small> O'C<small>ONNOR</small>, with whom J<small>USTICE</small> W<small>HITE</small> and J<small>USTICE</small> R<small>EHNQUIST</small> join, dissenting.

. . . [I]t is apparent from the Court's opinion that neither sound constitutional theory nor our need to decide cases based on the application of neutral principles can accommodate an analytical framework that varies according to the "stages" of pregnancy, where those stages, and their concomitant standards of review, differ according to the level of medical technology available when a particular challenge to state regulation occurs. The Court's analysis of the Akron regulations is inconsistent both with the methods of analysis employed in previous cases dealing with abortion, and with the Court's approach to fundamental rights in other areas.

Our recent cases indicate that a regulation imposed on "a lawful abortion 'is not unconstitutional unless it unduly burdens the right to seek an abortion.' " *Maher v. Roe.* In my view, this "unduly burdensome" standard should be applied to the challenged regulations throughout the entire pregnancy without reference to the particular "stage" of pregnancy involved. If the particular regulation does not "unduly burde[n]" the fundamental right, then our evaluation of that regulation is limited to our determination that the regulation rationally relates to a legitimate state purpose. . . .

The trimester or "three-stage" approach adopted by the Court in *Roe,* and, in a modified form, employed by the Court to analyze the regulations in these cases, cannot be supported as a legitimate or useful framework for accommodating the woman's right and the State's interests. . . . [T]he trimester approach is a completely unworkable method of accommodating the conflicting personal rights and compelling state interests that are involved in the abortion context. . . .

. . . [D]espite the Court's purported adherence to the trimester approach, . . . the lines . . . have now been "blurred" because of what the Court accepts as technological advancement in the safety of abortion procedure. The State may no longer rely on a "bright line" that separates permissible from impermissible regulation, and it is no longer free to consider the second trimester as a unit and weigh the risks posed by all abortion procedures throughout that trimester. Rather, the State must continuously and conscientiously study contemporary medical and scientific literature in order to determine whether the effect of a particular regulation is to "depart from accepted medical practice" insofar as particular procedures and particular periods within the trimester are concerned. Assuming that legislative bodies are able to engage in this exacting task, it is difficult to believe that our Constitution *requires* that they do it as a prelude to protecting the health of their citizens. It is even more difficult to believe that this Court, without the resources available to those bodies entrusted with making legislative choices, believes itself competent to make these inquiries. . . . As today's decision indicates, medical technology is changing, and this change will necessitate our continued functioning as the Nation's *"ex officio* medical board with powers to approve or disapprove medical and operative practices and standards throughout the United States." *Planned Parenthood of Central Missouri v. Danforth* (WHITE, J., concurring in part and dissenting in part).

Just as improvements in medical technology inevitably will move *forward* the point at which the State may regulate for reasons of maternal health, different technological improvements will move *backward* the point of viability at which the State may proscribe abortions except when necessary to preserve the life and health of the mother. . . .

The *Roe* framework, then, is clearly on a collision course with itself. As the medical risks of various abortion procedures decrease, the point at which the State may regulate for reasons of maternal health is moved further forward to actual childbirth. As medical science becomes better able to provide for the separate existence of the fetus, the point of viability is moved further back toward conception. . . . The *Roe* framework is inherently tied to the state of medical technology that exists whenever particular litigation ensues. Although legislatures are better suited to make the necessary factual judgments in this area, the Court's framework forces legislatures, as a matter of constitutional law, to speculate about what constitutes "accepted medical practice" at any given time. Without the necessary expertise or ability, courts must then pretend to act as science review boards and examine those legislative judgments. . . .

Even assuming that there is a fundamental right to terminate pregnancy in some situations, there is no justification in law or logic for the trimester framework adopted in *Roe* and employed by the Court today. . . .

The state interest in potential human life is ... extant throughout pregnancy. In *Roe,* the Court held that ... that interest could not become compelling until the point at which the fetus was viable. The difficulty with this analysis is clear: *potential* life is no less potential in the first weeks of pregnancy than it is at viability or afterward. At any stage in pregnancy, there is the *potential* for human life. Although the Court refused to "resolve the difficult question of when life begins," the Court chose the point of viability ... to permit the complete proscription of abortion. The choice of viability as the point at which the state interest in *potential* life becomes compelling is no less arbitrary than choosing any point before viability or any point afterward. Accordingly, I believe that the State's interest in protecting potential human life exists throughout pregnancy.

Although the State possesses compelling interests in the protection of potential human life and in maternal health throughout pregnancy, not every regulation ... must be ... examined with strict scrutiny. ... "Rather, the right [to an abortion] protects the woman from unduly burdensome interference with her freedom to decide whether to terminate her pregnancy." The Court and its individual Justices have repeatedly utilized the "unduly burdensome" standard in abortion cases. ...

The "undue burden" required in the abortion cases represents the required threshold inquiry that must be conducted before this Court can require a State to justify its legislative actions under the exacting "compelling state interest" standard. ...

The abortion cases demonstrate that an "undue burden" has been found for the most part in situations involving absolute obstacles or severe limitations on the abortion decision. ...

## Thornburgh v. American College of Obstetricians and Gynecologists

### 476 U.S. 747 (1986)

JUSTICE BLACKMUN delivered the opinion of the Court.

... Less than three years ago, this Court, in *Akron,* ... reviewed challenges to state and municipal legislation regulating the performance of abortions. In *Akron,* the Court specifically reaffirmed *Roe.* Again today, we reaffirm the general principles laid down in *Roe* and in *Akron.*

In the years since this Court's decision in *Roe,* States and municipalities have adopted a number of measures seemingly designed to prevent a woman, with the advice of her physician, from exercising her freedom of choice. ... But the constitutional principles that led this Court to its decisions in 1973 still provide the compelling reason for recognizing the constitutional dimensions of a woman's right to decide whether to end her pregnancy. ... Close analysis of [the provisions challenged here] shows that they wholly subordinate constitutional privacy interests and concerns with maternal health in an effort to deter a woman from making a decision that, with her physician, is hers to make. ...

Our cases long have recognized that the Constitution embodies a promise that a certain private sphere of individual liberty will be kept largely beyond the reach of government. That promise extends to women as well as to men. Few decisions are more personal and intimate, more properly private, or more basic to individual dignity and autonomy, than a woman's decision—with the guidance of her physician and within the limits specified in *Roe*—whether to end her pregnancy. A woman's right to make that choice freely is fundamental. Any other result, in our view, would protect inadequately a central part of the sphere of liberty that our law guarantees equally to all. ...

Justice Stevens, concurring.

The scope of the individual interest in liberty that is given protection by the Due Process Clause of the Fourteenth Amendment is a matter about which conscientious judges have long disagreed. Although I believe that that interest is significantly broader than Justice White does, . . . [we agree that] the aspect of liberty at stake in this case is the freedom from unwarranted governmental intrusion into individual decisions in matters of childbearing. . . .

. . . Justice White agrees that "a woman's ability to choose an abortion is a species of 'liberty' that is subject to the general protections of the Due Process Clause." His agreement with that "indisputable" proposition is not qualified or limited to decisions made by pregnant women who are married and, indeed, it would be a strange form of liberty if it were so limited. . . . Up to this point in Justice White's analysis, his opinion is fully consistent with the accepted teachings of the Court and with the major premises of *Roe v. Wade.* For reasons that are not entirely clear, however, Justice White abruptly announces that the interest in "liberty" that is implicated by a decision not to bear a child that is made a few days after conception is *less* fundamental than a comparable decision made before conception. There may, of course, be a significant difference in the strength of the countervailing state interest, but I fail to see how a decision on childbearing becomes *less* important the day after conception than the day before. Indeed, if one decision is more "fundamental" to the individual's freedom than the other, surely it is the postconception decision that is the more serious. Thus, it is difficult for me to understand how Justice White reaches the conclusion that restraints upon this aspect of a woman's liberty do not "call into play anything more than the most minimal judicial scrutiny."[4]

If Justice White were correct in regarding the postconception decision of the question whether to bear a child as a relatively unimportant, second-class sort of interest, I might agree with his view that the individual should be required to conform her decision to the will of the majority. But if that decision commands the respect that is traditionally associated with the "sensitive areas of liberty" protected by the Constitution, as Justice White characterized reproductive decisions in *Griswold,* no individual should be compelled to surrender the freedom to make that decision for herself simply because her "value preferences" are not shared by the majority. In a sense, the basic question is whether the "abortion decision" should be made by the individual or by the majority "in the unrestrained imposition of its own, extra-constitutional value preferences." But

---

[4]At times Justice White's rhetoric conflicts with his own analysis. For instance, his emphasis on the lack of a decision by "the people . . . in 1787, 1791, 1868, or any time since" stands in sharp contrast to his earlier, forthright rejection of "the simplistic view that constitutional interpretation can possibly be limited to 'the plain meaning' of the Constitution's text or to the subjective intention of the Framers." Similarly, his statement that an abortion decision should be subject to "the will of the people," does not take us very far in determining *which* people—the majorities in state legislatures or the individuals confronted with unwanted pregnancies. In view of his agreement that the decision about abortion is "a species of liberty" protected by the Constitution, moreover, and in view of the fact that "liberty" plays a rather prominent role in our Constitution, his suggestion that the Court's evaluation of that interest represents the imposition of "extra-constitutional value preferences" seems to me inexplicable. This characterization of the Court's analysis as "extraconstitutional" also does not reflect Justice White's simultaneous recognition that "[t]he Constitution . . . is a document announcing fundamental principles in value-laden terms that leave ample scope for the exercise of normative judgment by those charged with interpreting and applying it." Finally, I fail to see how the fact that "men and women of good will and high commitment to constitutional government" are on both sides of the abortion issue helps to resolve the difficult constitutional question before us; I take it that the disputants in most constitutional controversies in our free society can be similarly characterized.

surely JUSTICE WHITE is quite wrong in suggesting that the Court is imposing value preferences on anyone else.[6]

JUSTICE WHITE is also surely wrong in suggesting that the governmental interest in protecting fetal life is equally compelling during the entire period from the moment of conception until the moment of birth. Again, I recognize that a powerful theological argument can be made for that position, but I believe our jurisdiction is limited to the evaluation of secular state interests. I should think it obvious that the State's interest in the protection of an embryo—even if that interest is defined as "protecting those who will be citizens"—increases progressively and dramatically as the organism's capacity to feel pain, to experience pleasure, to survive, and to react to its surroundings increases day by day. . . .

Nor is it an answer to argue that life itself is not a static condition, and that "there is no nonarbitrary line separating a fetus from a child, or indeed, an adult human being." For, unless the religious view that a fetus is a "person" is adopted—a view JUSTICE WHITE refuses to embrace—there is a fundamental and well-recognized difference between a fetus and a human being; indeed, if there is not such a difference, the permissibility of terminating the life of a fetus could scarcely be left to the will of the state legislatures.[8] And if distinctions may be drawn between a fetus and a human being in terms of the state interest in their protection—even though the fetus represents one of "those who will be citizens"—it seems to me quite odd to argue that distinctions may not also be drawn between the state interest in protecting the freshly fertilized egg and the state interest in protecting the 9-month-gestated, fully sentient fetus on the eve of birth. . . .

Turning to JUSTICE WHITE's comments on *stare decisis,* he is of course correct in pointing out that the Court "has not hesitated to overrule decisions, or even whole lines of cases, where experience, scholarship, and reflection demonstrated that their fundamental premises were not to be found in the Constitution." But JUSTICE WHITE has not disavowed the "fundamental premises" on which the decision in *Roe v. Wade* rests. He has not disavowed the Court's prior approach to the interpretation of the word "liberty" or, more narrowly, the line of cases that culminated in the unequivocal holding, applied to unmarried persons and married persons alike, "that the Constitution protects individual decisions in matters of childbearing from unjustified intrusion by the State." . . .

Nor does the fact that the doctrine of *stare decisis* is not an absolute bar to the reexamination of past interpretations of the Constitution mean that the values underlying that doctrine may be summarily put to one side. There is a strong public interest in stability, and in the orderly conduct of our affairs, that is served by a consistent course of constitutional adjudication. Acceptance of the fundamental premises that underlie the decision in *Roe v. Wade,* as well as the application of those premises in that case, places the primary responsibility for decision in matters of childbearing squarely in the private sector of our society. The majority remains free to preach the evils of birth control and abortion and to persuade others to make correct decisions while the individual faced with the reality of a difficult choice having serious and personal consequences of major importance to her own future—perhaps to the salvation of her own immortal soul—remains

---

[6]JUSTICE WHITE's characterization of the governmental interest as "protecting those who will be citizens if their lives are not ended in the womb," reveals that his opinion may be influenced as much by his own value preferences as by his view about the proper allocation of decisionmaking responsibilities between the individual and the State. For if federal judges must allow the State to make the abortion decision, presumably the State is free to decide that a woman may *never* abort, may *sometimes* abort, or, as in the People's Republic of China, must *always* abort if her family is already too large. In contrast, our cases represent a consistent view that the individual is primarily responsible for reproductive decisions, whether the State seeks to prohibit reproduction, *Skinner v. Oklahoma,* or to require it, *Roe v. Wade.*

[8]No Member of this Court has ever suggested that a fetus is a "person" within the meaning of the Fourteenth Amendment.

free to seek and to obtain sympathetic guidance from those who share her own value preferences.

In the final analysis, the holding in *Roe v. Wade* presumes that it is far better to permit some individuals to make incorrect decisions than to deny all individuals the right to make decisions that have a profound effect upon their destiny. Arguably a very primitive society would have been protected from evil by a rule against eating apples; a majority familiar with Adam's experience might favor such a rule. But the lawmakers who placed a special premium on the protection of individual liberty have recognized that certain values are more important than the will of a transient majority.

CHIEF JUSTICE BURGER, dissenting.

I agree with much of JUSTICE WHITE's and JUSTICE O'CONNOR's dissents. . . .

I based my concurring statements in *Roe* and *Maher* on the principle expressed in the Court's opinion in *Roe* that the right to an abortion "is not unqualified and must be considered against important state interests in regulation." In short, every Member of the *Roe* Court rejected the idea of abortion on demand. The Court's opinion today, however, plainly undermines that important principle. . . .

The Court's opinion today is but the most recent indication of the distance travelled since *Roe*. Perhaps the first important road marker was the Court's holding in *Planned Parenthood of Central Missouri v. Danforth*, in which the Court held . . . that the State may not require that minors seeking an abortion first obtain parental consent. . . .

Yet today the Court goes beyond *Danforth* by remanding . . . the provisions of Pennsylvania's statute requiring that a minor seeking an abortion without parental consent petition the appropriate court for authorization. Even if I were to agree that the Constitution requires that the states may not provide that a minor receive parental consent before undergoing an abortion, I would certainly hold that judicial approval may be required. This is in keeping with the long-standing common-law principle that courts may function *in loco parentis* when parents are unavailable or neglectful. . . .

In discovering constitutional infirmities in state regulations of abortion that are in accord with our history and tradition, we may have lured judges into "roaming at large in the constitutional field." The soundness of our holdings must be tested by the decisions that purport to follow them. If *Danforth* and today's holding really mean what they seem to say, I agree we should reexamine *Roe*.

JUSTICE WHITE, with whom JUSTICE REHNQUIST joins, dissenting.

Today the Court carries forward the "difficult and continuing venture in substantive due process" that began with the decision in *Roe v. Wade* and has led the Court further and further afield in the 13 years since that decision was handed down. I was in dissent in *Roe v. Wade* and am in dissent today. . . .

I

The rule of *stare decisis* is essential if case-by-case judicial decisionmaking is to be reconciled with the principle of the rule of law, for when governing legal standards are open to revision in every case, deciding cases becomes a mere exercise of judicial will, with arbitrary and unpredictable results. But *stare decisis* is not the only constraint upon judicial decisionmaking. . . . [D]ecisions that find in the Constitution principles or values that cannot fairly be read into that document usurp the people's authority, for such decisions represent choices that the people have never made and that they cannot disavow through corrective legislation. For this reason, it is essential that this Court maintain the power to restore authority to its proper possessors by correcting constitutional decisions that, on reconsideration, are found to be mistaken.

The Court has therefore adhered to the rule that *stare decisis* is not rigidly applied in cases involving constitutional issues, and has not hesitated to overrule decisions, or even whole lines of cases, where experience, scholarship, and reflection demonstrated that their fundamental premises were not to be found in the Constitution. . . .

In my view, the time has come to recognize that *Roe v. Wade* . . . "departs from a proper understanding" of the Constitution and to overrule it. I do not claim that the arguments in support of this proposition are new ones or that they were not considered by the Court in *Roe* or in the cases that succeeded it. . . . [But that] the flaws in an opinion were evident at the time it was handed down is hardly a reason for adhering to it.

## A

*Roe v. Wade* posits that a woman has a fundamental right to terminate her pregnancy, and that this right may be restricted only in the service of two compelling state interests: the interest in maternal health (which becomes compelling only at the stage in pregnancy at which an abortion becomes more hazardous than carrying the pregnancy to term) and the interest in protecting the life of the fetus (which becomes compelling only at the point of viability). A reader of the Constitution might be surprised to find that it encompassed these detailed rules, for the text obviously contains no references to abortion, nor, indeed, to pregnancy or reproduction generally; and, of course, it is highly doubtful that the authors of any of the provisions of the Constitution believed that they were giving protection to abortion. As its prior cases clearly show, however, this Court does not subscribe to the simplistic view that constitutional interpretation can possibly be limited to the "plain meaning" of the Constitution's text or to the subjective intention of the Framers. The Constitution is not a deed setting forth the precise metes and bounds of its subject matter; rather, it is a document announcing fundamental principles in value-laden terms that leave ample scope for the exercise of normative judgment by those charged with interpreting and applying it. In particular, the Due Process Clause of the Fourteenth Amendment, which forbids the deprivation of "life, liberty, or property without due process of law," has been read by the majority of the Court to be broad enough to provide substantive protection against state infringement of a broad range of individual interests.

In most instances, the substantive protection afforded the liberty or property of an individual by the Fourteenth Amendment is extremely limited. . . . Only "fundamental" rights are entitled to the added protection provided by strict judicial scrutiny of legislation that impinges upon them. I can certainly agree with the proposition—which I deem indisputable—that a woman's ability to choose an abortion is a species of "liberty" that is subject to the general protections of the Due Process Clause. I cannot agree, however, that this liberty is so "fundamental" that restrictions upon it call into play anything more than the most minimal judicial scrutiny.

Fundamental liberties and interests are most clearly present when the Constitution provides specific textual recognition of their existence and importance. Thus, the Court is on relatively firm ground when it deems certain of the liberties set forth in the Bill of Rights to be fundamental and therefore finds them incorporated in the Fourteenth Amendment's guarantee that no State may deprive any person of liberty without due process of law. When the Court ventures further and defines as "fundamental" liberties that are nowhere mentioned in the Constitution (or that are present only in the so-called "penumbras" of specifically enumerated rights), it must, of necessity, act with more caution, lest it open itself to the accusation that, in the name of identifying constitutional principles to which the people have consented in framing their Constitution, the Court has done nothing more than impose its own controversial choices of value upon the people . . .

. . . One approach has been to limit the class of fundamental liberties to those interests that are "implicit in the concept of ordered liberty" such that "neither liberty nor justice would exist if [they] were sacrificed." Another, broader approach is to define fundamental liberties as those that are "deeply rooted in this Nation's history and tradition." . . . Whether either of these approaches can, as JUSTICE HARLAN hoped, prevent "judges from roaming at large in the constitutional field" is debatable. What for me is not subject to debate, however, is that either of the basic definitions of fundamental liberties, taken seriously, indicates the illegitimacy of the Court's decision in *Roe v. Wade*.

The Court has justified the recognition of a woman's fundamental right to terminate her pregnancy by invoking decisions upholding claims of personal autonomy in connection with the conduct of family life, the rearing of children, marital privacy, the use of contraceptives, and the preservation of the individual's capacity to procreate. Even if each of these cases was correctly decided and could be properly grounded in rights that are "implicit in the concept of ordered liberty" or "deeply rooted in this Nation's history and tradition," the issues in the cases cited differ from those at stake where abortion is concerned. As the Court appropriately recognized in *Roe v. Wade*, "[t]he pregnant woman cannot be isolated in her privacy;" the termination of a pregnancy typically involves the destruction of another entity: the fetus. . . . [T]here is no nonarbitrary line separating a fetus from a child or, indeed, an adult human being. Given that the continued existence and development—that is to say, the *life*—of such an entity are so directly at stake in the woman's decision whether or not to terminate her pregnancy, that decision must be recognized as *sui generis*, different in kind from the others that the Court has protected under the rubric of personal or family privacy and autonomy.[2] . . .

. . . The Court's opinion in *Roe* itself convincingly refutes the notion that the abortion liberty is deeply rooted in the history or tradition of our people, as does the continuing and deep division of the people themselves over the question of abortion. As for the notion that choice in the matter of abortion is implicit in the concept of ordered liberty, it seems apparent to me that a free, egalitarian, and democratic society does not presuppose any particular rule or set of rules with respect to abortion. And again, the fact that many men and women of good will and high commitment to constitutional government place themselves on both sides of the abortion controversy strengthens my own conviction that the values animating the Constitution do not compel recognition of the abortion liberty as fundamental. In so denominating that liberty, the Court engages not in constitutional interpretation, but in the unrestrained imposition of its own, extraconstitutional value preferences.[3]

[2]That the abortion decision . . . concerns childbearing (or, more generally, family life) in no sense necessitates a holding that the liberty to choose abortion is "fundamental." That the decision involves the destruction of the fetus renders it different in kind from the decision not to conceive in the first place. This difference does not go merely to the weight of the state interest in regulating abortion; it affects as well the characterization of the liberty interest itself. For if the liberty to make certain decisions with respect to contraception without governmental constraint is "fundamental," it is not only because those decisions are "serious" and "important" to the individual but also because some value of privacy or individual autonomy that is somehow implicit in the scheme of ordered liberties established by the Constitution supports a judgment that such decisions are none of government's business. The same cannot be said where, as here, the individual is not "isolated in her privacy."

My point can be illustrated by drawing on a related area in which fundamental liberty interests have been found: childrearing. The Court's decisions . . . can be read for the proposition that parents have a fundamental liberty to make decisions with respect to the upbringing of their children. But no one would suggest that this fundamental liberty extends to assaults committed upon children by their parents. It is not the case that parents have a fundamental liberty to engage in such activities and that the State may intrude to prevent them only because it has a compelling interest in the well-being of children; rather, such activities, by their very nature, should be viewed as outside the scope of the fundamental liberty interest.

[3]JUSTICE STEVENS asserts that I am "quite wrong in suggesting that the Court is imposing value

## B

A second, equally basic error infects the Court's decision in *Roe v. Wade.* The detailed set of rules governing state restrictions on abortion that the Court first articulated in *Roe* and has since refined and elaborated presupposes not only that the woman's liberty to choose an abortion is fundamental, but also that the State's countervailing interest in protecting fetal life (or, as the Court would have it, "potential human life") becomes "compelling" only at the point at which the fetus is viable. As Justice O'Connor pointed out three years ago in her dissent in *Akron,* the Court's choice of viability as the point at which the State's interest becomes compelling is entirely arbitrary....

The governmental interest at issue is in protecting those who will be citizens if their lives are not ended in the womb.... The State's interest is in the fetus as an entity in itself, and the character of this entity does not change at the point of viability under conventional medical wisdom. Accordingly, the State's interest, if compelling after viability, is equally compelling before viability.[4]

## C

... Abortion is a hotly contested moral and political issue. Such issues, in our society, are to be resolved by the will of the people, either as expressed through legislation or through the general principles they have already incorporated into the Constitution they have adopted. *Roe v. Wade* implies that the people have already resolved the debate by weaving into the Constitution the values and principles that answer the issue. As I have argued, I believe it is clear that the people have never—not in 1787, 1791, 1868, or at any time since—done any such thing. I would return the issue to the people by overruling *Roe v. Wade....*

The decision today appears symptomatic of the Court's own insecurity over its handiwork in *Roe* and the cases following that decision. Aware that in *Roe* it essentially created something out of nothing and that there are many in this country who hold that decision to be basically illegitimate, the Court responds defensively. Perceiving, in a statute implementing the State's legitimate policy of preferring childbirth to abortion, a threat to or criticism of the decision in *Roe,* the majority indiscriminately strikes down statutory provisions that in no way contravene the right recognized in *Roe.* I do not share the warped point of view of the majority, nor can I follow the tortuous path the majority tread in proceeding to strike down the statute before us. I dissent.

preferences on anyone else" when it denominates the liberty to choose abortion as "fundamental" (in contradistinction to such other, nonfundamental liberties as the liberty to use dangerous drugs or to operate a business without governmental interference) and thereby disempowers state electoral majorities from legislating in this area. I can only respond that I cannot conceive of a definition of the phrase "imposing value preferences" that does not encompass the Court's action.

Justice Stevens also suggests that it is the legislative majority that has engaged in "the unrestrained imposition of its own, extraconstitutional value preferences" when a state legislature restricts the availability of abortion. But a legislature, unlike a court, has the inherent power to do so unless its choices are constitutionally *forbidden,* which, in my view, is not the case here.

[4]Contrary to Justice Stevens' suggestion, this is no more a "theological" position than is the Court's own judgment that viability is the point at which the state interest becomes compelling.... The point is that the specific interest the Court has recognized as compelling after the point of viability— that is, the interest in protecting "potential human life"—is present as well before viability, and the point of viability seems to bear no discernible relationship to the strength of that interest....

Further, it is self-evident that neither the legislative decision to assert a state interest in fetal life before viability nor the judicial decision to recognize that interest as compelling constitutes an impermissible "religious" decision merely because it coincides with the belief of one or more religions. Certainly the fact that the prohibition of murder coincides with one of the Ten Commandments does not render a State's interest in its murder statutes less than compelling, nor are legislative and judicial decisions concerning the use of the death penalty tainted by their correspondence to varying religious views on that subject....

## Webster v. Reproductive Health Services
### 109 S.CT. 3040 (1989)

CHIEF JUSTICE REHNQUIST announced the judgment of the Court and delivered the opinion of the Court with respect to Parts I, II-A, II-B, and II-C, and an opinion with respect to Parts II-D and III, in which JUSTICE WHITE and JUSTICE KENNEDY join. . . .

### II

Decision of this case requires us to address four sections of the Missouri Act: (a) the preamble; (b) the prohibition on the use of public facilities or employees to perform abortions; (c) the prohibition on public funding of abortion counseling; and (d) the requirement that physicians conduct viability tests prior to performing abortions. . . .

### A

The Act's preamble . . . sets forth "findings" by the Missouri legislature that "[t]he life of each human being begins at conception," and that "[u]nborn children have protectable interests in life, health, and well-being." The Act then mandates that state laws be interpreted to provide unborn children with "all the rights, privileges, and immunities available to other persons, citizens, and residents of this state," subject to the Constitution and this Court's precedents. In invalidating the preamble, the Court of Appeals relied on this Court's dictum that " 'a State may not adopt one theory of when life begins to justify its regulation of abortions.' " *Akron,* citing *Roe.* . . . The court thought that . . . "the state intended its abortion regulations to be understood against the backdrop of its theory of life." . . .

In our view, the Court of Appeals misconceived the meaning of the *Akron* dictum, which was only that a State could not "justify" an abortion regulation otherwise invalid under *Roe* on the ground that it embodied the State's view about when life begins. Certainly the preamble does not by its terms regulate abortion. . . . The Court has emphasized that *Roe* "implies no limitation on the authority of a State to make a value judgment favoring childbirth over abortion." The preamble can be read simply to express that sort of value judgment. . . .

. . . It will be time enough for federal courts to address the meaning of the premable should it be applied to restrict the activities of appellees in some concrete way. . . . We therefore need not pass on the constitutionality of the Act's preamble.

### B

[The next provision which is challenged] provides that "[i]t shall be unlawful for any public employee within the scope of his employment to perform . . . an abortion, not necessary to save the life of the mother," [and that it is] "unlawful for any public facility to be used for the purpose of performing . . . an abortion not necessary to save the life of the mother." . . .

. . . [T]he State's decision here to use public facilities and staff to encourage childbirth over abortion "places no governmental obstacle in the path of a woman who chooses to terminate her pregnancy." Just as Congress' refusal to fund abortions in *Harris v. McRae* left "an indigent woman with at least the same range of choice in deciding whether to obtain a medically necessary abortion as she would have had if Congress had chosen to subsidize no health care costs at all," Missouri's refusal to allow public employees to perform abortions in public hospitals leaves a pregnant woman with the same choices as if the State had chosen not to operate any public hospitals at all. . . . Having held that the State's refusal to fund abortions does not violate *Roe,* it strains logic to reach a contrary result for the use of public facilities and employees. . . .

D

. . . [T]he Missouri Act provides:

"Before a physician performs an abortion on a woman he has reason to believe is carrying an unborn child of twenty or more weeks gestational age, the physician shall first determine if the unborn child is viable by using and exercising that degree of care, skill, and proficiency commonly exercised by the ordinarily skillful, careful, and prudent physician engaged in similar practice under the same or similar conditions. In making this determination of viability, the physician shall perform or cause to be performed such medical examinations and tests as are necessary to make a finding of the gestational age, weight, and lung maturity of the unborn child and shall enter such findings and determination of viability in the medical record of the mother."

As with the preamble, the parties disagree over the meaning of this statutory provision. The State emphasizes the language of the first sentence, which speaks in terms of the physician's determination of viability being made by the standards of ordinary skill in the medical profession. Appellees stress the language of the second sentence, which prescribes such "tests as are necessary" to make a finding of gestational age, fetal weight, and lung maturity. . . .

We think the viability-testing provision makes sense only if the second sentence is read to require only those tests that are useful to making subsidiary findings as to viability. If we construe this provision to require a physician to perform those tests needed to make the three specified findings *in all circumstances,* including when the physician's reasonable professional judgment indicates that the tests would be irrelevant to determining viability or even dangerous to the mother and the fetus, the second sentence . . . would conflict with the first sentence's *requirement* that a physician apply his reasonable professional skill and judgment. . . .

The viability testing provision . . . is concerned with promoting the State's interest in potential human life rather than in maternal health. [It] creates what is essentially a presumption of viability at 20 weeks, which the physician must rebut with tests indicating that the fetus is not viable prior to performing an abortion. It also directs the physician's determination as to viability by specifying consideration, if feasible, of gestational age, fetal weight, and lung capacity. The District Court found that "the medical evidence is uncontradicted that a 20-week fetus is *not* viable," . . . but . . . that there may be a 4-week error in estimating gestational age which supports testing at 20 weeks. . . .

. . . To the extent that [the provision] regulates the method for determining viability, it undoubtedly does superimpose state regulation on the medical determination of whether a particular fetus is viable. The Court of Appeals and the District Court thought it unconstitutional for this reason. To the extent that the viability tests increase the cost of what are in fact second-trimester abortions, their validity may also be questioned under *Akron,* where the Court held that a requirement that second-trimester abortions must be performed in hospitals was invalid because it substantially increased the expense of those procedures.

We think that the doubt cast upon the Missouri statute by these cases is not so much a flaw in the statute as it is a reflection of the fact that the rigid trimester analysis of the course of a pregnancy enunciated in *Roe* has resulted in subsequent cases . . . making constitutional law in this area a virtual Procrustean bed. . . .

*Stare decisis* is a cornerstone of our legal system, but it has less power in constitutional cases, where, save for constitutional amendments, this Court is the only body able to make needed changes. We have not refrained from reconsideration of a prior construction of the Constitution that has proved "unsound in principle and unworkable in practice." We think the *Roe* trimester framework falls into that category.

In the first place, the rigid *Roe* framework is hardly consistent with the notion of a Constitution cast in general terms, as ours is, and usually speaking in general principles, as ours does. The key elements of the *Roe* framework—trimesters and viability—are not found in the text of the Constitution or in any place else one would expect to find a constitutional principle. . . .

In the second place, we do not see why the State's interest in protecting potential human life should come into existence only at the point of viability, and that there should therefore be a rigid line allowing state regulation after viability but prohibiting it before viability. . . .

The tests that [the statute] requires the physician to perform are designed to determine viability. The State here has chosen viability as the point at which its interest in potential human life must be safeguarded. It is true that the tests in question increase the expense of abortion, and regulate the discretion of the physician in determining the viability of the fetus. Since the tests will undoubtedly show in many cases that the fetus is not viable, the tests will have been performed for what were in fact second-trimester abortions. But we are satisfied that the requirement of these tests permissibly furthers the State's interest in protecting potential human life, and we therefore believe [the viability testing requirement] to be constitutional.

. . . *Griswold,* unlike *Roe,* did not purport to adopt a whole framework, complete with detailed rules and distinctions, to govern the cases in which the asserted liberty interest would apply. As such, it was far different from the opinion, if not the holding, of *Roe,* which sought to establish a constitutional framework for judging state regulation of abortion during the entire term of pregnancy. . . . The experience of the Court in applying *Roe* in later cases suggests to us that there is wisdom in not unnecessarily attempting to elaborate the abstract differences between a "fundamental right" to abortion, a "limited fundamental constitutional right," which JUSTICE BLACKMUN's dissent today treats *Roe* as having established, or a liberty interest protected by the Due Process Clause, which we believe it to be . . .

### III

Both appellants and the United States as *Amicus Curiae* have urged that we overrule our decision in *Roe v. Wade.* The facts of the present case, however, differ from those at issue in *Roe.* Here, Missouri has determined that viability is the point at which its interest in potential human life must be safeguarded. In *Roe,* on the other hand, the Texas statute criminalized the performance of *all* abortions, except when the mother's life was at stake. This case therefore affords us no occasion to revisit the holding of *Roe,* which was that the Texas statute unconstitutionally infringed the right to an abortion derived from the Due Process Clause, and we leave it undisturbed. To the extent indicated in our opinion, we would modify and narrow *Roe* and succeeding cases. . . .

JUSTICE O'CONNOR, concurring in part and concurring in the judgment.

I concur in Parts I, II-A, II-B, and II-C of the Court's opinion.

Nothing in the record before us or the opinions below indicates that [the] preamble to Missouri's abortion regulation statute will affect a woman's decision to have an abortion. JUSTICE STEVENS suggests that the preamble may also "interfere[] with contraceptive choices," because certain contraceptive devices act on a female ovum after it has been fertilized by a male sperm. . . . It may be correct that the use of postfertilization contraceptive devices is constitutionally protected by *Griswold* and its progeny but, as with a woman's abortion decision, nothing in the record or the opinions below indicates that the preamble will affect a woman's decision to practice contraception. . . . Neither is there any indication of the possibility that the preamble might be applied to prohibit the performance of *in vitro* fertilization. I agree with the Court, therefore, that all of these intimations of unconstitutionality are simply too hypothetical to support the use of declaratory judgment procedures and injunctive remedies in this case. . . .

In its interpretation of Missouri's "determination of viability" provision, the plurality has proceeded in a manner unnecessary to deciding the question at hand. . . .

[While I agree with the plurality's interpretation of the statute,] [u]nlike the plurality, I do not understand these viability testing requirements to conflict with any of the Court's past decisions concerning state regulation of abortion. Therefore, there is no necessity to accept the State's invitation to reexamine the constitutional validity of *Roe v. Wade.* Where there is no need to decide a constitutional question, it is a venerable principle of this Court's adjudicatory process not to do so. . . . Neither will [the Court] generally "formulate a rule of constitutional law broader than is required by the precise facts to which it is to be applied." . . . [R]econsideration of *Roe* falls not into any "good-cause exception" to this "fundamental rule of judicial restraint. . . ." When the constitutional invalidity of a State's abortion statute actually turns on the constitutional validity of *Roe v. Wade,* there will be time enough to reexamine *Roe.* And to do so carefully. . . .

I do not think the second sentence of [the viability testing provision] . . . imposes a degree of state regulation on the medical determination of viability that in any way conflicts with prior decisions of this Court. As the plurality recognizes, the requirement that, where not imprudent, physicians perform examinations and tests useful to making subsidiary findings to determine viability "promote[s] the State's interest in potential human life rather than in maternal health." No decision of this Court has held that the State may not directly promote its interest in potential life when viability is possible. . . .

It is clear to me that requiring the performance of examinations and tests useful to determining whether a fetus is viable, when viability is possible, and when it would not be medically imprudent to do so, does not impose an undue burden on a woman's abortion decision. On this ground alone I would reject the suggestion that [the requirement] is unconstitutional.

JUSTICE SCALIA, concurring in part and concurring in the judgment.

I join Parts I, II-A, II-B, and II-C of the opinion of the CHIEF JUSTICE. As to Part II-D, I share JUSTICE BLACKMUN's view that it effectively would overrule *Roe v. Wade.* I think that should be done, but would do it more explicitly. Since today we contrive to avoid doing it, and indeed to avoid almost any decision of national import, I need not set forth my reasons, some of which have been well recited in dissents of my colleagues in other cases.

The outcome of today's case will doubtless be heralded as a triumph of judicial statesmanship. It is not that, unless it is statesmanlike needlessly to prolong this Court's self-awarded sovereignty over a field where it has little proper business since the answers to most of the cruel questions posed are political and not juridical—a sovereignty which therefore quite properly, but to the great damage of the Court, makes it the object of the sort of organized public pressure that political institutions in a democracy ought to receive.

JUSTICE O'CONNOR's assertion that a " 'fundamental rule of judicial restraint' " requires us to avoid reconsidering *Roe,* cannot be taken seriously. . . . We have not disposed of this case on some statutory or procedural ground, but have decided, and could not avoid deciding, whether the Missouri statute meets the requirements of the United States Constitution. The only choice available is whether, in deciding that constitutional question, we should use *Roe* as the benchmark, or something else. What is involved, therefore, is not the rule of avoiding constitutional issues where possible, but the quite separate principle that we will not " 'formulate a rule of constitutional law broader than is required by the precise facts to which it is to be applied.' " The latter is a sound general principle, but one often departed from when good reason exists. . . . I have not identified with certainty the first instance of our deciding a case on broader constitutional grounds than absolutely necessary, but it is assuredly no later than *Marbury v. Madison*. . . .

The real question, then, is whether there are valid reasons to go beyond the most stingy possible holding today. It seems to me there are not only valid but compelling ones. Ordinarily, speaking no more broadly than is absolutely required avoids throwing settled law into confusion; doing so today preserves a chaos that is evident to anyone who can read and count. . . . We can now look forward to at least another Term with carts full of mail from the public, and streets full of demonstrators, urging us—their unelected and life-tenured judges who have been awarded those extraordinary, undemocratic characteristics precisely in order that we might follow the law despite the popular will—to follow the popular will. . . .

It was an arguable question today whether [the viability testing provision] contravened this Court's understanding of *Roe v. Wade*,[1] and I would have examined *Roe* rather than examining the contravention. Given the Court's newly contracted abstemiousness, what will it take, one must wonder, to permit us to reach that fundamental question? The result of our vote today is that we will not reconsider that prior opinion, even if most of the Justices think it is wrong, unless we have before us a statute that in fact contradicts it—and even then (under our newly discovered "no-broader-than-necessary" requirement), only minor problematical aspects of *Roe* will be reconsidered, unless one expects State legislatures to adopt provisions whose compliance with *Roe* cannot even be argued with a straight face. It thus appears that the mansion of constitutionalized abortion-law, constructed overnight in *Roe v. Wade*, must be disassembled door-jamb by door-jamb, and never entirely brought down, no matter how wrong it may be.

Of the four courses we might have chosen today—to reaffirm *Roe*, to overrule it explicitly, to overrule it *sub silentio*, or to avoid the question—the last is the least responsible. On the question of the constitutionality of [the law], I concur in the judgment of the Court and strongly dissent from the manner in which it has been reached.

JUSTICE BLACKMUN, with whom JUSTICE BRENNAN and JUSTICE MARSHALL join, concurring in part and dissenting in part.

Today, *Roe v. Wade* and the fundamental constitutional right of women to decide whether to terminate a pregnancy, survive but are not secure. Although the Court extricates itself from this case without making a single, even incremental, change in the law of abortion, the plurality and JUSTICE SCALIA would overrule *Roe* (the first silently, the other explicitly) and would return to the States virtually unfettered authority to control the quintessentially intimate, personal, and life-directing decision whether to carry a fetus to term. Although today, no less than yesterday, the Constitution and the decisions of this Court prohibit a State from enacting laws that inhibit women from the meaningful exercise of that right, a plurality of this Court implicitly invites every state legislature to enact more and more restrictive abortion regulations in order to provoke more and more test cases, in the hope that sometime down the line the Court will return the law of procreative freedom to the severe limitations that generally prevailed in this country before January 22, 1973.

[1]That question, compared with the question whether we should reconsider and reverse *Roe*, is hardly worth a footnote, but I think JUSTICE O'CONNOR answers that incorrectly as well. . . .

Similarly irrational is the new concept that JUSTICE O'CONNOR introduces into the law in order to achieve her result, the notion of a State's "interest in potential life when viability is possible." Since viability means the mere *possibility* (not the certainty) of survivability outside the womb, "possible viability" must mean the possibility of a possibility of survivability outside the womb. Perhaps our next opinion will expand the third trimester into the second even further, by approving state action designed to take account of "the chance of possible viability."

. . . The plurality opinion is filled with winks, and nods, and knowing glances to those who would do away with *Roe* explicitly, but turns a stone face to anyone in search of what the plurality conceives as the scope of a woman's right under the Due Process Clause to terminate a pregnancy free from the coercive and brooding influence of the State. The simple truth is that *Roe* would not survive the plurality's analysis, and that the plurality provides no substitute for *Roe*'s protective umbrella.

I fear for the future. I fear for the liberty and equality of the millions of women who have lived and come of age in the 16 years since *Roe* was decided. I fear for the integrity of, and public esteem for, this Court.

I dissent.

* * *

. . . [T]ucked away at the end of its opinion, the plurality suggests a radical reversal of the law of abortion; and there, primarily, I direct my attention.

. . . In flat contradiction to *Roe,* the plurality concludes that the State's interest in potential life is compelling before viability, and upholds the testing provision because it "permissibly furthers" that state interest. . . .

Had the plurality read the statute as written, it would have had no cause to reconsider the *Roe* framework. As properly construed, the viability-testing provision does not pass constitutional muster under even a rational-basis standard, the least restrictive level of review applied by this Court. By mandating tests to determine fetal weight and lung maturity for every fetus thought to be more than 20 weeks gestational age, the statute requires physicians to undertake procedures, such as amniocentesis, that, in the situation presented, have no medical justification, impose significant additional health risks on both the pregnant woman and the fetus, and bear no rational relation to the State's interest in protecting fetal life. . . .

The plurality eschews this straightforward resolution, in the hope of precipitating a constitutional crisis. Far from avoiding constitutional difficulty, the plurality attempts to engineer a dramatic retrenchment in our jurisprudence by exaggerating the conflict between its untenable construction of [the law] and the *Roe* trimester framework.

No one contests that under the *Roe* framework the State, in order to promote its interest in potential human life, may regulate and even proscribe non-therapeutic abortions once the fetus becomes viable. If, as the plurality appears to hold, the testing provision simply requires a physician to use appropriate and medically sound tests to determine whether the fetus is actually viable when the estimated gestational age is greater than 20 weeks (and therefore within what the District Court found to be the margin of error for viability), then I see little or no conflict with *Roe*. . . .

How ironic it is, then, and disingenuous, that the plurality scolds the Court of Appeals for adopting a construction of the statute that fails to avoid constitutional difficulties. By distorting the statute, the plurality manages to avoid invalidating the testing provision on what should have been noncontroversial constitutional grounds; having done so, however, the plurality rushes headlong into a much deeper constitutional thicket, brushing past an obvious basis for upholding [the law] in search of a pretext for scuttling the trimester framework. . . .

. . . [T]he plurality summarily discards *Roe*'s analytic core as " 'unsound in principle and unworkable in practice.' " . . . The plurality does not bother to explain the[] alleged flaws in *Roe.* Bald assertion masquerades as reasoning. The object, quite clearly, is not to persuade, but to prevail.

The plurality opinion is far more remarkable for the arguments that it does not advance than for those that it does. The plurality does not even mention, much less join, the true jurisprudential debate underlying this case: whether the Constitution includes an "unenumerated" general right to privacy . . . and, more specifically, whether and to what extent such a right to privacy extends to matters of childbearing and family life, including abortion. . . .

. . . [R]ather than arguing that the text of the Constitution makes no mention of the right to privacy, the plurality complains that the critical elements of the *Roe* framework—trimesters and viability—do not appear in the Constitution and are, therefore, somehow inconsistent with a Constitution cast in general terms. Were this a true concern, we would have to abandon most of our constitutional jurisprudence. . . .

With respect to the *Roe* framework, the general constitutional principle, indeed the fundamental constitutional right, for which it was developed is the right to privacy, a species of "liberty" protected by the Due Process Clause, which under our past decisions safeguards the right of women to exercise some control over their own role in procreation. . . . The trimester framework simply defines and limits that right to privacy in the abortion context to accommodate, not destroy, a State's legitimate interest in protecting the health of pregnant women and in preserving potential human life. Fashioning such accommodations between individual rights and the legitimate interests of government, . . . lies at the very heart of constitutional adjudication. To the extent that the trimester framework is useful in this enterprise, it is not only consistent with constitutional interpretation, but necessary to the wise and just exercise of this Court's paramount authority to define the scope of constitutional rights.

The plurality next alleges that the result of the trimester framework has "been a web of legal rules that have become increasingly intricate, resembling a code of regulations rather than a body of constitutional doctrine." Again, if this were a true and genuine concern, we would have to abandon vast areas of our constitutional jurisprudence. . . . Are these distinctions any finer, or more "regulatory," than the distinctions we have often drawn in our First Amendment jurisprudence, where, for example, we have held that a "release time" program permitting public-school students to leave school grounds during school hours to receive religious instruction does not violate the Establishment Clause, even though a release-time program permitting religious instruction on school grounds does violate the Clause? Our Fourth Amendment jurisprudence recognizes factual distinctions no less intricate. . . .

Finally, the plurality asserts that the trimester framework cannot stand because the State's interest in potential life is compelling throughout pregnancy, not merely after viability. The opinion contains not one word of rationale for its view of the State's interest. This "it-is-so-because-we-say-so" jurisprudence constitutes nothing other than an attempted exercise of brute force; reason, much less persuasion, has no place. . . .

For my own part, I remain convinced, as six other Members of this Court 16 years ago were convinced, that the *Roe* framework, and the viability standard in particular, fairly, sensibly, and effectively functions to safeguard the constitutional liberties of pregnant women while recognizing and accommodating the State's interest in potential human life. . . . Although I have stated previously for a majority of this Court that "[c]onstitutional rights do not always have easily ascertainable boundaries," to seek and establish those boundaries remains the special responsibility of this Court. . . .

Having contrived an opportunity to reconsider the *Roe* framework, and then having discarded that framework, the plurality finds the testing provision unobjectionable because it "permissibly furthers the State's interest in protecting potential human life." This newly minted standard is circular and totally meaningless. Whether a challenged abortion regulation "permissibly furthers" a legitimate state interest is the *question* that courts must answer in abortion cases, not the standard for courts to apply. . . . The plurality's novel test appears to be nothing more than a dressed-up version of rational-basis review, this Court's most lenient level of scrutiny. One thing is clear, however: were the plurality's "permissibly furthers" standard adopted by the Court, for all practical purposes, *Roe* would be overruled.

The "permissibly furthers" standard completely disregards the irreducible minimum of *Roe:* the Court's recognition that a woman has a limited fundamental constitutional right to decide whether to terminate a pregnancy. . . . Since, in the plurality's view, the

State's interest in potential life is compelling as of the moment of conception, and is therefore served only if abortion is abolished, every hindrance to a woman's ability to obtain an abortion must be "permissible."

The plurality pretends that *Roe* survives, explaining that the facts of this case differ from those in *Roe:* here, Missouri has chosen to assert its interest in potential life only at the point of viability, whereas, in *Roe,* Texas had asserted that interest from the point of conception . . . This, of course, is a distinction without a difference. The plurality repudiates every principle for which *Roe* stands; in good conscience, it cannot possibly believe that *Roe* lies "undisturbed" merely because this case does not call upon the Court to reconsider the Texas statute, or one like it. . . . It is impossible to read the plurality opinion . . . without recognizing its implicit invitation to every State to enact more and more restrictive abortion laws, and to assert their interest in potential life as of the moment of conception. All these laws will satisfy the plurality's non-scrutiny, until sometime, a new regime of old dissenters and new appointees will declare what the plurality intends: that *Roe* is no longer good law.

Thus, "not with a bang, but a whimper," the plurality discards a landmark case of the last generation, and casts into darkness the hopes and visions of every woman in this country who had come to believe that the Constitution guaranteed her the right to exercise some control over her unique ability to bear children. The plurality does so either oblivious or insensitive to the fact that millions of women, and their families, have ordered their lives around the right to reproductive choice, and that this right has become vital to the full participation of women in the economic and political walks of American life. The plurality would clear the way once again for the government to force upon women the physical labor and specific and direct medical and psychological harms that may accompany carrying a fetus to term. The plurality would clear the way again for the State to conscript a woman's body and to force upon her a "distressful life and future."

The result, as we know from experience, would be that every year hundreds of thousands of women, in desperation, would defy the law, and place their health and safety in the unclean and unsympathetic hands of back-alley abortionists, or they would attempt to perform abortions upon themselves with disastrous results. Every year, many women, especially poor and minority women, would die or suffer debilitating physical trauma, all in the name of enforced morality or religious dictates or lack of compassion, as it may be.

\* \* \*

. . . Today's decision involves the most politically divisive domestic legal issue of our time. By refusing to explain or to justify its proposed revolutionary revision in the law of abortion, and by refusing to abide not only by our precedents, but also by our canons for reconsidering those precedents, the plurality invites charges of cowardice and illegitimacy to our door. I cannot say that these would be undeserved.

For today, at least, the law of abortion stands undisturbed. For today, the women of this Nation still retain the liberty to control their destinies. But the signs are evident and very ominous, and a chill wind blows.

I dissent.

JUSTICE STEVENS, concurring in part and dissenting in part.

. . . It seems to me that in Part II-D of its opinion, the plurality strains to place a construction on [the testing provision] that enables it to conclude, "[W]e would modify and narrow *Roe* and succeeding cases." That statement is ill-advised because there is no need to modify even slightly the holdings of prior cases in order to uphold [the provision]. For the most plausible nonliteral construction, as both JUSTICE BLACKMUN and JUS-

TICE O'CONNOR have demonstrated, is constitutional and entirely consistent with our precedents.

I am unable to accept JUSTICE O'CONNOR's construction of the second sentence, however. . . . [T]he meaning of the second sentence is too plain to be ignored. The sentence twice uses the mandatory term "shall," and contains no qualifying language. If it is implicitly limited to tests that are useful in determining viability, it adds nothing to the requirement imposed by the preceding sentence.

My interpretation of the plain language is supported by the structure of the statute as a whole, particularly the preamble, which "finds" that life "begins at conception" and further commands that state laws shall be construed to provide the maximum protection to "the unborn child at every stage of development." I agree with the District Court that "[o]bviously, the purpose of this law is to protect the potential life of the fetus, rather than to safeguard maternal health." . . . I am also satisfied . . . that the testing provision is manifestly unconstitutional "irrespective of the *Roe* framework."

The Missouri statute defines "conception" as "the fertilization of the ovum of a female by a sperm of a male." . . . Missouri's declaration therefore implies regulation not only of previability abortions, but also of common forms of contraception such as the IUD and the morning-after pill. . . .

To the extent that the Missouri statute interferes with contraceptive choices, I have no doubt that it is unconstitutional under the Court's holdings in *Griswold, Eisenstadt v. Baird,* and *Carey.* . . .

. . . I am [also] persuaded that the absence of any secular purpose for the legislative declarations that life begins at conception and that conception occurs at fertilization makes the relevant portion of the preamble invalid under the Establishment Clause of the First Amendment to the Federal Constitution. This conclusion does not, and could not, rest on the fact that the statement happens to coincide with the tenets of certain religions, or on the fact that the legislators who voted to enact it may have been motivated by religious considerations. Rather, it rests on the fact that the preamble, an unequivocal endorsement of some but by no means all Christian faiths, serves no identifiable secular purpose. That fact alone compels a conclusion that the statute violates the Establishment Clause. . . .

. . . There is, of course, an important and unquestionably valid secular interest in "protecting a young pregnant woman from the consequences of an incorrect decision." Although that interest is served by a requirement that the woman receive medical and, in appropriate circumstances, parental, advice, it does not justify the state legislature's official endorsement of the theological tenet of the [the preamble].

. . . Contrary to the theological "finding" of the Missouri Legislature, a woman's constitutionally protected liberty encompasses the right to act on her own belief that— to paraphrase St. Thomas Aquinas—until a seed has acquired the powers of sensation and movement, the life of a human being has not yet begun.

## *Hodgson v. Minnesota*
### 110 S.CT. 2926 (1990)

JUSTICE STEVENS announced the judgment of the Court and delivered the opinion of the Court with respect to Parts I, II, IV and VII, an opinion with respect to Part III in which JUSTICE BRENNAN joins, an opinion with respect to Parts V and VI in which JUSTICE O'CONNOR joins, and a dissenting opinion with respect to Part VIII.

A Minnesota statute provides, with certain exceptions, that no abortion shall be performed on a woman under 18 years of age until at least 48 hours after both of her parents have been notified. . . . [T]he notice is mandatory unless (1) the attending physician certifies that an immediate abortion is necessary to prevent the woman's death and there is insufficient time to provide the required notice; (2) both of her parents have consented in writing; or (3) the woman declares that she is a victim of parental abuse or neglect, in which event notice of her declaration must be given to the proper authorities. . . . Subdivision 6 of the same statute provides that if a court enjoins the enforcement of [the notification requirement], the same notice requirement shall be effective unless the pregnant woman obtains a court order permitting the abortion to proceed. . . .

For reasons that follow, we now conclude that the requirement of notice to both of the pregnant minor's parents is not reasonably related to legitimate state interests. . . . A different majority of the Court, for reasons stated in separate opinions, concludes that subdivision 6 is constitutional. . . .

## III

There is a natural difference between men and women: only women have the capacity to bear children. A woman's decision to beget or to bear a child is a component of her liberty that is protected by the Due Process Clause of the Fourteenth Amendment to the Constitution. That Clause . . . protects the woman's right to make such decisions independently and privately, free of unwarranted governmental intrusion. . . . [T]he right to make this decision "do[es] not mature and come into being magically only when one attains the state-defined age of majority." Thus, the constitutional protection against unjustified state intrusion into the process of deciding whether or not to bear a child extends to pregnant minors as well as adult women.

. . . [T]he identification of the constitutionally protected interest is merely the beginning of the analysis. . . . [T]he regulation of constitutionally protected decisions . . . must be predicated on legitimate state concerns other than disagreement with the choice the individual has made. In the abortion area, a state may have no obligation to spend its own money, or use its own facilities, to subsidize nontherapeutic abortions for minors or adults. See *Maher v. Roe; Webster v. Reproductive Health Services.* . . . A state policy favoring childbirth over abortion is not in itself a sufficient justification for overriding the woman's decision or for placing "obstacles—absolute or otherwise—in the pregnant woman's path to an abortion."

In these cases the State of Minnesota does not rest its defense of this statute on any such value judgment. . . . Because the Minnesota statute unquestionably places obstacles in the pregnant minor's path to an abortion, the State has the burden of establishing its constitutionality. Under any analysis, the Minnesota statute cannot be sustained if the obstacles it imposes are not reasonably related to legitimate state interests.

## IV

. . . [The Court reviewed the findings of the District Court with respect to the number of minors in Minnesota living with one or neither parent; the physical and psychological harm that may result from forced notification of an absent parent; and the practical effects of a two-parent notification requirement. The District Court concluded, "[F]ive weeks of trial have produced no factual basis upon which this court can find that [the statute] on the whole furthers in any meaningful way the state's interest in protecting pregnant minors or assuring family integrity."]

## V

Three separate but related interests—the interest in the welfare of the pregnant minor, the interest of the parents, and the interest of the family unit—are relevant to our consideration of the constitutionality of the 48-hour waiting period and the two-parent notification requirement.

The State has a strong and legitimate interest in the welfare of its young citizens, whose immaturity, inexperience, and lack of judgment may sometimes impair their ability to exercise their rights wisely. That interest . . . extends . . . to the minor's decision to terminate her pregnancy. Although the Court has held that parents may not exercise "an absolute, and possibly arbitrary veto" over that decision, it has never challenged a State's reasonable judgment that the decision should be made after notification to and consultation with a parent. . . .

. . . [T]he family has a privacy interest in the upbringing and education of children. . . . The family may assign one parent to guide the children's education and the other to look after their health. . . . We have long held that there exists a "private realm of family life which the State cannot enter." Thus, when the government intrudes on choices concerning the arrangement of the household, this Court has carefully examined the "governmental interests advanced and the extent to which they are served by the challenged regulation." . . .

## VI

We think it is clear that a requirement that a minor wait 48 hours after notifying a single parent of her intention to get an abortion would reasonably further the legitimate state interest in ensuring that the minor's decision is knowing and intelligent. We have held that when a parent or another person has assumed "primary responsibility" for a minor's well-being, the State may properly enact "laws designed to aid discharge of that responsibility." To the extent that [the statute] requires notification of only one parent, it does just that. The brief waiting period provides the parent the opportunity to consult with his or her spouse and a family physician, and it permits the parent to . . . provide the daughter needed guidance and counsel in evaluating the impact of the decision on her future.

The 48-hour delay imposes only a minimal burden on the right of the minor to decide whether or not to terminate her pregnancy. Although the District Court found that scheduling factors . . . may combine, in many cases, to create a delay of a week or longer between the initiation of notification and the abortion, there is no evidence that the 48-hour period itself is unreasonable. . . .

## VII

It is equally clear that the requirement that *both* parents be notified . . . does not reasonably further any legitimate state interest. The usual justification for a parental consent or notification provision is that it supports the authority of a parent who is presumed to act in the minor's best interest and thereby assures that the minor's decision is knowing, intelligent, and deliberate. To the extent that such an interest is legitimate, it would be fully served by a requirement that the minor notify one parent. . . .

The State . . . argues that, in the ideal family, the minor should make her decision only after consultation with both parents who should naturally be concerned with the child's welfare and that the State has an interest in protecting the independent right of the parents "to determine and strive for what they believe to be best for their children." . . . [But while] full communication among all members of a family [may be] desirable in some cases, [such] communication may not be decreed by the State. The State has no more interest in requiring all family members to talk with one another than it has in requiring certain of them to live together. . . .

Nor can any state interest in protecting a parent's interest in shaping a child's values and lifestyle overcome the liberty interests of a minor acting with the consent of a single parent or court. . . .

## VIII

The Court holds that the constitutional objection to the two-parent notice requirement is removed by the judicial bypass option provided in subdivision 6 of the Minnesota statute. I respectfully dissent from that holding.

A majority of the Court has previously held that a statute requiring one parent's consent to a minor's abortion will be upheld if the State provides an " 'alternate procedure whereby a pregnant minor may demonstrate that she is sufficiently mature to make the abortion decision herself or that, despite her immaturity, an abortion would be in her best interests.' " . . .

. . . We have concluded that the State has a strong and legitimate interest in providing a pregnant minor with the advice and support of a parent during the decisional period. A general rule requiring the minor to obtain the consent of one parent reasonably furthers that interest. An exception from the general rule is necessary to protect the minor from an arbitrary veto that is motivated by the separate concerns of the parent rather than the best interest of the child. But the need for an exception does not undermine the conclusion that the general rule is perfectly reasonable. . . .

A judicial bypass that is designed to handle exceptions from a reasonable general rule, and thereby preserve the constitutionality of that rule, is quite different from a requirement that a minor—or a minor and one of her parents—must apply to a court for permission to avoid the application of a rule that is not reasonably related to legitimate state goals. . . .

Justice O'Connor, concurring in part and concurring in the judgment in part.

## I

I join all but Parts III and VIII of Justice Stevens' opinion. While I agree with some of the central points made in Part III, I cannot join the broader discussion. I agree that the Court has characterized "[a] woman's decision to beget or to bear a child [as] a component of her liberty that is protected by the Due Process Clause of the Fourteenth Amendment to the Constitution." This Court extended that liberty interest to minors, albeit with some important limitations: "[P]arental notice and consent are qualifications that typically may be imposed by the State on a minor's right to make important decisions. As immature minors often lack the ability to make fully informed choices that take account of both immediate and long-range consequences, a State reasonably may determine that parental consultation often is desirable and in the best interest of the minor."

It has been my understanding in this area that "[i]f the particular regulation does not 'unduly burde[n]' the fundamental right, . . . then our evaluation of that regulation is limited to our determination that the regulation rationally relates to a legitimate state purpose." *Akron v. Akron Center for Reproductive Health;* see also *Webster.* It is with that understanding that I agree with Justice Stevens' statement that the "statute cannot be sustained if the obstacles it imposes are not reasonably related to legitimate state interests."

I agree with Justice Stevens that Minnesota has offered no sufficient justification for its interference with the family's decisionmaking processes created by . . . two-parent notification. . . .

The Minnesota exception to notification for minors who are victims of neglect or abuse is, in reality, a means of notifying the parents. . . . [T]o avail herself of the neglect or abuse exception, the minor must report the abuse. A report requires the welfare agency to immediately "conduct an assessment." If the agency interviews the victim, it must notify the parent of the fact of the interview; if the parent is the subject of an investigation, he has a right of access to the record of the investigation. . . . The combination of the abused minor's reluctance to report sexual or physical abuse with the likelihood that invoking the abuse exception for the purpose of avoiding notice will result in notice, makes the abuse exception less than effectual.

Minnesota's two-parent notice requirement is all the more unreasonable when one considers that only half of the minors in the state of Minnesota reside with both biological parents. A third live with only one parent. Given its broad sweep and its failure to serve the purposes asserted by the State in too many cases, I join the Court's striking of [the two-parent notice requirement].

## II

In a series of cases, this Court has explicitly approved judicial bypass as a means of tailoring a parental consent provision so as to avoid unduly burdening the minor's limited right to obtain an abortion. . . . Subdivision 6 passes constitutional muster because the interference with the internal operation of the family required by [the notification requirement] simply does not exist where the minor can avoid notifying one or both parents by use of the bypass procedure.

JUSTICE MARSHALL, with whom JUSTICE BRENNAN and JUSTICE BLACKMUN join, concurring in part, concurring in the judgment in part, and dissenting in part.

I concur in Parts I, II, IV, and VII of JUSTICE STEVENS' opinion for the Court . . . Although I do not believe that the Constitution permits a State to require a minor to notify or consult with a parent before obtaining an abortion, I am in substantial agreement with the remainder of the reasoning in Part V of the Court's opinion. For the reasons stated by JUSTICE STEVENS, Minnesota's two-parent notification requirement is not even reasonably related to a legitimate state interest. Therefore, that requirement surely would not pass the strict scrutiny applicable to restrictions on a woman's fundamental right to have an abortion.

I dissent from the judgment of the Court, however, that the judicial bypass option renders the parental notification and 48-hour delay requirements constitutional. The bypass procedure cannot save those requirements because the bypass itself is unconstitutional both on its face and as applied. At the very least, this scheme substantially burdens a woman's right to privacy without advancing a compelling state interest. More significantly, in some instances it usurps a young woman's control over her own body by giving either a parent or a court the power effectively to veto her decision to have an abortion.

This Court has consistently held since *Roe v. Wade* that the constitutional right . . . [to decide] "whether or not to terminate [pregnancy]" . . . "is fundamental." . . .

*Roe* remains the law of the land. Indeed, today's decision reaffirms the vitality of *Roe*, as five Justices have voted to strike down a state law restricting a woman's right to have an abortion. Accordingly, to be constitutional, state restrictions on abortion must meet the rigorous test set forth [in *Roe*].

## II

I strongly disagree with the Court's conclusion that the State may constitutionally force a minor woman either to notify both parents . . . and then wait 48 hours before proceeding with an abortion, or disclose her intimate affairs to a judge and ask that he grant her permission to have an abortion. . . .

Neither the scope of a woman's privacy right nor the magnitude of a law's burden is diminished because a woman is a minor. Rather, a woman's minority status affects only the nature of the State's interests. Although the Court considers the burdens that the two-parent notification requirement imposes on a minor woman's exercise of her right to privacy, it fails to recognize that forced notification of only one parent also significantly burdens a young woman's right to have an abortion.

A substantial proportion of pregnant minors voluntarily consult with a parent regardless of the existence of a notification requirement. . . . For these women, the notification requirement by itself does not impose a significant burden. But for those young women who would choose not to inform their parents, the burden is evident: the notification requirement destroys their right to avoid disclosure of a deeply personal matter.

A notification requirement can also have severe physical and psychological effects on a young woman. . . . The impact of any notification requirement is especially devastating for minors who live in fear of physical, psychological, or sexual abuse. . . .

Second, the prospect of having to notify a parent causes many young women to delay their abortions, thereby increasing the health risks of the procedure. . . .

. . . Clearly, then, requiring notification of one parent significantly burdens a young woman's right to terminate her pregnancy.

The 48-hour delay *after* notification further aggravates the harm caused by the *pre-*notification delay that may flow from a minor's fear of notifying a parent. . . . Even a brief delay can have a particularly detrimental impact if it pushes the abortion into the second trimester, when the operation is substantially more risky and costly. . . .

. . . [C]ompelled notification is unlikely to result in productive communication in families in which a daughter does not feel comfortable consulting her parents about intimate or sexual matters. . . .

. . . [I]ronically, the State's requirements here affirmatively interfere in family life by trying to force families to conform to the State's archetype of the ideal family. . . .

. . . The judicial bypass procedure cannot salvage [the notice and delay requirements] because that procedure . . . effectively gives a judge "an absolute veto over the decision of the physician and his patient." . . . No person may veto *any* minor's decision, made in consultation with her physician, to terminate her pregnancy. An "immature" minor has no less right to make decisions regarding her own body than a mature adult. . . .


Justice Scalia, concurring in the judgment in part and dissenting in part.

As I understand the various opinions today: One Justice holds that two-parent notification is unconstitutional [without] judicial bypass, but constitutional with bypass (O'Connor, J.); four Justices would hold that two-parent notification is constitutional with or without bypass (Kennedy, J.); four Justices would hold that two-parent notification is unconstitutional with or without bypass, though the four apply two different standards (Stevens, J.; Marshall, J.); six Justices hold that one-parent notification with bypass is constitutional, though for two different sets of reasons (Stevens, J.); and three Justices would hold that one-parent notification with bypass is unconstitutional (Blackmun, J.). One will search in vain the document we are supposed to be construing for text that provides the basis for the argument over these distinctions; and will find in our society's tradition regarding abortion no hint that the distinctions are constitutionally relevant, much less any indication how a constitutional argument about them ought to be resolved. The random and unpredictable results of our consequently unchanneled individual views make it increasingly evident, Term after Term, that the tools for this job are not to be found in the lawyer's—and hence not in the judge's—workbox. I continue to dissent from this enterprise of devising an Abortion Code, and from the illusion that we have authority to do so.


Justice Kennedy, with whom the Chief Justice, Justice White, and Justice Scalia join, concurring in the judgment in part and dissenting in part.

... I dissent from the portion of the Court's judgment affirming ... that Minnesota['s] two-parent notice statute is unconstitutional.

The Minnesota statute also provides, however, that if the two-parent notice requirement is invalidated, the same notice requirement is effective unless the pregnant minor obtains a court order permitting the abortion to proceed.... Five Members of the Court, the four who join this opinion and JUSTICE O'CONNOR, agree with the Court of Appeals' decision [to sustain] this aspect of the statute....

I acknowledge that in some cases notifying both parents will not produce desirable results.... [But] a law is not invalid if it fails to further the governmental interest in every instance....

The difference between notice and consent ... is apparent.... Unlike parental consent laws, a law requiring parental notice does not give any third party the legal right to make the minor's decision for her, or to prevent her from obtaining an abortion should she choose to have one performed.... The law before us does not place an absolute obstacle before any minor seeking to obtain an abortion....

Because a majority of the Court holds that the two-parent notice requirement ... is unconstitutional, it is necessary for the Court to consider whether the same notice requirement is constitutional if the minor has the option of obtaining a court order.... Assuming ... that the notice provisions standing alone are invalid, I conclude that the two-parent notice requirement with the judicial bypass alternative is constitutional....

In providing for the bypass, Minnesota has done nothing other than attempt to fit its legislation into the framework that we have supplied in our previous cases....

In this case, the Court rejects a legislature's judgment that parents should at least be aware of their daughter's intention to seek an abortion, even if the state does not empower the parents to control the child's decision. That judgment is rejected although it rests upon a tradition of a parental role in the care and upbringing of children that is as old as civilization itself. Our precedents do not permit this result.

... [T]he Court errs in serious degree when it commands its own solutions to the cruel consequences of individual misconduct, parental failure and social ills. The legislative authority is entitled to attempt to meet these wrongs by taking reasonable measures to recognize and promote the primacy of the family tie, a concept which this Court now seems intent on declaring a constitutional irrelevance.

[In the companion case of *Ohio v. Akron Center for Reproductive Health,* Justice Kennedy, joined by Chief Justice Rehnquist, and Justices White, Stevens, O'Connor and Scalia, upheld an Ohio statute prohibiting any person from performing an abortion on a minor absent notice to one of her parents or a court order.

[In Part V, joined only by Justices Rehnquist, White, and Scalia, Justice Kennedy wrote that "[A] free and enlightened society may decide that each of its members should attain a clearer, more tolerant understanding of the profound philosophic choices confronted by a woman who is considering whether to seek an abortion. Her decision will embrace her own destiny and personal dignity, and the origins of the other human life that lie within the embryo." Justice Stevens filed a concurrence, and Justice Blackmun, joined by Justices Brennan and Marshall, filed a dissenting opinion.]

# Index